ENGLISH SKILLS

OTHER BOOKS BY JOHN LANGAN

English Skills with Readings
College Writing Skills
College Writing Skills with Readings
Sentence Skills (Forms A, B, and C)
Reading and Study Skills (Form A and Form B)

ENGLISH SKILLS

FOURTH EDITION

JOHN LANGAN
Atlantic Community College

McGraw-Hill, Inc.
New York St. Louis San Francisco Auckland Bogotá
Caracas Hamburg Lisbon London Madrid Mexico Milan Montreal
New Delhi Paris San Juan São Paulo Singapore Sydney Tokyo Toronto

ENGLISH SKILLS

4567890 DOC/DOC 9987654321

ISBN 0-07-036327-7

This book was set in Times Roman by Monotype Composition Company.
The editors were Susan Hurtt and Susan Gamer;
the designer was Rafael Hernandez;
the production supervisor was Diane Renda.
R. R. Donnelley & Sons Company was printer and binder.

Library of Congress Cataloging-in-Publication Data

Langan, John, (date).
English skills.

Includes index.
1. English language—Rhetoric. I. Title.
PE1408.L318 1989 808'.042 88-23078
ISBN 0-07-036327-7

ABOUT THE AUTHOR

John Langan has taught reading and writing courses at Atlantic Community College near Atlantic City, New Jersey, since 1971. The author of a popular series of college textbooks on both subjects, he enjoys the challenge of developing materials that teach skills in an especially clear and lively way. Before teaching, he earned advanced degrees in writing at Rutgers University and in reading at Glassboro State College. Prior to graduate school, he spent a year writing fiction that, he says, "is now at the back of a drawer waiting to be discovered and acclaimed posthumously." He supported himself during this time and while in school by working as a truck driver, machinist, car battery assembler, hospital attendant, and apple packer. He presently lives with his wife, Judith Nadell, near Philadelphia. Among his everyday pleasures are listening to Phillies games, running, cooking, reading, and watching the television shows *60 Minutes* and *L.A. Law*.

**To my wife,
Judith Nadell**

CONTENTS

TO THE INSTRUCTOR

English Skills will help students learn and apply the basic principles of effective composition as well as master important grammar, punctuation, and usage skills. It is a nuts-and-bolts book based on a number of assumptions or beliefs about the writing process:

- First of all, *English Skills* assumes that four principles in particular are keys to effective writing: unity, support, coherence, and sentence skills. These four principles are highlighted on the inside front cover and reinforced throughout the book. Part One focuses on the first three principles; Part Six fully treats sentence skills. The rest of the book shows how the four principles apply in different types of paragraph development (Part Three), in several-paragraph essays (Part Four), and in specialized types of writing (Part Five). The success of the earlier editions of *English Skills* supports the fact that the four principles are easily grasped, remembered, and followed by students.
- The book reflects the belief that the best way to begin writing is with personal experience. After students have learned to support a point by providing material from their own experience, they are ready to develop an idea by drawing upon their own reasoning abilities and upon information in notes, articles, and books. Students are asked to write on both experiential and objective topics in Parts Three and Four. And Part Five offers guidance in many practical writing situations: exam essays, summaries, reports, the job application letter, and the research paper.
- The book also assumes that beginning writers are more likely to learn

composing skills through lively, engaging, and realistic models than through materials remote from the common experiences that are part of everyday life. For example, when a writer argues that proms should be banned, or catalogs ways to harass a teacher, or talks about why some teenagers take drugs, students are more apt to remember and follow the writing principles that may be involved. A related belief is that students are especially interested in and challenged by the writing of their peers. After reading vigorous papers composed by other students and understanding the power that good writing can have, students will be more encouraged to aim for a similar honesty, realism, and detail in their own work.

- Another premise of *English Skills* is that mastery of the paragraph should precede work on the several-paragraph essay. Thus Part One illustrates the basic principles of composition using paragraph models, and the assignments in Part Three aim at developing the ability to support ideas within a variety of paragraph forms. The essential principles of paragraph writing are then applied to the several-paragraph essays in Part Four.
- Other parts of the book reflect additional beliefs about the needs of an English text. Part Two describes several factors important for writing effectively, including the evaluation of one's own attitude about writing, the use of prewriting techniques, and the ability to create logical outlines. Part Five includes skills that will help in a variety of writing situations. Among the skills covered are writing reports and summaries, using the library, and documenting a research paper following the revised MLA guidelines. And last, the grammar, punctuation, and usage skills that make up Part Six are explained in a clear and direct way, without unnecessary technical terms. Here, as elsewhere, abundant exercise material is provided, especially for the mistakes most likely to interfere with clear communication.
- A final assumption is that, since no two people will use an English text in exactly the same way, the material should be organized in a highly accessible manner. Because each of the six parts of the book deals with a distinct writing area, instructors can turn quickly and easily to the skills they want to present. At the same time, ideas for sequencing material are provided by three boxes titled "Some Suggestions on What to Do Next"; the boxes appear at the end of the opening chapters of the book. And a detailed syllabus is provided in the Instructor's Manual.

NOTES ON THE FOURTH EDITION

With pleasure and gratitude, I have watched the audience for *English Skills* expand each year. Teachers continue to say that the four bases really do help students learn to write effectively. And they continue to comment that students find the activities, assignments, and model passages in the book especially interesting and worthwhile.

Along with such favorable remarks has come the occasional suggestion that the book might better start with the material now in Part Two, "Other Important Factors in Writing." I understand the reasons for this suggestion, but I have decided to keep the existing sequence. I think there is great value in presenting the two basic writing guidelines in the first lines of the first chapter. For students adrift in the choppy waters of learning to write competently, these principles become anchors. However, I have been careful to make Part Two self-contained so that teachers who want to start there can easily do so.

While I have not changed any of the basic features of the book, I have freshened some materials and made additions that I believe teachers will find helpful. Here is a list of what is new:

1 Sections added to Part Two include "Reading as an Aid to Writing," "Writing for a Specific Purpose and Audience," and writing as a process of discovery in "Know or Discover Your Subject." Also new is a review test for all the sections in Part Two.

2 A fifth writing assignment is now included with each type of paragraph development in Part Three. The new final assignment requires writing with a specific purpose to a specific audience. Students are asked, for example, to write as an apartment tenant complaining to a landlord about neighbors, or as a company employee describing a job position for an employment service. This fifth assignment completes a sequence of assignments that progress from personal to objective topics. (Note that the fourth assignment in each case requires some simple research.) The last assignment helps students prepare all the more for the real-world writing that may be part of their working lives.

3 Added to Part Six are eight combined mastery tests (pages 504–511) that reinforce a number of basic sentence skills. There are two tests apiece on fragments and run-ons, verbs, capital letters and punctuation, and effective word use.

4 Other changes have also been made in Part Six. The chapter on run-on sentences has been expanded, and the distinction between fused sentences and comma splices has been made explicit. The chapter on consistent verb tense includes more activities. Introductory projects have been added for punctuation marks, effective word use, and commonly confused words. Wordiness is now treated as part of a chapter on effective word use.

5 Materials in other parts of the book have been freshened. For example, there is a new model research paper, there is new material on transitions, and a number of changes have been made in the practice sentences in Part Six.

6 A second color has been added to the book, further enhancing the clarity of presentation and making the text that much more inviting to read.

7 Finally, a newly revised computer disk accompanies a set of twenty-five ditto masters and a comprehensive Instructor's Manual. Richard D. Hathaway, Professor of English at the State University of New York in New Paltz, has done the computer programming; the result is that the previous version of a disk for *English Skills* has been much improved. The disk runs very quickly and is truly "user-friendly"; features include an opening menu of the lessons on the disk, explanations of all answers, automatic scorekeeping, and frequent use of the student's first name. A guide in the Instructor's Manual provides further information and a partial printout of material on the disk.

The computer disk, as well as the Instructor's Manual and the ditto masters, is available from the local McGraw-Hill representative or by writing to the College English Editor, McGraw-Hill Book Company, 1221 Avenue of the Americas, New York, 10020.

ACKNOWLEDGMENTS

Reviewers who have assisted through their helpful comments include Barbara Beauchamp, County College of Morriss; Jose E. Benavides, Laredo Junior College; Janet Bickal, Mercer County Community College; Toni Empringham, El Camino College; Robert M. Esch, University of Texas at El Paso; Lydia S. Godfrey, Northern Virginia Community College; Elaine A. Greenwood, Valencia Community College; Charles Johnson, Tyler Junior College; Sue Ellen Meyer, Meramec Community College; Marsha Newman, Diablo Valley College; Ray Peterson, Santa Rosa Community College; June Siegel, City University of New York; Mary Jean Steenburg, Elkhorn Valley Metropolitan Technical Community College; and Sandra Stewart, Gavilan College.

I am grateful also for help provided by Janet M. Goldstein. And I am endlessly thankful to my students. The vitality and the specialness of their lives are amply demonstrated on many pages of this text. My last acknowledgment goes to my parents—if for nothing in particular, then for much in general.

John Langan

ENGLISH SKILLS

PART ONE

BASIC PRINCIPLES OF EFFECTIVE WRITING

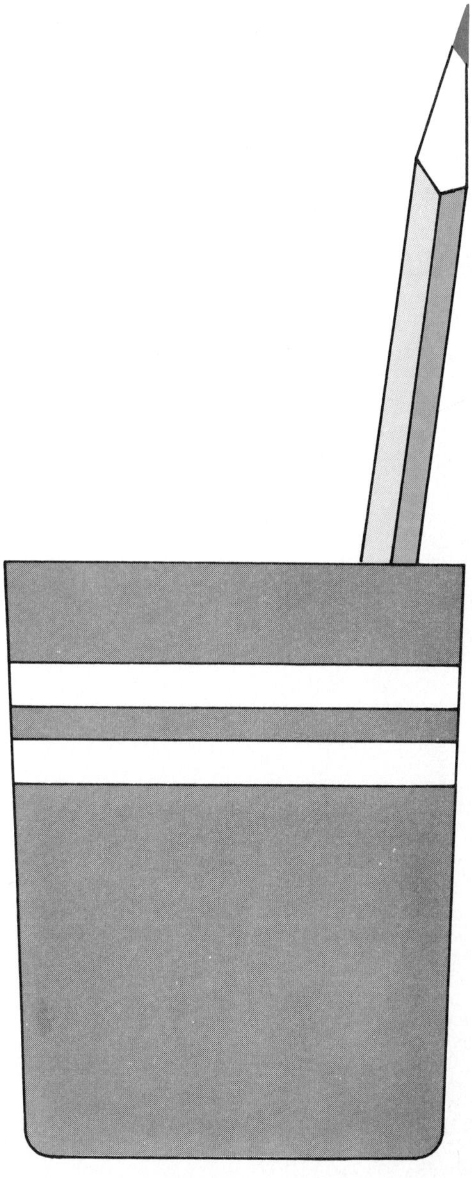

PREVIEW

Part One begins by introducing you to the book. As you work through the brief activities in the introduction, you will gain a quick understanding of the book's purpose, the way it is organized, and how it will help you develop your writing skills. Part One then describes the four basic steps that can make you an effective writer. The four steps are:

1 Make a point
2 Support the point with specific evidence
3 Organize and connect the specific evidence
4 Write clear, error-free sentences

Explanations, examples, and activities for the first three steps are provided so that you can master the steps. (You will be referred to Part Six of the book for a detailed treatment of the fourth step.) After seeing how the steps can help you write a competent paper, you will learn how they lead to the four standards, or "bases," of effective writing. You will then practice evaluating a number of papers in terms of the four bases of unity, support, coherence, and sentence skills.

INTRODUCTION TO THIS BOOK

This chapter will help you

- Understand how the book is organized
- Learn a sequence for using the book
- Explore your thoughts about writing

English Skills grows out of experiences I had when learning how to write. My early memories of writing in school are not pleasant. In the middle grades I remember getting back paper after paper on which the only comment was "Handwriting very poor." In high school, the night before a book report was due, I recall working anxiously at a card table in my bedroom. I was nervous and sweaty because I felt so out of my element, like a person who knows only how to open a can of soup being asked to cook a five-course meal. The act of writing was hard enough, and my feeling that I wasn't any good at it made me hate the process all the more.

Luckily, in college I had a teacher who changed my negative attitude about writing. During my first semester in composition, I realized that my teacher repeatedly asked two questions of any paper I wrote: "What is your point?" and "What is your support for that point?" I learned that sound writing consists basically of making a point and then providing evidence to support or develop that point. As I understood, practiced, and mastered these and other principles, I began to write effective papers. By the end of the semester, much of the uneasiness and bad feeling that I had had about writing had disappeared. I knew that competent writing was a skill that I or anyone could learn with practice. It was a nuts-and-bolts process consisting of a number of principles and skills that could be studied and mastered. Further, I learned that while there was no alternative to the work required for competent writing, there was satisfaction to be gained through such work. I no longer feared or hated writing, for I knew I could work at it and be good at it.

English Skills explains in a clear and direct way the basic principles and skills you must learn to write effectively. And it provides a number of practice materials so that you can work on the skills enough to make them habits. This introduction will show you how to use *English Skills*. By completing the brief activities here, you will learn exactly how the book is organized and how it can help you become an effective writer.

HOW THE BOOK IS ORGANIZED

The book is divided into six parts. Each part will be discussed in turn.

Part One (Pages 1–84)

A good way to get a quick sense of any part of the book is to look at the table of contents. Turn back to the contents at the beginning of the book (pages *vii–x*) and answer the following questions:

- What is the title of Part One?

  ____

- ''Introduction to This Book'' is the opening chapter of Part One. What is the title of the next chapter in Part One, and what two subheads follow the title?

  Title ______________________________

  Subhead ______________________________

  Subhead ______________________________

- The title of the following chapter in Part One is ''The Third and Fourth Steps in Writing.'' What two subheads follow the title?

  Subhead ______________________________

  Subhead ______________________________

At this point, you have already learned the central idea in the book. The idea is that there are four steps in effective writing: (1) make a point; (2) support the point with specific evidence; (3) organize and connect the specific evidence; and (4) write clear, error-free sentences. Part One describes three of the four writing steps. The fourth step, which includes all the skills involved in writing clear, error-free sentences, would take up too much space if treated in detail in Part One. Therefore, sentence skills have been placed in a later part of the book, where they can be easily referred to as needed. Use the table of contents (pages *vii–x*) to answer the following question:

■ In what part of the book are sentence skills treated?

____

The final chapter in Part One is titled "The Four Bases for Evaluating Writing." Look at the contents (pages *vii–viii*) again and fill in the first four subheads following the title of that chapter.

■ Subhead ________________

Subhead ________________

Subhead ________________

Subhead ________________

The four bases are another way of looking at the four steps in writing.

Inside Front Cover

Turn now to the inside front cover. You will see there a (*fill in the missing word*) ________________ of the four bases of effective writing. These four standards can be used as a guide for every paper that you write. They are summarized on the inside front cover for easy reference. If you follow them, you are almost sure to write effective papers.

Part Two (Pages 85–112)

The title of Part Two is ____.

Part Two, as the title indicates, explains other important factors in the writing process. Look at the preview on page 86 and record here what the factors are:

1. ____
2. ____
3. ____
4. ____
5. ____

Along with the four steps already described, these factors will help you with any paper that you write. Put here the factor that you think might be the most important for you:

____.

Part Three (Pages 113–211)

The title of Part Three is ____.

Part Three, as the title explains, is concerned with different ways to develop paragraphs. Read the preview on page 114 and record here how many types of paragraph development are presented: ____________________.

Turn to the first method of paragraph development, "Providing Examples," on page 117. You will see that the chapter opens with a brief introduction followed by several paragraphs written by students. Then you will see a series of six (*fill in the missing word*) ____________________ to help you evaluate the example paragraphs in terms of unity, support, and coherence. Finally, a number of writing topics that can be developed by means of examples are presented. The same format is used for each of the other methods of paragraph development in Part Three.

Part Four (Pages 213–244)

The title of Part Four is ____.

As the preview on page 214 notes, in Part Three you were asked to write single paragraphs; in Part Four, you are asked to write papers of more than one (*fill in the missing word*) ____________________.

Part Five (Pages 245–313)

The title of Part Five is ____.

Part Five gives you advice on a number of important writing-related skills. You can refer to this part of the book whenever the need develops.

- Which section will help you write effective answers to essay questions?

  ____

- Which sections will help you prepare papers on books or articles you must read for other classes?

  ____

  ____

  ____

Part Six (Pages 315–528)

The title of Part Six is ______________________________.

Part Six is the largest part of the book. It gives you practice in skills needed to write clear and effective sentences. You will note from the table of contents (pages *vii–x*) that it contains a diagnostic test, the skills themselves, editing activities, and an achievement test. The skills are grouped into four sections: "Grammar," "Mechanics," (*fill in the missing word*) ______________, and "Word Use."

Inside Back Cover

Given on the inside back cover is an alphabetical list of (*fill in the missing words*) ______________________________.
Your instructor may use these symbols in marking your papers. Also, you can use the page numbers in the list for quick reference to a specific sentence skill.

Charts in the Book

In addition to the guides on the inside front and back covers, several charts have been provided in the book to help you take responsibility for your own learning.

- What are the names of the charts on pages 535–538?

  ____

  ____

  ____

  ____

HOW TO USE THIS BOOK

Here is a suggested sequence for using this book if you are working on your own.

1 After completing this introduction, read the next three chapters in Part One and work through as many of the activities as you need to master the ideas in the chapters. Your instructor may give you answer sheets so that you can check your answers. Then do the same thing with Part Two. At that point, you will have covered all the basic theory needed to write effective papers.

2 Turn to Part Six and take the diagnostic test. The test will help you determine what sentence skills you need to review. Study those skills one or two at a time while you continue to work on other parts of the book.

3 What you do next depends on course requirements and/or individual needs. You will want to practice at least several different kinds of paragraph development in Part Three. If your time is limited, be sure to include "Providing Examples," "Explaining a Process," "Comparing and Contrasting," and "Arguing a Position." After that, you could logically go on to write one or more of the several-paragraph essays described in Part Four. And the writing-related skills in Part Five can be referred to whenever they are needed.

AN IMPORTANT FINAL NOTE

English Skills will help you learn, practice, and apply the writing skills you need to communicate clearly and effectively. But the starting point must be your personal determination to do the work needed to become an independent writer. If you decide—*and only you can decide*—that you want to learn to write effectively, this book will help you reach that goal.

Activity

To evaluate your attitude about writing, check the statement or statements that most closely apply to you.

_______ I intend to learn how to write effectively. I feel that clear writing is a necessary skill for me to have.

_______ I honestly don't think that good writing is a skill that I need. I just want to pass this course with a satisfactory grade.

_______ I'd like to learn how to write well, but the cards are stacked against me. I always did poorly in writing in school. Some people have the knack and some don't. I just happen to be one of the have-nots, and there may be little I can do to change this.

Now take a few minutes to examine your attitude about writing. Jot down on a piece of paper your reasons for checking the statement or statements that you did. What experiences in your life help explain your choice or choices? If you are in a class, your instructor may then ask you to share your ideas with a small group of other students.

By doing this activity, you may discover that you have a positive attitude about writing. However, even if you have mixed or negative feelings, you are probably now more aware of that fact. Such an awareness can be a vital first step in changing your attitude. *English Skills* is based on the belief that competent writing is necessary—not just in a composition class but in other courses, in everyday life, and in a career. The book is also based on the belief that people can learn how to write effectively by working at it. If you share these beliefs, or gradually come to share them, the chances are excellent that you will become a competent writer.

THE FIRST AND SECOND STEPS IN WRITING

This chapter will show you how to

- Begin a paper by making a point of some kind
- Provide specific evidence to support that point
- Write a simple paragraph

The first two steps in effective writing are:

1 Make a point
2 Support the point with specific evidence

The importance of these two steps will become clear after you read the brief introductory sections that follow.

AN IMPORTANT DIFFERENCE BETWEEN WRITING AND TALKING

In everyday conversation, you make all kinds of points, or assertions. You say, for example, "I hate my job"; "Sue's a really generous person"; or "That exam was unfair." The points that you make concern such personal matters as well as, at times, larger issues: "A lot of doctors are arrogant"; "The death penalty should exist for certain crimes"; "Tobacco and marijuana are equally dangerous."

The people you are talking with do not always challenge you to give reasons for your statements. They may know why you feel as you do, or they may already agree with you, or they simply may not want to put you on the spot; and so they do not always ask "Why?" But the people who *read* what you write may not know you, agree with you, or feel in any way obliged to you. So if you want to communicate effectively with them, you must provide solid evidence for any point you make. An important difference, then, between writing and talking is this: *In writing, any idea that you advance must be supported with specific reasons or details.*

Think of your readers as reasonable persons. They will not take your views on faith, but they *are* willing to accept what you say as long as you support it. So remember to support any statement that you make with specific evidence.

A POINT SUPPORTED BY SPECIFIC EVIDENCE

In conversation you might say to a friend, "I'm not going out with Tony anymore" or "Tony is a real loser as a date." If your friend already knows Tony, you won't have to explain your statement. But in writing, your point would have to be backed up with specific reasons or details. In the following paragraph, the decision to stop seeing Tony is supported by evidence. Note that a *paragraph* is simply a collection of specifics, in the form of sentences, that support a general idea or point; this point is often expressed in the first sentence of the paragraph.

Good-Bye, Tony

I have decided not to go out with Tony anymore. He said that he would be at my house by 8:30, but he did not arrive until 9:20. Then he told me that it was too late to go to the new Woody Allen movie I wanted to see, and that we would go to a horror classic, The Night of the Living Dead, instead. I told him that I didn't like gruesome movies, but he said that I could shut my eyes during the gory parts. After the movie, rather than suggesting a hamburger or a drink, he drove right out to a back road near Oakcrest High School and started necking with me. What Tony did a half hour later angered me most of all. He cut his finger on a pin I was wearing and said we had to go right home. He was afraid the scratch would get infected if he did not put Mercurochrome and a Band-Aid on it. When he dropped me off, I said, "Good-bye, Tony," in a friendly enough way, but in my head I thought, "Good-bye forever, Tony."

Notice what the details have done. They have provided you, the reader, with the basis for understanding why the writer made the decision that she did. Through specific evidence, the writer has explained and communicated her point successfully.

Activity 1

Write in the space provided the point that all the specifics in the above paragraph support. Then summarize, using several key words, each of the four reasons that support the point. The first reason is summarized for you as an example.

Point

Why She will not go out with tony.

Reasons

1. Arrived late for our date
2. Took her To a Gruesome movie
3. Did not Suggest Something To eat or drink
4. Started necking with her

Activity 2

See if you can complete the statements below.

1. An important difference between writing and talking is that in writing we absolutely must Support any statement that we make.
2. A Paragraph is a collection of specifics that support a point.

Step 1: Make a Point

Your first step in writing is to decide what point you want to make and to write that point in a single sentence. The point is commonly known as a *topic sentence*. As a guide to yourself and to the reader, put that point in the first sentence of your paragraph. Everything else in the paragraph should then develop and support in specific ways the single point given in the first sentence.

Activity

Read the two paragraphs below, written by students on the topic "Cheating in Everyday Life." Which paragraph starts with a clear, single point and goes on to support that point? Which paragraph fails to start with a clear point and rambles on in many directions, introducing a number of ideas but developing none of them?

Cheating

Cheating has always been a part of life, and it will be so in the future. An obvious situation is that students have many ways of cheating in school. This habit can continue after school is over and become part of their daily lives. There are steps that can be taken to prevent cheating, but many teachers do not seem to care. Maybe they are so burned out by their jobs that they do not want to bother. The honest student is often the one hurt by the cheating of others. Cheating at work occurs also. This cheating may be more dangerous, because employers watch out for it more. Businesses have had to close down because cheating by employees took away a good deal of their profits. A news story recently concerned a waiter who was fired for taking a steak home from the restaurant where he worked, but his taking the steak may have been justified. Cheating in the sense of being unfaithful to a loved one is a different story because emotions are involved. People will probably never stop cheating unless there is a heavy penalty to be paid.

Everyday Cheating

Cheating is common in everyday life. For one thing, cheating at school is common. Many students will borrow a friend's homework and copy it in their own handwriting. During a test, students will use a tiny sheet of answers stored in their pockets or sit near a friend to copy answers. People also cheat on the job. They use the postal meter at work for personal mail or take home office supplies such as tape, paper, or pens. Some people who are not closely supervised or who are out on the road may cheat an employer by taking dozens of breaks or using work time for personal chores. Finally, many people cheat when they deal with large businesses. For instance, few customers will report an incorrect bill in their favor. Visitors in a hotel may take home towels, and restaurant patrons may take home silverware. A customer in a store may change price tags because "This is how much the shirt cost last month." For many people, daily cheating is an acceptable way to behave.

Complete the following statement: The 2nd________ paragraph is effective, for it makes a clear, single point in the first sentence and goes on in the remaining sentences to support that single point.

The second paragraph starts with the single idea that people cheat in everyday life and then supports that idea with several different examples. But the first paragraph does not begin by making a definite point. Instead, we get two broad, obvious statements—that cheating "has always been a part of life" and "will be so in the future." Because the author has not focused in on a clear, single point, what happens in this paragraph is not surprising.

The line of thought in the first paragraph on cheating swerves about like a car without a steering wheel. In the second sentence, we read that ". . . students have many ways of cheating in school," and we think for a moment that this will be the author's point: he or she will give us supporting details about different ways students cheat in school. But the next sentence makes another point: that after school is over, students may continue to cheat as "part of their daily lives." We therefore expect the author to give us details backing up the idea that students who cheat continue to cheat after they leave or finish school. However, the next sentence makes two additional points: "There are steps that can be taken to prevent cheating, but many teachers do not seem to care." These are two more ideas that could be—but are not—the focus of the paragraph. By now we are not too surprised at what happens in the following sentences. Several more points are made: "The honest student is often the one hurt by the cheating of others," cheating at work "may be more dangerous," an employee who stole a steak "may have been justified," and cheating by being unfaithful is different "because emotions are involved." No single idea is developed; the result is confusion.

Step 2: Support the Point with Specific Evidence

The first essential step in writing effectively is to start with a clearly stated point. The second basic step is to support that point with specific evidence. Following are the two examples of supported points that you've already read.

Point

I've decided not to go out with Tony anymore.

Support

1. Arrived late for our date
2. Took me to a chiller movie
3. Didn't take me for a snack afterward
4. Stopped necking because of a scratch

Point

Cheating is common in everyday life.

Support

1. At school
   a. Copying homework
   b. Cheating on tests
2. At work
   a. Using postage meter
   b. Stealing office supplies
   c. Taking breaks and doing errands on company time
3. With large businesses
   a. Not reporting error on bill
   b. Stealing towels and silverware
   c. Switching price tags

The supporting evidence is needed so that we can *see and understand for ourselves* that each writer's point is a sound one. By providing us with particulars about Tony's actions, the first writer shows why she has decided not to go out with him anymore. We can see that she has made a sound point. Likewise, the author of "Everyday Cheating" has supplied specific supporting examples of how cheating is common in everyday life. That paragraph, too, has provided the evidence that is needed for us to understand and agree with the writer's point.

Activity

Both of the paragraphs on the following page resulted from an assignment to "Write a paper that details your reasons for being in college." Both writers make the point that they have various reasons for attending college. Which paragraph then goes on to provide plenty of specific evidence to back up its point? Which paragraph is vague and repetitive and lacks the concrete details needed to show us the exact reasons why the author decided to attend college?

Hint: Imagine that you were asked to make a short film based on each paragraph. Which one suggests specific pictures, locations, words, and scenes you could shoot?

Reasons for Going to College

I decided to attend college for various reasons. One reason is self-respect. For a long time now, I have felt little self-respect. I spent a lot of time doing nothing, just hanging around or getting into trouble, and eventually I began to feel bad about it. Going to college is a way to start feeling better about myself. By accomplishing things, I will improve my self-image. Another reason for going to college is that things happened in my life that made me think about a change. For one thing, I lost the part-time job I had. When I lost the job, I realized I would have to do something in life, so I thought about school. I was in a rut and needed to get out of it but did not know how. But when something happens out of your control, then you have to make some kind of decision. The most important reason for college, though, is to fulfill my dream. I know I need an education, and I want to take the courses I need to reach the position that I think I can handle. Only by qualifying yourself can you get what you want. Going to college will help me fulfill this goal. These are the main reasons why I am attending college.

Why I'm in School

There are several reasons why I'm in school. First of all, my father's attitude made me want to succeed in school. One night last year, after I had come in at 3 A.M., my father said, "Mickey, you're a bum. When I look at my son, all I see is a good-for-nothing bum." I was angry, but I knew my father was right in a way. I had spent the last two years working odd jobs at a pizza parlor and luncheonette, taking "uppers" and "downers" with my friends. That night, though, I decided I would prove my father wrong. I would go to college and be a success. Another reason why I'm in college is my girlfriend's encouragement. Marie has already been in school for a year, and she is doing well in her computer courses. Marie helped me fill out my application and register for courses. She even lent me sixty-five dollars for textbooks. On her day off, she lets me use her car so I don't have to take the college bus. The main reason why I am in college is to fulfill a personal goal: I want to finish something for the first time in my life. For example, I quit high school in the eleventh grade. Then I enrolled in a government job-training program, but I dropped out after six months. I tried to get a high school equivalency diploma, but I started missing classes and eventually gave up. Now I am in a special program where I will earn my high school degree by completing a series of five courses. I am determined to accomplish this goal and to then go on and work for a degree in hotel management.

Complete the following statement: The __2nd__ paragraph provides clear, vividly detailed reasons why the writer decided to attend college.

The second paragraph is the one that solidly backs up its point. The writer gives us specific reasons why he is in school. On the basis of such evidence, we can clearly understand his opening point. The writer of the first paragraph offers only vague, general reasons for being in school. We do not get specific examples of how the writer was "getting into trouble," what events occurred that forced the decision, or even what kind of job he or she wants to qualify for. We sense that the feeling expressed is sincere; but without the benefit of particular examples, we cannot really see why the writer decided to attend college.

THE IMPORTANCE OF SPECIFIC DETAILS

The point that opens a paper is a general statement. The evidence that supports a point is made up of specific details, reasons, examples, and facts.

Specific details have two key values. First of all, details *excite the reader's interest.* They make writing a pleasure to read, for we all enjoy learning particulars about other people—what they do and think and feel. Second, details *support and explain a writer's point;* they give the evidence needed for us to see and understand a general idea. For example, the writer of "Good-bye, Tony" provides details that make vividly clear her decision not to see Tony anymore. She specifies the exact time Tony was supposed to arrive (8:30) and when he actually arrived (9:20). She mentions the kind of film she wanted to see (a new Woody Allen movie) and the one that Tony took her to instead (*The Night of the Living Dead*). She tells us what she may have wanted to do after the movie (have a hamburger or a drink) and what Tony did instead (went necking); she even specifies the exact location of the place Tony took her (a back road near Oakcrest High School). She explains precisely what happened next (Tony "cut his finger on a pin I was wearing") and even mentions by name (Mercurochrome and a Band-Aid) the treatments he planned to use.

The writer of "Why I'm in School" provides equally vivid details. He gives clear reasons (his father's attitude, his girlfriend's encouragement, and his wish to fulfill a personal goal) for being in school and backs up each reason with specific details. His details give us many sharp pictures. For instance, we hear the exact words his father spoke: "Mickey, you're a bum." He tells us exactly how he was spending his time ("working odd jobs at a pizza parlor and luncheonette, taking 'uppers' and 'downers' with my friends"). He describes how his girlfriend helped him (filling out the college application, lending money and her car). Finally, instead of stating generally that "you have to make some kind of decision," as the writer of "Reasons for Going to College" does, he specifies that he has a strong desire to finish college because he dropped out of many schools and programs in the past: high school, a job-training program, and a high school equivalency course.

In both "Good-bye, Tony" and "Why I'm in School," then, the vivid, exact details capture our interest and enable us to share in the writer's experience. We see people's actions and hear their words; the details provide pictures that make each of us feel "I am there." The particulars also allow us to understand clearly each writer's point. We are shown exactly why the first writer has decided not to see Tony anymore and exactly why the second writer is attending college.

Activity

Each of the five points below is followed by two selections. Put an S (for *specific*) in front of the selection that provides specific support for the point. Put an X in front of the selection that lacks supporting details.

1. My two-year-old son was in a stubborn mood today.

   ___X___ a. When I asked him to do something, he gave me nothing but trouble. He seemed determined to make things difficult for me, for he had his mind made up.

   ___S___ b. When I asked him to stop playing in the yard and come indoors, he looked me square in the eye and shouted "No!" and then spelled it out, "N . . . O!"

2. The prices in the amusement park were outrageously high.

   ___X___ a. The food seemed to cost twice as much as it would in a supermarket and was sometimes of poor quality. The rides also cost a lot, and so I had to tell the children that they were limited to a certain number of them.

   ___S___ b. The cost of the log flume, a ride that lasts roughly 3 minutes, was $3.75 a person. Then I had to pay 95 cents for a 6-ounce cup of Coke and $2.50 for a hot dog.

3. My brother-in-law is accident-prone.

   ___S___ a. Once he tried to open a tube of Krazy Glue by his teeth. When the cap came loose, glue squirted out and sealed his lips shut. They had to be pried open in a hospital emergency room.

   ___X___ b. Even when he does seemingly simple jobs, he seems to get into trouble. This can lead to hilarious, but sometimes dangerous, results. Things never seem to go right for him, and he often needs the help of others to get out of one predicament or another.

4. The bargains at the yard sale were junk.

X a. The tables at the yard sale were filled with useless stuff no one could possibly want. They were the kinds of things that should be thrown away, not sold.

S b. The bargains at the yard sale included two headless dolls, blankets filled with holes, scorched pot holders, and a plastic Christmas tree with several branches missing.

5. The key to success in college is organization.

X a. Knowing what you're doing, when you have to do it, and so on is a big help for a student. A system is crucial in achieving an ordered approach to study. Otherwise, things become very disorganized, and it is not long before grades will begin to drop.

S b. Organized students never forget paper or exam dates, which are marked on a calendar above their desks. And instead of having to cram for exams, they study their clear, neat classroom and textbook notes on a daily basis.

The specific support for the first point is answer *b*. The writer does not just tell us that the little boy was stubborn but provides an example that shows us. In particular, the detail of the son's spelling out "N . . . O!" makes the stubbornness vividly real for the reader. Under the second point, answer *b* gives specific prices ($3.75 for a ride, 95 cents for a Coke, and $2.50 for a hot dog) to support the idea that the amusement park was expensive. Answer *a* under the third point vividly backs up the idea that the brother-in-law is accident-prone by detailing an accident with Krazy Glue. The fourth point is supported by answer *b*, which lists specific examples of useless items that were offered for sale—from headless dolls to a broken plastic Christmas tree. We cannot help agreeing with the writer's point that the items were not bargains, but junk. The final point is backed up by answer *b*, which identifies two specific strategies of organized students: they mark important dates on calendars above their desks, and they take careful notes and study them on a daily basis.

In each of the five cases, then, specific evidence is presented to enable us to *see for ourselves* that the writer's point is a valid one.

THE IMPORTANCE OF ADEQUATE DETAILS

One of the most common and serious problems in student writing is inadequate development. You must provide *enough* specific details to support fully a point you are making. You could not, for example, submit a paragraph about how your brother-in-law is accident-prone and provide only a short example. You would have to add several other examples or provide an extended example of your brother-in-law's ill luck. Without such additional support, your paragraph would be underdeveloped.

At times, students try to hide an undersupported point through repetition and wordy generalities. You saw this, for example, in the paragraph titled "Reasons for Going to College" on page 16. Be prepared to do the plain hard work needed to ensure that each of your paragraphs has full and solid support.

Activity

Both of the following paragraphs were written on the same topic, and both have clear opening points. Which one is adequately developed? Which one, on the other hand, has only several particulars and uses mostly vague, general, wordy sentences to conceal the fact that it is starved for specific details?

Abuse of Public Parks

Some people abuse public parks. Instead of using the park for recreation, they go there, for instance, to clean their cars. Park caretakers regularly have to pick up the contents of dumped ashtrays and car litter bags. Certain juveniles visit parks with cans of spray paint to deface buildings, fences, fountains, and statues. Other offenders are those who dig up and cart away park flowers, shrubs, and trees. One couple was even arrested for stealing park sod, which they were using to fill in their back lawn. Perhaps the most widespread offenders are the people who use park tables and benches and fireplaces but do not clean up afterward. Picnic tables are littered with trash, including crumpled bags, paper plates smeared with catsup, and paper cups half-filled with stale soda. On the ground are empty beer bottles, dented soda cans, and sharp metal pop tops. Parks are made for people, and yet--ironically--their worst enemy is people pollution.

Mistreatment of Public Parks

Some people mistreat public parks. Their behavior is evident in many ways, and the catalog of abuses could go on almost without stopping. Different kinds of debris are left by people who have used the park as a place for attending to their automobiles. They are not the only individuals who mistreat public parks, which should be used with respect for the common good of all. Many young people come to the park and abuse it, and their offenses can occur in any season of the year. The reason for their inconsiderate behavior is best known only to themselves. Other visitors have a lack of personal cleanliness in their personal habits when they come to the park, and the park suffers because of it. Such people seem to have the attitude that someone else should clean up after them. It is an undeniable fact that people are the most dangerous thing that parks must contend with.

Complete the following statement: The 1ST paragraph provides an adequate number of specific details to support its point.

The first paragraph offers a series of well-detailed examples of how people abuse parks. The second paragraph, on the other hand, is underdeveloped. The second paragraph speaks only of "different kinds of debris," while the first paragraph refers specifically to "dumped ashtrays and car litter bags"; the second paragraph talks in a general way of young people abusing the park, while the first paragraph supplies such particulars as "cans of spray paint" and defacing "buildings, fences, fountains, and statues." And there is no equivalent in the second paragraph for the specifics in the first paragraph about people who steal park property and litter park grounds. In summary, the second paragraph lacks the full detailed support needed to develop its opening point convincingly.

■ Review Activity

To check your understanding of the chapter so far, see if you can answer the following questions.

1. It has been observed: "To write well, the first thing that you must do is decide what nail you want to drive home." What is meant by *nail*?
   Point you want to make
2. How do you drive home the nail in a paper?
   by using specific details
3. What are the two reasons for using specific details in your writing?
   a. To Excite The reader
   b. TO EXPlain a writers Point

Practice in Making and Supporting a Point

You now know the two most important steps in competent writing: (1) making a point and (2) supporting that point with specific evidence. The purpose of this section is to expand and strengthen your understanding of these two basic steps.

You will first work through a series of activities on *making* a point:

1 Identifying Common Errors in Writing a Topic Sentence
2 Understanding the Two Parts of a Topic Sentence
3 Writing a Topic Sentence: I
4 Writing a Topic Sentence: II

You will then sharpen your understanding of specific details by working through a series of activities on *supporting* a point:

5 Making Words and Phrases Specific
6 Making Sentences Specific
7 Providing Specific Evidence
8 Identifying Adequate Supporting Evidence
9 Adding Details to Complete a Paragraph

Finally, you will practice writing a paragraph of your own:

10 Writing a Simple Paragraph

1 IDENTIFYING COMMON ERRORS IN WRITING A TOPIC SENTENCE

When writing a point, or topic sentence, people sometimes make one of several mistakes that undermine their chances of producing an effective paper. One mistake is to substitute an announcement of the topic for a true topic sentence. Other mistakes include writing statements that are too broad or too narrow. Below are examples of all three errors.

Announcements

Automobile drivers are the concern of this paragraph.

I want to talk about increases in the divorce rate.

The subject of this paper will be my apartment.

Statements That Are Too Broad

People do not always behave responsibly in public places.

Many people have trouble getting along with others.

The places where people live have definite effects on their lives.

Statements That Are Too Narrow

The driver in front of me suddenly slowed for a turn without signaling.

Almost one out of every two marriages ends in divorce.

I have no hot water in my apartment between midnight and 6 A.M.

In the first group above, the statements are not topic sentences; they are, rather, simple announcements of a topic idea. For instance, "Automobile drivers are the concern of this paragraph" does not make a point; it merely identifies, in a rather weak and unimaginative way, the writer's general subject. A topic sentence must advance a point about a limited subject. An effective point would be: "Some automobile drivers have dangerous habits."

In the second group above, all the statements are too broad to be supported adequately. For example, "Many people have trouble getting along with others" could not be supported with specific details in a single paragraph. The statement is broad enough to cover every kind of problem from marital difficulties to quarrels among neighbors to international conflicts. A limited point that could be covered in a paragraph would be: "The divorce rate is increasing for several reasons."

In the third group above, there is no room in any of the three statements for support to be given. For instance, "I have no hot water in my apartment between midnight and 6 A.M." is too narrow to be expanded into a paragraph. Such a statement is sometimes called a *dead-end statement;* there is no place to go with it. Because it is a simple fact, it needs no support. On the other hand, "My landlord is cheating me in several ways" is a point that could be expanded into a paragraph.

Activity 1

Put A beside the sentence that *only announces* a topic in each pair of sentences below. Put OK beside the sentence that *advances an idea* about the topic.

1. __A__ a. This paper will deal with flunking math.
   __OK__ b. I flunked math last semester for several reasons.
2. __A__ a. I am going to write about my job as a gas station attendant.
   __OK__ b. Working as a gas station attendant was the worst job I ever had.
3. __A__ a. Obscene phone calls are the subject of this paragraph.
   __OK__ b. People should know what to do when they receive an obscene phone call.

4. OK a. In several ways, my college library is inconvenient to use.
 A b. This paragraph will deal with the college library.

5. A a. My paper will discuss the topic of procrastinating.
 OK b. The following steps will help you stop procrastinating.

Activity 2

Put TN beside the statement in each pair that is too narrow to be developed into a paragraph. Such a narrow statement is also known as a *dead-end sentence.* Put OK beside the statement in each pair that calls for support or development of some kind.

1. TN a. I do push-ups and sit-ups each morning.
 OK b. Exercising every morning has had positive effects on my health.

2. OK a. José works nine hours a day and then goes to school three hours a night.
 TN b. José is an ambitious man.

3. TN a. I started college after being away from school for seven years.
 OK b. Several of my fears about returning to school have proved to be groundless.

4. OK a. Parts of Walt Disney's *Bambi* make it a frightening movie for children.
 TN b. Last summer I visited Disneyland in Anaheim, California.

5. OK a. My brother was depressed yesterday for several reasons.
 TN b. Yesterday my brother had to pay fifty-two dollars for a motor tune-up.

Activity 3

Put TB beside the statement in each pair that is too broad to be supported adequately in a short paper. Put OK beside the statement that makes a limited point.

1. OK a. Professional football is a dangerous sport.
 TB b. Professional sports are violent.

2. +B a. Married life is the best way of living.
ok b. Teenage marriages often end in divorce for several reasons.

3. ok a. Aspirin can have several harmful side effects.
+B b. Drugs are dangerous.

4. +B a. I've always done poorly in school.
ok b. I flunked math last semester for several reasons.

5. +B a. Computers are changing our society.
ok b. Using computers to teach schoolchildren is a mistake.

2 UNDERSTANDING THE TWO PARTS OF A TOPIC SENTENCE

As stated earlier, the point that opens a paragraph is often called a *topic sentence.* When you look closely at a point, or topic sentence, you can see that it is made up of two parts:

1 The *limited topic*

2 The writer's *idea* about the limited topic

The writer's idea is usually expressed in a *key word* or *words.* All the details in a paragraph should support the idea expressed in the key words. In each of the topic sentences below, a single line appears under the topic and a double line under the idea about the topic (expressed in a key word or words):

My girlfriend is very aggressive.

Highway accidents are often caused by absentmindedness.

The kitchen is the most widely used room in my house.

Voting should be required by law in America.

My pickup truck is the most reliable vehicle I have ever owned.

In the first sentence, the topic is *girlfriend,* and the key word that expresses the writer's idea about his topic is that his girlfriend is *aggressive.* In the second sentence, the topic is *highway accidents,* and the key word that determines the focus of the paragraph is that such accidents are often caused by *absentmindedness.* Notice each topic and key word or words in the other three sentences as well.

Activity

For each point below, put a single line under the topic and a double line under the idea about the topic.

1. Billboards should be abolished.
2. Single life has several advantages for me.
3. The middle child is often a neglected member of the family.
4. The apartment needed repairs.
5. Television commercials use many propaganda techniques.
6. My parents have rigid racial attitudes.
7. The language in many movies today is offensive.
8. Homeowners today are more energy-conscious than ever before.
9. My friend Debbie, who is only nineteen, is extremely old-fashioned.
10. Looking for a job can be a degrading experience.
11. Certain regulations in the school cafeteria should be strictly enforced.
12. My car is a temperamental machine.
13. Living in a one-room apartment has its drawbacks.
14. The city's traffic-light system has both values and drawbacks.
15. Consumers' complaints can often have positive results.

3 WRITING A TOPIC SENTENCE: I

Activity

This activity will give you practice in writing an accurate point, or topic sentence—one that is neither too broad nor too narrow for the supporting material in a paragraph. An added value of the activity is that sometimes you will construct your topic sentence after you have decided what details you want to discuss. You will need to know, then, how to write a topic sentence that will match exactly the details that you have developed.

1. ***Topic sentence:*** Some Causes of Forest Fires ________________

a. Some are caused by careless people tossing matches out car windows.
b. A few are started when lightning strikes a tree.
c. Some result from campers who fail to douse cooking fires.
d. The majority of forest fires are deliberately set by arsonists.

2. ***Topic sentence:*** ______________________________

____

a. We had to wait a half hour even though we had reserved a table.
b. Our appetizers and main courses all arrived at the same time.
c. The busboy ignored our requests for more water.
d. The wrong desserts were delivered to us.

3. ***Topic sentence:*** I have bad Phone

____

a. My phone goes dead at certain times of the day.
b. When I talk long distance, I hear conversations in the background.
c. The line to the phone service center is busy for hours.
d. My telephone bill includes three calls I never made.

4. ***Topic sentence:*** ______________________________

____

a. The crowd scenes were crudely spliced from another film.
b. Mountains and other background scenery were just painted cardboard cutouts.
c. The ''sync'' was off, so that you heard voices even when the actors' lips were not moving.
d. The so-called monster was just a spider that had been filmed through a magnifying lens.

5. ***Topic sentence:*** ______________________________

____

a. In early grades we had spelling bees, and I would be among the first ones sitting down.
b. In sixth-grade English, my teacher kept me busy diagraming sentences on the board.
c. In tenth grade we had to recite poems, and I always forgot my lines.
d. In my senior year, my compositions had more red correction marks than anyone else's.

4 WRITING A TOPIC SENTENCE: II

Often you will start with a general topic or a general idea of what you want to write about. You may, for example, want to write a paragraph about some aspect of school life. To come up with a point about school life, begin by limiting your topic. One way to do this is to make a list of all the limited topics you can think of that fit under the general topic.

Activity

Given below are five general topics and a series of limited topics that fit under them. Make a point out of one of the limited topics in each group.

Hint: To create a topic sentence, ask yourself, "What point do I want to make about ________________ (*my limited topic*)?"

Example Recreation

- Movies
- Dancing
- TV shows
- Reading
- Amusement parks

Your point: *Amusement parks today have some truly terrifying rides.*

1. Your school
   - Teacher
   - Cafeteria
   - Specific class
   - Particular room or building
   - Particular policy (attendance, grading, etc.)
   - Classmate

   Your point: my classmates are in the same grade

2. Job
   - Pay
   - Boss
   - Working conditions
   - Duties
   - Coworkers
   - Customers or clients

   Your point: the Pay for this Job is very low

3. Money
   - Budgets
   - Credit cards
   - Dealing with a bank
   - School expenses
   - Ways to get it
   - Ways to save it

   Your point: Budgets can save money

4. Cars
   - First car
   - Driver's test
   - Road conditions
   - Accident
   - Mandatory speed limit
   - Safety problems

   Your point: The Car accident looked bad

5. Sports
   - A team's chances
   - At your school
   - Women's teams
   - Recreational versus spectator
   - Favorite team
   - Outstanding athlete

   Your point: outstanding Atheletes Go to the Pro's

5 MAKING WORDS AND PHRASES SPECIFIC

To be an effective writer, you must use specific, rather than general, words. Specific words create pictures in the reader's mind. They help capture interest and make your meaning clear.

Activity

This activity will give you practice at changing vague, indefinite words into sharp, specific ones. Add three or more specific words to replace the general word or words underlined in each sentence. Make changes in the wording of a sentence as necessary.

Example My bathroom cabinet contains many drugs.

My bathroom cabinet contains aspirin, antibiotics, tranquilizers, and codeine cough medicine.

1. At the shopping center, we visited several stores.

   At the shopping center, we visited Bergners, meis and Pages.

2. Sunday is my day to take care of chores.

   Sunday is my day to wax Floors, clean the car, and mow the lawn.

3. Lola enjoys various activities in her spare time.

   Lola enjoys Skating and boating in her spare time.

4. I spent most of my afternoon doing homework.

   I spent most of my afternoon doing math and reading.

5. We returned home from vacation to discover that several pests had invaded the house.

   We returned home from vacation to discover that ants, and termites had invaded the house.

6 MAKING SENTENCES SPECIFIC

Again, you will practice changing vague, indefinite writing into lively, image-filled writing that captures your reader's interest and makes your meaning clear. Compare the following sentences:

General	*Specific*
The boy came down the street.	Jerry ran down Woodlawn Avenue.
A bird appeared on the grass.	A blue jay swooped down on the frost-covered lawn.
She stopped the car.	Wanda slammed on the brakes of her Escort.

The specific sentences create clear pictures in your reader's mind. The details *show* readers exactly what has happened.

Here are four ways to make your words and sentences specific:

1 Use exact names.

She loves her *motorbike.*
Lola loves her *Honda.*

2 Use lively verbs.

The garbage truck *went* down Front Street.
The garbage truck *rumbled* down Front Street.

3 Use descriptive words (modifiers) before nouns.

A girl peeked out the window.
A *chubby, six-year-old* girl peeked out the *dirty kitchen* window.

4 Use words that relate to the five senses: sight, hearing, taste, smell, and touch.

That woman is a karate expert.
That *tiny, silver-haired* woman is a karate expert. (*Sight*)

When the dryer stopped, a signal sounded.
When the *whooshing* dryer stopped, a *loud buzzer* sounded. (*Hearing*)

Lola offered me an orange slice.
Lola offered me a *juicy* orange slice. (*Taste*)

The real estate agent opened the door of the closet.
The real estate agent opened the door of the *cedar-scented* closet. (*Smell*)

I pulled the blanket around me to fight off the wind.
I pulled the *scratchy* blanket around me to fight off the *chilling* wind. (*Touch*)

Activity

With the help of the methods described above, add specific details to any eight of the ten sentences that follow. Use separate paper.

Examples The person got out of the car.
The elderly man painfully lifted himself out of the white Buick station wagon.

The fans enjoyed the victory.
Many of the fifty thousand fans stood, waved blankets, and cheered wildly when Barnes scored the winning touchdown.

1. The lunch was not very good.
2. The animal ran away.
3. An accident occurred.
4. The teacher came into the room.
5. The machine did not work.
6. The crowd grew restless.
7. I relaxed.
8. The room was cluttered.
9. The child threw the object.
10. The driver was angry.

7 PROVIDING SPECIFIC EVIDENCE

Activity

Provide three details that logically support each of the following points, or topic sentences. Your details can be drawn from your direct experience, or they can be invented. In each case, the details should show in a specific way what the point expresses in only a general way. State your details briefly in several words rather than in complete sentences.

Example The student had several ways of passing time during the dull lecture.

1. *Shielded his eyes with his hand and dozed awhile.*
2. *Read the sports magazine he had brought to class.*
3. *Made an elaborate drawing on a page of his notebook.*

1. I could tell I was coming down with the flu.

I could not Keep Food Down,
I Had chills
I Kept Coughing

2. The food at the cafeteria was terrible yesterday.

the Hamburger was Cold
The Ice cream was hot
the Chips were Stale

3. I had car problems recently.

My Car did not start
the Altenator went out
The tire was Flat

4. When your money gets tight, there are several ways to economize.

Put money in Savings
Stop eating out
Shop at Discount Stores

5. Some people have dangerous driving habits.

they Swerve From Lane to Lane
Poor usage OF Signals
They Drive too Fast

8 IDENTIFYING ADEQUATE SUPPORTING EVIDENCE

Activity

Two of the following paragraphs provide sufficient details to support their topic sentences convincingly. Write AD for *adequate development* beside those paragraphs. There are also three paragraphs that, for the most part, use vague, general, or wordy sentences as a substitute for concrete details. Write U for *underdeveloped* beside those paragraphs.

AD 1. My Husband's Stubbornness

My husband's worst problem is his stubbornness. He simply will not let any kind of weakness show. If he isn't feeling well, he refuses to admit it. He will keep on doing whatever he is doing and will wait until the symptoms get almost unbearable before he will even hint that anything is the matter with him. Then things are so far along that he has to spend more time recovering than he would with another attitude. He also hates to be wrong. If he is wrong, he will be the last to admit it. This happened once when we went shopping, and he spent an endless amount of time going from one place to the next. He insisted that one of them had a fantastic sale on things he wanted. We never found a sale, but the fact that this situation happened will not change his attitude. Finally, he never listens to anyone else's suggestions on a car trip. He always knows he's on the right road, and the results have led to a lot of time wasted getting back in the right direction. Every time one of these incidents happens, it only means it is going to happen again in the future.

AD 2. Dangerous Games

Because they feel compelled to show off in front of their friends, some teenagers play dangerous games. In one incident, police found a group of boys performing a dangerous stunt with their cars. The boys would perch on the hoods of cars going thirty-five or forty miles an hour. Then the driver would brake sharply, and the boy who flew the farthest off the car would win. Teenagers also drive their cars with the lights off and pass each other on hills or curves as ways of challenging each other. Water, as well as cars, seems to tempt young people to invent dangerous contests. Some students dared each other to swim through a narrow pipe under a four-lane highway. The pipe carried water from a stream to a pond, and the swimmer would have to hold his or her breath for several minutes before coming out on the other side. Another contest involved diving off the rocky sides of a quarry. Large stones sat under the water in certain places, so that any dive could result in a broken neck. But the students would egg each other on to go "rock diving." Playing deadly games like these is a horrifying phase of growing up for some teenagers.

U ________ 3.

Attitudes about Food

Attitudes about food that we form as children are not easily changed. In some families, food is love. Not all families are like this, but some children grow up with this attitude. Some families think of food as something precious and not to be wasted. The attitudes children pick up about food are hard to change in adults. Some families celebrate with food. If a child learns an attitude, it is hard to break this later. Someone once said: "As the twig is bent, so grows the tree." Children are very impressionable, and they can't really think for themselves when they are small. Children learn from the parent figures in their lives, and later from their peers. Some families have healthy attitudes about food. It is important for adults to teach their children these healthy attitudes. Otherwise, the children may have weight problems when they are adults.

U ________ 4.

Qualities in a Friend

There are several qualities I look for in a friend. A friend should give support and security. A friend should also be fun to be around. Friends can have faults, like anyone else, and sometimes it is hard to overlook them. But a friend can't be dropped because he or she has faults. A friend should stick by you, even in bad times. There is a saying that "a friend in need is a friend indeed." I believe this means that there are good friends and fair-weather friends. The second type is not a true friend, since he or she is the kind of person who runs when there's trouble. Friends don't always last a lifetime. Someone you believed to be your best friend may lose contact with you if you move to a different area or go around with a different group of people. A friend should be generous and understanding. A friend does not have to be exactly like you. Sometimes friends are opposites, but they still like each other and get along. Since I am a very quiet person, I can't say that I have many friends. But these are the qualities I believe a friend should have.

U ________ 5.

A Special Joy

I experience a special joy when I stand at the doorway and see my infant son wake up to confront his day. Unaware of my presence, he lies on his back and gurgles and sings to himself. He uses his hands to hit the bells on the red carousel mounted on the side of his crib, and he then examines his hands as if they made the jingling sound. He inspects the corner of his fuzzy white thermal blanket and eventually kicks himself free of the blanket. Then he looks carefully at his toes and legs and gets his foot stuck momentarily between the bars of the crib. Grunting, he turns himself on his side and grasps the slats of the crib. His foot comes free as he pulls himself up to a

standing position, and he seems to laugh and gurgle with pleasure at his accomplishment. For a while, he busies himself banging the side of the crib and reaching out to pull at the blue lace window curtain nearby. I say, "Well, hello there," as I enter the room, and he turns and greets me with a huge smile. He makes excited sounds as he moves toward me along the side of the crib and extends an arm in anticipation. With a smile, I reach down to pick up my son.

9 ADDING DETAILS TO COMPLETE A PARAGRAPH

Activity

Each of the following paragraphs needs specific details to back up its supporting points. In the spaces provided, add a sentence or two of realistic details for each supporting point. The more specific you are, the more convincing your details are likely to be.

1. A Pushover Instructor

We knew after the first few classes that the instructor was a pushover. First of all, he didn't seem able to control the class.

The whole class seem to talk while he attempted to talk. We often hand in homework late

In addition, he made some course requirements easier when a few students complained. He cancelled the midterm and reduced the 3 assignments to 1.

Finally, he gave the easiest quiz we had ever taken. by leting the class use an open Book, and only gave true or False questions.

2. Helping a Parent in College

There are several ways a family can help a parent who is attending college. First, family members can take over some of the household chores that the parent usually does. ______________________________

____

____

____

Also, family members can make sure that the student has some quiet study time. ______________________________

____

____

____

Last, families can take an interest in the student's problems and accomplishments. ______________________________

____

____

____

10 WRITING A SIMPLE PARAGRAPH

You know now that an effective paragraph does two essential things: (1) it makes a point, and (2) it provides specific details to support that point. You have considered a number of paragraphs that have been effective or ineffective because they have or have not followed these two basic steps.

You are ready, then, to write a simple paragraph of your own. Choose either of the assignments ahead, and follow carefully the guidelines provided.

■ Assignment 1

Turn back to the activity on page 33 and select the point for which you have the best supporting details. Develop the point into a paragraph by following these steps:

a If necessary, rewrite the point so that the first sentence is more specific or more exactly suits your purpose. For example, you might want to rewrite the second point so that it includes a specific time and place: "Dinner at the Union Building Cafeteria was terrible yesterday."

b Provide several sentences of information to develop fully each of your three supporting details. Make sure that all the information in your paragraph truly supports your point. Use as an outlining aid the paragraph form on the inside back cover of this book.

c Use the words *First of all, Second,* and *Finally* to introduce each of your three supporting details.

d Conclude your paragraph with a sentence that refers to your opening point. This last sentence "rounds off" the paragraph and lets the reader know that your discussion is complete. For example, the second paragraph about cheating on page 13 begins with "Cheating is common in everyday life." It closes with a statement that refers to, and echoes, the opening point: "For many people, daily cheating is an acceptable way to behave."

e Supply a title based on the point. For instance, the fourth point might have the title "Ways to Economize."

Use the following list to check your paragraph for each of the above items:

Yes	*No*	
____	____	Do you begin with a point?
____	____	Do you provide relevant, specific details that support the point?
____	____	Do you use the words *First of all, Second,* and *Finally* to introduce each of your three supporting details?
____	____	Do you have a closing sentence?
____	____	Do you have a title based on the point?
____	____	Are your sentences clear and free from obvious errors?

■ Assignment 2

You have read two paragraphs in this chapter (page 16) on reasons for being in college. For this assignment, write a paragraph describing your own reasons for being in college. You might want to look first at the following list of common reasons students give for going to school. Use the ones that apply to you (making them as specific as possible) or supply your own. Select three of your most important reasons for being in school and generate specific supporting details for each reason. To write the paragraph, follow steps *b* through *e* under Assignment 1.

Apply in My Case	*Reasons Students Go to College*
________	■ To have some fun before getting a job
________	■ To prepare for a specific career
________	■ To please their families
________	■ To educate and enrich themselves
________	■ To be with friends who are going to college
________	■ To take advantage of an opportunity they didn't have before in their lives
________	■ To find a husband or wife
________	■ To see if college has anything to offer them
________	■ To do more with their lives than they've done so far
________	■ To take advantage of Veterans' Administration benefits or other special funding
________	■ To earn the status that they feel comes with a college degree
________	■ To get a new start in life

Some Suggestions on What to Do Next

1 Work through the next chapter in Part One: "The Third and Fourth Steps in Writing."

2 Read "Providing Examples" (page 117) in Part Three and do the first writing assignment.

3 Work through "Using the Dictionary" (page 455) and "Improving Spelling" (page 463) in Part Six.

4 Read the first two skills under "Key Study Skills" (page 247) in Part Five.

5 Take the "Sentence-Skills Diagnostic Test" (page 317) in Part Six and begin working on the sentence skills you need to review.

THE THIRD AND FOURTH STEPS IN WRITING

This chapter will show you how to

- Organize the specific evidence in a paper by using a clear method of organization
- Connect the specific evidence by using transitions and other connecting words
- Write clear, error-free sentences by referring to the rules in Part Six of this book

The third and fourth steps in effective writing are:

3 Organize and connect the specific evidence
4 Write clear, error-free sentences

You know from the previous chapter that the first two steps in writing an effective paragraph are stating a point and supporting it with specific evidence. The third step is to organize and connect the specific evidence. Most of this chapter will deal with the chief ways to organize and connect this supporting information in a paper. The chapter will then look briefly at the sentence skills that make up the fourth and final step in writing a successful paper.

Step 3: Organize and Connect the Specific Evidence

At the same time that you are generating the specific details needed to support a point, you should be thinking about ways to organize and connect those details. All the details in your paper must cohere, or stick together; in this way, your reader will be able to move smoothly and clearly from one bit of supporting information to the next. This chapter will discuss the following ways to organize and connect supporting details: (1) common methods of organization, (2) transitions, and (3) other connecting words.

COMMON METHODS OF ORGANIZATION: TIME ORDER AND EMPHATIC ORDER

Time order and emphatic order are common methods used to organize the supporting material in a paper. You will learn more specialized methods of development in Part Three of the book.

Time order simply means that details are listed as they occur in time. *First* this is done; *next* this; *then* this; *after* that, this, and so on. Here is a paragraph that organizes its details through time order:

How I Relax

The way I relax when I get home from school on Thursday night is, first of all, to put my three children to bed. Next, I run hot water in the tub and put in lots of perfumed bubble bath. As the bubbles rise, I undress and get into the tub. The water is relaxing to my tired muscles, and the bubbles are tingly on my skin. I lie back and put my feet on the water spigots, with everything but my hair under the water. I like to stick my big toe up the spigot and spray water over the tub. After about ten minutes of soaking, I wash myself with scented soap, get out and dry myself off, and put on my nightgown. Then I go downstairs and make myself two ham, lettuce, and tomato sandwiches on white bread and pour myself a tall glass of iced tea with plenty of sugar and ice cubes. I carry these into the living room and turn on the television. To get comfortable, I sit on the couch with a pillow behind me and my legs under me. I enjoy watching the Tonight Show or a late movie. The time is very peaceful after a long, hard day of housecleaning, cooking, washing, and attending night class.

Fill in the missing words: The paragraph on the preceding page uses the following words to help show time order: ______________, ______________, ______________, ______________, and ______________.

Emphatic order is sometimes described as "save-the-best-till-last" order. It means that the most interesting or important detail is placed in the last part of a paper. (In cases where all the details seem equal in importance, the writer should impose a personal order that seems logical or appropriate to the details in question.) The last position in a paper is the most emphatic position because the reader is most likely to remember the last thing read. *Finally, last of all,* and *most important* are typical words showing emphasis. The following paragraph organizes its details through emphatic order.

The National Enquirer

There are several reasons why the National Enquirer is so popular. First of all, the paper is heavily advertised on television. In the ads, attractive-looking people say, with a smile, "I want to know!" as they scan the pages of the Enquirer. The ads reassure people that it's all right to want to read stories such as "Grace Kelly's Ghost Haunts Her Family" or "Burt's Secret Affair with Schoolgirl." In addition, the paper is easily available. In supermarkets, convenience stores, and drugstores, the Enquirer is always placed in racks close to the cash register. As customers wait in line, they can't help being attracted by the paper's glaring headlines. Then, on impulse, customers will add the paper to their other purchases. Most of all, people read the Enquirer because of a love of gossip. We find other people's lives fascinating, especially if those people are rich and famous. We want to see and read about their homes, their clothes, their friends, lovers, and families. We also take a kind of mean delight in their problems and mistakes, perhaps because we're jealous of them. It's hard to resist buying a paper that promises to show "Liz's Fabulous Jewels," "The Husband Barbra Dumped," or even--though we may feel ashamed of our interest--"Michael's Secret Love." The Enquirer knows how to get us interested and make us buy.

Fill in the missing words: The paragraph lists a total of ______ different reasons why people read the *National Enquirer*. The writer of the paragraph feels that the most important reason is ____.
He or she signals this reason by using the emphasis words ______________.

Some paragraphs use a *combination of time order and emphatic order*. For example, the paragraph about Tony on page 11 includes a time order: it moves from the time Tony arrived to the end of the evening. In addition, the writer uses an emphatic order, ending with her most important reason (signaled by the words "most of all") for not wanting to see Tony anymore.

TRANSITIONS

Transitions are signals that help readers follow the direction of the writer's thought. They are like signposts on the road that guide travelers. In the box below are some common transitional words and phrases, grouped according to the kind of signal they give to readers. Note that certain words provide more than one kind of signal.

Addition signals: first of all, for one thing, second, the third reason, also, next, another, and, in addition, moreover, furthermore, finally, last of all

Time signals: first, then, next, after, as, before, while, meanwhile, now, during, finally

Space signals: next to, across, on the opposite side, to the left, to the right, in front, in back, above, below, behind, nearby

Change-of-direction signals: but, however, yet, in contrast, otherwise, still, on the contrary, on the other hand

Illustration signals: for example, for instance, specifically, as an illustration, once, such as

Conclusion signals: therefore, consequently, thus, then, as a result, in summary, to conclude, last of all, finally

Activity

1. Underline the three *addition* signals in the following selection:

   I am opposed to state-supported lotteries for a number of reasons. First of all, by supporting lotteries, states are supporting gambling. I don't see anything morally wrong with gambling, but it is a known cause of suffering for many people who do it to excess. The state should be concerned with relieving suffering, not causing it. Another objection I have to the state lotteries is the kind of advertising they do on television. The commercials promote the lotteries as an easy way to get rich. In fact, the odds against getting rich are astronomical. Last of all, the lotteries take advantage of the people who can least afford them. Studies have shown that people with lower incomes are more likely to play the lottery than people with higher incomes. This is the harshest reality of the lotteries: the state encouraging people of limited means not to save their money but to throw it away on a state-supported pipe dream.

2. Underline the four *time* signals in the following selection:

It is often easy to spot bad drivers on the road because they usually make more than one mistake: they make their mistakes in series. First, for example, you notice that a man is tailgating you. Then, almost as soon as you notice, he has passed you in a no-passing zone. That's two mistakes already in a matter of seconds. Next, almost invariably, you see him speed down the road and pass someone else. Finally, as you watch in disbelief, glad that he's out of your way, he speeds through a red light or cuts across oncoming traffic in a wild left turn.

3. Underline the three *space* signals in the following selection:

Standing in the burned-out shell of my living room was a shocking experience. Above my head were charred beams, all that remained of our ceiling. In front of me, where our television and stereo had once stood, were twisted pieces of metal and chunks of blackened glass. Strangely, some items seemed little damaged by the fire. For example, I could see the TV tuner knob and a dusty record under the rubble. I walked through the gritty ashes until I came to what was left of our sofa. Behind the sofa had been a wall of family photographs. Now, the wall and the pictures were gone. I found only a water-logged scrap of my wedding picture.

4. Underline the four *change-of-direction* signals in the following selection:

In some ways, train travel is superior to air travel. People always marvel at the speed with which airplanes can zip from one end of the country to another. Trains, on the other hand, definitely take longer. But sometimes longer can be better. Traveling across the country by train allows you to experience the trip more completely. You get to see the cities and towns, mountains and prairies that too often pass by unnoticed when you fly. Another advantage of train travel is comfort. Traveling by plane means wedging yourself into a narrow seat with your knees bumping the back of the seat in front of you and being handed a "snack" consisting of a bag of ten roasted peanuts. In contrast, the seats on most trains are spacious and comfortable, permitting even the most long-legged traveler to stretch out and watch the scenery just outside the window. And when train travelers grow hungry, they can get up and stroll to the dining car, where they can order anything from a simple snack to a gourmet meal. There's no question that train travel is definitely slow and old-fashioned compared to air travel. However, in many ways it is much more civilized.

5. Underline the three *illustration* signals in the following selection:

   Status symbols are all around us. The cars we drive, for instance, say something about who we are and how successful we have been. The auto makers depend on this perception of automobiles, designing their commercials to show older, well-established people driving Cadillacs and young, fun-loving people driving to the beach in sports cars. Television, too, has become something of a status symbol. Specifically, school children are often measured by their classmates according to whether or not their family has a cable television hookup. Another example of a status symbol is the video cassette recorder. This device, not so long ago considered a novelty, is now considered as common as the television set itself. To be without a VCR today is like having a car without whitewalls in the fifties.

6. Underline the *conclusion* signal in the following selection:

   A hundred years ago, miners used to bring caged canaries down into the mines with them to act as warning signals. If the bird died, the miner knew that the oxygen was running out. The smaller animal would be affected much more quickly than the miners. In the same way, animals are acting as warning signals to us today. Baby birds die in the shell because pesticides in the environment cause the adults to lay paper-thin eggs. Fish die when lakes are contaminated with acid rain or poisonous mercury. The dangers in our environment will eventually affect all life on earth, including humans. Therefore, we must pay attention to these early warning signals. If we don't, we will be as foolish as a miner who ignored a dead canary--and we will die.

OTHER CONNECTING WORDS

In addition to transitions, there are three other kinds of connecting words that help tie together the specific evidence in a paper: repeated words, pronouns, and synonyms. Each will be discussed in turn.

Repeated Words

Many of us have been taught by English teachers—correctly so—not to repeat ourselves in our writing. On the other hand, repeating key words can help tie together the flow of thought in a paper. In the selection that follows, the word *retirement* is repeated to remind readers of the key idea around which the discussion is centered. Underline the word the five times it appears.

Oddly enough, retirement can pose more problems for the spouse than for the retired person. For a person who has been accustomed to a demanding job, retirement can mean frustration and a feeling of uselessness.

This feeling will put pressure on the spouse to provide challenges at home equal to those of the workplace. Often, these tasks will disrupt the spouse's well-established routine. Another problem arising from retirement is filling up all those empty hours. The spouse may find himself or herself in the role of social director or tour guide, expected to come up with a new form of amusement every day. Without sufficient challenges or leisure activities, a person can become irritable and take out the resulting boredom and frustration of retirement on the marriage partner. It is no wonder that many of these partners wish their spouses would come out of retirement and do something--anything--just to get out of the house.

Pronouns

Pronouns (*he, she, it, you, they, this, that,* and others) are another way to connect ideas as you develop a paper. Using pronouns to take the place of other words or ideas can help you avoid needless repetition in a paper. (Be careful, though, to use pronouns with care in order to avoid the unclear or inconsistent pronoun references described in this book on page 000.) Underline the eight pronouns in the passage below, noting at the same time the words that the pronouns refer to.

A professor of nutrition at a major university recently advised his students that they could do better on their examinations by eating lots of sweets. He told them that the sugar in cakes and candy would stimulate their brains to work more efficiently, and that if the sugar were eaten for only a month or two, it would not do them any harm.

Synonyms

Using synonyms (that is, words that are alike in meaning) also can help move the reader clearly from one thought in a paper to the next. In addition, the use of synonyms increases variety and interest by avoiding needless repetition of the same words. Underline the three words used as synonyms for *fallacies* in the following selection.

There are many fallacies about suicide. One false idea is that the person who talks about suicide never follows through. The truth is that about three out of every four people who commit suicide notify one or more persons ahead of time. Another misconception is that the person who commits suicide is poor or downtrodden. Poverty, however, appears to be a deterrent to suicide rather than a predisposing factor. A final myth about suicide is that suicide-bent persons will eventually take their lives one way or another, whether or not the most obvious means of suicide is removed from their reach. Since an attempt at suicide is a kind of cry for help, removing convenient means of taking one's life, such as a gun, shows to the people bent on suicide that someone cares enough about them to try to prevent it.

Activity

Read the selection below and then answer the questions about it that follow.

My Worst Experience of the Week

The registration process at State College was a nightmare. The night before registration officially began, I went to bed anxious about the whole matter, and nothing that happened the next day served to ease my tension. First, even though I had paid my registration fee early last spring, the people at the bursar's office had no record of my payment. And for some bizarre reason, they wouldn't accept the receipt I had. Consequently, I had to stand in line for two hours, waiting for someone to give me a slip of paper which stated that I had, in fact, paid my registration fee. The need for this new receipt seemed ludicrous to me since, all along, I had proof that I had paid. I was next told that I had to see my adviser in the Law and Justice Department and that the department was in Corridor C of the Triad Building. I had no idea what or where the Triad was. But, finally, I found my way to the ugly, gray-white building. Then I began looking for Corridor C. When I found it, everyone there was a member of the Communications Department. No one seemed to know where Law and Justice had gone. Finally, one instructor said she thought Law and Justice was in Corridor A. "And where is Corridor A?" I asked. "I don't know," the teacher answered. "I'm new here." She saw the bewildered look on my face and said sympathetically, "You're not the only one who's confused." I nodded and walked numbly away. I felt as if I were fated to spend the rest of the semester trying to complete the registration process, and I wondered if I would ever become an official college student.

■ Questions

1. How many times is the key idea *registration* repeated? ______________
2. Write here the pronoun that is used for *people at the bursar's office* (lines 4–5): ______________; *Corridor C* (line 13): ______________; *instructor* (line 15): ______________.
3. Write here the words that are used as a synonym for *receipt* (line 6): ____; the words that are used as a synonym for *Triad* (line 12): ____; the word that is used as a synonym for *instructor* (line 15): ____.

Step 4: Write Clear, Error-Free Sentences

The fourth step in writing an effective paper is to follow the agreed-upon rules, or conventions, of written English. These conventions, or, as they are called in this book, *sentence skills,* must be followed if your sentences are to be clear and error-free. Here are the most common of these conventions.

1 Write complete sentences rather than fragments.
2 Do not write run-on sentences.
3 Use verb forms correctly.
4 Make sure that subjects and verbs agree.
5 Eliminate faulty parallelism and faulty modifiers.
6 Use pronoun forms correctly.
7 Use capital letters where needed.
8 Use correctly the following marks of punctuation: apostrophe, quotation marks, comma, semicolon, colon, hyphen, dash, parentheses.
9 Use correct paper format.
10 Eliminate wordiness.
11 Choose words carefully.
12 Check for possible spelling errors.
13 Eliminate careless errors.
14 Vary your sentences.

Space will not be taken here to explain and offer activities in all the sentence skills. Rather, they will be treated in detail in Part Six of the book, where they can be referred to easily as needed. A diagnostic test on page 317 will help you identify skills you may need to review. You teacher will also identify such skills in marking your papers and may use the correction symbols shown on the inside back cover. Note that the correction symbols, and also the checklist of sentence skills on the inside front cover, contain page references, so that you can turn quickly to those skills that give you problems.

■ Review Activity

Complete the following statements.

1. The four steps in writing a paper are:

   a. ______________________________

   b. ______________________________

   c. ______________________________

   d. ______________________________

2. *Time order* means ______________________________

   ____

3. *Emphatic order* means ______________________________

   ____

4. ____________ are word signals that help readers follow the direction of a writer's thought.

5. In addition to transitions, three other kinds of connecting words that help link sentences and ideas are repeated words, ________, and ________.

Practice in Organizing and Connecting Specific Evidence

You now know the third step in effective writing: organizing the specific evidence used to support the main point of a paper. You also know that the fourth step—writing clear, error-free sentences—will be treated in detail in Part Six of the book. This closing section will expand and strengthen your understanding of the third step in writing.

You will work through the following series of activities:

1 Organizing through Time Order
2 Organizing through Emphatic Order
3 Organizing through a Combination of Time and Emphatic Order
4 Identifying Transitions
5 Providing Transitions
6 Identifying Transitions and Other Connecting Words

1 ORGANIZING THROUGH TIME ORDER

Activity

Use time order to organize the scrambled list of sentences below. Put the number 1 beside the point that all other sentences support. Then number each supporting sentence as it occurs in time.

_______ The table is right near the garbage pail.

_______ So you reluctantly select a gluelike tuna-fish sandwich, a crushed-in apple pie, and watery hot coffee.

_______ You sit at the edge of the table, away from the garbage pail, and gulp down your meal.

_______ Trying to eat in the cafeteria is an unpleasant experience.

_______ Suddenly you spot a free table in the corner.

_______ With a last swallow of the lukewarm coffee, you get up and leave the cafeteria as rapidly as possible.

_______ Flies are flitting in and out of the pail.

_______ By the time it is your turn, the few things that are almost good are gone.

_______ There does not seem to be a free table anywhere.

_______ Unfortunately, there is a line in the cafeteria.

_______ The hoagies, coconut-custard pie, and iced tea have all disappeared.

_______ You hold your tray and look for a place to sit down.

_______ You have a class in a few minutes, and so you run in to grab something to eat quickly.

2 ORGANIZING THROUGH EMPHATIC ORDER

Activity

Use emphatic order (order of importance) to arrange the scrambled list of sentences below. Put the number 1 beside the point that all other sentences support. Then number each supporting sentence, starting with what seems the least important detail and ending with the most important detail.

_______ The people here are all around my age and seem to be genuinely friendly and interested in me.

_______ The place where I live has several important advantages.

_______ The schools in this neighborhood have a good reputation, so I feel that my daughter is getting a good education.

_______ The best thing of all about this area, though, is the school system.

_______ Therefore, I don't have to put up with public transportation or worry about how much it's going to cost to park each day.

_______ The school also has an extended day-care program, so I know my daughter is in good hands until I come home from work.

_______ First of all, I like the people who live in the other apartments near mine.

_______ Another positive aspect of this area is that it's close to where I work.

_______ That's more than I can say for the last place I lived, where people stayed behind locked doors.

_______ The office where I'm a receptionist is only a six-block walk from my house.

_______ In addition, I save a lot of wear and tear on my car.

3 ORGANIZING THROUGH A COMBINATION OF TIME ORDER AND EMPHATIC ORDER

Activity

Use a combination of time and emphatic order to arrange the scrambled list of sentences below. Put the number 1 beside the point that all other sentences support. Then number each supporting sentence. Paying close attention to transitional words and phrases will help you organize and connect the supporting sentences.

_______ I did not see the spider but visited my friend in the hospital where he suffered through a week of nausea and dizziness because of the poison.

_______ We were listening to the radio when we discovered that nature was calling.

_______ As I got back into the car, I sensed, rather than felt or saw, a presence on my left hand.

_______ After my two experiences, I suspect that my fear of spiders will be with me until I die.

_______ The first experience was when my best friend received a bite from a black widow spider.

_______ I looked down at my hand but could not see anything because it was so dark.

_______ I had two experiences when I was sixteen that are the cause of my *arachniphobia,* or terrible and uncontrollable fear of spiders.

_______ We stopped the car, walked into the woods a few feet, and watered the leaves.

_______ My friend then entered the car, putting on the dashboard light, and I almost passed out with horror.

_______ I saw the bandage on his hand and the puffy swelling when the bandage was removed.

_______ Then it flew off my hand and into the dark bushes nearby.

_______ I sat in the car for an hour afterward, shaking and sweating and rubbing the fingers of my hand to reassure myself that the spider was no longer there.

_______ But my more dramatic experience with spiders happened one evening when another friend and I were driving around in his car.

_______ Almost completely covering my fingers was a monstrous brown spider, with white stripes running down each of an endless number of long, furry legs.

_______ Most of all, I saw the ugly red scab on his hand and the yellow pus that continued oozing from under the scab for several weeks.

_______ I imagined my entire hand soon disappearing as the behemoth devoured it.

_______ At the same time I cried out ''Arghh!'' and flicked my hand violently back and forth to shake off the spider.

_______ For a long, horrible second it clung stickily, as if intertwined for good among the fingers of my hand.

4 IDENTIFYING TRANSITIONS

Activity

Locate the major transitions used in the following two selections. Then write the transitions in the spaces provided. Mostly you will find addition words such as *another* and *also.* You will also find several change-of-direction words such as *but* and *however.*

1. Hints for Runners

Watching a football game on television may seem like the easiest thing in the world to do. However, like the game of football itself, watching a game correctly is far more complicated than it appears. First is the matter of who you will watch the game with. The ideal number of people depends on the size of your living room. Also, at least one of your companions should be rooting for the opposite team. There's nothing like a little rivalry to increase the enjoyment of a football game. Next, you must attend to the refreshments. Make sure that plenty of everyone's favorite drinks are on hand, along with the essential chips, dips, and pretzels. You may even want something more substantial on hand, like sandwiches or pizza. If you do, make everyone wait until the moment of kickoff before eating. This will make everything taste much better. Finally, there is one last piece of equipment you should have on hand: a football. The purpose of this object is not to send lamps hurtling from tables or to smash the television screen, but to toss around--outside--during halftime. If your team happens to be getting trounced, you may decide not to wait until halftime.

a. ______________________ d. ______________________

b. ______________________ e. ______________________

c. ______________________

2. Avoidance Tactics

Getting down to studying for an exam or writing a paper is hard, and so it is tempting for students to use one of the following five avoidance tactics in order to put the work aside. For one thing, students may say to themselves, "I can't do it." They adopt a defeatist attitude at the start and give up without a struggle. They could get help with their work by using such college services as tutoring programs and skills labs. However, they refuse to even try. A second avoidance tactic is to say, "I'm too busy." Students may take on an extra job, become heavily involved in social activities, or allow family problems to become so time-consuming that they cannot concentrate on their studies. Yet if college really matters to a student, he or she will make sure that there is enough time to do the required work. Another avoidance tactic is expressed by the phrase "I'm too tired." Typically, sleepiness occurs when it is time to study or go to class and then vanishes when the school pressure is off. This sleepiness is a sign of work avoidance. A fourth excuse is to say, "I'll do it later." Putting things off until the last minute is practically a guarantee of poor grades on tests and papers. When everything else seems more urgent than studying--watching TV, calling a friend, or even cleaning an oven--a student may simply be escaping academic work. Last, some students avoid work by saying to themselves, "I'm here and that's what counts." Such students live under the dangerous delusion that, since they possess a college ID, parking sticker, and textbooks, the course work will somehow take care of itself. But once a student has a college ID in a pocket, he or she has only just begun. Doing the necessary studying, writing, and reading will bring real results: good grades, genuine learning, and a sense of accomplishment.

a.	____________________	e.	____________________
b.	____________________	f.	____________________
c.	____________________	g.	____________________
d.	____________________	h.	____________________

5 PROVIDING TRANSITIONS

Activity

In the spaces provided, add logical transitions to tie together the sentences and ideas in the following paragraphs. Use the words in the boxes that precede each paragraph.

1.

however	a second	last of all
for one thing	also	on the other hand

Why School May Frighten a Young Child

Schools may be frightening to young children for a number of reasons. ______________, the regimented environment may be a new and disturbing experience. At home children may have been able to do what they wanted when they wanted to do it. In school, ______________, they are given a set time for talking, working, playing, eating, and even going to the bathroom. ______________ source of anxiety may be the public method of discipline that some teachers use. Whereas at home children are scolded in private, in school they may be held up to embarrassment and ridicule in front of their peers. "Bonnie," the teacher may say, "why are you the only one in the class who didn't do your homework?" Or, "David, why are you the only one who can't work quietly at your seat?" Children may ______________ be frightened by the loss of personal attention. Their little discomforts or mishaps, such as tripping on the steps, may bring instant sympathy from a parent; in school, there is often no one to notice, or the teacher is frequently too busy to care and just says, "Go do your work. You'll be all right."

_____________, a child may be scared by the competitive environment of the school. At home, one hopes, such competition for attention is minimal. In school, _____________, children may vie for the teacher's approving glance or tone of voice, or for stars on a paper, or for favored seats in the front row. For these and other reasons, it is not surprising that children may have difficulty adjusting to school.

2.

for example	finally	first of all
then	such as	as a result
but	another	

Job Burnout

Job burnout has several causes. _____________, successful workers may be given more to do just because they do their jobs well. Soon they become overloaded and must work even harder just to keep up with the pace. _____________, the work load becomes impossible, and exhaustion sets in. _____________ cause of burnout is conflicting demands. Many career women, _____________, find themselves trapped between one set of expectations in the workplace and another at home. They are expected to perform competently for eight hours a day and then come home to cook a gourmet meal or help a child or spouse with a problem. _____________, certain occupations are high burnout risks. People in the service professions, _____________ nurses, social workers, and teachers, begin their careers filled with idealism and commitment. _____________ the long hours, heavy case loads or enrollments, and miles of red tape become overwhelming, and the rewards--the few people they can help--are all too few. _____________, burnout for these people is almost inevitable.

6 IDENTIFYING TRANSITIONS AND OTHER CONNECTING WORDS

Activity

The following selections use transitions, repeated words, synonyms, and pronouns to help tie together ideas. The connecting words you are to identify have been underlined. In the space provided, write T for *transition,* RW for *repeated word,* S for *synonym,* and P for *pronoun.*

________ 1. I decided to pick up a drop-add form from the registrar's office. However, I changed my mind when I saw the long line of students waiting there.

________ 2. We absorb radiation from many sources in our environment. Our color television sets and microwave ovens, among other things, give off low-level radiation.

________ 3. I checked my car's tires, oil, water, and belts before the trip. But the ungrateful machine blew a gasket about fifty miles from home.

________ 4. At the turn of the century, bananas were still an oddity in America. Some people even attempted to eat them with the skins on.

________ 5. Many researchers believe that people have weight set-points their bodies try to maintain. This may explain why many dieters return to their original weight.

________ 6. Women's clothes, in general, use less material than men's clothes. Yet women's garments are usually more expensive than men's.

________ 7. In England, drivers use the left-hand side of the road. Moreover, steering wheels are on the right-hand side of their cars.

________ 8. At the end of the rock concert, thousands of fans held up Bic lighters in the darkened arena. The sea of lights signaled that the fans wanted an encore.

________ 9. The temperance movement in this country sought to ban alcohol. Drinking liquor, movement leaders said, led to violence, poverty, prostitution, and insanity.

________ 10. Crawling babies will often investigate new objects by putting them in their mouths. Therefore, parents should be alert for any pins, tacks, or other dangerous items on floors and carpets.

________ 11. One technique that advertisers use is to have a celebrity endorse a product. The consumer then associates the star qualities of the celebrity with the product.

________ 12. Canning vegetables is easy and economical. It can also be very dangerous.

_______ 13. For me, apathy quickly sets in when the weather becomes hot and humid. This listlessness disappears when the humidity decreases.

_______ 14. Establishing credit is important for a woman. A good credit history is often necessary when applying for a loan or charge account.

_______ 15. The restaurant table must have had uneven legs. Every time we tried to eat, it wobbled like a seesaw.

Some Suggestions on What to Do Next

1 Work through the final chapter in Part One: "The Four Bases for Evaluating Writing."

2 Read "Explaining a Process" (page 135) in Part Three and do the first writing assignment.

3 Read the rest of "Key Study Skills" in Part Five and "Vocabulary Development" in Part Six.

4 Continue your review of sentence skills in Part Six. If you plan to make a general review of all the key skills, here is an appropriate sequence to follow: (1) Paper Format, (2) Capital Letters, (3) Subjects and Verbs, (4) Sentence Fragments, (5) Run-Ons, (6) Standard English Verbs, (7) Irregular Verbs, (8) Subject-Verb Agreement, (9) Apostrophe, (10) Comma, (11) Quotation Marks, (12) Sentence Variety.

THE FOUR BASES FOR EVALUATING WRITING

This chapter will show you how to evaluate a paper for

- Unity
- Support
- Coherence
- Sentence Skills

In the preceding chapters, you learned the four essential steps in writing an effective paper. The box below shows how the steps lead to four bases, or standards, you can use in evaluating a paper.

Four Steps →		*Four Bases*
1	If you make one point and stick to that point,	you will have *unity* in your paper.
2	If you support the point with specific evidence,	you will have *support* in your paper.
3	If you organize and connect the specific evidence,	you will have *coherence* in your paper.
4	If you write clear, error-free sentences,	you will have effective *sentence skills* in your paper.

This chapter will discuss the four bases of unity, support, coherence, and sentence skills and will show how the four bases can be used to evaluate a paper.

Base 1: Unity

Activity

The following two paragraphs were written by students on the topic "Why Students Drop Out of College." Read them and decide which one makes its point more clearly and effectively, and why.

Why Students Drop Out

Students drop out of college for many reasons. First of all, some students are bored in school. These students may enter college expecting nonstop fun or a series of fascinating courses. When they find out that college is often a routine, they quickly lose interest. They do not want to take dull required courses or spend their nights studying, and so they drop out. Students also drop out of college because the work is harder than they thought it would be. These students may have made decent grades in high school simply by showing up for class. In college, however, they may have to prepare for two-hour exams, write fifteen-page term papers, or make detailed presentations to a class. The hard work comes as a shock, and students give up. Perhaps the most common reason students drop out is because they are having personal or emotional problems. Younger students, especially, may be attending college at an age when they are also feeling confused, lonely, or depressed. These students may have problems with roommates, family, boyfriends, or girlfriends. They become too unhappy to deal with both hard academic work and emotional troubles. For many types of students, dropping out seems to be the only solution they can imagine.

Student Dropouts

There are three main reasons why students drop out of college. Some students, for one thing, are not really sure they want to be in school and lack the desire to do the work. When exams come up, or when a course requires a difficult project or term paper, these students will not do the required studying or research. Eventually, they may drop out because their grades are so poor they are about to flunk out anyway. Such students sometimes come back to school later with a completely different attitude about school. Other students drop out for financial reasons. The pressures of paying tuition, buying textbooks, and possibly having to support themselves can be overwhelming. These students can often be helped by the school because financial aid is available, and some schools offer work-study programs. Finally, students drop out because they have personal problems. They cannot concentrate on their courses because they are unhappy at home, they are lonely, or they are having trouble with boyfriends or girlfriends. Teachers should suggest that such troubled students see counselors or join support groups. If teachers would take a more personal interest in their students, more students would make it through troubled times.

Fill in the blanks: The ________________ paragraph makes its point more clearly and effectively because ______________________________

____

____.

UNDERSTANDING UNITY

The first paragraph is more effective because it is *unified.* All the details in the paragraph are *on target;* they support and develop the single point expressed in the first sentence—that there are many reasons students drop out of college. On the other hand, the second paragraph contains some details irrelevant to the opening point—that there are three main reasons why students drop out. These details should be omitted in the interest of paragraph unity. Go back to the second paragraph and cross out the sections that are off target, the sections that do not support the opening idea.

You should have crossed out the following sections: "Such students sometimes . . . attitude about school"; "These students can often . . . work-study programs"; and "Teachers should suggest . . . through troubled times."

The difference between the first two paragraphs leads us to the first base, or standard, of effective writing: *unity.* To achieve unity is to have all the details in your paper related to the single point expressed in the topic sentence, the first sentence of your paper. Each time you think of something to put into your paper, ask yourself whether it relates to your main point. If it does not, leave it out. For example, if you were writing a paper about a certain job as the worst job you ever had and then spent a couple of sentences talking about the interesting people that you met there, you would be missing the first and most essential base of good writing. The pages ahead will consider the other three bases that you must touch in order to "score" in your writing.

CHECK FOR UNITY

To check a paper for unity, ask yourself these questions:

1 Is there a clear opening statement of the point of the paper?

2 Is all the material on target in support of the opening point?

Base 2: Support

Activity

The following student paragraphs were written on the topic "A Quality of Some Person You Know." Both are unified, but one communicates more clearly and effectively. Which one, and why?

My Quick-Tempered Father

My father is easily angered by normal everyday mistakes. One day my father told me to wash the car and cut the grass. I did not hear exactly what he said, and so I asked him to repeat it. Then he went into a hysterical mood and shouted, "Can't you hear?" Another time he asked my mother to go to the store and buy groceries with a fifty-dollar bill, and told her to spend no more than twenty dollars. She spent twenty-two dollars. As soon as he found out, he immediately took the change from her and told her not to go anywhere else for him; he did not speak to her the rest of the day. My father even gives my older brothers a hard time with his irritable moods. One day he told them to be home from their dates by midnight; they came home at 12:15. He informed them that they were grounded for three weeks. To my father, making a simple mistake is like committing a crime.

My Generous Grandfather

My grandfather is the most generous person I know. He has given up a life of his own in order to give his grandchildren everything they want. Not only has he given up many years of his life to raise his children properly, but he is now sacrificing many more years to his grandchildren. His generosity is also evident in his relationship with his neighbors, friends, and the members of his church. He has been responsible for many good deeds and has always been there to help all the people around him in times of trouble. Everyone knows that he will gladly lend a helping hand. He is so generous that you almost have to feel sorry for him. If one day he suddenly became selfish, it would be earthshaking. That's my grandfather.

Fill in the blanks: The ________________ paragraph makes its point more clearly and effectively because ____

____

____.

UNDERSTANDING SUPPORT

The first paragraph is more effective, for it offers specific examples that show us the father in action. We see for ourselves why the writer describes the father as quick-tempered. The second writer, on the other hand, gives us no specific evidence. The writer tells us repeatedly that the grandfather is generous but never shows us examples of that generosity. Just how, for instance, did the grandfather sacrifice his life for his children and grandchildren? Did he hold two jobs so that his son could go to college, or so that his daughter could have her own car? Does he give up time with his wife and friends to travel every day to his daughter's house to baby-sit, go to the store, and help with the dishes? Does he wear threadbare suits and coats and eat Hamburger Helper and other inexpensive meals (with no desserts) so that he can give money to his children and toys to his grandchildren? We want to see and judge for ourselves whether the writer is making a valid point about the grandfather, but without specific details we cannot do so. In fact, we have almost no picture of him at all.

Consideration of these two paragraphs leads us to the second base of effective writing: *support*. After realizing the importance of specific supporting details, one student writer revised a paper she had done on a restaurant job as the worst job she ever had. In the revised paper, instead of talking about "the unsanitary conditions in the kitchen," she referred to such specifics as "the green mold on the bacon" and "the ants in the potato salad." All your papers should include many vivid details!

CHECK FOR SUPPORT

To check a paper for support, ask yourself these questions:

1 Is there *specific* evidence to support the opening point?
2 Is there *enough* specific evidence?

Base 3: Coherence

Activity

The following two paragraphs were written on the topic "The Best or Worst Job You Ever Had." Both are unified and both are supported. However, one communicates more clearly and effectively. Which one, and why?

Pantry Helper

My worst job was as a pantry helper in one of San Diego's well-known restaurants. I had an assistant from three to six in the afternoon who did little but stand around and eat the whole time she was there. She kept an ear open for the sound of the back door opening, which was a sure sign the boss was coming in. The boss would testily say to me, "You've got a lot of things to do here, Alice. Try to get a move on." I would come in at two o'clock to relieve the woman on the morning shift. If her day was busy, that meant I would have to prepare salads, slice meat and cheese, and so on. Orders for sandwiches and cold platters would come in and have to be prepared. The worst thing about the job was that the heat in the kitchen, combined with my nerves, would give me an upset stomach by seven o'clock almost every night. I might be going to the storeroom to get some supplies, and one of the waitresses would tell me she wanted a bacon, lettuce, and tomato sandwich on white toast. I would put the toast in and head for the supply room, and a waitress would holler out that her customer was in a hurry. Green flies would come in through the torn screen in the kitchen window and sting me. I was getting paid only $1.60 an hour. At five o'clock when the dinner rush began, I would be dead tired. Roaches scurried in all directions whenever I moved a box or picked up a head of lettuce to cut.

My Worst Job

The worst job I ever had was as a waiter at the Westside Inn. First of all, many of the people I waited on were rude. When a baked potato was hard inside or a salad was flat or their steak wasn't just the way they wanted it, they blamed me, rather than the kitchen. Or they would ask me to light their cigarettes, or chase flies from their tables, or even take their children to the bathroom. Also, I had to contend with not only the customers but the kitchen staff as well. The cooks and busboys were often undependable and surly. If I didn't treat them just right, I would wind up having to apologize to customers because their meals came late or their water glasses weren't filled. Another reason I didn't like the job was that I was always moving. Because of the constant line at the door, as soon as one group left, another would take its place. I usually had only a twenty-minute lunch break and a ten-minute break in almost nine hours of work. I think I could have put up with the job if I had been able to pause and rest more often. The last and most important reason I hated the job was my boss. She played favorites with the waiters and waitresses, giving some the best-tipping repeat customers and preferences on holidays. She would hover around during my break to make sure I didn't take a second more than the allotted time. And even when I helped out by working through a break, she never had an appreciative word but would just tell me not to be late for work the next day.

Fill in the blanks: The ________________ paragraph makes its point more clearly and effectively because ______________________________

____

____.

UNDERSTANDING COHERENCE

The second paragraph is more effective because the material is organized clearly and logically. Using emphatic order, the writer gives us a list of four reasons why the job was so bad: rude customers, unreliable kitchen staff, constant motion, and most of all, an unfair boss. Further, the writer includes transitional words that act as signposts, making movement from one idea to the next easy to follow. The major transitions include *First of all, Also, Another reason,* and *The last and most important reason.*

While the first paragraph is unified and supported, the writer does not have any clear and consistent way of organizing the material. Partly, emphatic order is used, but this is not made clear by transitions or by saving the most important reason for last. Partly, a time order is used, but it moves inconsistently from two to seven to five o'clock.

These two paragraphs lead us to the third base of effective writing: *coherence.* The supporting ideas and sentences in a composition must be organized so that they cohere or "stick together." As has already been mentioned, key techniques for tying together the material in a paper are a clear method of organization (such as time order or emphatic order), transitions, and other connecting words.

CHECK FOR COHERENCE

To check a paper for coherence, ask yourself these questions:

1 Does the paper have a clear method of organization?
2 Are transitions and other connecting words used to tie together the material?

Base 4: Sentence Skills

Activity

Two versions of a paragraph are given below. Both are unified, supported, and organized, but one version communicates more clearly and effectively. Which one, and why?

Falling Asleep Anywhere

There are times when people are so tired that they fall asleep almost anywhere. For example, there is a lot of sleeping on the bus or train on the way home from work in the evenings. A man will be reading the newspaper, and seconds later it appears as if he is trying to eat it. Or he will fall asleep on the shoulder of the stranger sitting next to him. Another place where unplanned naps go on is in the lecture hall. In some classes, a student will start snoring so loudly that the professor has to ask another student to shake the sleeper awake. A more embarrassing situation occurs when a student leans on one elbow and starts drifting off to sleep. The weight of the head pushes the elbow off the desk, and this momentum carries the rest of the body along. The student wakes up on the floor with no memory of getting there. The worst time to fall asleep is when driving a car. Police reports are full of accidents that occur when people lose consciousness and go off the road. If the drivers are lucky, they are not seriously hurt. One woman's car, for instance, went into the river. She woke up in four feet of water and thought it was raining. When people are really tired, nothing will stop them from falling asleep--no matter where they are.

Falling Asleep Anywhere

[1]There are times when people are so tired that they fall asleep almost anywhere. [2]For example, on the bus or train on the way home from work. [3]A man will be reading the newspaper, seconds later it appears as if he is trying to eat it. [4]Or he will fall asleep on the shoulder of the stranger sitting next to him. [5]Another place where unplanned naps go on are in the lecture hall. [6]In some classes, a student will start snoring so loudly that the professor has to ask another student to shake the sleeper awake. [7]A more embarrassing situation occurs when a student leans on one elbow and starting to drift off to sleep. [8]The weight of the head push the elbow off the desk, and this momentum carries the rest of the body along. [9]The student wakes up on the floor with no memory of getting there. [10]The worst time to fall asleep is when driving a car. [11]Police reports are full of accidents that occur when people conk out and go off the road. [12]If the drivers are lucky they are not seriously hurt. [13]One womans car, for instance went into the river. [14]She woke up in four feet of water. [15]And thought it was raining. [16]When people are really tired, nothing will stop them from falling asleep--no matter where they are.

Fill in the blanks: The ________________ paragraph makes its point more clearly and effectively because ____

____

____.

UNDERSTANDING SENTENCE SKILLS

The first paragraph is more effective because it properly uses *sentence skills,* the fourth base of competent writing. See now if you can identify the ten sentence-skills mistakes made in the second paragraph. Do this, first of all, by going back and underlining the ten spots in the second paragraph that differ in wording or punctuation from the first paragraph. Then try to identify the ten sentence-skills mistakes by circling what you feel is the correct answer in each of the ten statements below.

Note: Comparing the second paragraph with the correct version may help you guess correct answers even if you are not familiar with the names of certain skills.

1. In word group 2, there is a
   a. missing comma
   b. missing apostrophe
   c. sentence fragment
   d. dangling modifier

2. In word group 3, there is a (an)
   a. run-on
   b. sentence fragment
   c. mistake in subject-verb agreement
   d. irregular verb mistake

3. In word group 5, there is a
   a. sentence fragment
   b. spelling error
   c. run-on
   d. mistake in subject-verb agreement

4. In word group 7, there is a
   a. misplaced modifier
   b. dangling modifier
   c. mistake in parallelism
   d. run-on

5. In word group 8, there is a
   a. nonstandard English verb
   b. run-on
   c. comma mistake
   d. missing capital letter

6. In word group 11, there is a (an)
   a. irregular verb mistake
   b. sentence fragment
   c. slang phrase
   d. mistake in subject-verb agreement

7. In word group 12, there is a (an)
   a. missing apostrophe
   b. missing comma
   c. irregular verb mistake
   d. sentence fragment

8. In word group 13, there is a (an)
   a. mistake in parallelism
   b. irregular verb mistake
   c. missing apostrophe
   d. missing capital letter

9. In word group 13, there is a
   a. missing comma around an interrupter
   b. dangling modifier
   c. run-on
   d. cliché

10. In word group 15, there is a (an)
   a. missing quotation mark
   b. irregular verb mistake
   c. sentence fragment
   d. mistake in pronoun point of view

You should have chosen the following answers:

1. c	3. d	5. a	7. b	9. a
2. a	4. c	6. c	8. c	10. c

Part Six of this book carefully explains these and other sentence skills. You should review all the skills carefully. Doing so will ensure that you know the most important grammar, punctuation, and usage rules needed to write clear, error-free sentences.

CHECK FOR SENTENCE SKILLS

Sentence skills are summarized in the chart on the following page and on the inside front cover of the book.

A Summary of the Four Bases of Effective Writing

2
Support

- Specific evidence?
- Plenty of it?

1
Unity

- Clear opening statement of the point of your paper?
- All material on target in support of opening point?

3
Coherence

- Clear method of organization?
- Transitions and other connective devices?

4
Sentence Skills

- Fragments eliminated?
- Run-ons eliminated?
- Correct verb forms?
- Subject and verb agreement?
- Faulty parallelism and faulty modifiers eliminated?
- Faulty pronouns eliminated?
- Capital letters used correctly?
- Punctuation marks where needed?
  (a) Apostrophe
  (b) Quotation marks
  (c) Comma
  (d) Semicolon; colon
  (e) Hyphen; dash
  (f) Parentheses
- Correct paper format?
- Needless words eliminated?
- Correct word choices?
- Possible spelling errors checked?
- Careless errors eliminated through proofreading?
- Sentences varied?

Practice in Using the Four Bases

You are now familiar with the four bases, or standards, of effective writing: unity, support, coherence, and sentence skills. In this closing section, you will expand and strengthen your understanding of the four bases as you work through the following activities:

1 Evaluating Scratch Outlines for Unity
2 Evaluating Paragraphs for Unity
3 Evaluating Paragraphs for Support
4 Evaluating Paragraphs for Coherence
5 Revising Paragraphs for Coherence
6 Evaluating Paragraphs for All Four Bases:
Unity, Support, Coherence, and Sentence Skills

1 EVALUATING SCRATCH OUTLINES FOR UNITY

The best time to check a paper for unity is when it is in outline form. A scratch outline, as explained on page 95, is one of the best techniques for getting started with a paper.

Look at the following scratch outline that one student prepared and then corrected for unity:

I had a depressing weekend.

1. Hay fever bothered me
2. Had to pay seventy-seven-dollar car bill
3. Felt bad
4. Boyfriend and I had a fight
5. Did poorly in my math test today as a result
6. My mother yelled at me unfairly

Four reasons support the opening statement that the writer was depressed over the weekend. The writer crossed out "Felt bad" because it was not a specific reason for her depression. (Saying that she felt bad is almost another way of saying that she was depressed.) She also crossed out the item about the day's math test because the point she is supporting is that she was depressed over the weekend.

Activity

Cross out the items that do not support the opening point in each outline. These items must be omitted in order to achieve paragraph unity.

1. The cost of raising a child keeps increasing.
   a. School taxes get higher every year.
   b. It is estimated that a pair of children's shoes will cost $200 by 1990.
   c. Overpopulation is a worldwide problem.
   d. Providing nutritious food is more costly because of inflated prices.
   e. Children should work at age sixteen.
2. My father's compulsive gambling hurt our family life.
   a. We were always short of money for bills.
   b. Luckily, my father didn't drink.
   c. My father ignored his children to spend time at the racetrack.
   d. Gamblers' Anonymous can help compulsive gamblers.
   e. My mother and father argued constantly.
3. There are several ways to get better mileage in your car.
   a. Check air pressure in tires regularly.
   b. Drive at the fifty-five mile-per-hour speed limit.
   c. Orange and yellow cars are the most visible.
   d. Avoid jackrabbit starts at stop signs and traffic lights.
   e. Always have duplicate ignition and trunk keys.
4. My swimming instructor helped me overcome my terror of the water.
   a. He talked with me about my fears.
   b. I was never good at sports.
   c. He showed me how to hold my head underwater and not panic.
   d. I held on to a floating board until I was confident enough to give it up.
   e. My instructor was on the swimming team at his college.
5. Fred Wilkes is the best candidate for state governor.
   a. He has fifteen years' experience in the state senate.
   b. His son is a professional football player.
   c. He has helped stop air and water pollution in the state.
   d. His opponent has been divorced.
   e. He has brought new industries and jobs to the state.

2 EVALUATING PARAGRAPHS FOR UNITY

Activity

Each of the following five paragraphs contains sentences that are off target. The sentences do not support the opening point, and so the paragraphs are not unified. In the interest of paragraph unity, such sentences must be omitted.

Cross out the irrelevant sentences and put the numbers of those sentences in the spaces provided. The number of spaces will tell you the number of irrelevant sentences in each paragraph.

1. A Kindergarten Failure

[1]In kindergarten I experienced the fear of failure that haunts many schoolchildren. [2]My moment of panic occurred on my last day in kindergarten at Charles Foos Public School in Riverside, California. [3]My family lived in California for three years before we moved to Omaha, Nebraska, where my father was a personnel manager for Mutual of Omaha. [4]Our teacher began reading a list of names of all those students who were to line up at the door in order to visit the first-grade classroom. [5]Our teacher was a pleasant-faced woman who had resumed her career after raising her own children. [6]She called off every name but mine, and I was left sitting alone in the class while everyone else left, the teacher included. [7]I sat there in absolute horror. [8]I imagined that I was the first kid in human history who had flunked things like crayons, sandbox, and sliding board. [9]Without getting the teacher's permission, I got up and walked to the bathroom and threw up into a sink. [10]Only when I ran home in tears to my mother did I get an explanation of what had happened. [11]Since I was to go to a parochial school in the fall, I had not been taken with the other children to meet the first-grade teacher at the public school. [12]My moment of terror and shame had been only a misunderstanding.

The numbers of the irrelevant sentences: ______ ______

2. How to Prevent Cheating

[1]Teachers should take steps to prevent students from cheating on exams. [2]To begin with, teachers should stop reusing old tests. [3]Even a test that has been used once is soon known on the student grapevine. [4]Students will check with their friends to find out, for example, what was on Dr. Thompson's biology final last term. [5]They may even manage to turn up a copy of the test itself, "accidentally" not turned in by a former student of Dr. Thompson's. [6]Teachers should also take some commonsense precautions at test time. [7]They should make students separate themselves--by at least one seat--during an exam, and they should watch the class closely. [8]The best place for the teacher to sit is in the rear of the room, so that a student is never sure if the teacher is looking at him or her. [9]Last of all, teachers must make it clear to students that there will be stiff penalties for cheating. [10]One of the problems with our school systems is a lack of discipline. [11]Teachers never used to give in to students' demands or put up with bad behavior, as they do today. [12]Anyone caught cheating should immediately receive a zero for the exam. [13]A person even suspected of cheating should be forced to take an alternative exam in the teacher's office. [14]Because cheating is unfair to honest students, it should not be tolerated.

The numbers of the irrelevant sentences: ______ ______

3. A Dangerous Cook

[1]When my friend Tom sets to work in the kitchen, disaster often results. [2]Once he tried to make toasted cheese sandwiches for us by putting slices of cheese in the toaster along with the bread; he ruined the toaster. [3]Unfortunately, the toaster was a fairly new one that I had just bought for him three weeks before, on his birthday. [4]On another occasion, he had cut up some fresh beans and put them in a pot to steam. [5]I was really looking forward to the beans, for I eat nothing but canned vegetables in my dormitory. [6]I, frankly, am not much of a cook either. [7]The water in the Teflon pan steamed away while Tom was on the telephone, and both the beans and the Teflon coating in the pan were ruined. [8]Finally, another time Tom made spaghetti for us, and the noodles stuck so tightly together that we had to cut off slices with a knife and fork. [9]In addition, the meatballs were burned on the outside but almost raw inside. [10]The tomato sauce, on the other hand, turned out well. [11]For some reason, Tom is very good at making meat and vegetable sauces. [12]Because of Tom's kitchen mishaps, I never eat at his place without an Alka-Seltzer in my pocket, or without money in case we have to go out to eat.

The numbers of the irrelevant sentences:

______ ______ ______ ______ ______

4. Why Adults Visit Amusement Parks

[1]Adults visit amusement parks for several reasons. [2]For one thing, an amusement park is a place where it is acceptable to "pig-out" on junk food. [3]At the park, everyone is drinking soda and eating popcorn, ice cream, or hot dogs. [4]No one seems to be on a diet, and so buying all the junk food you can eat is a guilt-free experience. [5]Parks should provide stands where healthier food, such as salads or cold chicken, would be sold. [6]Another reason people visit amusement parks is to prove themselves. [7]They want to visit the park that has the newest, scariest ride in order to say that they went on the Parachute Drop, the seven-story Elevator, the Water Chute, or the Death Slide. [8]Going on a scary ride is a way to feel courageous and adventurous without taking much of a risk. [9]Some rides, however, can be dangerous. [10]Rides that are not properly inspected or maintained have killed people all over the country. [11]A final reason people visit amusement parks is to escape from everyday pressures. [12]When people are poised at the top of a gigantic roller coaster, they are not thinking of bills, work, or personal problems. [13]A scary ride empties the mind of all worries--except making it to the bottom alive. [14]Adults at an amusement park may claim they have come for their children, but they are there for themselves as well.

The numbers of the irrelevant sentences: ______ ______ ______

5. My Color Television

[1]My color television has given me nothing but heartburn. [2]I was able to buy it a little over a year ago because I had my relatives give me money for my birthday instead of a lot of clothes that wouldn't fit. [3]My first dose of stomach acid came when I bought the set. [4]I let a salesclerk fool me into buying a discontinued model. [5]I realized this a day later, when I saw newspaper advertisements for the set at seventy-five dollars less than I had paid. [6]The set worked so beautifully when I first got it home that I would keep it on until stations signed off for the night. [7]Fortunately, I didn't get any channels showing all-night movies, or I would never have gotten to bed. [8]Then I started developing a problem with the set that involved static noise. [9]For some reason, when certain shows switched into a commercial, a loud buzz would sound for a few seconds. [10]Gradually, this sound began to appear during a show, and to get rid of it, I had to click the dial to another channel and click it back. [11]Sometimes this technique would not work, and I had to pick up the set and shake it to remove the buzzing sound. [12]I actually began to build up my arm muscles shaking my set; I could feel the new muscles working whenever I shot a basketball. [13]When neither of these methods removed the static noise, I would sit popping Tums and wait for the sound to go away. [14]Eventually I wound up slamming the set with my hand again, and it stopped working altogether. [14]My trip to the repair shop cost me $62. [16]The set is working well now, but I keep expecting more trouble.

The numbers of the irrelevant sentences: ______ ______ ______ ______

3 EVALUATING PARAGRAPHS FOR SUPPORT

Activity

The five paragraphs that follow lack sufficient supporting details. Identify the spot or spots where more specific details are needed in each paragraph.

1. Hamburger: Our Best Friend

[1]Hamburger is the best-selling meat today for a number of good reasons. [2]First of all, its reasonable cost puts it within everyone's reach. [3]Hamburger is popular, too, because it can be prepared in so many different ways. [4]It can, for example, be cooked by itself, in spaghetti sauce, or with noodles and gravy. [5]It can be baked, boiled, broiled, or fried. [6]Hamburger also is convenient. [7]Last and most important, hamburger has a high nutritional value. [8]Four ounces of hamburger contain twenty-eight grams of protein, which is almost half the recommended daily dietary allowance.

Fill in the blanks: The first spot where supporting details are needed occurs after sentence number ______. The second spot occurs after sentence number ______.

2. A Car Accident

[1]I was on my way home from work when my terrible car accident took place. [2]As I drove my car around the curve of the expressway exit, I saw a number of cars ahead of me, backed up because of a red light at the main road. [3]I slowly came to a stop behind a dozen or more cars. [4]In my rear-view mirror, I then noticed a car coming up behind me that did not slow down or stop. [5]I had a horrible, helpless feeling as I realized the car would hit me. [6]I knew there was nothing I could do to signal the driver in time, nor was there any way I could get away from the car. [7]Minutes after the collision, I picked up my glasses, which were on the seat beside me. [8]My lip was bleeding, and I got out a tissue to wipe it. [9]The police arrived quickly, along with an ambulance for the driver of the car that hit me. [10]My car was so damaged that it had to be towed away. [11]Today, eight years after the accident, I still relive the details of the experience whenever a car gets too close behind me.

Fill in the blank: The point where details are clearly needed occurs after sentence number ______.

3. Tips on Bringing Up Children

[1]In some ways, children should be treated as mature individuals. [2]For one thing, adults should not use baby talk with children. [3]Using real words with children helps them develop language skills faster. [4]Baby talk makes children feel patronized, frustrated, and confused, for they want to understand and communicate with adults by learning their speech. [5]So animals should be called cows and dogs, not "moo-moos" and "bow-wows." [6]Second, parents should be consistent when disciplining children. [7]For example, if a parent tells a child, "You cannot have dessert unless you put away your toys," it is important that the parent follow through on the warning. [8]By being consistent, parents will teach children responsibility and give them a stable center around which to grow. [9]Finally, and most important, children should be allowed and encouraged to make simple decisions. [10]Parents will thus be helping their children prepare for the complex decisions that they will have to deal with in later life.

Fill in the blank: The spot where supporting details are needed occurs after sentence number ______.

4. Telephone Answering Machines

[1]Telephone answering machines are beginning to annoy me. [2]First of all, I am so surprised when a machine answers the phone that I become tongue-tied or flustered. [3]As the metallic voice says, "Please leave your message when you hear the tone," my mind goes blank. [4]I don't like to hang up, but I know I'll sound like a fool when the owner plays back the message: "Uh, uh, Dr. Spencer, uh, I wanted to make an appointment, uh, wait a minute, for the fifth, no the second, uh, I'm not sure. . . ." [5]Another problem I have with the machines is that they can malfunction. [6]I sometimes call big catalog companies to place orders, and the order is taken by a recording machine. [7]Just as I'm trying to say, "Two blouses, number B107, size 10," the machine clicks off. [8]When I call back, another mix-up will occur. [9]Above all, I dislike the so-called funny tapes that some people now use to answer their phones. [10]One of my coworkers recently bought an answering machine and uses one of these tapes. [11]Answering machines seem to be spreading all over the country, but I would rather talk to a human voice anytime.

Fill in the blanks: The first spot where supporting details are needed occurs after sentence number ______. The second spot occurs after sentence number ______.

5. Being on TV

[1]People act a little strangely when a television camera comes their way. [2]Some people behave as if a crazy puppet-master is pulling their strings. [3]Their arms jerk wildly about, and they begin jumping up and down for no apparent reason. [4]Often they accompany their body movements with loud screams, squeals, and yelps. [5]Another group of people engage in an activity known as the cover-up. [6]They will be calmly watching a sports game or other televised event when they realize the camera is focused on them. [7]The camera operator can't resist zooming in for a close-up of these people. [8]Then there are those who practice their funny faces on the unsuspecting public. [9]They take advantage of the television time to show off their talents, hoping to get that big break that will carry them to stardom. [10]Finally, there are those who pretend they are above reacting for the camera.[11]They wipe all expression from their faces and appear to be interested in something else. [12]Yet if the camera stays on them long enough, they will slyly check to see if they are still being watched. [13]Everybody's behavior seems to be slightly strange in front of a TV camera.

Fill in the blanks: The first spot where supporting details are needed occurs after sentence number ______. The second spot occurs after sentence number ______.

4 EVALUATING PARAGRAPHS FOR COHERENCE

Activity

Answer the questions about coherence that follow each of the two paragraphs below.

1. Why I Bought a Handgun

[1]I bought a handgun to keep in my house for several reasons. [2]Most important, I have had a frightening experience with an obscene phone caller. [3]For several weeks, a man has called me once or twice a day, sometimes as late as three in the morning. [4]As soon as I pick up the phone, he whispers something obscene or threatens me by saying, "I'll get you." [5]I decided to buy a gun because crime is increasing in my neighborhood. [6]One neighbor's house was burglarized while she was at work; the thieves not only stole her appliances, but they also threw paint around her living room and slashed her furniture. [7]Not long after this incident, an elderly woman from the apartment house on the corner was mugged on her way to the supermarket. [8]The man grabbed her purse and threw her to the ground, breaking her hip. [9]I started thinking about buying a gun about a year ago when I was listening to the news one night. [10]It seemed that every news story involved violence of some

kind--rapes, murders, muggings, and robberies. [11]I wondered if some of the victims in the stories would still be alive if they had been able to frighten off the criminal with a gun. [12]As time passed, I became more convinced that I should keep a gun in the house.

a. What words show emphasis in sentence 2? ________________

b. What is the number of the sentence to which the transition *In addition* could be added? ________________

c. In sentence 8, to whom does the pronoun *her* refer? ______________

d. How many times is the key word *gun* repeated in the paragraph? ________________

e. The paragraph should use emphatic order. Put a 1 before the reason that is slightly less important than the other two, a 2 before the second-most-important reason, and a 3 before the most important reason.

______ Obscene phone caller

______ Crime increase in neighborhood

______ News stories about crime victims

2. Joining a Health Club

[1]You should do some investigating before you decide to join a health club. [2]Make sure that the contract you sign is accurate. [3]Check the agreement to be certain that the fees listed are correct, that the penalties for breaking the contract are specified, and that no hidden charges are included. [4]As soon as you begin thinking about joining a health club, make a list of your needs and requirements. [5]Decide if you want (or will ever use) facilities such as a swimming pool, jogging track, steam room, weight machines, racquet-ball courts, or a bar and lounge. [6]Your requirements will determine what kind of club you should join and where you will truly get your money's worth. [7]After you have decided what type of exercise club is best for you, visit some local clubs and check out the facilities. [8]Make sure that the equipment is in good order, that the changing rooms and exercise areas are clean, and that there are enough instructors for everyone. [9]Talk to some of the members to see if they are satisfied with the club and its management. [10]Ask them if they have had any problems with contracts, the club's hours, or lack of equipment. [11]Once you have found the best club, you are ready to sign a membership contract.

a. What is the number of the sentence to which the word *Also* could be added? ______

b. To whom does the pronoun *them* in sentence 10 refer? ____________

c. What is a synonym for *contract* in sentence 3? ______________

d. What is the number of a sentence to which the words *For example* could be added? ______

e. The paragraph should use time order. Put a 1 before the step that should come first, a 2 before the intermediate step, and a 3 before the final step.

______ Make sure the contract is accurate.

______ Make a list of your needs and requirements.

______ Visit some local clubs to check facilities.

5 REVISING PARAGRAPHS FOR COHERENCE

The two paragraphs in this section begin with a clear point, but the supporting material that follows the point is not coherent. Read each paragraph and the comments that follow it on how to organize and connect the supporting material. Then do the activity provided in each case.

A Difficult Period

Since I arrived in the Bay Area in midsummer, I have had the most difficult period of my life. I had to look for an apartment. I found only one place that I could afford, but the landlord said I could not move in until it was painted. When I first arrived in San Francisco, my thoughts were to stay with my father and stepmother. I had to set out looking for a job so that I could afford my own place, for I soon realized that my stepmother was not at all happy having me live with them. A three-week search led to a job shampooing rugs for a housecleaning company. I painted the apartment myself, and at least that problem was ended. I was in a hurry to get settled because I was starting school at the University of San Francisco in September. A transportation problem developed because my stepmother insisted that I return my father's bike which I was using at first to get to school. I had to rely on a bus that often arrived late, with the result that I missed some classes and was late for others. I had already had a problem with registration in early September. My counselor had made a mistake with my classes, and I had to register all over again. This meant that I was one week late for class. Now I'm riding to school with a classmate and no longer have to depend on the bus. My life is starting to order itself, but I must admit that at first I thought it was hopeless to stay here.

Comments: The writer provided a good deal of specific evidence to support the opening point. The evidence, however, needs to be organized. Before starting the paragraph, the writer should have decided to arrange the details by using time order. He or she could then have listed in a scratch outline the exact sequence of events that made for such a difficult period.

Activity

Here is a list of the various events described by the writer. Number the events in the correct time sequence by placing a 1 in front of the first event that occurred, a 2 in front of the second event that occurred, and so on.

Since I arrived in the Bay Area in midsummer, I have had the most difficult period of my life.

_____ I had to search for an apartment I could afford.

_____ I had to find a job so that I could afford my own place.

_____ My stepmother objected to my living with her and my father.

_____ I had to paint the apartment before I could move in.

_____ I had to find an alternative to unreliable bus transportation.

_____ I had to reregister for my college courses because of a counselor's mistake.

Your instructor may now have you rewrite the paragraph on separate paper. If so, be sure to use time signals such as *first, next, then, during, when, after,* and *now* to help guide your reader from one event to the next.

Childhood Cruelty

When I was in grade school, my classmates and I found a number of excuses for being cruel to a boy named Andy Poppovian. Sometimes Andy gave off a strong body odor, and we knew that several days had passed since he had taken a bath. Andy was very slow in speaking, as well as very careless in personal hygiene. The teacher would call on him during a math or grammar drill. He would sit there silently for so long before answering that she sometimes said, "Are you awake, Andy?" Andy had long fingernails that he never seemed to cut, with black dirt caked under them. We called him "Poppy," or we accented the first syllable in his name and mispronounced the rest of it and said to him, "How are you today, POP-o-van?" His name was funny. Other times we called him "Popeye," and we would shout at him, "Where's your spinach today, Popeye?" Andy always had sand in the corners of his eyes. When we played tag games at recess, Andy was always "it" or the first one who was caught. He was so physically slow that five guys could dance around him and he wouldn't be able to touch any of them. Even when we tried to hold a regular conversation with him about sports or a teacher, he was so slow in responding to a question that we got bored talking with him. Andy's hair was always uncombed, and it was often full of white flakes of dandruff. Only when Andy died suddenly of spinal meningitis in seventh grade did some of us begin to realize and regret our cruelty toward him.

Comments: The writer provides a number of specifics that support the opening point. However, the supporting material has not been organized clearly. Before writing this paragraph, the author should have (1) decided to arrange the supporting evidence by using emphatic order and (2) listed in a scratch outline the reasons for the cruelty to Andy Poppovian and the supporting details for each reason. The writer could also have determined which reason to use in the emphatic final position of the paper.

Activity

Create a clear outline for the paragraph by filling in the scheme below. The outline is partially completed.

When I was in grade school, my classmates and I found a number of excuses for being cruel to a boy named Andy Poppovian.

Reason 1. *Physically slow* ____________________

Details a. ____________________

b. *Five guys could dance around him.* ____________________

Reason 2. ____________________

Details a. ____________________

b. *Sand in eyes* ____________________

c. ____________________

d. ____________________

Reason 3. *Funny name* ____________________

Details a. ____________________

b. ____________________

Reason 4. ______________________________

Details a. ______________________________

b. *In regular conversation*

Your instructor may have you rewrite the paragraph on separate paper. If so, be sure to introduce each of the four reasons with transitions such as *First, Second, Another reason,* and *Finally*. You may also want to use repeated words, pronouns, and synonyms to help further tie your sentences together.

6 EVALUATING PARAGRAPHS FOR ALL FOUR BASES: UNITY, SUPPORT, COHERENCE, AND SENTENCE SKILLS

Activity

In this activity, you will evaluate paragraphs in terms of the four bases of unity, support, coherence, and sentence skills. Evaluative comments follow each paragraph below. Circle the letter of the statement that most applies in each case.

1. Ponderosa Steak House

There are a number of advantages to eating at Ponderosa Steak House. The first advantage is that the meals are moderate in price. Another reason is that the surroundings are clean, and the people are pleasant. Also, I have a variety of dinners to choose from. The last and main advantage is that I don't have to plan and prepare the meal.

a. The paragraph is not unified.
b. The paragraph is not adequately supported.
c. The paragraph is not well-organized.
d. The paragraph does not show a command of sentence skills.
e. The paragraph is well-written in terms of the four bases.

2. A Frustrating Moment

A frustrating moment happened to me several days ago. When I was shopping. I had picked up a tube of crest toothpaste, a bottle of secret deodorant, and a jar of noxema skin cream. After the cashier rang up the purchases, which came to $4.15. I handed her $10. Then got back my change, which was only $0.85. I told the cashier that she had made a mistake. Giving me change for $5 instead of $10. But she insist that I had only gave her $5, I became very upset and insist that she return the rest of my change. She refused to do so instead she asked me to step aside so she could wait on the next customer. I stood very rigid, trying not to lose my temper. I simply said to her, I'm not going to leave here, Miss, without my change for $10. Giving in at this point a bell was rung and the manager was summoned. After the situation was explain to him, he ask the cashier to ring off her register to check for the change. After doing so, the cashier was $5 over her sale receipts. Only then did the manager return my change and apologize for the cashier mistake.

a. The paragraph is not unified.
b. The paragraph is not adequately supported.
c. The paragraph is not well-organized.
d. The paragraph does not show a command of sentence skills.
e. The paragraph is well-written in terms of the four bases.

3. Asking Girls Out

There are several reasons I have trouble asking girls to go out with me. I have asked some girls out and have been turned down. This is one reason that I can't talk to them. At one time I was very shy and quiet, and people sometimes didn't even know I was present. I can talk to girls now as friends, but as soon as I want to ask them out, I usually start to become quiet, and a little bit of shyness comes out. When I get the nerve up finally, the girl will turn me down, and I swear that I will never ask another one out again. I feel sure I will get a refusal, and I have no confidence in myself. Also, my friends mock me, though they aren't any better than I am. It can become discouraging when your friends get on you. Sometimes I just stand there and wait to hear what line the girl will use. The one they use a lot is "We like you as a friend, Ted, and it's better that way." Sometimes I want to have the line put on a tape recorder, so they won't have to waste their breath on me. All my past experiences with girls have been just as bad. One girl used me to make her old boyfriend jealous. Then when she succeeded, she started going out with him again. I had a bad experience when I took a girl to the prom. I spent a lot of money on her. Two days later, she told me that she was going steady with another guy. I feel that when I meet a girl I have to be sure I can trust her. I don't want her to turn on me.

a. The paragraph is not unified.
b. The paragraph is not adequately supported.
c. The paragraph is not well-organized.
d. The paragraph does not show a command of sentence skills.
e. The paragraph is well-written in terms of the four bases.

4. A Change in My Writing

A technique in my present English class has corrected a writing problem that I've always had. In past English courses, I had major problems with commas in the wrong places, bad spelling, capitalizing the wrong words, sentence fragments, and run-on sentences. I never had any big problems with unity, support, or coherence, but the sentence skills were another matter. They were like little bugs that always appeared to infest my writing. My present teacher asked me to rewrite papers, just concentrating on sentence skills. I thought that the teacher was crazy because I didn't feel that rewriting would do any good. I soon became certain that my teacher was out of his mind, for he made me rewrite my first paper four times. It was very frustrating, for I became tired of doing the same paper over and over. I wanted to belt my teacher against the wall when I'd show him each new draft and he'd find skills mistakes and say "Rewrite." Finally, my papers began to improve and the sentence skills began to fall into place. I was able to see them and correct them before turning in a paper, whereas I couldn't before. Why or how this happened I don't know, but I think that rewriting helped a lot. It took me most of the semester, but I stuck it out and the work paid off.

a. The paragraph is not unified.
b. The paragraph is not adequately supported.
c. The paragraph is not well-organized.
d. The paragraph does not show a command of sentence skills.
e. The paragraph is well-written in terms of the four bases.

5. Luck and Me

I am a very lucky young man, which has not been the case with the rest of my family. Sometimes when I get depressed, which is too frequently, it's hard to see just how lucky I am. I'm lucky that I'm living in a country that is free. I'm allowed to worship the way I want to, and that is very important to me. Without a belief in God a person cannot live with any real certainty in life. My family cares about me, though maybe not as much as I would like. My relationship with my girlfriend is a source of good fortune for me. She gives me security and that's something I need a lot. Even with these positive realities in my life, I still seem to find time for insecurity, worry, and, worst of all, depression. At times in my life I have had bouts of terrible luck. But overall, I'm a very lucky guy. I plan to further develop the positive aspects of my life and try to eliminate the negative ones.

a. The paragraph is not unified.
b. The paragraph is not adequately supported.
c. The paragraph is not well-organized.
d. The paragraph does not show a command of sentence skills.
e. The paragraph is well-written in terms of the four bases.

Some Suggestions on What to Do Next

1 Work through Part Two, ‘‘Other Important Factors in Writing.’’

2 Read ‘‘Providing Examples’’ (117) or ‘‘Narrating an Event’’ (182) in Part Three and do the writing assignments given. Then go on to the other types of paragraph development in Part Three.

3 When you have mastered the different types of paragraph development, you may want to work through ‘‘Essay Development’’ in Part Four and do one or more of the writing assignments presented.

4 Continue review of sentence skills in Part Six.

5 Begin to do any ‘‘Special Skills’’ in Part Five that you may need to know.

PART TWO

OTHER IMPORTANT FACTORS IN WRITING

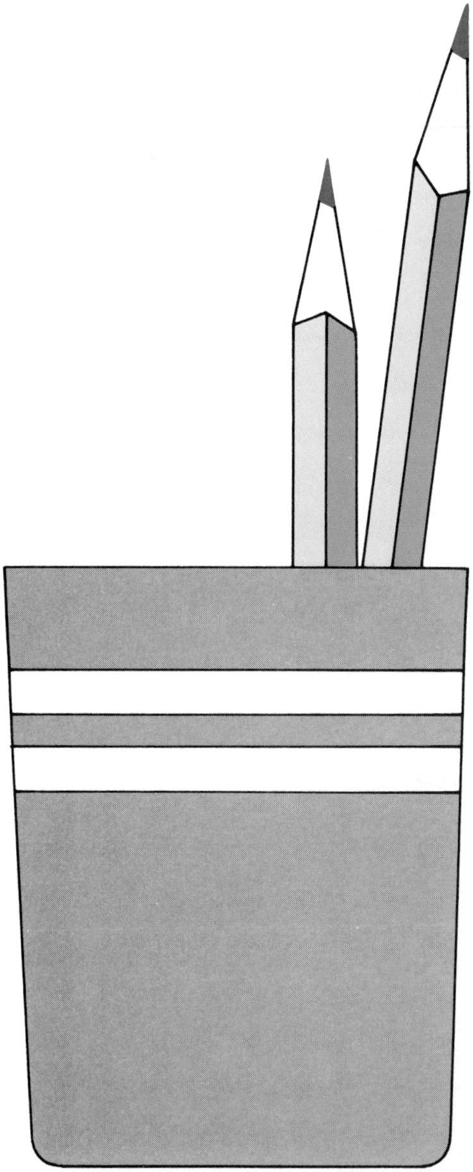

PREVIEW

Part Two helps you, first of all, to consider your own attitude about writing. You will learn that while writing is hard work for almost everyone, it is a skill that most people can master with practice. Part Two then encourages you to choose writing topics you know about, or to research a topic until you have enough information to write about it effectively. Next, you learn four prewriting techniques to help you get started with an assignment. The techniques are brainstorming, freewriting, making a list, and preparing a scratch outline. The following section offers extensive practice in outlining skills important to clear thinking and writing. Part Two concludes by asking you to view your own writing as a process—a series of drafts which move toward the final version of a paper. To illustrate the point that rewriting is essential, a student paper is shown in several of the stages it goes through while being written.

KEY FACTORS IN WRITING

This part of the book will discuss the importance of

- Having the right attitude
- Writing for a specific purpose and audience
- Knowing or discovering your subject
- Prewriting
- Outlining
- Revising, editing, and proofreading

In addition to the four principles of effective writing, there are several other factors that will help you turn out good papers. These factors, which will be discussed on the following pages, include (1) having the right attitude about writing; (2) writing for a specific purpose and audience; (3) knowing or discovering your subject; (4) prewriting, or having ways of getting started in writing; (5) outlining; and (6) revising, editing, and proofreading.

Having the Right Attitude

One sure way to wreck your chances of learning how to write competently is to believe that writing is a natural gift. People with this attitude think that they are the only ones for whom writing is an unbearably difficult activity. They feel that everyone else finds writing easy or at least tolerable. Such people typically say, "I'm not any good at writing" or "English was not one of my good subjects."

They imply that they simply do not have a talent for writing, while others do. The result of this attitude is that people don't do their best when they write, or, even worse, they hardly try at all. Their self-defeating attitude becomes a reality; their writing fails chiefly because they have brainwashed themselves into thinking that they don't have the natural talent needed to write. Until their attitude is changed, they probably will not learn how to write effectively.

A realistic attitude about writing, rather than the mistaken notion that writing is a "natural gift," should build on the following two ideas.

1 ***Writing is hard work for almost everyone.*** It is painful to do the intense and active thinking that clear writing demands. (Perhaps television has made us all so passive that the active thinking necessary in both writing and reading now seems doubly hard.) It is scary to sit down before a blank sheet of paper and know that, an hour later, nothing on it may be worth keeping. It is frustrating to discover how difficult it is to transfer thoughts and feelings from one's head onto a sheet of paper. It is upsetting to find how an apparently simple writing subject often turns out to be complicated. But writing is not an automatic process: we will not get something for nothing, and we cannot expect something for nothing. Competent writing results only through plain hard work—through determination, sweat, and head-on battle.

2 ***Writing is a skill.*** Writing is a skill like driving, typing, or cooking. Like any skill, it can be learned—if you decide that you are going to learn and then really work at it. This book will give you the extensive practice needed to develop your writing skills.

Activity

Answering the following questions will help you evaluate your attitude about writing.

1. How much practice were you given in writing compositions in high school?

   ______Much ______Some ______Little

2. How much feedback (positive or negative comments) did your instructors give you on your compositions?

   ______Much ______Some ______Little

3. How did your teachers seem to regard your writing?

   ______Good ______Fair ______Poor

4. Do you feel that some people simply have a gift for writing and others do not?

   ______Yes ______Sometimes ______No

5. When do you start writing a paper?

   ______Several days before it is due

   ______About a day before it is due

   ______At the last possible minute

Many people who answer *Little* to questions 1 and 2 also answer *Poor, Yes,* and *At the last possible minute* to the other questions. On the other hand, people who answer *Much* or *Some* to questions 1 and 2 also tend to have more favorable responses to the other questions. The point is that people with little practice in the skill of writing often have understandably negative feelings about their writing ability. They need not have such feelings, however, because writing is a skill that they can learn with practice.

Writing for a Specific Purpose and Audience

The three most common purposes of writing are to inform, to entertain, and to persuade. Most of the writing you will do in this book will involve some form of persuasion. You will advance a point or topic sentence and then support it in a variety of ways. To some extent, also, you will write papers to inform—to provide readers with information about a particular subject.

Your audience will be primarily your instructor, and sometimes other students as well. Your instructor is really a symbol of the larger audience you should see yourself as writing for—an educated, adult audience that expects you to present your ideas in a clear, direct, organized way. If you can learn to write to persuade or inform such a general audience, you will have accomplished a great deal.

It will also be helpful for you to write some papers for a more specific audience. By so doing, you will develop an ability to choose words and adopt a tone of voice that is just right for a given purpose and a given group of people. In this book, then, there is an assignment at the end of each chapter in Part Three that asks you to write with a very specific purpose in mind and for a very specific audience.

You will be asked, for example, to imagine yourself as a TV critic addressing parents at your local school, as a graduate of a local high school advising a counselor there about a drug problem, as an aide at a day care center preparing instructions for children, as an apartment tenant complaining to a landlord about neighbors, or as a client of a video dating service introducing himself or herself to potential dates. Through these and other assignments, you will learn how to adjust your style and tone of voice to a given writing situation.

Knowing or Discovering Your Subject

KNOWING A SUBJECT

Whenever possible, try to write on a subject which interests you. You will then find it easier to put more time into your work. Even more important, try to write on a subject that you know about. If you do not have direct experience with the subject, you should at least have indirect experience—knowledge gained through thinking, reading, or talking about the subject. The section that follows, "Prewriting," will provide specific techniques that will help you think about and accumulate ideas and details on a topic. In addition, many of the writing assignments in Part Three of this book will provide hints and guidelines on how to develop the knowledge needed in writing a paper. Without direct or indirect experience, or both, you will not be able to provide the specific evidence needed to develop whatever point you are trying to make. Your writing will be starved for specifics.

If you are asked to write on a topic about which you have no experience, you should do whatever research is required to gain the knowledge you need. For example, you may want to go to the library to look up relevant information. "Using the Library" on pages 284 to 297 will show you how to consult helpful library resources. And in Part Three, the next-to-last assignment in each chapter will suggest some practical research that you can do to gain needed information on a subject.

DISCOVERING A SUBJECT

At times you will not know your subject when you begin to write. Instead, you will discover it in the process of writing. For example, when a student named Gene first sat down to write a paper about his work in an apple plant (see page 104), his topic was going to be the worst boss he ever had. He then quickly realized as he began to accumulate details that his topic was really the job itself and all the drawbacks of the job. Gene only thought he knew his paper's focus when he began to write. In fact, he *discovered his subject in the course of writing.*

Another example involves the paper titled "How I Relax" on page 41. A student named Rhonda, talking afterwards about her paper, explained that at first her topic was how she relaxed with her children. As she accumulated details, she realized after a page of writing that the words "relax" and "children" simply did not go together. Her details were examples of how she *enjoyed* her children but not how she *relaxed* with them. She now sensed that the real focus of her writing should be what she did by herself to relax. And then she thought suddenly that her best time of the week was on Thursday after school. "A light clicked on in my head," she explained. "I knew I had my paper." Then it was a matter of detailing exactly what she did to relax on Thursday evening.

The moral of these examples is that sometimes you must write a bit in order to find out just what you want to write. Writing can help you think about and explore your topic and to discover just what the final direction of your paper will be. Don't be surprised, then, if you sometimes find yourself shifting gears and changing your topic while working on a paper. The act of writing itself may help you find your point and a convincing set of details that support that point.

One related feature of the writing process bears mention. Do not feel that you must proceed in a linear fashion when you write. That is, do not assume that the writing process is a railroad track where you must go straight from your central point to supporting detail one to supporting detail two to supporting detail three. Instead, proceed in whatever way seems most comfortable as you draft the paper. You may want to start by writing the closing section or by developing supporting detail three.

Do whatever is easiest—and as you get material down on the page, it will make what you have left to do a bit easier. And sometimes, of course, as you work on one section, it may happen that another focal point for your paper will emerge. That's fine—if your writing tells you that it wants to be something else, then revise or start over as needed to take advantage of that discovery. Your goal is to wind up with a paper that solidly makes and supports a point. Be ready and open to change direction and to make whatever adjustments are needed to reach your goal.

Prewriting

If you are like many people, you may have trouble at times getting started with your writing. A mental block may develop when you sit down before a blank sheet of paper. Or after you have started a paper, you may hit snags or moments of "Where to go next?" The following pages describe four techniques that will help you think about your topic and get words down on paper. The techniques are often called *prewriting techniques* because they come before the actual writing of a paper. They are (1) brainstorming, (2) freewriting, (3) making a list, and (4) making a scratch outline. You will have a chance to apply all these techniques as you work on specific assignments in Part Three.

TECHNIQUE 1: BRAINSTORMING

In *brainstorming* you generate ideas and details by asking all the questions you can think of about your subject. Such questions include *What? When? Why? How? Where?* and *Who?*

Below is an example of how one person, Sal, used the brainstorming technique to generate material for a paper. Sal felt he could write about a painful moment he experienced, but he was having trouble getting started. So he asked himself a series of brainstorming questions about the experience. As a result, he accumulated a series of details that provided the basis for the paper he finally wrote. Here are the questions Sal asked, and the answers he wrote in response to them:

Questions	Answers
Where did the experience happen?	In my girlfriend's dorm room at Penn State.
When did it happen?	A week before Thanksgiving.
Who was involved?	My girlfriend, her roommate (briefly), and I.
What happened?	I discovered my girlfriend was dating someone else.
Why was the experience so painful?	Bonnie and I were engaged. She had never mentioned Blake. My surprise visit turned into a terrible surprise for me.

How did Bonnie react?	She was nervous and tried to avoid answering my questions.
How did I react?	I felt sick and angry. I wanted to do something violent. I wanted to tear up the poster with Blake's name on it. I wanted to slam the door, but I walked out quietly. My knees were shaking.

After brainstorming, Sal's next step was to prepare a scratch outline. He then prepared several drafts of the paper. The effective paragraph that eventually resulted from Sal's prewriting technique appears on page 183.

TECHNIQUE 2: FREEWRITING

When you do not know what to write about a particular subject or when you have a mental block, freewriting sometimes helps. In *freewriting* you write on your topic for ten minutes. You do not worry about spelling, punctuation, erasing mistakes, or finding exact words. You just write without stopping. If you get stuck for words, you write "I am looking for something to say" or repeat words until something comes. There is no need to feel inhibited, for mistakes do not count and you do not have to hand in your paper.

Freewriting will limber up your writing muscles and make you familiar with the act of writing. It is a way to break through mental blocks about writing and the fear of making errors. Since you do not have to worry about making mistakes, you can concentrate on discovering what you want to say about a subject. Your initial ideas and impressions will often become clearer after you have gotten them down on paper. Through continued practice in freewriting, you will develop the habit of thinking as you write. And you will learn a technique that is a helpful way to get started on almost any paper that you do.

Here is the freewriting that one student did to accumulate details for a paper on why he stopped smoking:

> I was way overdue to stop smoking cigarettes and I finally did. I had a friend who went to the hospital with lung cancer. No one can say that he's going to recover. He's in Eagleville Hospital. When I heard about him, it was the last straw for me. Smoking is a life and death matter. My friend is the one who brought this message home to me. Smoking is a life and death matter just like the ads say. When I think about it, I hated the fact that I was helping corporations make a lot of money all the while that I smoked. The corporations produced all this slick advertising and I felt I was one of the puppets who listened to it. I marched to their tune. I didn't want to make

wealthy corporations even richer, and I hated it every time I gave over hard earned dollars for a carton of cigarettes. Cigarettes were a very expensive habit. I can hardly say how much a year I had to put out for them. You could see I smoked as you walked through my house. There were ashtrays in the living room, dining room, bathroom, and kitchen. My wife said there was a smell of smoke in the house. I couldn't tell. I had a nose so clogged that I couldn't smell much at all. Cigarettes were a bum trip that I am not going to take any longer.

The writer's next step was to use the freewriting as the basis for a scratch outline. The effective paper that eventually resulted from the author's freewriting, a scratch outline, and a good deal of rewriting appears on page 127.

TECHNIQUE 3: MAKING A LIST

List all the different items you can think of concerning your topic. Don't worry about repeating yourself, about sorting out major details from minor ones, or about spelling or punctuating correctly. Simply make a list of everything about your subject that occurs to you. Your aim is to generate details and to accumulate as much raw material for writing as possible.

Below is a list prepared by one student, Linda, who decided to write a paper on the abuse of public parks. Her first stage in doing the paper was simply to make a list of thoughts about the topic that occurred to her. Here is her list:

Messy picnickers (most common)
Noisy radios
Spray graffiti on buildings and fences
Frisbee games that disturb others
Dumping car ashtrays
Stealing park property
Nude sunbathing
Destroying flowers
Damaging fountains and statues
Litter
Muggings

Notice that Linda puts in parentheses a note to herself that messy picnickers are the most common type of park abusers. Very often as you make a list, ideas about how to develop a paper will occur to you. Jot them down.

Making a list is an excellent way to get started. Often you can then go on to make a scratch outline and write the first draft of your paper. A scratch outline for Linda's list is shown in the next section.

TECHNIQUE 4: PREPARING A SCRATCH OUTLINE

A scratch outline may be the *most helpful single technique* for writing a good paper. It is an excellent follow-up to the prewriting techniques already mentioned: brainstorming, freewriting, and making a list. In a scratch outline, you think carefully about the exact point you are making, about the exact items you are going to use to support that point, and about the exact order in which you want to arrange those items. The scratch outline is, then, a plan, or blueprint, that will help you achieve a unified, supported, and organized composition.

Here is the scratch outline that the student Linda prepared from her general list on the preceding page:

Some people abuse public parks.

1. Cleaning out cars
   a. Ashtrays
   b. Litter bags
2. Defacing park property
3. Stealing park property
   a. Flowers, trees, shrubs
   b. Park sod
4. Not cleaning up after picnics
   a. Paper trash
   b. Bottles and cans

This scratch outline enabled Linda to think about her paper—to decide exactly which items to include and in what order. Without writing a great many sentences, she has taken a giant step toward a paper that is unified (she has left out items that are not related); supported (she has added items that develop her point); and organized (she has arranged the items in a logical way—here, in emphatic order). The effective paragraph that eventually resulted from Linda's list and scratch outline is on page 20.

USING ALL FOUR TECHNIQUES

Very often the scratch outline follows brainstorming, freewriting, or making a list. At other times, the scratch outline may substitute for the other three techniques. Also, you may use several techniques almost simultaneously when writing a paper. You may, for example, ask questions while making a list; you may organize and outline the list as you write it; you may ask yourself questions and then freewrite answers to them. The four techniques are all ways to help you go about writing a paper. In the next section, the process of writing a paper is illustrated, and you will see all four techniques used as writing aids.

Activity 1

Answer the following questions.

1. Which of the prewriting techniques do you already practice?

   ______Brainstorming ______Freewriting

   ______Making a list ______Making a scratch outline

2. Which prewriting technique involves asking questions about your topic?

   ____

3. Which prewriting technique involves writing quickly about your topic without being concerned about grammar and spelling?

   ____

4. Which prewriting technique is almost always part of doing a paper?

   ____

5. Which techniques are the ones that will work best for you?

   ____

Activity 2

Given below are examples of the four prewriting techniques used to develop the topic "How to Make Five Dollars Last a Week." Put a B before the brainstorming selection, an F before the freewriting, an L before the list, and an SO before the scratch outline.

________ Avoid toll roads
Eat all the old food in the refrigerator
Eat things like pancakes, potato cakes, oatmeal
Don't use much gas
Mail overdue bills with postdated checks
Ride bike
Drive slowly to stretch gas
Hide when paperboy comes
Look for change in chairs, car, pockets
Break into penny jar
Make kids' school lunches with jelly sandwiches
Mail bills at midnight of deadline

_______ Sometimes I find that it's Friday and I have only five dollars to last until the next Friday. The five dollars must last the entire week. This happens when it's the end of the month usually. And my paycheck will be coming on the last Friday of the month. There are ways to get around this. But it's not a very pleasant experience. Makes you realize what it's like to watch every single cent. I never drive on the parkway or any toll road or toll bridge. I nurse the gas in the car. I can usually take a bike to the shopping mall. I save the car for getting back and forth from work. Food is necessary. I use what I have. Things like pancake flour, cereals, potatoes and onions stored in the drawer. Pancakes can be filling and are made with only flour, egg, and milk. Use any leftovers in the refrigerator. Whatever is on hand. Sometimes bills are overdue. I'll mail the checks as late as possible. I postdate the checks. And hope that they don't arrive too fast. Bounced the fuel oil check last winter. I ignore the paperboy at the door. I'm always searching for change in my pockets and under the car seat and the couch cushions in living room. Pennies can add up and help.

____

<u>What</u> do I do when I have only five dollars to last for a week?	I have to avoid buying food, gas; I have to put off paying bills; I keep looking for extra money.
<u>When</u> does this happen?	The last week of the month before I receive my monthly paycheck.
<u>Why</u> does it happen?	Sometimes an unexpected bill will come up during the month or my check will be delayed.
<u>Whom</u> do I avoid?	Anybody collecting money, like the paperboy, the Avon lady, the volunteer fire fighters, the Girl Scout cookie sellers.

_______ This is how I make five dollars last for a week.

1. Food
   a. Use up old food in refrigerator, like eggs, old vegetables
   b. Give the kids jelly sandwiches for school lunch
   c. Serve pancakes, oatmeal, potato cakes for dinner
2. Transportation
   a. Use bike or walk when possible
   b. Stretch gas mileage in car by driving slowly
   c. Avoid toll roads
3. Paying bills
   a. Mail overdue bills with postdated checks
   b. Avoid paperboy
4. Locating extra money
   a. Search chairs, car, pockets, bottom of washing machine for change
   b. Break into penny jar and take rolls to bank

Outlining

As already mentioned, often the best way to write an effective paragraph is to outline it first. (At times, you may have to do a fair amount of writing first to discover your topic, but a stage will come when outlining, or re-outlining, will help.) Outlining is an organizational skill that will develop your ability to think in a clear and logical manner. An outline lets you work on, and see, the bare bones of a paper, without the distraction of a clutter of words and sentences. Outlining provides a quick check on whether your paper is *unified*. It suggests right at the start whether your paper will be adequately *supported*. And it shows you how to plan a paper that is *well organized*.

The following series of exercises will help develop the outlining skills that are so important to writing an effective paper.

Activity 1

One key to effective outlining is the ability to distinguish between major ideas and the details that fit under those ideas. The exercise below will develop your ability to generalize from a list of details and to determine a major thought. In each case, write in the heading that describes accurately the list provided.

Examples

Signs of a cold
Headache
Runny nose
Fever
Chills

Fuels
Wood
Oil
Gas
Kerosene

1. ______________________
Vanilla fudge
Strawberry
Chocolate
Butter almond

2. ______________________
Lincoln
Reagan
Jefferson
Roosevelt

3. ______________________
Birthday
Get well
Anniversary
Graduation

4. ______________________
Anacin
Bufferin
Alka-Seltzer
Tylenol

5. ______________________
Robbery
Murder
Assault
Kidnapping

6. ______________________
Loafers
Moccasins
Sneakers
Sandals

7. ______________________
Russian
Oil and vinegar
Blue cheese
French

8. ______________________
Washing dishes
Taking out trash
Making meals
Dusting

9. ______________________
Cash
Check
Money order
Credit card

10. ______________________
Writing
Speaking
Listening
Reading

Activity 2

Major and minor ideas are mixed together in the two paragraphs outlined below. Put the ideas in logical order by filling in the outlines.

1. ***Topic sentence:*** People can be classified by how they treat their cars.

Never wash, wax, or vacuum car
Protective owners
Clean car only if someone writes in dirt on the trunk
Indifferent owners
Deliberately ignore needed maintenance
Abusive owners
Service car only when it breaks down
Wash and polish car every week
Keep every mechanical item in top shape

a. ______________________
(1) ______________________
(2) ______________________
b. ______________________
(1) ______________________
(2) ______________________
c. ______________________
(1) ______________________
(2) ______________________

2. ***Topic sentence:*** Living with an elderly parent has many benefits.

Advantages for elderly person	a. ______________
Live-in baby-sitter	(1) ______________
Learn about the past	(2) ______________
Advantages for adult children	b. ______________
Serve useful role in family	(1) ______________
Help with household tasks	(2) ______________
Advantages for grandchildren	c. ______________
Stay active and interested in young people	(1) ______________
More attention from adults	(2) ______________

Activity 3

Again, major and minor ideas are mixed together. In addition, in each outline one of the three major ideas is missing and must be added. Put ideas in logical order by filling in the outlines that follow and adding a third major idea.

1. ***Topic sentence:*** Extending the school day would have several advantages.

Help children academically	a. ______________
Parents know children are safe at the school	(1) ______________
More time to spend on basics	(2) ______________
Less pressure to cover subjects quickly	b. ______________
More time for extras like art, music, and sports	(1) ______________
Help working parents	(2) ______________
More convenient to pick up children at 4 or 5 P.M.	c. ______________
Teachers' salaries would be raised	(1) ______________
	(2) ______________

2. ***Topic sentence:*** Living in a mobile home has many disadvantages.

Cost of site rental can go up every year	a. __________
Tiny baths and bedrooms	(1) __________
Few closets or storage areas	(2) __________
Crowded conditions in park	b. __________
Lack of space	(1) __________
Noise from neighbors	(2) __________
Resale value low compared to houses	c. __________
No privacy outside in tiny yards	(1) __________
	(2) __________

Activity 4

Read the following two paragraphs. Then outline each one in the space provided. Write out the topic sentence in each case and summarize in a few words the primary and secondary supporting material that fits under the topic sentence.

1. Why I'm a Stay-at-Home Baseball Fan

I'd much rather stay at home and watch the ball game on television than go to the ball park. First of all, it's cheaper to watch the game at home. I don't have to spend $6 for a ticket and another $3 for a parking space. If I want some refreshments, I can have what's already in the refrigerator instead of shelling out another $2.50 for a limp, lukewarm hot dog and a watery Coke. Also, it's more comfortable at home. I avoid a bumper-to-bumper drive to the ball park and pushy crowds who want to go through the same gate I do. I can lie quietly on my living-room sofa instead of sitting on a hard stadium seat with noisy people all around me. Most of all, watching the game on television is more informative. Not only do I see every play, which I might not from my $6 seat, but I see some of them two and three times on instant replay. In addition, I get each play explained to me in glorious detail. If I were at the ball park, I wouldn't know that the pitch our third baseman hit was a high and inside slider or that his grand-slam home run was a record-setting seventh in his career. So I'll let the other fans spend their money, put up with traffic, crowds, and hard seats, and guess at the plays. I'll take my baseball lying down--at home.

Topic sentence: __________

____

a. __________

(1) __________

(2) __________

b. ______________________________

(1) ______________________________

(2) ______________________________

c. ______________________________

(1) ______________________________

(2) ______________________________

2. Why Teenagers Take Drugs

There are several reasons why teenagers take drugs. First of all, it is easy for young people to get drugs. Drugs are available almost anywhere, from a school cafeteria to a movie line to a football game. Teens don't have to risk traveling to the slums or dealing with shady types on street corners. It is also easy to get drugs because today's teens have spending money, which comes from allowances or earnings from part-time jobs. Teens can use their money to buy the luxuries they want--records, makeup, clothes, or drugs. Second, teens take drugs because the adolescent years are filled with psychological problems. For a teenager, one of these problems is facing the pressure of making important life decisions, such as choosing a career path. Another problem is establishing a sense of self. The teen years are the time when young people must become more independent from their parents and form their own values. The enormous mental pressures of these years can make some people turn to drugs. A final, and perhaps most important, reason why teenagers take drugs is peer pressure to conform. Teens often become very close to special friends, for one thing, and they will share a friend's interests, even if one of them is drugs. Teenagers also attend parties and other social events where it's all-important to be one of the crowd, to be "cool." Even the most mature teenager might be tempted to use drugs rather than risk being an outcast. For all these reasons, drugs are a major problem facing teenagers.

Topic sentence: ______________________________

____

a. ______________________________

(1) ______________________________

(2) ______________________________

b. ______________________________

(1) ______________________________

(2) ______________________________

c. ________________________________

(1) ________________________________

(2) ________________________________

Revising, Editing, and Proofreading

Writing an effective paper is almost never done all at once. Rather, it is a step-by-step process in which you take your paper through a series of stages—from prewriting to final draft.

In the first stage, you get your initial ideas and impressions about the subject down on paper; *you accumulate raw material.* You do this through brainstorming, freewriting, and making lists and scratch outlines.

In the second stage, *you shape, add to, and perhaps subtract from your raw material* as you take your paper through a series of two or three or four rough drafts. You work to make clear the single point of your paper, to develop fully the specific evidence needed to support that point, and to organize and connect the specific evidence. For example, perhaps in the second draft you will concentrate on adding details that will further support the main idea of your paper. At the same time you also may eliminate details that, you realize, do not truly back up your main point. And perhaps in the next draft, you will work on reorganizing the details and adding connections between sentences so that your material will hold together.

In the last stage, you *edit* and *proofread.* You *edit* the next-to-final draft—that is, you check it carefully for the correctness of sentence skills—grammar, mechanics, punctuation, and usage. Then you *proofread* the final copy of the paper for any typing or handwriting mistakes. Editing and proofreading are important steps that some people avoid, often because they have worked so hard (or so little) on the previous stages.

Ideally, you should have enough time to set your paper aside for a while, so that you can check it later with a fresh, rested mind. Remember that locating and correcting sentence-skills mistakes can turn an average paper into a better one and a good paper into an excellent one. A later section of this book will give you practice in editing and proofreading in the form of a series of editing tests (pages 512–522).

This section will show you the stages that can be involved in writing an effective paper. You will see what one student, Gene, did in preparing a paper on his worst job.

There is no single sequence that all people follow in writing a composition. However, the different stages in composing that Gene goes through in writing his paper are fairly representative of the writing process.

Note: To keep Gene's drafts as readable as possible, all spelling and sentence-skills mistakes have been corrected. Ordinarily, a number of such mistakes might be present, and editing a paper for them would be a part of the writing process.

First Stage: Making a List

Apple factory job—worst one I ever had

Boss was a madman
Working conditions were poor
Went to work at 5 P.M., got back at 7 A.M.
Lifted cartons of apple juice for ten hours
Slept, ate, and worked—no social life
Gas money to and from work
Cold outside
Floors of trucks cold metal
Had to clean apple vats

■ Comments and Activity

Fill in the missing words: Gene is fortunate enough to know almost from the start what the ________________ in his paper will be. Most of his work can thus go into developing details to support the point. Details seldom come automatically; they must be dug for, and Gene's sketchy list of unpleasant items about the job is an early stage in the development of his subject. Making a ________________ is an excellent way to get started.

Note that, in his list, Gene is not concerned about ordering the details in any way, or about deciding whether any detail really fits, or even about repeating himself. He is just doing first things first: getting raw material down on paper. In the second stage, Gene will also concentrate on accumulating raw material and will start to give attention to shaping that material.

Second Stage: More Prewriting

I hated my job in the apple factory. I hated it because the work was hard. I loaded cartons of apple juice onto wooden skids in tractor trailers. Two parts to job: ten hours on line; two hours cleaning. I hated the job because the working conditions were bad and the pay was poor.

Why were working conditions bad?

Outside weather cold

Usually zero degrees

Floor of tractor trailer was cold steel

Breaks were limited--
10 minutes every 2½ hours

½ hour for lunch

Why was pay poor?

Two dollars an hour (minimum wage at the time)

Nickel more for working the second shift

Only money was in overtime--when you got time-and-a-half

No double time

I would work twenty hours Friday through Saturday to get as much overtime as possible

1 Work hard
3 Working conditions were poor
(temperature outside, cleaning of the vats)
2 Money poor

■ Comments and Activity

Fill in the missing words: The second stage of Gene's paper is a mix of freewriting, brainstorming, and a scratch ________________. Gene uses all these techniques as he continues to draw out and accumulate ______________. At the same time, he also has realized how to organize his details. He decides to focus *not* on his unpleasant boss but on the job itself. In a rough scratch outline, he lists his three reasons (hard work, bad working conditions, poor wages) for hating the job. He then tentatively decides on working conditions as the worst part of the job and numbers the reasons 1, 2, 3 in the order in which he might develop them. Keep in mind that as you accumulate and develop details, you should, like Gene, be thinking of a way to ________________ them.

Third Stage: An Initial Draft

Working in an apple plant was the worst job I ever had. The work was physically hard. For a ~~long time~~ ten hours a night, I stacked cartons in a tractor trailer. The cartons rolled down a metal track. ~~Each carton was very heavy Each carton was heavy with with cans or bottles of apple juice~~ Each carton contained twelve thirty-two-ounce cans or bottles of apple juice, and they were heavy. ~~At the same time, I had to keep a mental count of all the cartons I had loaded.~~ The pay for the job was another bad feature. I was getting the minimum wage at that time plus a nickel extra for night shift. I worked ~~long hours~~ over sixty hours a week. I still did not take home much ~~money~~ more than one hundred dollars. Working conditions were poor at the plant. During work we were limited to ~~short breaks~~ two ten-minute breaks and unpaid lunch. . . . The truck-loading dock had zero temperatures. . . . Lonely on the job . . . no interests with other loaders . . . worked by myself at the end of the shift . . . cleaned up the apple vats.

■ Comments and Activity

Fill in the missing words: At this stage, Gene has enough details to write the initial draft of his paper. Notice that he continues to accumulate specific supporting details as he writes the draft. For example, he crosses out and replaces "long hours" with the more specific ________________; he crosses out and replaces "short breaks" with the more specific ________________. He also works to improve some of his sentences (for instance, he writes three different versions of the ________________ sentence in the paragraph). In addition, he crosses out and eliminates a sentence about a ________________ because he realizes it does not develop his first supporting point that the work was physically hard.

Toward the end of the paper, Gene either can't find the right words to say what he wants to say or he doesn't quite know yet what he wants to say. So he freewrites (shown by the ellipses . . .), putting down on paper all the impressions that come into his head. He knows that the technique of ________________ may help him move closer to the right thought and the right words.

In a second and third draft, Gene continues to work on and improve his paper. He then edits carefully his next-to-final draft, and the result is the final draft that follows.

Last Stage: The Final Draft

My Job in an Apple Plant

Working in an apple plant was the worst job I ever had. First of all, the work was physically hard. For ten hours a night, I took cartons that rolled down a metal track and stacked them onto wooden skids in a tractor trailor. Each carton contained twelve thirty-two-ounce cans or bottles of apple juice, and they were heavy. The second bad feature of the job was the pay. I was getting the minimum wage at that time, two dollars an hour, plus the minimum of a nickel extra for working the night shift. Even after working over sixty hours a week, I still did not take home much more than one hundred dollars. The worst feature of the apple plant job was the working conditions. During work we were limited to two ten-minute breaks and an unpaid half hour for lunch. Most of my time was spent outside on the truck-loading dock in near-zero-degree temperatures. And I was very lonely on the job, since I had no interests in common with the other truck loaders. I felt this isolation especially when the production line shut down for the night, and I worked by myself for two hours cleaning the apple vats. The vats were an ugly place to be on a cold morning, and the job was a bitter one to have.

■ Comments and Activity

Fill in the missing words: Notice the many improvements that Gene has made as a result of his second and third drafts. He has added transitional words that mark clearly the three supporting points of his paper. The transitional words are "first of all," ________________, and ________________. He has sharpened his details, improved the phrasing of his sentences, and found the words needed to complete the last section of his paper. He has also edited and proofread his paper carefully, checking the spelling of words he was unsure about and correcting several sentence-skills mistakes.

Almost every effective writer, like Gene, is engaged in a continuing process of moving toward a completely realized paper. The final version is seldom, almost never, attained all at once. Instead, it is the end result of a series of ________________. All too often, people stop writing when they are only part way through the writing process; they turn in a paper that is really only an early draft. They have the mistaken notion that a paper is something you should be able to do "all at once." But for almost everyone, writing means hard work and lots of ________________. Be sure, then, to take your paper through the entire series of drafts that you probably will need to write an effective composition.

ADDITIONAL ACTIVITIES FOR REVISING, EDITING, AND PROOFREADING

Activity 1

Answering the questions below will help you evaluate your attitude about revising, editing, and proofreading.

1. When do you typically start to work on a paper?

   ______Several nights before it's due

   ______Night before it's due

   ______Day it's due

2. How many drafts do you typically write when doing a paper?

   ______One ______Two ______Three ______Four or more

3. How would you describe your editing (checking the next-to-final draft for sentence-skills mistakes)?

   ______Do little or no editing

   ______Look quickly for and correct obvious errors

   ______Consult a sentence-skills handbook and a dictionary about all possible errors

4. How would you describe your proofreading (checking the final draft for typing or handwriting errors)?

   ______Do not look at paper again after the last word is written

   ______May glance quickly through the paper

   ______Read paper over carefully to find mistakes

5. Do you ever get back papers marked for obvious errors?

   ______Frequently ______Sometimes ______Almost never ______Never

Activity 2

Listed in the box below are five different stages in the process of composing a paragraph titled "Dangerous Places":

1. Prewriting (list)
2. Prewriting (list, brainstorming, and outline)
3. First draft
4. Second draft
5. Final draft

The five stages appear in scrambled order below. Place the number 1 in front of the first stage of development and number the remaining stages in sequence.

_______ There are some places where I never feel safe. For example, bus stations. The people there look ~~strange look~~ tired and scared. The security guards there makes me feel ~~something bad is going to happen~~ a fight is going to start. I'm also afraid in parking lots. ~~Late at night, I don't like walking in the lot After class, I don't like the parking lot.~~ When I leave my night class or the shopping mall late the walk to the car is scary. ~~Most parking lots have large lights which make me feel at least a little better.~~ I feel least safe in our laundry room . . . It is a depressing place . . . bars on the windows . . . pipes making noises . . . cement steps the only way out . . .

_______ There are some places where I never feel completely safe. For example, I never feel safe in bus stations. The people in bus stations often look tired and scared as they hang on to their suitcases. The security guards add to my feeling that a fight is about to start. I also feel unsafe in large, dark parking lots. When I leave my night class a little late or I leave the mall at 10 P.M., the walk to the car is scary. I'm afraid that someone may be behind a car. Also that my car won't start. The place where I feel least safe is the basement laundry room in our apartment building. No matter when I do the laundry, I'm the only person there. The windows are barred and there are steep steps. I feel trapped when I fold the clothes. The pipes in the room make frightening noises such as hisses and clanks. Places like bus stations, parking lots, and our laundry room give me the shivers.

_______ <u>Dangerous Places</u>

Highways
Cars—especially parking lots
Feel frightened in our laundry room
Big crowds—concerts, movies
Closed-in places
Bus and train stations
Airplane
Elevators and escalators

_______ Dangerous Places

There are some places where I never feel completely safe. For example, I never feel safe in bus stations. The people in bus stations often look tired and scared as they keep one hand protectively on their suitcases. The security guards roaming around bus stations add to my feeling that a fight is about to break out, that someone is going to be mugged, or that a man will force me into a dark corner. I also feel unsafe in large, dark parking lots. When I leave my night class a little late, or I am one of the few leaving the mall at 10

P.M., I dread the walk to my car. I am afraid that someone may be lurking behind another car, ready to mug me. And I fear that my car will not start, leaving me stuck in the dark parking lot. The place where I feel least safe is the basement laundry room in our apartment building. No matter what time I do my laundry, I seem to be the only person there. The windows are barred, and the only exit is a steep flight of cement steps. While I'm folding the clothes, I feel trapped. If anyone unfriendly came down those steps, I would have nowhere to go. The pipes in the room make sudden gurgles, clanks, and hisses, adding to my uneasiness. Places like bus stations, dark parking lots, and our laundry room give me the shivers.

________ Some places seem dangerous and unsafe to me. For example, last night I stayed till 10:15 after night class and walked out to parking lot alone. Very scary. Also, other places I go to every day, such as places in my apartment building. Also frightened by big crowds and lonely bus stations.

Why was the parking lot scary?	What places in my building scare me?
Dark	Laundry room (especially)
Only a few cars	Elevators
No one else in lot	Lobby at night sometimes
Could be someone behind a car	Outside walkway at night
Cold	

2 Parking lots
3 Laundry room
1 Bus stations

Activity 3

The author of "Dangerous Places" in the preceding activity made a number of editing changes between the second draft and the final draft. Compare the two drafts and identify five of the changes in the spaces provided below.

1. ________________________________
2. ________________________________
3. ________________________________
4. ________________________________
5. ________________________________

A Review of Part Two

Fill in the missing words in the following summary of this chapter.

Having the Right Attitude: Some people feel that in order to be a good writer, writing must come easily. This idea is a false one that can interfere with the ability to make progress in writing. A more realistic and productive attitude includes the understanding that, for most people, writing is _______________. In addition, it helps to realize that, like driving or typing, writing is a _______________ that can be learned with lots of _______________.

Writing for a Specific Purpose and Audience: The three most common purposes of writing are to _______________, to _______________, and to _______________. In this book, you will have a lot of practice in writing to persuade people and some practice in writing to provide information.

Your main audience in class is your _______________. But he or she is really a symbol for a general audience of well-educated adults. Writing for this audience should be clear and well organized.

This book will also give you practice in writing for a specific audience. That practice will help you develop the knack of choosing the words and tone of voice that suit specific purposes and people.

Knowing or Discovering Your Subject: It is best to write about a subject that _______________ you and that you know something about, either directly or indirectly. When you must write on a topic about which you have little or no background, you should do _______________ to gain the necessary knowledge. The library is one good place to do that.

There are times, however, when you won't know your exact subject until after you have written for a while. Writing will help you think about and explore your material. On occasion you will write for a page or two and discover that it will make sense to change the _______________ of your paper.

As you work on a paper, remember that it is not necessary to write a paper straight through from _______________ to end. You should proceed in whatever way seems easiest, including starting at the middle or even the end. Make whatever adjustments are needed to reach your goal of a paper that makes and _______________ a point.

Prewriting: There are four types of prewriting techniques. One type, called ________________, is a process of generating ideas by asking questions about your subject. Such questions include *What? When?* and *Why?*

Freewriting is another prewriting technique. It involves writing on your topic for ten minutes without ________________ or worrying about being correct. In this process, your thoughts about your paper often become clearer.

Making a ________________ is another excellent prewriting technique for getting you started on a paper. The goal is to generate many possible details for your paper and maybe even ways of developing that paper.

Finally, perhaps the most helpful technique for writing a good paper is preparing a scratch outline. It is an excellent follow-up to the other prewriting techniques. Sometimes you may even skip the other techniques and concentrate on this one. In a scratch outline, you think about the specific point you will make in your paper, the exact ________________ that will support that point, and the exact ________________ in which you will arrange those items.

Outlining: Often the best way to write an effective paragraph is to ________ it. Outlining develops your ability to think clearly and logically. It helps you to see and work with the fundamental ideas of a paper, and it helps you to focus on producing a paper that is unified, well supported, and well organized.

Revising, Editing, and Proofreading: Writing a paper is usually a step-by-step process. It begins with prewriting, during which you accumulate raw material. In the second stage, you shape your paper by writing and revising it several times. Finally, you edit and proofread. Editing involves checking your paper for mistakes in sentence ________________. Proofreading involves checking the final copy of your paper for typing or handwriting ____________.

PART THREE

TYPES OF PARAGRAPH DEVELOPMENT

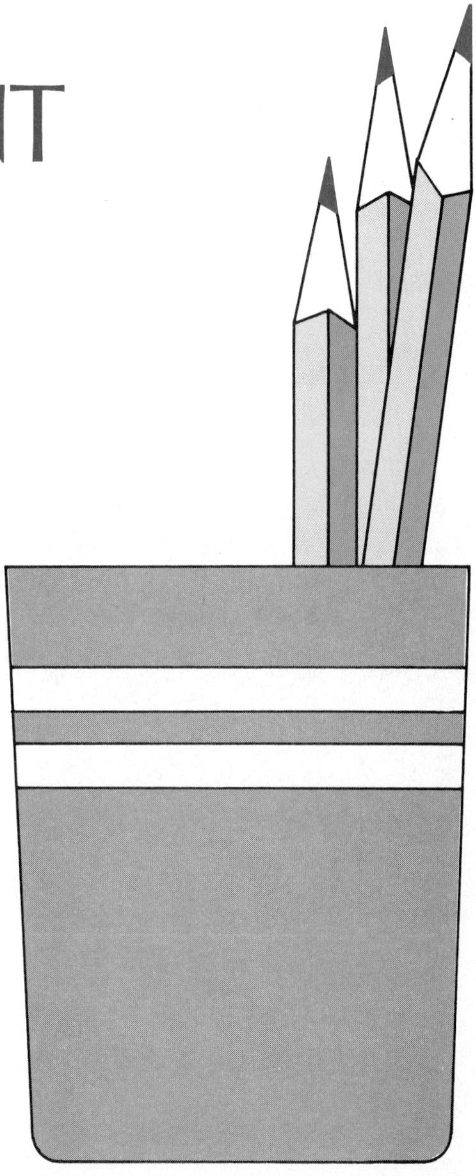

PREVIEW

Part Three gives you practice in the following common types of paragraph development:

Providing Examples
Examining Cause and Effect
Explaining a Process
Comparing and Contrasting
Defining a Term
Dividing and Classifying
Describing a Scene or Person
Narrating an Event
Arguing a Position

After a brief explanation of each type of paragraph development, student paragraphs illustrating each type are presented, followed by questions about those paragraphs. The questions relate to the standards of effective writing described in Part One. You are then asked to write your own paragraph. In each case, writing assignments progress from personal-experience topics to more formal and objective topics, with the last assignment in each section requiring some simple research. At times, points or topic sentences for development are suggested, so that you can concentrate on (1) making sure your evidence is on target in support of your opening idea, (2) providing plenty of specific supporting details to back up your point, and (3) organizing your supporting material clearly.

INTRODUCTION TO PARAGRAPH DEVELOPMENT

THE FOUR TRADITIONAL MODES OF WRITING

Traditionally, all writing has been divided into four major forms, or modes. They are as follows:

- Exposition

Examples	Comparison-contrast
Cause and effect	Definition
Process	Division and classification

- Description
- Narration
- Persuasion or argumentation

In exposition, the writer provides information about a particular subject. The methods of development in exposition include (1) providing examples, (2) examining cause and effect, (3) explaining a process, (4) comparing and contrasting, (5) defining a term, and (6) dividing and classifying. A description is a verbal picture of a person, place, or object. In a narration, a writer tells the story of something that happened. Persuasion or argumentation is an attempt to prove a point or defend an opinion.

In this part of the book, each of the six types of expository development is presented in a separate chapter. There are also individual chapters devoted to description, narration, and argument.

WRITING AS A FORM OF PERSUASION

Most of the paragraphs you write will probably involve some form of persuasion. You will advance a point or topic sentence and then support it in a variety of ways. To convince the reader that your point is valid, you may use description or narration or some method of exposition. In the paragraphs you will read in Part Three, for example, one writer supports the point that a certain pet shop is depressing by providing a number of descriptive details. Another writer labels a certain experience in his life as heartbreaking and then uses a narrative to demonstrate the truth of his statement. A third writer advances the opinion that good horror movies can be easily distinguished from bad horror movies and then supplies comparative information about both to support her claim. All your writing, in short, has the purpose of persuading your reader that the idea you have advanced is a valid one.

THE ORDER OF EACH CHAPTER

After each type of paragraph development is explained, student papers illustrating that type are presented, followed by questions about the papers. The questions relate to unity, support, and coherence, the principles of effective writing explained earlier in the book. You are then asked to write your own paragraph. In most cases, the first assignment is fairly structured and provides a good deal of guidance for the writing process. The other assignments offer an unusually wide and interesting choice of writing topics.

PROVIDING EXAMPLES

In our daily conversations, we often provide *examples*—that is, details, particulars, specific instances—to explain statements that we make. In the box below are several statements and supporting examples:

Statement	*Examples*
The A&P was crowded today.	There were at least four carts waiting at each of the checkout lines, and it took me forty-five minutes to get through a line.
The corduroy shirt I bought is poorly made.	When I washed it, the colors began to fade, one button cracked and another fell off, a shoulder seam opened, and the sleeves shrank almost two inches.
My son Peter is unreliable.	If I depend on him to turn off a pot of beans in ten minutes, the family is likely to eat burned beans. If I ask him to turn down the thermostat before he goes to bed, the heat is likely to stay on all night.

In each case, the examples help us *see for ourselves* the truth of the statement that has been made. In paragraphs, too, explanatory examples help the audience fully understand a point. Lively, specific examples also add interest to a paper.

In this chapter, you will be asked to provide a series of examples to support a topic sentence. Providing examples to support a point is one of the most common and simple methods of paragraph development. First read the paragraphs ahead; they all use examples to develop their points. Then answer the questions that follow.

PARAGRAPHS TO CONSIDER

The Cruelty of Children

Children can be very cruel. Very early, for example, they learn that words can wound. Little three-year-olds in nursery school call each other "dum-dum" or "weirdo," and older children invent cruel nicknames, like "fatty" or "four-eyes," to tease their schoolmates. And children who are just a bit older learn facts about other kids from their parents, and use those facts to make someone break down and cry. Children also attack each other physically. Whenever a group of grade-schoolers troops home from school, there is a lot of pushing, tripping, punching, and pinching. An argument will end in shoving and hair-pulling. But far worse than harsh words or physical violence is the emotional hurt children can cause their classmates. By junior high school days, young teenagers start to shut out people they do not like. They ignore the kids whose looks, clothes, interests, or finances differ from their own. Popular kids gather together in cliques, and the unpopular ones face social isolation, loneliness, and depression. The kids who are shunned endure a hurt that is worse than cruel words and fistfights. Many adults think that childhood is an ideal time, but there are terribly cruel things that can happen.

A Dangerous Playing Field

We play touch football on a local field. First of all, the grass on the field is seldom mowed. The result is that we have to run through tangled weeds that wrap around our ankles like trip wires. The tall grass also hides the gaping holes lurking beneath. The best players know the exact positions of all the holes and manage to detour around them like soldiers zigzagging across a minefield. Most of us, though, endure at least one sprained ankle per game. Another danger is the old baseball infield that we use as the last twenty yards of our gridiron. This area is covered with stones and broken glass. No matter how often we clean it up, we can never keep pace with the broken bottles hurled on the field by the teenagers we call the "night shift." These people apparently hold drinking parties every night in the abandoned dugout and enjoy throwing the empties out on the field. During every game, we try to avoid falling on especially big chunks of Budweiser bottles. Finally, encircling the entire field is an old, rusty chain-link fence full of tears and holes. Being slammed into the fence during the play can mean a painful stabbing by the jagged wires. All these dangers have made us less afraid of opposing teams than of the field where we play.

An Egotistical Neighbor

I have an egotistical neighbor named Alice. If I tell Alice how beautiful I think the dress she is wearing is, she will take the time to tell me the name of the store where she bought it, the type of material that was used in making it, and the price. Alice is also egotistical when it comes to her children. Because they are hers, she thinks they just have to be the best children on the block. I am wasting my time by trying to tell her I have seen her kids expose themselves on the street or take things from parked cars. I do not think parents should praise their children too much. Kids have learned how to be good at home and simply awful when they are not at home. Finally, Alice is quick to describe the furnishings of her home for someone who is meeting her for the first time. She tells how much she paid for the paneling in her dining room. She mentions that she has two color television sets and that they were bought at an expensive furniture store. She lets the person know that the stereo set in her living room cost more than six hundred dollars, and that she has such a collection of records that she would not be able to play them all in one week. Poor Alice is so self-centered that she never realizes how boring she can be.

■ Questions

About Unity

1. Which paragraph uses a topic sentence that is too narrow?

   ____

   Write an effective topic sentence for the paragraph. (*Hint:* Use the key word given in the title).

   ____

   ____

2. Which two sentences in "Neighbor" are irrelevant to the point that Alice is egotistical?

   ____

   ____

About Support

3. How many examples are given of Alice's egotism?

   ______1 ______2 ______3 ______4

4. After which sentence in "Cruelty" are specific details needed?

   ____

   ____

About Coherence

5. What are the three main transition words used in "Playing Field"?

   a. ________________

   b. ________________

   c. ________________

6. Does "Cruelty" organize its details through time order, emphatic order, or a combination of both?

   ____

   ____

WRITING THE PARAGRAPH

■ Writing Assignment 1

The assignment here is to complete an unfinished paragraph. The paragraph on the following page has as its topic sentence, "My husband Roger is a selfish person." Provide the supporting details needed to fill out the examples of Roger's selfishness. The first example has been done for you.

How to Proceed: To do this assignment, first jot down on separate paper a couple of answers for each of the following questions.

a What specific vacations did the family go on because Roger wanted to go? Give places, length of stay, time of year. What vacations has the family never gone on (for example, to visit the wife's relatives) even though the wife has wanted to?

b What specific items has Roger bought for himself (rather than for the whole family's use) with leftover budget money?

c What chores and duties involved in the everyday caring for the children has Roger never done?

A Selfish Person

My husband Roger is a selfish person. For one thing, he refuses to move out of the city, even though it is a bad place to raise the children. *We inherited some money when my parents died, and it might be enough for a down payment on a small house in a nearby town. But Roger says he would miss his buddies in the neighborhood.* Also, when we go on vacation, we always go where Roger wants to go. ____________________

____

____

____

Another example of Roger's selfishness is that he always spends any budget money that is left over. ____________________

____

____

____

____

Finally, Roger leaves all the work of caring for the children to me. ______

____

____

____

____

Here and in general in your writing, try to generate *more* supporting material than you need. You are then in a position to choose the most convincing details for your paper. Now take your best details, reshape them as needed, and use them to complete the paragraph about Roger.

Writing Assignment 2

Write a paragraph about one quality of a person you know well. The person might be a member of your family, a friend, a roommate, a boss or supervisor, a neighbor, a teacher, or someone else. Listed below are some descriptive words that can be applied to people. They are only suggestions; you can write about any other specific quality.

Honest	Hardworking	Jealous
Bad-tempered	Supportive	Materialistic
Ambitious	Suspicious	Sarcastic
Bigoted	Open-minded	Self-centered
Considerate	Lazy	Spineless
Argumentative	Independent	Good-humored
Softhearted	Stubborn	Cooperative
Energetic	Flirtatious	Disciplined
Patient	Irresponsible	Sentimental
Reliable	Stingy	Defensive
Generous	Trustworthy	Dishonest
Persistent	Aggressive	Insensitive
Shy	Courageous	Unpretentious
Sloppy	Compulsive	Neat

How to Proceed

a Begin by making a list of examples that will support your topic sentence. For example, if you decide to write about your brother's irresponsibility, jot down several examples of times when he showed this quality. Part of your list might look like this:

Lost rent money
Forgot to return borrowed textbooks
Didn't show up for big family dinner
Left dog alone in the apartment for two days
Left my bike out in the rain
Missed conference with teacher

Another way to get started is to ask yourself questions about your topic and write down the answers. Again, if you were writing about your brother's irresponsibility, you might ask yourself questions such as these:

How has Bill been irresponsible?
What are examples of times he's shown this quality?

What happened on these occasions?
Who was involved?
What were the results of his actions?

The answers to these questions should serve as an excellent source of details for the paragraph.

b Then prepare a scratch outline made up of the strongest examples from the prewriting material you generated above. Note that as you make this outline, you should group related details together. For example, the items in the list about the irresponsible brother might be categorized as follows:

At apartment

Lost rent money

Left dog alone in apartment

At home

Missed family dinner

Left bike in rain

At school

Didn't return textbooks

Missed conference

c Next, write out your topic sentence. This first sentence should tell the name of the person you are writing about, your relationship to the person, and the specific quality you are focusing on. For example, you might write, "Linda is a flirtatious girl I know at school," or "Stubbornness is Uncle Carl's outstanding characteristic."

Do not make the mistake of beginning with more than one quality ("I have a cousin named Alan who is softhearted and generous") or with a general quality ("My boss is a good person"). Focus on *one specific quality*.

d Develop your examples with specific details. Remember that you don't want to *tell* us about the person; rather, you want to *show* the person to us by detailing words, actions, or both. You might want to go back and reread the examples provided in the paragraph on an egotistical neighbor.

e As you are writing drafts of your paragraph, ask yourself repeatedly: "Do my examples truly show that my subject has a certain quality?" Your aims in this assignment are twofold: (1) to provide *adequate* specific details for the quality in question and (2) to provide *enough* specific details so that you solidly support your point.

f When you are satisfied that you have provided effective examples, edit your paragraph carefully for the sentence-skills mistakes listed on the inside front cover. In addition, make sure you can answer *Yes* to the questions on unity, support, and coherence.

■ Writing Assignment 3

Write a paragraph that uses examples to develop one of the following statements or a related statement of your own.

1. ________________ is a distracting place to try to study.
2. The daily life of a student is filled with conflicts.
3. Abundant evidence exists that America has become a health-conscious nation.
4. Despite modern appliances, many household chores are still drudgery.
5. One of my professors, ________________, has some good (*or* unusual) teaching techniques.
6. Wasted electricity is all around us.
7. Life in America is faster-paced than ever before.
8. Violence on television is widespread.
9. Women today are wearing some ridiculous fashions.
10. Many students here at ________________ do not care about learning (*or* are overly concerned about grades).

Be sure to choose examples that truly support your point. They should be relevant facts, statistics, personal experiences, or incidents you have heard or read about.

Organize your paragraph by grouping several examples that support your point. Save the most vivid, convincing, or important example for last.

■ Writing Assignment 4

Research some magazine articles or recent books to back up the topic sentence, "The diet of the average American is unhealthy." You might want to check for articles dealing with such topics as fat, fiber, fast food, junk food, caffeine, food additives, heart disease, and cancer. The *Readers' Guide to Periodical Literature* and your library card catalog (subject index) will direct you to the material you need. Try looking under such headings as nutrition, food habits, diet, vitamins, and health.

■ Writing Assignment 5

Imagine that you are a television critic and are still living near the high school you attended. The principal is planning a special parents' evening and would like you to make a speech then on the topic of "Television and the Responsible Parent." You accept the invitation and decide to organize your talk around this thesis: "There are three television programs that represent worthwhile viewing for families." Write a one-paragraph summary of your talk.

To make an outline for your speech, think of three programs you would recommend for viewing by all members of a family. Write down the titles of the programs, and then list under each the specific features that made you choose that show.

EXAMINING CAUSE AND EFFECT

What caused Pat to drop out of school? Why are soap operas so popular? Why does our football team do so poorly each year? How has retirement affected Dad? What effects does divorce have on children? Every day we ask questions similar to those above and look for answers. We realize that many actions do not occur without causes, and we realize also that a given action can have a series of effects—for good or bad. By examining the causes or effects of an action, we seek to understand and explain things that happen in our lives.

You will be asked in this section to do some detective work by examining the causes of something or the effects of something. First read the three paragraphs that follow and answer the questions about them. All three paragraphs support their opening points by explaining a series of causes or a series of effects.

PARAGRAPHS TO CONSIDER

New Puppy in the House

Buying a new puppy can have drastic effects in a quiet household. For one thing, the puppy keeps the entire family awake for at least two solid weeks. Every night when the puppy is placed in its box, it begins to howl, yip, and whine. Even after the lights go out and the house quiets down, the puppy continues to moan. Since it is impossible to sleep while listening to a heartbreaking, trembling "Woo-wooo," the family soon begins to suffer the effects of loss of sleep. Everyone becomes hostile, short-tempered, depressed, and irritable. A second effect is that the puppy tortures the family by destroying its material possessions. Every day something different is damaged. Family members find chewed belts and shoes, gnawed table legs, and leaking sofa cushions. In addition, the puppy usually ruins the wall-to-wall carpeting and makes the house smell like a public rest room at a big-city bus station. Worst of all, though, the puppy causes family arguments. Parents argue with children about who is supposed to feed and walk the dog. Children argue among themselves about whose turn it is to play with the puppy. Everyone argues about whose idea it was to get the puppy in the first place. These continual arguments, along with the effects of sleeplessness and the loss of valued possessions, seriously disrupt a household. Only when the puppy gets a bit older will the house be peaceful again.

My Car Accident

Several factors led to my recent car accident. First of all, because a heavy snow and freezing rain had fallen the day before, the road that I was driving on was hazardous. The road had been plowed but was dangerously icy in spots where dense clusters of trees kept the early morning sun from hitting the road. Second, despite the slick patches, I was stupidly going along at about fifty miles an hour instead of driving more cautiously. I have a daredevil streak in my nature and sometimes feel I want to become a stock-car racer after I finish school, rather than an accountant as my parents want me to be. Another contributing factor to my accident was a dirty green Gremlin that suddenly pulled onto the road from a small intersecting street about fifty yards ahead of me. The road was a sheet of ice at that point, but I was forced to apply my brake and also swing my car into the next lane. Unfortunately, the fourth and final cause of my accident now presented itself. The rear of my Volkswagen was heavy because the engine is there and also because I had a barbell set in the backseat. I was selling the fairly new weight-lifting set to someone at school, since the weights had failed to build up my muscles immediately and I had gotten tired of practicing with them. The result of all the weight in the rear was that after I passed the Gremlin, my car spun completely around on the slick road. For a few horrifying, helpless moments, I was sliding down the highway backwards at fifty miles an hour, with no control whatsoever over the car. Then, abruptly, I slid off the road, thumping into a high plowed snowbank. I felt stunned for a moment but then also relieved. I saw a telephone pole about six feet to the right of me and realized my accident could have been really disastrous.

Why I Stopped Smoking

For one thing, I realized that my cigarette smoke bothered others, particularly my wife and children, irritating their eyes and causing them to cough and sneeze. Also, cigarettes are a messy habit. Our house was littered with ashtrays piled high with butts, matchsticks, and ashes, and the children were always knocking them over. Cigarettes are expensive, and I estimated that the carton a week that I was smoking cost me about $650 a year. Another reason I stopped was that the message about cigarettes being harmful to health finally got through to me. A heavy smoker I know from work is in Eagleville Hospital now with lung cancer. Cigarettes were also inconvenient. When I would smoke, I would have to drink something to wet down my dry throat, and that meant I had to keep going to the bathroom all the time. I sometimes seemed to spend whole weekends doing nothing but smoking, drinking, and going to the bathroom. Most of all, I resolved to stop smoking because I felt exploited. I hated the thought of wealthy, greed-filled corporations making money off my sweat and blood. The rich may keep getting richer, but--at least as regards to cigarettes--with no thanks to me.

Questions

About Unity

1. Which two sentences in ''My Car Accident'' are not on target in support of the opening idea and so should be omitted?

   a. ______________________________

   b. ______________________________

2. Which paragraph lacks a topic sentence?

   ____

About Support

3. How many causes are given to support the opening idea in ''My Car Accident''?

   ______1 ______2 ______3 ______4

   In ''Smoking''?

   ______1 ______2 ______3 ______4

4. How many effects of bringing a new puppy into the home are given in ''New Puppy in the House''?

   ______1 ______2 ______3 ______4

About Coherence

5. What are the five major transition words used in ''Why I Stopped Smoking''?

   a. ____________ b. ____________ c. ____________

   d. ____________ e. ____________

6. What words signal the most important effect in ''Puppy''?

   ____

Activity 1

Complete the following outline of the paragraph on ''Why I Stopped Smoking.'' The effect is that the author stopped smoking; the causes are what make up the paragraph. Summarize each in a few words. The first cause and details are given for you as an example.

Point

There are a number of reasons why I stopped smoking.

1. Reason: *Bothered others* ____________________
 Details: *Eye irritation, coughing, sneezing* ____________________
2. Reason: ____________________
 Details: ____________________
3. Reason: ____________________
 Details: ____________________
4. Reason: ____________________
 Details: ____________________
5. Reason: ____________________
 Details: ____________________
6. Reason: ____________________
 Details: ____________________

Activity 2

The exercise here will help you tell the difference between reasons that back up a point and the supporting details that go with each one of the reasons. The scrambled list ahead contains both reasons and supporting details. Complete the outline following the list by writing the reasons in the lettered blanks (A, B, C, D) and the appropriate supporting details in the numbered blanks (1, 2, 3). Arrange the reasons in what *you feel* is their order of importance. Also, summarize the reasons and details in a few words rather than writing them out completely.

Point

There are a number of reasons why people enjoy eating at Burger Village.

Reasons and Details

An order is ready no more than three minutes or so after it is placed.
A hostess is present in the dining room to help parents with children.
The workers wear clean uniforms, and their hands are clean.
There are french fries in two sizes.
The hostess hands out moistened cloths to wash the children after they eat.

The waiting line moves quickly.

Customers can order hamburgers or fish, chicken, or ham sandwiches.

The hostess helps with the children's coats and gets a highchair for the baby.

The place is clean.

There are several flavors of milk shakes and several kinds of soft drinks, as well as coffee and hot chocolate.

Someone is always sweeping the floor, collecting trays, and wiping off tables.

The kitchen area is all clean and polished stainless steel.

The service is fast and convenient.

The hostess gives the children small cups to drink from and special hats.

There are a variety of items on the menu.

Orders come packaged in bags or boxes for easy carrying out.

Outline

a. ______________________________

 (1) ______________________________

 (2) ______________________________

 (3) ______________________________

b. ______________________________

 (1) ______________________________

 (2) ______________________________

 (3) ______________________________

c. ______________________________

 (1) ______________________________

 (2) ______________________________

 (3) ______________________________

d. ______________________________

 (1) ______________________________

 (2) ______________________________

 (3) ______________________________

WRITING THE PARAGRAPH

■ Writing Assignment 1

Listed below are topic sentences and brief outlines for four potential cause or effect paragraphs. Choose one of them to develop into a paragraph.

1. Topic sentence: There are several reasons why some high school graduates are unable to read.
   a. Failure of parents (cause)
   b. Failure of schools (cause)
   c. Failure of students themselves (cause)
2. Topic sentence: Having poor vision has had a major impact on my life.
   a. Expenses for doctors and glasses (effect)
   b. Inconvenience in daily life (effect)
   c. Occasional danger (effect)
3. Topic sentence: Attending college has changed my personality in positive ways.
   a. More confident (effect)
   b. More knowledgeable (effect)
   c. More assertive (effect)
4. Topic sentence: Living with roommates makes attending college difficult.
   a. Late night hours (cause)
   b. More temptations to cut class (cause)
   c. More distractions from studying (cause)

How to Proceed

a On separate paper, make a list of details that might go under each of the supporting points. Provide more details than you can possibly use. Here, for example, are some of the details generated by the writer of "New Puppy in the House" while working on the paragraph:

Whines and moans
Arguments about walking dog
Arguments about feeding dog
Purchase collar, leash, food
Chewed belts and shoes
Arguments about playing with dog
Loss of sleep
Visits to vet
Short tempers
Accidents on carpet
Chewed cushions and tables

b Decide which details you will use to develop the paragraph. Also, number the details in the order in which you will present them. Here is how the writer of "New Puppy in the House" made decisions about details:

2 Whines and moans
6 Arguments about walking dog
6 Arguments about feeding dog
~~Purchase collar, leash, food~~
4 Chewed belts and shoes
6 Arguments about playing with dog
1 Loss of sleep
~~Visits to vet~~
3 Short tempers
5 Accidents on carpet
4 Chewed cushions and tables

Notice that the writer has put the same number in front of certain details that go together. For example, there is a "4" in front of "Chewed belts and shoes" and also in front of "Chewed cushions and tables."

c As you are working on your paper, keep checking your material to make sure it is unified, supported, and coherent.

d Finally, edit the next-to-final draft of your paper for sentence-skills mistakes, including spelling.

■ Writing Assignment 2

Below are ten possible topic sentences for a cause or an effect paper. In scratch outline form on separate paper, provide brief supporting points for five of the ten statements.

List the Causes

1. There are several reasons why so many accidents occur on ____________ (*name a local road, traffic circle, or intersection*).
2. ____________ is (*or* is not) a good teacher (*or* employer).
3. ____________ is a sport that cannot be appreciated on television.
4. ____________ is the most difficult course I have ever taken.
5. Mothers with very young children should not work outside the home.

List the Effects

6. In several ways, cars have made our lives more complicated.
7. When I heard the news that ________________, I was affected in various ways.
8. Children no longer respect their teachers.
9. Breaking my bad habit of ________________ has changed my life (*or* would change my life).
10. My fear of ________________ has affected my everyday life.

Decide which of your outlines would be most promising to develop into a paragraph. Make sure that your causes or effects are logical ones that truly support the point in the topic sentence. Then follow the directions on "How to Proceed" in Writing Assignment 1.

■ Writing Assignment 3

Most of us criticize others readily, but we find it more difficult to give compliments. For this assignment, write a one-paragraph letter praising someone. The letter may be to a person you know (parent, relative, friend); to a public figure (actor, politician, leader, sports star, and so on); or to a company or organization (for example, the people who manufactured a product you own, a newspaper, a TV network, or a government agency).

To start, make a list of reasons why you admire the person or organization. Here are examples of reasons for praising an automobile manufacturer:

My car's dependability
Prompt action on a complaint
Well-thought-out design
Friendly dealer service

Here are reasons for admiring a parent:

Sacrifices you made
Patience with me
Your sense of humor
Your fairness
Your encouragement

Then follow the suggestions on "How to Proceed" in Writing Assignment 1.

■ Writing Assignment 4

Investigate the reasons behind a currently breaking news event. For example, you may want to investigate the causes of:

A labor strike

A military action by our or some other government

A Supreme Court decision or some other court decision

Murder or some other act of violence

A particular tax increase

A natural disaster, a traffic accident, a plane crash, or some other catastrophe

Research the reasons for the event by reading current newspapers (especially big-city dailies with detailed stories), by reading weekly news magazines (such as *Time, Newsweek,* and *U.S. News & World Report*), by watching television news shows and specials, or by asking authorities on the subject (a professor of law, history, or political science, for example).

Decide on the three or four major causes of the event, and write a paragraph detailing those causes.

■ Writing Assignment 5

Option 1: Assume that there has been an alarming increase in drug abuse among the students at the high school you attended. What might be the causes of this increase? Spend some time thinking about the several possible causes for the rise in substance abuse. Then, as a concerned member of the local community, write a letter to the high-school guidance counselor explaining the reasons for the increased drug use. Your purpose in the letter is to provide helpful information that the counselor may be able to use in dealing with the problem.

Option 2: Your roommate has been complaining that it's impossible to succeed in Mr. X's class because the class is too stressful. You volunteer to attend the class and see for yourself. Afterwards, you decide to write an anonymous letter to the teacher, calling attention to the stressful conditions in the class and suggesting concrete ways that the instructor could deal with these conditions. Write this letter dealing with the causes and effects of stress in the class.

EXPLAINING A PROCESS

Every day we perform many activities that are processes—that is, a series of steps carried out in a definite order. Many of these processes are familiar and automatic: for example, tying shoelaces, changing bed linen, using a vending machine, or starting a car. We are thus seldom aware of the sequence of steps that makes up each activity. In other cases, such as when we are asked for directions to a particular place, or when we try to read and follow the directions for a new table game, we may be painfully conscious of the whole series of steps involved in the process.

In this section, you will be asked to write a process paragraph—one that explains clearly how to do or make something. To prepare for this assignment, you should first read the student process papers below and then respond to the questions that follow.

PARAGRAPHS TO CONSIDER

Sneaking into the House at Night

The first step I take is bringing my key along with me. Obviously, I don't want to have to knock on the door at 1:30 in the morning and rouse my parents out of bed. Second, I make it a point to stay out past midnight. If I come in before then, my father is still up. I find it hard to face his disapproving look after a night out. All I need in my life right now is for him to make me feel guilty. Trying to make it as a college student is as much as I'm ready to handle. Next, I am careful to be very quiet upon entering the house. This involves lifting the front door up slightly as I open it, so that it does not creak. It also means treating the floor and steps to the second floor like a minefield, stepping carefully over the spots that squeak. Finally, I stop briefly in the bathroom without turning on the light and then tiptoe to my room, put my clothes in a pile on a chair, and slip quietly into bed. With my careful method of sneaking into the house at night, I have avoided some major hassles with my parents.

How to Harass a Teacher

You can use a number of time-proven techniques to harass a teacher. First of all, show up late for class, so that you can interrupt the beginning of the teacher's presentation. Saunter in nonchalantly and try to find a seat by a friend. In a normal tone of voice, speak some words of greeting to your friends as you sit down, and scrape your desk as loudly as possible while you make yourself comfortable in it. Then just sit there and do anything but pay attention. When the teacher sees that you are not involved in the class, he or she may pop a quick question, probably hoping to embarrass you. You should then say, in a loud voice, "I DON'T KNOW THE ANSWER." This declaration of ignorance will throw the teacher off guard. If the teacher then asks you why you don't know the answer, say "I don't even know what page we're on" or "I thought the assignment was boring so I didn't do it." Give the impression that there is no sane reason why you should be expected to know the answer. After the teacher calls on someone else, get up loudly from your seat, walk to the front of the classroom, and demand to be excused for an emergency meeting in the bathroom. Stay at least fifteen minutes and take your time coming back. If the teacher asks you where you've been when you reenter the room, simply ignore the question and go to your seat. Flop into your desk, slouching back and extending your legs as far out as possible. When the teacher informs you of the assignment that the class is working on, make an exaggerated sigh and very slowly open up and start turning the pages of your book. As soon as he or she stops looking at you, rest your elbows on the desk, hold your pencil between the fingertips of your hands, and gaze off into space. The teacher will look at you and wonder whether it wouldn't have been better to go into business instead of education.

Driving around a Traffic Circle

If you want to drive around one of our country's treacherous traffic circles and live to tell about it, there are a number of steps to follow. To begin, you must prepare yourself mentally as you approach the circle. Do not give in to panic or begin to quiver with terror. Instead, try repeating to yourself, in a calm tone of voice, "Other drivers do not want to kill me. They are sane people. We will all go around the circle in an orderly way." Next, as you actually begin to negotiate the circle, you should practice the technique of looking in all directions at once. Every second, check your rearview mirror, left mirror, right mirror, and then turn your head quickly to cover any blind spots. Following this, you must deal with the flow of traffic merging onto the circle from other roads. Try to maintain your speed at all costs. Do not slow down to read road signs or stop to allow another car to enter the circle. This will merely create a massive pileup behind you. Finally, the trickiest part of traffic-circle driving is exiting from the circle. At some point, you must stop going around and make a move, usually across two lanes of traffic, toward a side road. You can use your directional signals, although these will have little effect on the other drivers. The best way to exit is to check your rearview mirror until you spot a timid-looking driver slightly behind you in the next lane. This person will slow down as you cut into his or her lane and make a successful dash for the exit. Never cut across in front of a Cadillac driver smoking a thick cigar or in front of an eighteen-year-old in a Trans Am. Such people will speed up, not slow down. These instructions, then, should enable you to enter a traffic circle and come out in one piece on the other side.

■ Questions

About Unity

1. Which paragraph lacks a topic sentence?

 ____

2. Write the first several words of the two sentences in ''Sneaking'' that should be eliminated in the interest of paragraph unity.

 a. ______________________________

 b. ______________________________

About Support

3. After which sentence in ''Teacher'' are supporting details needed?

 ____

4. Summarize the four steps in the process of driving around a traffic circle.

 a. ______________________________

 b. ______________________________

 c. ______________________________

 d. ______________________________

About Coherence

5. Do the paragraphs use time order or emphatic order?

 ____

6. What are the four main transition words in ''Sneaking''?

 a. ______________ b. ______________

 c. ______________ d. ______________

WRITING THE PARAGRAPH

■ Writing Assignment 1

Choose one of the topics below to write about in a process paper.

How to change a car or bike tire
How to bathe a dog or cat
How to get rid of house or garden pests such as mice, roaches, or wasps
How to fall asleep (if you need to and can't)
How to play a simple game like checkers, tic-tac-toe, or an easy card game
How to load a van
How to learn a song
How to live on a limited budget
How to shorten a skirt or pants
How to plan a garden
How to take care of plants
How to fix a leaky faucet, a clogged drain, or the like
How to build a campfire
How to make your house look lived in when you are away
How to study for an important exam
How to paint a ceiling
How to conduct a yard or garage sale
How to wash dishes efficiently, clean a bathroom, do laundry, or the like

How to Proceed

a Now freewrite for ten minutes on the topic you have chosen. Do not worry about spelling, grammar, organization, or other matters of correct form. Just write whatever comes into your head regarding the topic. Keep writing for more than ten minutes if added details about the topic occur to you. This freewriting will give you a base of raw material that you can draw on in the next phase of your work on the paragraph. After freewriting, you should have a sense of whether there is enough material available for you to write a process paragraph about the topic. If so, continue as explained below. If not, choose another topic and freewrite about *it* for ten minutes.

b Write a clear, direct topic sentence about the process you are going to describe. In your topic sentence, you can (1) say that it is important for your audience to know about the process (''Knowing how to study effectively for a major exam can mean the difference between passing and failing a course''), or (2) state your opinion of the process (''My technique for building a campfire is almost foolproof''). Don't worry, at this point, about how each step fits and whether certain steps overlap. Instead, just get down all the steps you can think of. Here, for example, is the list prepared by the author of ''Sneaking into the House at Night'':

Quiet on stairs
Come in after Dad's asleep
House is freezing at night
Bring key
Know which steps to avoid
Lift up front door
Late dances on Saturday night
Don't turn on bathroom light
Avoid squeaky spots on floor
Get into bed quietly

c Number your items in time order; strike out items that do not fit in the list; add others that come to mind. Thus:

~~Quiet on stairs~~
2 Come in after Dad's asleep
~~House is freezing at night~~
1 Bring key
5 Know which steps to avoid
3 Lift up front door
~~Late dances on Saturday night~~
6 Don't turn on bathroom light
4 Avoid squeaky spots on floor
8 Get into bed quietly
7 *Undress quietly*

d Use your list as a guide to write the first rough draft of your paper. As you write, try to think of additional details that will support your opening sentence. Do not expect to finish your paper in one draft. You should, in fact, be ready to write a series of lists and drafts as you work toward the goals of unity, support, and coherence.

e Be sure that the point of view in your paragraph is consistent. For example, if you begin to write "How *I* got rid of mice" (first person), do not switch suddenly to "*You* must buy the right traps" (second person). Write your paragraph either from the first-person point of view (*I-we*) *or* from the second-person point of view (*you*).

Do not hesitate to use a second-person *you* point of view. A process paragraph in which you give instructions is one of the few situations in formal writing where the second-person *you* is acceptable.

f Be sure to use some transitions such as *first, next, also, then, after, now, during,* and *finally* so that your paper moves smoothly and clearly from one step in the process to the next.

g While working on your paper, refer to the checklist on the inside front cover to make sure you can answer *Yes* to the questions about unity, support, and coherence. Also, refer to the checklist when you edit the next-to-final draft of your paper for sentence-skills mistakes, including spelling.

■ Writing Assignment 2

For this assignment, you will be working with more general topics than the ones in the previous assignment. You will find, in many cases, that you must invent your own steps in a particular process. You will also have to make decisions about how many steps to include and what order to place them in.

How to break a bad habit such as smoking, overeating, or excess drinking
How to improve a course you have taken
How to make someone you know happy
How to go about meeting people
How to discipline a child
How to improve the place where you work
How to show appreciation to others
How to make someone forgive you
How to con a teacher
How to make yourself depressed
How to get over a broken relationship
How to procrastinate
How to flirt

Writing Assignment 3

Everyone is an expert at something. Write a process paragraph on some skill that you can perform very well. The skill might be, for example, "refereeing a game," "fishing for perch," "playing third base," "putting up a tent," "making an ice cream soda," "becoming a long-distance runner," or "fine-tuning a car engine." Write from the point of view that "This is how ____________ should be done."

Writing Assignment 4

Write a process paragraph on how to succeed at a job interview. Here are some ways to research this topic.

- Consult material that is available in your college placement center.
- Look in your college bookstore or any paperback bookstore for "how to" books on getting a job; many such books will contain a chapter on doing well in a job interview.
- In your library, look up relevant books under a subject heading such as *Career Planning, Vocational Guidance,* and *Occupations.*
- Browse through the magazine rack in your library or the magazine section of any newspaper store; articles on this common topic frequently appear in popular magazines.
- Look in a recent *Readers' Guide to Periodical Literature* in your library under the heading *Interviewing* for articles on the topic. (See "Using the Library" on pages 284–297 for information on the *Readers' Guide.*)

Condense the material you have consulted into three, four, or five basic steps. Pick out the steps, tips, and pointers that seem most important to you or that recur most often in the material. Remember that you are reading only to obtain background information for your paper. Do not copy material or repeat someone else's words or phrases in your own work.

Writing Assignment 5

Option 1: You have a part-time job helping out in a day-care center. The director is pleased with your work and wants to give you more responsibility, so she has assigned you to be in charge of a group activity (for example, an exercise session, an alphabet lesson, or a valentine-making project). But before you actually begin the activity, she wants to see a summary of how you would go about it. What advance preparation would be needed, and what exactly would you be doing throughout the time of the project? Write a paragraph explaining the steps you would follow in conducting the activity.

Option 2: Alternatively, write an explanation you might give to one of the children on how to do a simple classroom task—serving juice and cookies, getting ready for nap time, watering a plant, putting toys or other classroom materials away, or any other task you choose. Explain each step of the task in a way that a child would understand.

COMPARING AND CONTRASTING

Comparison and contrast are two thought processes we constantly perform in everyday life. When we *compare* two things, we show how they are similar; when we *contrast* two things, we show how they are different. We might compare or contrast two brand-name products (for example, Levi's versus Wrangler jeans), or two television shows, or two cars, or two teachers, or two jobs, or two friends, or two courses of action we could take within a given situation. The purpose of comparing or contrasting is to understand each of the two things more clearly and, at times, to make judgments about them.

You will be asked in this section to write a paper of comparison or contrast. First, however, you must learn the two common methods of developing a comparison or contrast paragraph. Read the two paragraphs that follow and try to explain the difference in the two methods of development.

PARAGRAPHS TO CONSIDER

My Senior Prom

My senior prom was nothing like what I had expected it to be. From the start of my senior year, I had pictured getting dressed in a blue gown that my aunt would make and that would cost ninety dollars in any store. No one else would have a gown as attractive as mine. I imagined my boyfriend coming to the door with a lovely blue corsage, and I pictured myself happily inhaling its perfume all evening long. I saw us setting off for the evening in his brother's 1983 burgundy Eldorado. We would make a flourish as we swept in and out of a series of parties before the prom. Our evening would be capped by a delicious shrimp dinner at the prom and our dancing closely together into the early morning hours. The prom was held on May 16, 1984, at the Pony Club on the Black Horse Pike. However, because of sickness in her family, my aunt had no time to finish my gown and I had to buy an ugly pink one at the last minute for forty dollars. My corsage of yellow carnations looked terrible on my pink gown, and I do not remember its having any scent. My boyfriend's brother was out of town, and I stepped outside to the stripped-down Chevy that he used at the races on weekends. We went to one party where I drank a lot of wine that made me sleepy and upset my stomach. After we arrived at the prom, I did not have much more to eat than a roll and some celery sticks. Worst of all, we left early without dancing because my boyfriend and I had had a fight several days before and at the time we did not really want to be with each other.

Electronic versus Electric Typewriters

The electronic typewriter I use in my job as a secretary is a great improvement over the electric model I use at home. First of all, the electronic Brother C-60 is more convenient to use than my ten-year-old Royal. The electronic typewriter has a one-step correction key. If I make mistakes on a page, all I have to do is hit the correction key. The typewriter then instantly removes the mistyped letter, word, or even line. In contrast, my electric has no correction key. If I spot an error, I have to paint it with correction fluid and wait for the fluid to dry before correcting the mistake. This is very time-consuming, especially when there are a lot of corrections to be made. Second, the electronic typewriter is fast and does not jam. When I type at top speed, the machine remembers all the letters I hit and keeps printing them even if I go a bit ahead of the machine's typing speed. On the other hand, my electric's keys will sometimes jam together if I type too fast. Then I have to reach in and separate the metal bars before I can type again. Finally, the electronic typewriter is a much quieter machine. The sound of typing on an electronic is a gentle, low-pitched series of taps. The electric, however, makes a loud, clattery noise as I type. The sound seems to echo through the room and continue in my head even after I stop typing. The convenience, speed, and quiet of the electronic Brother I use at work has spoiled me for my old-fashioned Royal at home. An electronic typewriter simply outclasses everything that has come before.

Complete this comment: The difference in the methods of contrast in the two paragraphs is ____

____

____

____.

Compare your answer with the following explanation of the two methods of development used in comparison or contrast paragraphs.

METHODS OF DEVELOPMENT

There are two common methods of development in a comparison or contrast essay. Details can be presented in a *one-side-at-a-time* format or in a *point-by-point* format. Each format is illustrated below.

One Side at a Time

Look at the outline of "My Senior Prom":

a. Expectations (first half of paper)
   (1) Gown (expensive, blue)
   (2) Corsage (lovely, fragrant blue)
   (3) Car (Eldorado)
   (4) Partying (much)
   (5) Dinner (shrimp)
   (6) Dancing (all night)
b. Reality (second half of paper)
   (1) Gown (cheap, pink)
   (2) Corsage (wrong color, no scent)
   (3) Car (stripped-down Chevy)
   (4) Partying (little)
   (5) Dinner (roll and celery sticks)
   (6) Dancing (didn't because of quarrel)

The first half of the paragraph explains fully one side of the contrast; the second half of the paragraph deals entirely with the other side. When you use this method, be sure to follow the same order of points of contrast (or comparison) for each side.

Point by Point

Now look at the outline of "Electronic versus Electric Typewriters":

a. Convenience
   (1) Electronic
   (2) Electric
b. Speed
   (1) Electronic
   (2) Electric
c. Noise level
   (1) Electronic
   (2) Electric

The outline shows how the two kinds of typewriters are contrasted point by point. First, the writer compares the correction convenience of the electronic with the lack of a correction key on the electric; next, the writer compares the speed of the electronic with the slowness of the electric; finally, the writer compares the quiet electronic with the noisy electric.

When you begin a comparison or contrast paper, you should decide right away whether you are going to use the one-side-at-a-time format or the point-by-point format. An outline is an essential step in helping you decide which format will be the most workable one for your topic.

Activity 1

Complete the partial outlines provided for the two paragraphs that follow.

1. How My Parents' Divorce Changed Me

In the three years since my parents' divorce, I have changed from a spoiled brat to a reasonably normal college student. Before the divorce, I expected my mother to wait on me. She did my laundry, cooked and cleaned up after meals, and even straightened up my room. My only response was to complain if the meat was too well done or if the sweater I wanted to wear was not clean. In addition, I expected money for anything I wanted. Whether it was an expensive bowling ball or a new school jacket, I expected Mom to hand over the money. If she refused, I would get it from Dad. However, he left when I was fifteen, and things changed. When Mom got a full-time job to support us, I was the one with the free time to do housework. Now, I did the laundry, started the dinner, and cleaned not only my own room but the whole house. Fortunately, Mom was tolerant. She did not even complain when my first laundry project left us with streaky blue underwear. Also, I no longer asked her for money, since I knew there was none to spare. Instead, I got a part-time job on weekends to earn my own spending money. Today I have my own car that I am paying for, and I am putting myself through college. Things have been hard sometimes, but I am glad not to be that spoiled kid any more.

In the three years since my parents' divorce, I have changed from a spoiled brat to a reasonably normal college student.

a. Before the divorce

(1) ______________________________

(2) ______________________________

b. After the divorce

(1) ______________________________

(2) ______________________________

Complete the following statement: Paragraph 1 uses a ______________ method of development.

2. Good and Bad Horror Movies

A good horror movie is easily separated from a bad one. A good horror movie, first of all, has both male and female victims. Both sexes suffer terrible fates at the hands of monsters and maniacs. Therefore, everyone in the audience has a chance to identify with the victim. Bad horror movies, on the other hand, tend to concentrate on women, especially half-dressed ones. These movies are obviously prejudiced against half the human race. Second, a good horror movie inspires compassion for its characters. For example, the audience will feel sympathy for the Wolfman's victims and also for the Wolfman, who is shown to be a sad victim of fate. In contrast, a bad horror movie encourages feelings of aggression and violence in viewers. For instance, in the Halloween films, the murder scenes use the murderer's point of view. The effect is that the audience stalks the victims along with the killer and feels the same thrill he does. Finally, every good horror movie has a sense of humor. In Dracula, the Count says meaningfully at dinner, "I don't drink wine" as he stares at a young woman's juicy neck. Humor provides relief from the horror and makes the characters more human. A bad horror movie, though, is humorless and boring. One murder is piled on top of another, and the characters are just cardboard figures. Bad horror movies may provide cheap thrills, but the good ones touch our emotions and live forever.

A good horror movie is easily distinguished from a bad one.

a. Kinds of victims

(1) ______________________________

(2) ______________________________

b. Effect on audience

(1) ______________________________

(2) ______________________________

c. Tone

(1) ______________________________

(2) ______________________________

Complete the following statement: Paragraph 2 uses a ____________ method of development.

Activity 2

Put a number 1 beside the point that all the other scrambled sentences in the list below support. Then number the rest of the sentences in a logical order. To do this, you will have to decide whether the sentences should be arranged according to an order of *one side at a time* or an order of *point by point.*

A Change in Attitude

_______ Eventually I could not find a dress or pair of slacks in my wardrobe that I could wear while still continuing to breathe.

_______ In the evening when I got hungry, I made myself tomato, lettuce, and onion salad with vinegar dressing.

_______ I have kicked my chocolate habit, saved my clothes wardrobe, and enabled myself to breathe again.

_______ I also could seldom resist driving over to the nearby Snack Shack in the evening to get a large chocolate shake.

_______ For dessert at lunch I had an orange or other fruit.

_______ I gobbled chocolate bars during breaks at work, had chocolate cake for dessert at lunch, and ate chocolate-covered butter creams in the evening.

_______ At this point I began using willpower to control my urge for chocolate.

_______ As a result, the twelve pounds that I didn't want dropped off steadily and eventually disappeared.

_______ When the pounds began to multiply steadily, I tried to console myself.

_______ I have been able to lose weight by changing my attitude about chocolate.

_______ I said, "Well, that's only three pounds; I can lose that next week."

_______ Also, I made myself go and step on the bathroom scale whenever I got the urge to drive over to the Snack Shack.

_______ There was a time when I made chocolate a big part of my daily diet.

_______ Instead of eating chocolate bars on my break, I munched celery and carrots.

Complete the following statement: The sentences can be organized using an order of ____________.

ADDITIONAL PARAGRAPHS TO CONSIDER

Read these additional paragraphs of comparison or contrast and then answer the questions that follow.

My Broken Dream

When I became a police officer in my town, the job was not as I had dreamed it would be. I began to dream about being a police officer at about age ten. I could picture myself wearing a fancy blue uniform and having an impressive-looking badge on my chest. I could also picture myself driving a powerful patrol car through town and seeing everyone stare at me with envy. But most of all, I dreamed of wearing a gun and using all the equipment that "TV cops" use. I just knew everyone would be proud of me. I could almost hear the guys on the block saying, "Boy, Steve made it big. Did you hear he's a cop?" I dreamed of leading an exciting life, solving big crimes, and meeting lots of people. I just knew that if I became a cop everyone in town would look up to me. However, when I actually did become a police officer, I soon found out that it was not as I had dreamed it would be. My first disappointment came when I was sworn in and handed a slightly worn-out and baggy uniform. My disappointment continued when I was given a badge that looked like something pulled out of a Cracker Jack box. I was assigned a beat-up old junker and told that it would be my patrol car. It had a striking resemblance to a car that had lost a demolition derby at a stock-car raceway. Disappointment seemed to continue. I soon found out that I was not the envy of all my friends. When I drove through town, they acted as if they had not seen me. I was told I was crazy doing this kind of job by people I thought would look up to me. My job was not as exciting as I had dreamed it would be either. Instead of solving robberies and murders every day, I found that I spent a great deal of time comforting a local resident because a neighborhood dog watered his favorite bush.

Two Views on Toys

There is a vast difference between children and adults where presents are concerned. First, there is the matter of taste. Adults pride themselves on taste, while children ignore the matter of taste in favor of things that are fun. Adults, especially grandparents, pick out tasteful toys that go unused, while children love the cheap playthings advertised on television. Then, of course, there is the matter of money. The new games on the market today are a case in point. Have you ever tried to lure a child away from some expensive game in order to get him or her to play with an old-fashioned game or toy? Finally, there is a difference between an adult's and a child's idea of what is educational. Adults, filled with memories of their own childhoods, tend to be fond of the written word. Today's children, on the other hand, concentrate on anything electronic. These things mean much more to them than to adults. Next holiday season, examine the toys that adults choose for children. Then look at the toys the children prefer. You will see the difference.

Mike and Helen

Like his wife Helen, Mike has a good sense of humor. Also, they are both short, dark-haired, and slightly pudgy. Both Mike and Helen can be charming when they want to be, and they seem to handle small crises in a calm, cool way. A problem such as an overflowing washer, stalled car, or sick child is not a cause for panic; they seem to take such events in stride. Unlike Helen, though, Mike tends to be disorganized. He is late for appointments and unable to keep important documents--bank records, receipts, and insurance papers--where he can find them. And unlike Helen, Mike tends to hold a grudge. He is slow to forget a cruel remark, careless joke, or unfriendly slight. Also, Mike enjoys swimming, camping, and tennis, unlike Helen, who is an indoors type.

■ Questions

About Unity

1. Which paragraph lacks a topic sentence?

   ____

2. Which paragraph has a topic sentence that is too broad?

   ____

About Support

3. Which paragraph contains virtually no specific details?

   ____

4. Which paragraph do you feel offers the most effective details?

   ____

About Coherence

5. What method of development (one side at a time or point by point) is used in the first paragraph?

   ____

   In the second paragraph?

   ____

6. Which paragraph offers specific details, but lacks a clear, consistent method of development?

   ____

WRITING THE PARAGRAPH

■ Writing Assignment 1

Given below are topic sentences and supporting points for three potential contrast paragraphs. Choose one of the three to develop into a paragraph.

Choice 1

Topic sentence: I abused my body when I was twenty, but I treat myself much differently at the age of thirty.

a. At twenty, I was a heavy smoker. . . .
Now, instead of smoking, I . . .

b. At twenty, I had a highly irregular diet. . . .
Today, on the other hand, I eat . . .

c. Finally, at twenty, I never exercised. . . .
Today, I work out regularly. . . .

Choice 2

Topic sentence: Dating is much easier for boys than it is for girls.

a. A boy can take the initial step of asking for a date without seeming too aggressive. . . .
In contrast, a girl . . .

b. The boy is usually in charge of deciding where to go and what to do. . . .
The girl, on the other hand, has to live with the choices. . . .

c. At the end of the night, the boy knows the moves he is planning to make, if any. . . .
But the girl waits nervously to see what will happen. . . .

Choice 3

Topic sentence: My sociology instructor teaches a class quite differently from my psychology instructor.

a. For one thing, Ms. ________________ demands many hours of homework each week. . . .

In contrast, Mr. ________________ does not believe in much work outside class. . . .

b. In addition, Ms. ________________ gives difficult tests—with no study aids. . . .

   Mr. ________________'s tests, on the other hand, are easy. . . .

c. Finally, Ms. ________________ keeps every class strictly on the subject of the day. . . .

   But Mr. ________________ will wander off onto any topic that snags his interest. . . .

How to Proceed

a To develop some supporting details for the paragraph, freewrite for five minutes on the topic sentence you have chosen.

b Then add to the material you have written by asking yourself questions. If you were writing about how you treat your body differently at thirty, for example, you might ask yourself:

   How many cigarettes did I smoke at twenty?

   What have I substituted for cigarettes?

   What kinds of food did I used to eat?

   How regularly did I eat?

   What foods do I eat today?

   Why didn't I exercise at twenty?

   What made me decide to start exercising?

   What kind of exercises do I do?

   How often do I exercise?

   Write down whatever answers occur to you for these and other questions. As with the freewriting, do not worry at this stage about writing correct answers. Instead, concentrate on getting down all the information you can think of that supports each point.

c Now go through all the material you have accumulated. Perhaps some of the details you have written down may help you think of even better details that would fit. If so, write them down.

d As you work on the drafts of your paper, use words such as *in contrast, but, on the other hand,* and *however* to tie together your material.

e Be sure to edit the next-to-final draft of your paper for sentence-skills mistakes, including spelling.

Writing Assignment 2

Write a comparison or contrast paragraph on one of the twenty topics below.

Two holidays
Two teachers
Two children
Two kinds of eaters
Two drivers
Two coworkers
Two members of a team (or two teams)
Two singers or groups
Two animals
Two parties
Two jobs
Two characters in the same movie or TV show
Two commercials
Two methods of studying
Two cartoon strips
Two cars
Two friends
Two crises
Two employees
Two magazines

How to Proceed

a You must begin by making two decisions: (1) what your topic will be and (2) whether you are going to do a comparison or a contrast. Many times, students choose to do essays centered on the differences between two things. For example, you might write about how a math teacher you have in college differs from one you had in high school. You might discuss important differences between two coworkers or between two of your friends. You might contrast a factory job you had packing vegetables with a white-collar job you had as a salesperson in a clothing store.

b After you choose a tentative topic, write a simple topic sentence expressing that topic. Then see what kind of support you can generate for that topic. For instance, if you plan to contrast two cars, see if you can think of and jot down three distinct ways they differ. In other words, prepare a scratch outline. An outline is an excellent prewriting technique to use when doing any paragraph; it is almost indispensable when planning a comparison or contrast paragraph. Look back at the outlines given on pages 145–148.

Keep in mind that this planning state is probably the *most important single phase* of work you will do on your paper. Without clear planning, you are not likely to write an effective paragraph.

c After you have decided on a topic and the main lines of support, you must decide whether to use a one-side-at-a-time or point-by-point method of development. Both methods are explained and illustrated in this chapter.

d Now, freewrite for ten minutes on the topic you have chosen. Do not worry about punctuation, spelling, or other matters relating to correct form. Just get as many details as you can onto the page. You want a base of raw material that you can add to and select from as you now work on the first draft of your paper.

After you do a first draft, try to put it aside for a day or at least several hours. You will then be ready to return with a fresh perspective on the material and build upon what you have already done.

e Use transition words like *first, in addition, also, in contrast, another difference, on the other hand, but, however,* and *most important* to link together points in your paper.

f As you continue working on your paper, refer to the checklist on the inside front cover. Make sure that you can answer *Yes* to the questions about unity, support, and coherence.

g Finally, use the checklist on the inside front cover to edit the next-to-final draft of your paper for sentence-skills mistakes, including spelling.

■ Writing Assignment 3

Write a contrast paragraph on one of the fifteen topics below.

Neighborhood stores versus a shopping mall
Driving on an expressway versus driving on country roads
People versus *Us* (or any other two popular magazines)
Camping in a tent versus camping in a recreational vehicle
Working parents versus stay-at-home parents
Last year's fashions versus this year's
Used car versus new car
Records versus tapes
PG-rated movies versus R-rated movies

News in a paper versus news on television
Yesterday's toys versus today's
Fresh food versus canned or frozen food
Winning locker room after a game versus losing one
Ad on television versus ad (for the same product) in a magazine
Amateur sport versus professional sport

Follow the directions on "How to Proceed" given in Writing Assignment 2.

■ Writing Assignment 4

Write a summary of a television show in which two contrasting points of view are presented. The show might be *Phil Donahue* or any other program which presents two different viewpoints on a subject. As you listen, take notes. You may want to organize your notes in two columns so that you can compare viewpoints at a glance.

In your topic sentence, include the date and subject of the show. For example:

> Two opposing views on abortion were presented on the *Phil Donahue* show on January 16, 1985.

Limit the points of support you will cover in your paragraph to three or four major areas. After you have generated your points of support, decide which method of organization you will use and prepare a brief outline of the paragraph. Be sure to use transition words and to edit the next-to-final draft carefully.

■ Writing Assignment 5

You are living in an apartment in which new tenants are making life unpleasant for you. Write a letter of complaint to your landlord comparing and contrasting life before and after the tenants arrived. You might want to focus on one or more of the following:

Noise level
Trash
Safety hazards
Parking situation

DEFINING A TERM

In talking with other people, we at times offer informal definitions to explain just what we mean by a particular term. Suppose, for example, we say to a friend, "Ted is an anxious person." We might then expand on our idea of "anxious" by saying, "He's always worrying about the future. Yesterday he was talking about how many bills he'll probably have this year. Then he was worrying about what he would ever do if he got laid off." In a written definition, we make clear in a more complete and formal way our own personal understanding of a term. Such a definition typically starts with one meaning of a term. The meaning is then illustrated with a series of examples or a story.

You will be asked in this section to write a paragraph in which you define a term. The three student papers below are all examples of definition paragraphs. Read them and then answer the questions that follow.

PARAGRAPHS TO CONSIDER

Disillusionment

Disillusionment is the feeling of having one of our most cherished beliefs stolen from us. I learned about disillusionment firsthand the day Mr. Keller, our eighth-grade teacher, handed out the grades on our class biology projects. I had worked hard to assemble what I thought was the best insect collection any school had ever seen. For weeks, I had set up homemade traps around our house, in the woods, and in vacant lots. At night, I would stretch a white sheet between two trees, shine a lantern on it, and collect the night-flying insects that gathered there. With my own money, I had bought killing jars, insect pins, gummed labels, and display boxes. I carefully arranged related insects together, with labels listing each scientific name and the place and date of capture. Slowly and painfully, I wrote and typed the report that accompanied my project at the school science fair. In contrast, my friend Eddie did almost nothing for his project. He had his father, a doctor, build an impressive maze complete with live rats and a sign that read, "You are the trainer." A person could lift a little plastic door, send a rat running through the maze, and then hit a button to release a pellet of rat food as a reward. This exhibit turned out to be the most popular one at the fair. I felt sure that our teacher would know that Eddie could not have built it, and I was certain that my hard work would be recognized and rewarded. Then the grades were finally handed out, and I was crushed. Eddie had gotten an A plus, but my grade was a B. I suddenly realized that honesty and hard work don't always pay off in the end. The idea that life is not fair, that sometimes it pays to cheat, hit me with such force that I felt sick. I will never forget that moment.

Luck

Luck is putting $1.25 into a cigarette machine and getting the money back with the pack. It is a teacher's decision to give a retest on a test where you first scored thirty. Luck refers to moments of good fortune that happen in everyday life. It is not going to the dentist for two years and then going and finding out that you do not have any cavities. It is calling up a plumber to fix a leak on a day when the plumber has no other work to do. Luck is finding a used car for sale at a good price at exactly the time when your car rolls its last mile. It is driving into a traffic bottleneck and choosing the lane that winds up moving most rapidly. Luck is being late for work on a day when your boss arrives later than you do. It is having a new checkout aisle at the supermarket open up just as your cart arrives. The best kind of luck is winning a new color TV set on a chance for which you paid only a quarter.

A Mickey Mouse Course

A Mickey Mouse course is any college course that is so easy that even Mickey or Minnie Mouses could achieve A grades. A student who is taking a heavy schedule, or who does not want four or five especially difficult courses, will try to sandwich in a Mickey Mouse course. A student can find out about such a course by consulting other students, since word of a genuine Mickey Mouse course spreads like wildfire. Or a student can study the college master schedule for telltale course titles like The Art of Pressing Wild Flowers, History of the Comic Book, or Watching Television Creatively. In an advanced course such as microbiology, though, a student had better be prepared to spend a good deal of time during the semester on that course. Students in a Mickey Mouse course can attend the classes while half-asleep, hung-over, or wearing stereo earphones or a blindfold; they will still pass. The course exams (if there are any) would not challenge a five-year-old. The course lecture usually consist of information that anyone with common sense knows anyway. Attendance may be required, but participation or involvement in the class is not. The main requirement for passing is that a student's body is there, warming a seat in the classroom. There are no difficult labs or special projects, and term papers are never mentioned. Once safely registered for such a course, all the students have to do is sit back and watch the credits accumulate on their transcripts.

Questions

About Unity

1. Which paragraph places its topic sentence within the paragraph rather than, more appropriately, at the beginning?

   ____

2. Write the first several words of the sentence in the paragraph on a Mickey Mouse course that should be omitted in the interest of paragraph unity.

   ____

About Support

3. Which two paragraphs develop their definitions through a series of short examples?

   ____

   ____

4. Which paragraph develops its definition through a single extended example?

   ____

About Coherence

5. Which paragraph uses emphatic order, saving its best detail for last?

   ____

6. Which paragraph uses time order to organize its details?

   ____

WRITING THE PARAGRAPH

Writing Assignment 1

Following are a topic sentence and three supporting points for a paragraph that defines the term *TV addict*. Using separate paper, plan out and write the secondary supporting details and closing sentence needed to complete the paragraph. Refer to the suggestions on "How to Proceed" that follow.

Topic Sentence

Television addicts are people who will watch all the programs they can, for as long as they can, rather than do anything else.

Supporting Points

1. TV addicts, first of all, will watch anything on the tube, no matter how bad it is. . . .
2. In addition, addicts watch TV more hours than normal people do. . . .
3. Finally, addicts feel that TV is more important than any other activities or events that might be going on. . . .

How to Proceed

a Prepare examples for each of the three qualities of a TV addict. For each quality, you should have at least two or three sentences that provide either an extended example or shorter examples of this quality in action.

b To generate these details, ask yourself the following questions:

What are some examples of terrible shows that I (or people I know) watch just because the television is turned on?

What are some examples of how frequently I (or people I know) watch TV?

What are some other activities or events that I (or people I know) give up in order to watch TV?

Write down quickly whatever answers occur to you for the questions. Do not worry about writing correct sentences; just concentrate on getting down all the details about television addicts that you can think of.

c Draw from and add to this material as you work on the paragraph. Make sure that your paragraph is unified, supported, and coherent.

d Finally, edit the next-to-final draft of your paper for sentence-skills mistakes, including spelling.

■ Writing Assignment 2

Write an essay that defines one of the following terms. Each term refers to a certain kind of person.

Bigmouth	Fair-weather friend	Good neighbor	Perfectionist
Charmer	Team player	Optimist	Pack rat
Loser	Clown	Pessimist	Hard worker
Lazybones	Jellyfish	Good example	Apple-polisher
Kibitzer	Leader	Hypocrite	Fusspot
Con artist	Nerd		

How to Proceed

a To write a topic sentence for your definition paragraph, your first step should be to *place the term in a class or category*. Then *describe what you feel are the special features that distinguish your term from all the other members of its class*.

In the sample topic sentence below, underline the class, or category, that the term belongs to and double-underline the distinguishing details of that class, or category. One is done for you as an example.

A klutz is a person who stumbles through life.

A worrywart is a person who sees danger everywhere.

The class clown is a student who gets attention in the wrong way.

A clotheshorse is a person who needs new clothes to be happy.

b In order to develop your definition, use one of the following methods:

Examples: Give several examples that support your topic sentence.

Extended example: Use one longer example to support your topic sentence.

Contrast: Support your topic sentence by showing what your term is *not*. For instance, you may want to define a ''fair-weather friend'' by contrasting his or her actions with those of a true friend.

c Once you have created a topic sentence and decided how to develop your paragraph, write a scratch outline. This step is especially important if you are using a contrast method of development.

d Be sure you touch the four bases of unity, support, coherence, and sentence skills in your writing.

■ Writing Assignment 3

Write an essay that defines one of the abstract terms below.

Persistence	Responsibility	Fear
Rebellion	Insecurity	Arrogance
Sense of humor	Assertiveness	Conscience
Escape	Jealousy	Class
Danger	Nostalgia	Innocence
Curiosity	Gentleness	Freedom
Common sense	Depression	Violence
Family	Obsession	Shyness
Practicality	Self-control	

As a guide in writing your paper, use the suggestions on ''How to Proceed'' in Writing Assignment 2. Remember to place your term in a class, or category, and to describe what *you* feel are the distinguishing features of that term. Three examples follow.

> Laziness is a quality that doesn't deserve its bad reputation.
>
> Jealousy is the emotion that hurts the most.
>
> Persistence is the quality of not giving up even during rough times.

■ Writing Assignment 4

Since it affects almost all of us, *stress* is an important word to define. In order to write a definition paragraph on stress, do some research in popular magazines, paperbacks, and textbooks.

How to Proceed

a Look up *stress* in the index of any psychology or sociology textbook.

b Using a recent issue of the *Readers' Guide to Periodical Literature* in your library, locate recent magazine articles listed under the heading *Stress.*

c Also in your library, look up books in the card catalog under the subject heading *Stress.* You may also want to check your public library, which will probably carry more popular paperbacks dealing with stress than your college library.

d Check your college bookstore, or any paperback bookstore, for recent books about stress; many of these will be in the category of ''self-help'' books.

e You should organize this definition paragraph in one of the ways listed below:

- Use a series of examples (see page 117) of stress.
- Use division and classification (see page 163) to describe several types of stress.
- Use narrative (see page 182); create, for example, a hypothetical person and show how stress affects this person in a typical morning or day.

Hints: Do not simply write a series of general, abstract sentences that repeat and reword your definition. If you concentrate on providing specific support, you will avoid the common trap of getting lost in a maze of generalities.

Make sure your paper is firmly anchored on the bases of unity, support, coherence, and good sentence skills. Edit carefully the next-to-final draft of the paragraph.

■ Writing Assignment 5

Option 1: An employee has just quit at the place where you work, creating a new job opening. Since you have been working there for a while, your boss has asked you to write a job description of the position. That description, which is really a detailed definition of the job, will be sent to employment services. These services will be responsible for interviewing candidates. Choose any position you know about, and write a job description for it. First give the purpose of the job, and then list its duties and responsibilities. Finally, give the qualifications for the position.

Option 2: Alternatively, imagine that a new worker has been hired, and your boss has asked you to explain "team spirit" to him or her. The purpose of your explanation will be to give the newcomer an idea of the teamwork that is expected in this place. Write a paragraph that defines in detail what your boss means by *team spirit.* Use examples or one extended example to illustrate your general statements.

DIVIDING AND CLASSIFYING

If you were doing the laundry, you would probably begin by separating the clothing into piles. You might put all the whites in one pile and all the colors in another. You might put all cottons in one pile, polyesters in another, silks in a third, and so on. Or you might divide and classify the laundry not according to color or fabrics but on the basis of use. You might put bath towels in one pile, bed sheets in another, personal garments in a third, and so on. Sorting clothes in various ways is just one small example of how we spend a great deal of time organizing our environment in one manner or another.

In this section, you will be asked to write a paragraph in which you divide or classify a subject according to a single principle. To prepare for this assignment, first read the division and classification paragraphs below and then work through the questions and the activity that follow.

PARAGRAPHS TO CONSIDER

Automobile Drivers

One type of automobile driver is the slowpoke driver. A woman who is a slowpoke, for instance, will drive forty miles per hour in a fifty-five-mile zone. She will slow down and start signaling for a left-hand turn three blocks before making it. Or her car will slow down while she is in avid conversation with other people in the car, or while she puzzles over street signs to get her bearings, or while she looks at displays and sale signs in shopwindows, or as she struggles to open the wrapping of her Burger King Whopper. A second type is the high-speed driver. A man who is a high-speed driver, for example, will limit his speed only when he suspects that the state police or radar traps are nearby. The state police must develop a system to ensure that they begin to catch this kind of driver. He typically speeds past cars on the left and right sides, weaving in and around them sharply, and he closely tailgates a car that holds him up until it shifts to another lane. He races to get through yellow or just-red lights at highway and city intersections, and he speeds down city streets, oblivious to the possibility of children who may run from between parked cars or people who may open a car door. The final type is the sensible-speed driver who, road conditions being normal, maintains the posted speed limits and drives at a consistent and moderate rate. If these drivers do change their rate, they do so because they are driving defensively. They are speeding up to pass the driver in front, who is creeping along to look at the pumpkins on display at a road stand. Or they are slowing down to allow the speed demon who has tried passing to get back in the lane and out of the path of an oncoming truck.

Studying for a Test

The time a student spends studying for a test can be divided into three distinct phases. Phase 1, often called the "no problem" phase, runs from the day the test is announced to approximately forty-eight hours before the dreaded exam is passed out. During phase 1, the student is carefree, smiling, and kind to helpless animals and small children. When asked by classmates if he or she has studied for the test yet, the reply will be an assured "No problem." During phase 1, no actual studying takes place. Phase 2 is entered two days prior to testing. For example, if the test is scheduled for 9 A.M. Friday, phase 2 begins at 9 A.M. Wednesday. During phase 2, again, no actual studying takes place. Phase 3, the final phase, is entered twelve hours before "zero hour." This is the acute phase, characterized by sweaty palms, nervous twitches, and confused mental patterns. For a test at nine on Friday morning, a student begins exhibiting these symptoms at approximately nine o'clock on Thursday night. Phase 3 is also termed the "shock" phase, since the student is shocked to discover the imminent nature of the exam and the amount of material to be studied. During this phase, the student will probably be unable to sleep and will mumble meaningless phrases like "$a^2 + c^2$." This phase will not end until the exam is over. If the cram session has worked, the student will fall gratefully asleep. On waking up, he or she will be ready to go through the whole cycle again with the next test.

The Dangers of Tools

Tools can be divided into three categories according to how badly people can injure themselves with them. The first group of tools causes dark-purple bruises to appear on the user's feet, fingers, or arms. Hammers are famous for this, as millions of cartoons and comic strips have shown. Mallets and crowbars, too, can go a bit off target and thud onto a bit of exposed flesh. But first-class bruises can also be caused by clamps, pliers, vise grips, and wrenches. In a split second, any one of these tools can lash out and badly squeeze a stray finger. Later, the victim will see blue-black blood forming under the fingernails. The second type of tool usually attacks by cutting or tearing. Saws seem to enjoy cutting through human flesh as well as wood. Keeping a hand too close to the saw, or using a pair of knees as a sawhorse, will help the saw satisfy its urge. Planes, chisels, and screwdrivers also cut into skin. And the utility knife--the kind with a razor blade projecting from a metal handle--probably cuts more people than linoleum. The most dangerous tools, however, are the mutilators, the ones that send people directly to the emergency room. People were definitely not made to handle monster tools like chain saws, table saws, power drills, and power hammers. Newspapers are filled with stories of shocking accidents people have had with power tools. In summary, if people are not careful, using tools can definitely be hazardous to their physical health.

■ Questions

About Unity

1. Which paragraph lacks a topic sentence?

 ____

2. Write the sentence in ''Drivers'' that should be omitted in the interest of paragraph unity.

 ____

 ____

About Support

3. Which of the three phases in ''Studying for a Test'' lacks specific details?

 ____

4. After which sentence in ''The Dangers of Tools'' are supporting details needed?

 ____

 ____

About Coherence

5. Which paragraph uses time order to organize its details?

 ____

6. Which paragraph uses emphatic order to organize its details?

 ____

7. What words in this paragraph signal the most important detail?

 ____

Activity

This activity will sharpen your sense of the classifying process. In each of the following ten groups, cross out the one item that has not been classified on the same basis as the other three. Also, indicate in the space provided the single principle of classification used for the three items. Note the examples.

Examples Water
a. Cold
b. Lake
c. Hot
d. Lukewarm
Unifying principle:
Temperature ____________

Household pests
a. Mice
b. Ants
c. Roaches
d. Flies
Unifying principle:
Insects ____________

1. Eyes
   a. Blue
   b. Nearsighted
   c. Brown
   d. Hazel
   Unifying principle:
   ____

2. Mattresses
   a. Double
   b. Twin
   c. Queen
   d. Firm
   Unifying principle:
   ____

3. Zoo animals
   a. Flamingo
   b. Peacock
   c. Polar bear
   d. Ostrich
   Unifying principle:
   ____

4. Vacation
   a. Summer
   b. Holiday
   c. Seashore
   d. Weekends
   Unifying principle:
   ____

5. College classes
   a. Enjoy
   b. Dislike
   c. Tolerate
   d. Morning
   Unifying principle:
   ____

6. Wallets
   a. Leather
   b. Plastic
   c. Stolen
   d. Fabric
   Unifying principle:
   ____

7. Newspaper
   a. Wrapping garbage
   b. Editorials
   c. Making paper planes
   d. Covering floor while painting

   Unifying principile:

   ____

8. Students
   a. Freshman
   b. Transfer
   c. Junior
   d. Sophomore

   Unifying principle:

   ____

9. Exercise
   a. Running
   b. Swimming
   c. Gymnastics
   d. Fatigue

   Unifying principle:

   ____

10. Leftovers
    a. Cold chicken
    b. Feed to dog
    c. Reheat
    d. Use in a stew

    Unifying principle:

    ____

WRITING THE PARAGRAPH

■ Writing Assignment 1

Given below are four possible division and classification writing assignments, along with possible divisions. Choose *one* of them to develop into a paragraph.

1. Supermarket shoppers
   a. Slow, careful shoppers
   b. Average shoppers
   c. Rushed, hurried shoppers
2. Eaters
   a. Super-conservative eaters
   b. Typical eaters
   c. Adventurous eaters
3. Methods of housekeeping
   a. Never clean
   b. Clean regularly
   c. Clean constantly
4. Attitudes toward money
   a. Tightfisted
   b. Sometimes splurge
   c. Spendthrift

How to Proceed

a To develop some ideas for the paragraph, freewrite for five or ten minutes on your topic.

b Add to the material you have written by asking yourself questions. If you were writing about supermarket shoppers, for example, you might ask:

How do the three kinds of shoppers pick out the items they want?
How many aisles will each type of shopper visit?
Which shoppers bring lists, calculators, coupons, and so on?
How much time does it take each type of shopper to finish shopping?

Write down whatever answers occur to you for these and other questions. As with freewriting, do not worry at this stage about writing correct answers. Instead, concentrate on getting down all the information you can think of that supports each of the three points.

c Now go through all the material you have accumulated. Perhaps some of the details you have written down may help you think of even better details that would fit. If so, write them down. Then make decisions about the exact information you will use to support each point. List the details 1, 2, 3, and so on in the order you will present them.

d As you work on the drafts of your paragraph, make sure that it touches the bases of unity, support, and coherence.

e Finally, edit the next-to-final draft of your paper for sentence-skills mistakes, including spelling.

■ Writing Assignment 2

Write a division and classification essay on one of the following subjects:

Teachers
Sports fans
Eating places
Attitudes toward life
Commercials
Employers
Jobs
Bars
Family get-togethers
Shoes
Drivers
Mothers or fathers
Women's or men's magazines
Presents
Neighbors
Rock or pop or country singers
Amusement parks or rides
Guests or company
Ways to get an A (or F) in a course
Car accessories

How to Proceed

a The first step in writing a division and classification paragraph is to divide your tentative topic into three reasonably complete parts. *Always use a single principle of division when you form your three parts.* For example, if your topic was "Automobile Drivers" and you divided them into slow, moderate, and fast drivers, your single basis for division would be "rate of speed." It would be illogical, then, to have as a fourth type "teenage drivers" (the basis of such a division would be "age") or "female drivers" (the basis of such a division would be "sex"). You probably could classify automobile drivers on the basis of age or sex or another division, for almost any subject can be analyzed in more than one way. What is important, however, is that in any single paper you choose only one basis for division and stick to it. Be consistent.

In "Studying for a Test," the writer divides the process of studying into three time phases: from the time the test is announced to forty-eight hours before; the day and a half before the test; the final twelve hours before the test. In "The Dangers of Tools," the single basis for dividing tools into three categories is the kind of injury each type inflicts: bruises, cuts, and major injuries.

b To ensure a clear three-part division in your own paragraph, fill in the outline below before starting your paper and make sure you can answer *Yes* to the questions that follow. You should expect to do a fair amount of thinking before coming up with a logical plan for your paper.

Topic: ______________________________

Three-part division of the topic:

1. ______________________________
2. ______________________________
3. ______________________________

Is there a single basis of division for the three parts? ______

Is the division reasonably complete? ______

c Refer to the checklist of the four bases on the inside front cover while writing the drafts of your paper. Make sure you can answer *Yes* to the questions about unity, support, coherence, and sentence skills. Also, use the checklist when you edit the next-to-final draft of your paper for sentence-skills mistakes, including spelling.

■ Writing Assignment 3

There are many ways you could classify the students around you. Pick out one of your courses and write a division and classification paragraph on the students in that class. You might want to categorize the students according to one of the principles of division below:

Attitude toward the class	Attendance
Participation in the class	Level of confidence
Method of taking notes in class	Performance during oral reports, speeches, presentations, lab sessions
Method of taking a test in class	
Punctuality	

Of course, you may use any other principle of division that seems appropriate. Follow the steps listed in "How to Proceed" for Writing Assignment 2.

■ Writing Assignment 4

Write a review of a restaurant by analyzing a particular restaurant's (1) food, (2) service, and (3) atmosphere. In order to do the assignment, you should visit a restaurant, take a notebook with you, and write down observations about such elements as:

Quantity of food you receive	Attitude of the servers
Taste of the food	Efficiency of the servers
Temperature of the food	Decor
Freshness of the ingredients	Level of cleanliness
How the food is presented (garnishes, dishes, and so on)	Noise level and music, if any

You may want to write about details other than the ones listed above. Just be sure they fit into one of your three categories of food, service, or atmosphere.

For your topic sentence, rate the restaurant by giving it from one to five stars, based on your overall impression. Include the restaurant's name and location in your topic sentence. Here are some examples:

Guido's, a center-city Italian restaurant, deserves three stars.

The McDonald's on Route 70 merits a four-star rating.

The Circle Diner in Westfield barely earns a one-star rating.

Writing Assignment 5

You are teaching a class in safe driving at a high school, and part of today's lecture is about types of drivers to avoid. For this part of your presentation, write a paragraph dividing the category of "unsafe drivers" into three or more types according to their driving habits. For each type, include both a description and suggestions to your students on how to avoid an accident with this type of driver.

DESCRIBING A SCENE OR PERSON

When you describe something or someone, you give a picture in words to your readers. To make the word picture as vivid and real as possible, you must observe and record specific details that appeal to your readers' senses (sight, hearing, taste, smell, and touch). More than any other type of writing, a descriptive paragraph needs sharp, colorful details. Here is a description in which only the sense of sight is used:

> A rug covers the living-room floor.

In contrast, here is a description rich in sense impressions:

> A thick, reddish-brown shag rug is laid wall to wall across the living-room floor. The long, curled fibers of the shag seem to whisper as you walk through them in your bare feet, and when you squeeze your toes into the deep covering, the soft fibers push back at you with a spongy resiliency.

Sense impressions include sight (*thick, reddish-brown shag rug; laid wall to wall; walk through them in your bare feet; squeeze your toes into the deep covering; push back*), hearing (*whisper*), and touch *(bare feet, soft fibers, spongy resiliency)*. The sharp, vivid images provided by the sensory details give us a clear picture of the rug and enable us to share in the writer's experience. In this section, you will be asked to describe a person, place, or thing for your readers through the use of words rich in sensory details. To help you prepare for the assignment, first read the three paragraphs ahead and then answer the questions that follow.

PARAGRAPHS TO CONSIDER

An Athlete's Room

As I entered the bright, cheerful space with its beige walls and practical, flat-pile carpet, I noticed a closet to my right with the door open. On the shelf above the bunched-together clothes were a red baseball cap, a fielder's glove, and a battered brown gym bag. Turning from the closet, I noticed a single bed with its wooden headboard against the far wall. The bedspread was a brown, orange, and beige print of basketball, football, and baseball action scenes. A lamp shaped like a baseball and a copy of Sports Illustrated were on the top of a nightstand to the left of the bed. A sports schedule and several yellowing newspaper clippings were tacked to the cork bulletin board on the wall above the nightstand. A desk with a bookcase top stood against the left wall. I walked toward it to examine it more closely. As I ran my fingers over the items on the dusty shelves, I noticed some tarnished medals and faded ribbons for track accomplishments. These lay next to a heavy gold trophy that read, "MVP: Pinewood Varsity Basketball." I accidentally tipped an autograph-covered, slightly deflated basketball off one shelf, and the ball bounced with a dull thud across the width of the room. Next to the desk was a window with brightly printed curtains that matched the bedspread. Between the window and the left corner stood a dresser with one drawer half open, revealing a tangle of odd sweat socks and a few stretched-out T-shirts emblazoned with team insignias. As I turned to leave the room, I carefully picked my way around scattered pairs of worn-out sneakers.

A Depressing Place

The mall pet shop is a depressing place. A display window attracts passers-by who stare at the prisoners penned inside. In the right-hand side of the window, two puppies press their forepaws against the glass and attempt to lick the human hands that press from the outside. A cardboard barrier separates the dogs from several black-and-white kittens piled together in the opposite end of the window. Inside the shop, rows of wire cages line one wall from top to bottom. At first, it is hard to tell whether a bird, hamster, gerbil, cat, or dog is locked inside each cage. Only an occasional movement or clawing, shuffling sound tells visitors that living creatures are inside. Running down the center of the store is a line of large wooden perches that look like coat racks. When customers pass by, the parrots and mynas chained to these perches flutter their clipped wings in a useless attempt to escape. At the end of this center aisle is a large plastic tub of dirty, stagnant-looking water containing a few motionless turtles. The shelves against the left-hand wall are packed with all kinds of pet-related items. The smell inside the entire shop is an unpleasant mixture of strong chemical deodorizers, urine-soaked newspapers, and musty sawdust. Because so many animals are crammed together, the normally pleasant, slightly milky smell of the puppies and kittens is sour and strong. The droppings inside the uncleaned birdcages give off a dry, stinging odor. Visitors hurry out of the shop, anxious to feel fresh air and sunlight. The animals stay on.

Karla

Karla, my brother's new girlfriend, is a catlike creature. Her face, with its wide forehead, sharp cheekbones, and narrow, pointed chin, resembles a triangle. Karla's skin is a soft, velvety brown. Her large brown eyes slant upward at the corners, and she emphasizes their angle with a sweep of maroon eye shadow. Karla's habit of looking sidelong out of the tail of her eye makes her look cautious, as if she were expecting something to sneak up on her. Her nose is small and flat. The sharply outlined depression under it leads the observer's eye to a pair of red-tinted lips. With their slight upward tilt at the corners, Karla's lips make her seem self-satisfied and secretly pleased. One reason Karla may be happy is that she recently was asked to be in a local beauty contest. Karla's face is framed by a smooth layer of brown hair that always looks just combed. Her long neck and slim body are perfectly in proportion with her face. Karla manages to look elegant and sleek no matter how she is standing or sitting, for her body seems to be made up of graceful angles. Her slender hands are tipped with long, polished nails. Her narrow feet are long, too, but they appear delicate even in flat-soled running shoes. Somehow, Karla would look perfect in a cat's jeweled collar.

■ Questions

About Unity

1. Which paragraph lacks a topic sentence?

   ____

2. Which sentence in the paragraph on Karla should be omitted in the interest of paragraph unity?

   ____

   ____

About Support

3. Label as *sight, touch, hearing,* or *smell* all the sensory details in the following sentences taken from the three paragraphs. The first one is done for you as an example.

   a. I accidentally tipped (*sight*) an autograph-covered (*sight*), slightly deflated (*sight*) basketball off one shelf (*sight*), and the ball bounced with a dull thud (*hearing*) across the width of the room (*sight*).

   b. Because so many animals are crammed together, the normally pleasant, slightly milky smell of the puppies and kittens is sour and strong.

c. Her slender hands are tipped with long, polished nails.

d. As I ran my fingers over the items on the dusty shelves, I noticed some tarnished medals and faded ribbons for track accomplishments.

4. After which sentence in "A Depressing Place" are specific details needed?

____

____

About Coherence

5. Spatial signals (*above, next to, to the right,* and so on) are often used to help organize details in descriptive paragraphs. List four space signals that appear in "An Athlete's Room":

__________ __________ __________ __________

6. The writer of "Karla" organizes the details by observing Karla in an orderly way. Which of Karla's features is described first? __________ Which is described last? __________ Check the method of spatial organization that best describes the paragraph:

_____ Interior to exterior

_____ Near to far

_____ Top to bottom

WRITING THE PARAGRAPH

■ Writing Assignment 1

Write a paragraph describing a special kind of room. Use the following line as your topic sentence: "I could tell by looking at the room that a __________ lived there." There are many kinds of people who could be the focus for such a paragraph. You can select any one of the following, or think of some other type of person.

Photographer	Outdoors person	Cheerleader	Cat or dog lover
Cook	Teacher	Football player	World traveler
Student	Music lover	Actor	Drug addict
Musician	TV addict	Prostitute	Little boy or girl
Hunter	Camper	Carpenter	Alcoholic
Slob	Grandparent	Baby	Roller skater

How to Proceed

a After choosing a topic, spend a few minutes making sure it will work. Prepare a list of all the details you can think of that support the topic. For example, the writer of ''An Athlete's Room'' made this list:

Sports trophy
Autographed basketball
Sports Illustrated
Baseball lamp
Sports schedule
Medals and ribbons
Sports print on bedspread, curtains
Sweat socks, T-shirts
Baseball cap
Baseball glove
Gym bag
Sports clippings

If you don't have enough details, then choose another type of person, and check your new choice with a list of details before committing yourself to the topic.

b As you work on the paragraph, you should keep in mind all four bases of effective writing.

Base 1: Unity. Everything in the paragraph should support your point. For example, if you are writing about an athlete's room, all the details should serve to show that the person who lives in the room is an athlete. Other details should be omitted. Then, after your paragraph is finished, imagine omitting the key word in your topic sentence. Your details alone should make it clear to the reader what word should fit in that empty space.

Base 2: Support. Description depends on the use of *specific* rather than *general* descriptive words. For example:

General	*Specific*
Old sports trophies	Tarnished medals and faded ribbons for track accomplishments
Ugly turtle tub	Large plastic tub of dirty, stagnant-looking water containing a few motionless turtles
Unpleasant smell	Unpleasant mixture of strong chemical deodorizers, urine-soaked newspapers, and musty sawdust
Nice skin	Soft, velvety brown skin

Remember that you want your readers to experience the room vividly as they read. Your words should be as detailed as a clear photograph and should give your readers a real feel for the room as well. Use as many senses as possible in describing the room. Chiefly you will use sight, but to an extent you may be able to use touch, hearing, and smell as well.

Base 3: Coherence. Organize your descriptive paragraph by using spatial order. Spatial order means that you move from right to left or from larger items to smaller ones, just as a visitor's eye might move around a room. For instance, the writer of "An Athlete's Room" presents an orderly description in which the eye moves from right to left around the room. Here are transition words that will help you connect your sentences as you describe the room:

to the left	above
to the right	below
next to	on the opposite side
across from	nearby

Such transitions will help prevent you—and your reader—from getting lost as the description proceeds.

Base 4: Sentence skills. In the later drafts of your paper, edit carefully for sentence-skills mistakes. Refer to the checklist of such skills on the inside front cover of the book.

■ Writing Assignment 2

Write a paragraph about a particular place that you can observe carefully or that you already know well. It might be one of the following or some other place:

Student lounge area	Hair salon
Car showroom	Doctor's or dentist's office
Gymnasium	Classroom
Fast-food restaurant	Bank
Inside of a car	Dressing room
Ladies' or men's room	Attic
Movie theater	Street market
Auto repair garage	Place where you work
Record shop	Porch

How to Proceed

a Remember that, like all paragraphs, a descriptive paper must have an opening point. This point, or topic sentence, should state a dominant impression about the place you are describing. State the place you want to describe and the dominant impression you want to make in a single short sentence. The sentence can be refined later. For now, you just want to find and express a workable topic. You might write, for example, a sentence like one of the following:

The student lounge was hectic.

The record shop was noisy.

The car's interior was very clean.

The dressing room in the department store was stifling.

The dentist's office was soothing.

The movie theater was freezing.

The gymnasium was tense.

The attic was gloomy.

The men's room was classy.

The office where I work was strangely quiet.

b Now make a list of all the details you can think of that support the general impression. For example, the writer of "A Depressing Place" made this list:

Puppies behind glass
Unpleasant smell
Chained birds
Rows of cages
Dirty tub of turtles
Stuffy atmosphere
Kittens in window
Sounds of caged animals
Droppings and urine on newspapers

c Organize your paper by using any one or a combination of the following methods.

In terms of physical order: That is, move from left to right, or far to near, or in some other consistent order

In terms of size: That is, begin with large features or objects and work down to smaller ones

In terms of a special order: Use a special order appropriate to the subject.

For instance, the writer of "A Depressing Place" organizes the paper in terms of physical order (from one side of the pet shop to the center to the other side).

d Use as many senses as possible in describing a scene. Chiefly you will use sight, but to an extent you may be able to use touch, hearing, smell, and perhaps even taste as well. Remember that it is through the richness of your sense impressions that the reader will gain a picture of the scene.

e As you are working on the drafts of your paper, refer to the checklist on the inside front cover. Make sure you can answer *Yes* to the questions about unity, support, coherence, and sentence skills.

■ Writing Assignment 3

Write a paragraph describing a person. Decide on a dominant impression you have about the person, and use only those details that will add to that impression. Here are some examples of interesting types of people you might want to write about.

TV or movie personality	Coworker
Teacher	Clergyman
Employer	Police officer
Child	Store owner or manager
Older person	Bartender
Close friend	Joker
Enemy	Neighbor

Before you begin, you may want to look carefully at the paragraph on Karla given earlier in this chapter and at the "How to Proceed" notes for Writing Assignment 2.

Here are some possible topic sentences. Your instructor may let you develop one of these or may require you to write your own.

Kate gives the impression of being permanently nervous.

The old man was as faded and brittle as a dying leaf.

The child was a cherubic little figure.

Our high-school principal resembled a cartoon drawing.

The young woman seemed to belong to another era.

Our neighbor is a fussy person.

The rock singer seemed to be plugged in to some kind of energy source.

The drug addict looked as lifeless as a corpse.

My friend Mike is a slow, deliberate person.

The owner of that grocery store seems burdened with troubles.

■ Writing Assignment 4

Visit a place you have never been to before and write a paragraph describing it. You may want to go to:

A restaurant

A classroom, laboratory, office, or other room in your school

A kind of store you ordinarily don't visit: for example, a certain men's or women's clothing store, hardware store, toy store, record shop, gun shop, or sports shop

A bus terminal, train station, airport

A church or synagogue

A park or vacant lot or street corner

You may want to jot down details about the place while you are there or very soon after you leave. Again, decide on a dominant impression you have about the place and use only those details which will add to that impression. Follow the notes on "How to Proceed" for Writing Assignment 2.

Writing Assignment 5

Option 1: You have just subscribed to a video dating service. Clients of this service are required to make a three-minute presentation, which will be recorded on videotape. In this presentation, clients describe the kind of person they would like to date. Write a one-paragraph description for your video presentation. Begin by brainstorming for a few minutes on what your "ideal date" would be like. Then arrange the details you come up with into some or all of the following categories:

- ***Character and personality*** (Are his or her attitudes important to you? Do you prefer someone who's quiet or someone who's outgoing?)
- ***Interests*** (Should your date have some of the same interests as you? If so, which ones?)
- ***Personal habits*** (Do you care, for instance, if your date is a nonsmoker?)
- ***Physical qualities*** (How might your ideal date look and dress?)

Option 2: Alternatively, write a similar presentation in which you describe *yourself.* Your aim is to present yourself as honestly as possible, so that interested members of the dating service will get a good sense of what you are like.

NARRATING AN EVENT

At times we make a statement clear by relating in detail something that has happened to us. In the story we tell, we present the details in the order in which they happened. A person might say, for example, "I was embarrassed yesterday," and then go on to illustrate the statement with the following narrative:

> I was hurrying across campus to get to a class. It had rained heavily all morning, so I was hopscotching my way around puddles in the pathway. I called to two friends ahead to wait for me, and right before I caught up to them, I came to a large puddle that covered the entire path. I had to make a quick choice of either stepping into the puddle or trying to jump over it. I jumped, wanting to seem cool since my friends were watching, but didn't clear the puddle. Water splashed everywhere, drenching my shoe, sock, and pants cuff, and also spraying the pants of my friends as well. "Well done, Dave!" they said. I felt the more embarrassed because I had tried to look so casual.

The speaker's details have made his moment of embarrassment vivid and real for us, and we can see and understand just why he felt as he did.

In this section, you will be asked to tell a story that illustrates some point. The paragraphs ahead all present narrative experiences that support a point. Read them and then answer the questions that follow.

PARAGRAPHS TO CONSIDER

Heartbreak

Bonnie and I had gotten engaged in August just before she left for college at Penn State. A week before Thanksgiving, I drove up to see her as a surprise. When I knocked on the door of her dorm room, she was indeed surprised but not in a pleasant way. She introduced me to her roommate, who looked uncomfortable and quickly left. I asked Bonnie how classes were going, and at the same time I tugged on the sleeve of my heavy sweater in order to pull it off. As I was pulling it off, a large poster caught my eye. It was decorated with paper flowers and yellow ribbon, and it said, "Bonnie and Blake." "What's going on?" I said. I stood there stunned and then felt an anger that grew rapidly. "Who is Blake?" I asked. Bonnie laughed nervously and said, "What do you want to hear about--my classes or Blake?" I don't really remember what she then told me, except that Blake was a sophomore math major. I felt a terrible pain in the pit of my stomach, and I wanted to rest my head on someone's shoulder and cry. I wanted to tear down the sign and run out, but I did nothing. Clumsily I pulled on my sweater again. My knees felt weak, and I barely had control of my body. I opened the room door, and suddenly more than anything I wanted to slam the door shut so hard that the dorm walls would collapse. Instead, I managed to close the door quietly. I walked away understanding what was meant by a broken heart.

A Childhood Disappointment

The time I almost won a car when I was ten years old was probably the most disappointing moment of my childhood. One hot summer afternoon I was wandering around a local department store, waiting for my mother to finish shopping. Near the toy department, I was attracted to a crowd of people gathered around a bright blue car that was on display in the main aisle. A sign indicated that the car was the first prize in a sweepstakes celebrating the store's tenth anniversary in the city. The sign also said that a person did not have to buy anything to fill out an entry form. White entry cards and shiny yellow pencils were scattered on a card table nearby, and the table was just low enough for me to write on, so I filled out a card. Then, feeling very much like an adult, I slipped my card into the slot of a heavy blue wooden box that rested on another table nearby. I then proceeded to the toy department, completely forgetting about the car. However, about a month later, just as I was walking into the house from my first day back at school, the telephone rang. When my mother answered it, a man asked to speak to a Michael Winchester. My mother said, "There's a Michael Williams here, but not a Michael Winchester." He asked, "Is this 862-9715 at 29 Williams Street?" My mother said, "That's the right number, but this is 29 Winchester Street." She then asked him, "What is this all about?" and he explained to her about the sweepstakes contest. My mother then called me to ask if I had ever filled out an application for a sweepstakes drawing. I said that I had, and she told me to get on the phone. The man by this time had realized that I had filled in my first name and street name on the line where my full name was to be. He told me I could not qualify for the prize because I had filled out the application incorrectly. For the rest of the day, I cried whenever I thought of how close I had come to winning the car. I am probably fated for the rest of my life to think of the "almost" prize whenever I fill out any kind of contest form.

A Frustrating Job

Working as a baby-sitter was the most frustrating job I ever had. I discovered this fact when my sister asked me to stay with her two sons for the evening. I figured I would get them dinner, let them watch a little TV, and then put them to bed early. The rest of the night I planned to watch TV and collect an easy twenty dollars. It turned out to be anything but easy. First, right before we were about to sit down for a pizza dinner, Rickie let the parakeet out of its cage. This bird is really intelligent and can repeat almost any phrase. The dog started chasing it around the house, so I decided to catch it before the dog did. Rickie and Jeff volunteered to help, following at my heels. We had the bird cornered by the fireplace when Rickie jumped for it and knocked over the hamster cage. Then the bird escaped again, and the hamsters began scurrying around their cage like crazy creatures. The dog had disappeared by this point, so I decided to clean up the hamsters' cage and try to calm them down. While I was doing this, Rickie and Jeff caught the parakeet and put it back in its cage. It was time to return to the kitchen and eat cold pizza. But upon entering the kitchen, I discovered why the dog had lost interest in the bird chase. What was left of the pizza was lying on the floor, and tomato sauce was dripping from the dog's chin. I cleaned up the mess and then served chicken noodle soup and ice cream to the boys. Only at nine o'clock did I get the kids to bed. I then returned downstairs to find that the dog had thrown up pizza on the living-room rug. When I finished cleaning the rug, my sister returned. I took the twenty dollars and told her that she should get someone else next time.

Questions

About Unity

1. Which paragraph lacks a topic sentence?

____

Write a topic sentence for the paragraph:

____

____

____

2. Which sentence in ''A Frustrating Job'' should be omitted in the interest of paragraph unity?

____

____

About Support

3. What is for you the best (most real and vivid) detail or image in the paragraph on ''Heartbreak''?

____

____

What is the best detail or image in ''A Childhood Disappointment''?

____

____

In ''A Frustrating Job''?

____

____

4. Which two paragraphs provide details in the form of the actual words used by the participants?

a. ____

b. ____

About Coherence

5. Do the three paragraphs use time order or emphatic order to organize the details?

____

6. Pick out four transition words used in ''A Frustrating Job.''

a. ________________

b. ________________

c. ________________

d. ________________

WRITING THE PARAGRAPH

■ Writing Assignment 1

Write an essay about an experience in which a certain emotion was predominant. The emotion might be fear, pride, satisfaction, embarrassment, or any of the following:

Frustration	Sympathy	Shyness
Love	Bitterness	Disappointment
Sadness	Violence	Happiness
Terror	Surprise	Jealousy
Shock	Nostalgia	Anger
Relief	Loss	Hate
Envy	Silliness	Nervousness

The experience should be limited in time. Note that the three paragraphs presented in this chapter all detail experiences that occurred within relatively short periods. One writer describes a heartbreaking surprise he received the day he visited his girlfriend; another describes the disappointing loss of a prize; the third describes a frustrating night of baby-sitting.

A good way to re-create an event is to include some dialog, as the writers of two of the three paragraphs in this chapter have done. Repeating what you have said or what you have heard someone else say helps make the situation come alive. Be sure, though, to check first the section on quotation marks on pages 432–439.

How to Proceed

a Think of an experience or event in your life in which you felt a certain emotion strongly. Then spend ten minutes freewriting about the experience. Do not worry at this point about such matters as spelling or grammar or putting things in the right order; instead, just try to get down all the details you can think of that seem related to the experience.

b This preliminary writing will help you decide whether your topic is promising enough to develop further. If it is not, choose another emotion. If it is, do two things:

- First, write your topic sentence, underlining the emotion you will focus on. For example, "My first day in kindergarten was one of the scariest days of my life."
- Second, make up a list of all the details involved in the experience. Then arrange these details in time order.

c Using the list as a guide, prepare a rough draft of your paper. Use time signals such as *first, then, next, after, while, during,* and *finally* to help connect details as you move from the beginning to the middle to the end of your narrative.

d As you work on the drafts of your paper, refer to the checklist on the inside front cover to make sure that you can answer *Yes* to the questions about unity, support, and coherence. Also use the checklist to edit the next-to-final draft of your paper for sentence-skills mistakes, including spelling.

Writing Assignment 2

Write a paper that shows, through some experience you have had, the truth *or* falsity of a popular belief. You might write about any one of the following statements or some other popular saying.

Every person has a price.

Do unto others as you would have them do unto you.

Haste makes waste.

Don't count your chickens before they're hatched.

A bird in the hand is worth two in the bush.

It isn't what you know, it's who you know.

Borrowing can get you into trouble.

What you don't know won't hurt you.

Keeping a promise is easier said than done.

You never really know people until you see them in an emergency.

If you don't help yourself, nobody will.

An ounce of prevention is worth a pound of cure.

Hope for the best but expect the worst.

Never give advice to a friend.

You get what you pay for.

A stitch in time saves nine.

If it isn't broken, don't fix it.

A fool and his money are soon parted.

There is an exception to every rule.

Nice guys finish last.

Begin your narrative paragraph with a topic sentence that expresses your agreement or disagreement with a popular saying. For example, "My sister learned recently that 'Keeping a promise is easier said than done.' " Or " 'Never give advice to a friend' is not always true, as I learned after helping a friend reunite with her boyfriend."

Refer to the suggestions about "How to Proceed" on pages 186–187 when doing your paper. Remember that the purpose of your story is to *support* your topic sentence. Feel free to select carefully from and even add to your experience so that the details truly support the point of your story.

■ Writing Assignment 3

Write an account of a memorable personal experience. Make sure that your story has a point, expressed in the first sentence of the paper. If necessary, tailor your narrative to fit your purpose. Use time order to organize your details (*first* this happened; *then* this; *after* that, this; *next,* this; and so on). Concentrate on providing as many specific details as possible so that the reader can really share your experience. Try to make it as vivid for the reader as it was for you when you first experienced it.

You might want to use one of the topics below, or a topic of your own choosing. Regardless, remember that your story must illustrate or support a point stated in the first sentence of your paper.

The first time you felt grown-up
A major decision
A moment you knew you were happy
The occasion of your best or worst date
A time you took a foolish risk
An argument you will never forget
An incident that changed your life
A time you did or did not do the right thing
Your best or worst holiday, birthday, or other special occasion
A time you learned a lesson or taught one to someone else
A moment of embarrassment, defeat, or disappointment
An occasion of triumph in sports or some other event

You may want to refer to the suggestions in Writing Assignment 1 on "How to Proceed."

Writing Assignment 4

For this assignment, you will re-create a real-life scene you have witnessed. Here are some places where you will find interesting interaction among people:

The traffic or small-claims court in your area

The dinner table at your or someone else's home

A waiting line at a supermarket, unemployment office, ticket counter, movie theater, or cafeteria

A doctor's office

An audience at a movie or sports event

A classroom

A restaurant

A student lounge

In your topic sentence, name the place where the incident happened and make some point about the incident. Here are some possibilities:

I witnessed a heartwarming incident at Burger King yesterday.

Two fans at last week's baseball game got into a hilarious argument.

The scene at our family dinner table Monday was one of complete confusion.

A painful dispute went on in Atlantic County small-claims court yesterday.

In your paragraph, describe the characters you watched: who they were, their facial expressions, their tones of voice, and so on. Use dialog to re-create what they said to each other. As you write the paragraph, keep in mind that your goal is to "photograph" the incident in writing. You want to achieve with words a sharp, clear re-creation of a limited subject.

Writing Assignment 5

Imagine that a younger brother or sister, or a young friend, has to make a difficult decision of some kind. Perhaps he or she must decide how to go about preparing for a job interview, whether or not to get help with a difficult class, or what to do about a co-worker who is taking money from the cash register. Write a narration from your own experience (or that of someone you know) that will teach a younger person something about the decision he or she must make. Include a comment or two in your paragraph about the lesson your story teaches.

You may narrate an experience about any problem young people face, including any of those already mentioned or those listed below.

Should he or she save a little from a weekly paycheck?

Should he or she live at home or move to an apartment with some friends?

How should he or she deal with a group of friends that are into drugs, stealing, or both?

ARGUING A POSITION

Most of us know someone who enjoys a good argument. Such a person usually challenges any sweeping statement we might make. "Why do you say that?" he or she will ask. "Give your reasons." Our questioner then listens carefully as we cite our reasons, waiting to see if we really do have solid evidence to support our point of view. Such a questioner may make us feel a bit nervous, but we may also feel grateful to him or her for helping us think through our opinions.

Our ability to advance sound and compelling arguments is an important skill in everyday life. We can use persuasion to get an extension on a term paper, obtain a favor from a friend, or convince an employer that we are the person for a job. Learning persuasion based on clear, logical reasoning can also help us see through the sometimes faulty arguments advanced by advertisers, editors, politicians, and others who try to bring us over to their side.

In this section, you will be asked to argue a position and defend it with a series of solid reasons. You are in a general way doing the same thing—making a point and then supporting it—with all the paragraphs in the book. The difference here is that, in a more direct and formal manner, you will advance a point about which you feel strongly and seek to convince others to agree with you.

PARAGRAPHS TO CONSIDER

Let's Ban Proms

High school proms should be banned. One reason is that even before the prom takes place it causes problems. Teens are separated into "the ones who were asked" and "the ones who weren't." Being one of those who weren't asked to go can be heartbreaking to a sensitive young person. Another pre-prom problem is money. The price of the various items needed can add up quickly to a lot of money. The prom itself can be unpleasant and frustrating, too. At the beginning of the evening, the girls enviously compare dresses while the boys sweat nervously inside their rented suits. During the dance, the couples who have gotten together only to go to the prom have split up into miserable singles. When the prom draws to a close, the popular teenagers drive off happily to other parties while the less-popular ones head home, as usual. Perhaps the main reason proms should be banned, however, is the drinking and driving that go on after the prom is over. Teenagers pile into their cars on their way to "after-proms" and pull out the bottles and cans stashed under the seat. By the time the big night is finally over, at 4 or 5 A.M., students are trying to weave home without encountering the police or a roadside tree. Some of them do not make it, and prom night turns into tragedy. For all these reasons, proms have no place in our schools.

A Terrible Vacation

Taking a cruise is a terrible way to spend a vacation. For one thing, there is too much food. You are force-fed seven times a day: breakfast, midmorning snack, lunch, afternoon punch and pastries, dinner, the midnight buffet, and the 1:30 A.M. pizza in the disco. Also, the waiters will not take "no" for an answer when they bring the food to your table. They think "no" means "give me a medium-sized portion." Another problem with a cruise is that there is too little genuine exercise. The swimming pool is the size of a large bathtub. Three strokes bring you to the other side. And if you want to jog around the deck, you will have to dodge flying Ping-Pong balls and leapfrog over the shuffleboard players as you go. Finally, the shipboard activities are boring. The big event of the afternoon is bingo, and at night, for excitement, there is the Kentucky Derby, complete with little wooden horses and a social director throwing dice to see which one wins. Many people are opposed to gambling anyway, and these games can be offensive to them. If you try to start a conversation on deck with one of the other passengers, you will find that most of them have sent their minds on vacation along with their bodies. All they are interested in is what kind of suntan lotion you are using or what you think will be served at the next meal. You will soon give up and join them in the chief activity on board--staring at the ocean. So the next time you look through your vacation folders, pick the mountains, the seashore--anything but a cruise ship. This way, your vacation will expand your mind and your muscles but not your waistline.

Living Alone

Living alone is quite an experience. People who live alone, for one thing, have to learn to do all kinds of tasks by themselves. They must learn--even if they have had no experience--to change fuses, put up curtains and shades, temporarily dam an overflowing toilet, cook a meal, and defrost a refrigerator. When there are no fathers, husbands, mothers, or wives to depend on, a person can't fall back on the excuse, "I don't know how to do that." Those who live alone also need the strength to deal with people. Alone, singles must face noisy neighbors, unresponsive landlords, dishonest repair people, and aggressive bill collectors. Because there are no buffers between themselves and the outside world, people living alone have to handle every visitor--friendly or unfriendly--alone. Finally, singles need a large dose of courage to cope with occasional panic and unavoidable loneliness. That weird thump in the night is even more terrifying when there is no one in the next bed or the next room. Frightening weather or unexpected bad news is doubly bad when the worry can't be shared. Even when life is going well, little moments of sudden loneliness can send shivers through the heart. Struggling through such bad times taps into reserves of courage that people may not have known they possessed. Facing everyday tasks, confronting all types of people, and handling panic and loneliness can shape singles into brave, resourceful, and more independent people.

■ Questions

About Unity

1. The topic sentence in "Living Alone" is too broad. Circle the topic sentence below that states accurately what the paragraph is about.
   a. Living alone takes courage.
   b. Living alone can create feelings of loneliness.
   c. Living alone should be avoided.
2. Which sentence in "Vacation" should be eliminated in the interest of paragraph unity? ______________________

About Support

3. How many reasons are given to support the topic sentence?
   a. In "Vacation" ______ 1 ______ 2 ______ 3 ______ 4
   b. In "Proms" ______ 1 ______ 2 ______ 3 ______ 4
   c. In "Living Alone" ______ 1 ______ 2 ______ 3 ______ 4
4. After which sentence in "Proms" are more specific details needed?

   ____

About Coherence

5. Which paragraph uses a combination of time and emphatic order to organize its details?

 ____

6. What are the three main transition words in "Living Alone"?

 a. ____________ b. ____________ c. ____________

Activity

Complete the outline below of the paragraph titled "A Terrible Vacation." Summarize in a few words the primary and secondary supporting material that fits under the topic sentence. Two items have been done for you as examples.

Topic sentence: Taking a cruise is a terrible way to spend a vacation.

a. ______________________________
 (1) ______________________________
 (2) ______________________________

b. ______________________________
 (1) ______________________________
 (2) *Little room for jogging*

c. ______________________________
 (1) ______________________________
 (2) *Dull conversations with other passengers*
 (3) ______________________________

WRITING THE PARAGRAPH

■ Writing Assignment 1

On separate paper, make up brief outlines for any four of the eight statements that follow. Note the example. Make sure that you have three separate and distinct reasons for each statement.

Example Large cities should outlaw passenger cars.
a. Cut down on smog and pollution
b. Cut down on noise
c. Create more room for pedestrians

1. A teenager makes a poor parent.
2. ________________ (*name a specific sports team*) should win its league championship.
3. Large cars should be banned from our highways.
4. ________________ is one of the best (worst) shows on television.
5. Americans spend too much money on ________________.
6. ________________s are the best (worst) pets.
7. ________________ was the best (worst) job I ever had.
8. This college needs a better ________________ (cafeteria, library, student center, grading policy, attendance policy, etc.).

How to Proceed

a Decide, perhaps through discussion with your instructor or classmates, which of your outlines would be most promising to develop into a paragraph. Make sure that your supporting points are logical ones that actually back up your topic sentence. Ask yourself in each case, "Does this item truly support my topic sentence?"

b Now prepare a list of all the details you can think of that might support your point. At this beginning point, prepare more details than you can possibly use. Here, for example, are details generated by the writer of "Let's Ban Proms" while working on the paragraph:

Car accidents (most important)
Drinking after prom
Competition over dates
Preparation for prom cuts into school hours
Rejection of not being asked
Waste of school money
Going with someone you don't like
License to stay out all night
Separates popular from unpopular
Expenses
Parents' interference

c Decide which details you will use to develop your paragraph. Also, number the details in the order in which you will present them. (You may also want to make an outline of your paragraph at this point.) Because emphatic order (most important reason last) is the most effective way to organize an argument paragraph, be sure to save your most powerful reason for last. Here is how the writer of ''Let's Ban Proms'' made decisions about details:

8 Car accidents (most important)
7 Drinking after prom
3 Competition over dates
~~Preparation for prom cuts into school hours~~
1 Rejection of not being asked
~~Waste of school money~~
4 Going with someone you don't like
6 License to stay out all night
5 Separates popular from unpopular
2 Expenses
~~Parents' interference~~

d Develop each reason with specific details. For example, in the model paragraph on high school proms, notice how the writer explains how unpleasant the prom can be by describing the boys ''who sweat nervously'' and the one-night-only dates splitting up into ''miserable singles.'' The writer also expands the idea of after-prom drinking by describing the ''bottles and cans stashed under the seat'' and the teenagers ''trying to weave home.''

e As you write, imagine that your audience is a jury that will ultimately believe or disbelieve your argument. Have you presented a convincing case? If *you* were on the jury, would you be favorably impressed with this argument?

f As you are working on the drafts of your paper, keep the four bases of unity, support, coherence, and sentence skills in mind.

g Finally, edit the next-to-final draft of your paper for sentence-skills mistakes, including spelling.

Writing Assignment 2

Write a paragraph that uses reasons to develop a point of some kind. You may advance and defend a point of your own about which you feel strongly, or you can support any one of the following statements:

1. ________________ is a dangerous invention.
2. Without ________________, many people's lives would be miserable.
3. A college diploma is now essential for any ambitious person.
4. Most Americans are poor drivers.
5. Fall is a sad season.
6. ________________ is (are) overpriced.
7. College instructors may know their subjects, but some of them are poor teachers.
8. ________________ is a sport that should be banned.
9. ________________ is a subject that should be taught in every school.
10. Being young is better than being old.
11. Being old is better than being young.
12. Every college should provide a day-care center.

Use the suggestions in ''How to Proceed'' on pages 195–196 as a guide in writing your paragraph.

Writing Assignment 3

Write a paragraph in which you take a stand on one of the controversial subjects below. As a lead-in to this writing project, your instructor might give the class a chance to ''stand up for what they believe in.'' One side of the front of the room should be designated *strong agreement* and the other side *strong disagreement,* with the space between for varying degrees of agreement or disagreement. As the class stands in front of the room, the instructor will read one value statement at a time from the list below, and students will move to the appropriate spot depending on their degree of agreement or disagreement. Some time will be allowed for students, first, to discuss with those near them the reasons they are standing where they are, and second, to state to those on the other end of the scale the reasons for their position.

1. Students should not be required to attend high school.
2. Prostitution should be legalized.
3. Homosexuals and lesbians should not be allowed to teach in schools.
4. Marijuana should be legalized.

5. The death penalty should exist for certain crimes.
6. Abortion should be illegal.
7. Federal prisons should be coed, and prisoners should be allowed to marry.
8. An act of Congress should ban the government from making any more nuclear weapons.
9. Parents of girls under eighteen should be informed if their daughters receive birth-control aids.
10. The government should set up centers where sick or aged persons can go voluntarily to commit suicide.
11. Any woman on welfare who has more than two illegitimate children should be sterilized.
12. The grade of F should be abolished.

Begin your paragraph by writing a sentence that expresses your attitude toward one of the value statements listed above. For example, "I feel that prostitution should be legalized."

Outline the reason or reasons you hold the opinion that you do. Your support may be based on your own experience, the experience of someone you know, or logic. For example, an outline of a paragraph based on one student's logic proceeded as follows:

> I feel that prostitution should be legalized for the following reasons:
>
> 1. Prostitutes would then have to pay their fair share of income tax.
> 2. Government health centers would administer regular checkups and thus help prevent the spread of venereal disease.
> 3. Prostitutes would be able to work openly and independently and would not be subject to exploitation by others.
> 4. Most of all, prostitutes would no longer be so much regarded as social outcasts--an attitude that is psychologically damaging to those who may already have emotional problems.

Another outline, based on experience, proceeded as follows:

> I do not feel that prostitution should be legalized, because of a woman I know who was once a prostitute.
>
> 1. The attention Linda received as a prostitute prevented her from seeing and working on her personal problems.
> 2. She became embittered toward all men, whom she always suspected of wanting to exploit her.
> 3. She developed a negative self-image and felt that no one could love her.

Use your outline as the basis for writing a paragraph. Be sure to refer to the suggestions on "How to Proceed" on pages 195–196.

Writing Assignment 4

Write a paper in which you use research findings to help support one of the following statements.

Wearing seat belts should be mandatory.

Many people do not need vitamin pills.

Disposable cans and bottles should be banned.

Everyone should own a pet.

Mandatory retirement ages should be abolished.

Cigarettes should be illegal.

Penalties against drunken drivers should be sharply increased.

Advertising should not be permitted on Saturday morning cartoon shows.

Research the topic you have chosen in one or more of the following ways:

- Look up the topic in the subject section of your library card catalog. (You may want to review "Using the Library" on page 284.) Possible subject headings for the above statements might be automobile safety, vitamin pills, pollution, pets, retirement, smoking, alcohol, and advertising. Select the books listed under your heading that seem likely to give you relevant information about your topic. Then find the books in the library stacks.
- Look up the topic in recent issues of *Readers' Guide to Periodical Literature*. (You may want to review "Using the Library.") Try the same headings suggested above. Select the articles listed under your heading that appear most likely to provide information on your topic. Then see if you can find some of these articles in the periodicals section of your library.
- You may also want to check a paperback bookstore. Ask a salesperson to help you find recent books on your topic.

Reading material on your topic will help you think about that topic. See if you can organize your paper in the form of three reasons that support the topic. Put these reasons into a scratch outline, and use it as a guide in writing your paragraph. Here is an example:

Wearing seat belts should be mandatory.

1. Seat belts are now comfortable and easy to use. . . .
2. A seat-belt law would be easy to enforce. . . .
3. Seat belts would save lives. . . .

Note that statistics (on how many lives could be saved) would support the last reason. Do not hesitate to cite studies and other data in a limited way; they make your argument more objective and compelling.

■ Writing Assignment 5

You have finally met Mr. or Ms. Right—but your parents don't approve of him or her. Specifically, they are against your doing one of the following:

Continuing to see this person
Going steady
Moving in together
Getting married at the end of the school year

Write a letter to your parents explaining in a fully detailed way why you have made the choice that you have. Do your best to convince them that it is a good choice.

ADDITIONAL PARAGRAPH ASSIGNMENTS

This section contains a variety of paragraph writing assignments. The earlier assignments are especially suited for writing practice at the very start of a course; the later ones can be used to measure progress at the close of a semester. More detailed instructions are provided with the earlier assignments; fewer guidelines appear for the later ones, so that writers must make more individual decisions about exactly how to proceed. In short, the section provides a wide number and range of writing assignments. Many choices are possible, then, depending on the needs and interests of students and the purposes of the instructor.

■ 1 Best or Worst Experience

Your instructor may pass out slips of paper and ask you to write, in the middle of the slip, your name; in the top left-hand corner, the best or worst job (or chore) you have ever had; in the top right-hand corner, the best or worst teacher you have ever had; in the lower left-hand corner, the best or worst place you have ever eaten in; in the lower right-hand corner, the best or worst thing that has happened to you in the past week. The instructor may also participate by writing on the board. Here is one student's paper.

Baby-sitting for my sister		*B. O. Sullivan (Tenth grade history teacher)*
	Gail Battaglia	
Fourth Street Diner		*Trying to register*

You should then get together with any person in the room whom you do not know, exchange papers, and talk for a bit about what you wrote. Then the two of you should join another pair, with members of the resulting group of four doing two things:

- Mastering the first names of all the members of the group, so that, if asked, they could introduce the teacher to everyone in the group.
- Giving a "mini" speech to the group in which they talk with *as much specific detail as possible* about any one of the four responses on their slip of paper. During or after this speech, other members of the group should ask questions to get as full a sense as possible of why the experience described was a "best" or "worst" one.

Finally, you should write a paper about any one of the best or worst experiences. The main purpose in writing this paper is to provide plenty of specific details that *show clearly* why your choice was a "best" or "worst" one. Student responses to this assignment include the papers on pages 63–64.

2 Interview Writing

Interview someone in the class. Take notes as you ask the person a series of questions.

How to Proceed

a Begin by asking a series of factual questions about the person. You might ask such questions as:

Where is the person from? Where does he or she live now?

Does the person have brothers or sisters? Does the person live with other people, or alone?

What kinds of jobs (if any) has the person had? Where does he or she work now?

What are the person's school or career plans? What courses is he or she taking?

What are the person's favorite leisure activities?

Work at getting specific details rather than general ones. You do not want your introduction to include lines such as "Regina graduated from high school and worked for a year." You want to state specific places and dates: "Regina graduated from DeWitt Clinton High School in the Bronx in 1984.

Within a week of graduation, she had gotten a job as keypunch operator for a branch of the Allstate Insurance Company located in Queens.'' Or if you are writing about a person's favorite activities, you do not want to simply say, ''Regina enjoys watching TV in her few spare hours.'' Instead, go on and add details such as ''Her favorite shows are *60 Minutes, Cheers, L.A. Law*, and *Dallas*.''

b Then ask a series of questions about the person's attitudes and thoughts on various matters. You might ask the person's feelings about his or her

Writing ability
Parents
Boss (if any)
Courses
Past schooling
Strengths and talents
Areas for self-improvement

You might also ask what things make the person angry or sad or happy, and why.

c After collecting all this information, use it in two paragraphs. Begin your introduction to the person with a line like ''This is a short introduction to ________________. Here is some factual information about him (her).'' Then begin your second paragraph with the line, ''Now let's take a brief look at some of ____________'s attitudes and beliefs.''

■ 3 Keeping a Journal

Keep a journal for one week or whatever time period your instructor indicates. At some point during each day—perhaps right before going to bed—write for ten minutes or more about some of the specific happenings, thoughts, and feelings of your day. You do not have to prepare what to write or be in the mood or worry about making mistakes; just write down whatever words come out. As a minimum, you should complete at least one page in each writing session.

Keeping a journal will help you develop the habits of thinking on paper and writing in terms of specific details. Also, the journal can serve as a sourcebook of ideas for possible papers. Read the following excerpt from one student's journal. (Sentence-skills mistakes have been corrected in the excerpt to improve readability.) As you read, look for a general point and supporting material that could be the basis for an interesting paper.

Wednesday

Today a woman came into our department at the store and wanted to know if we had any scrap lumber ten feet long. Ten feet! "Lady," I said, "anything we have that's ten feet long sure as heck isn't scrap." When the boss heard me say that, he almost canned me. My boss is a company man down to his toe tips. He wants to make a big impression on his bosses, and he'll run us around like mad all night to make himself look good. He's the most ambitious man I've ever met. If I don't transfer out of Hardware soon, I'm going to go crazy on this job. I'm not ready to quit, though. The time is not right. I want to be here for a year and have another job lined up and have other things right before I quit. It's good the boss wasn't around tonight when another person wanted me to carry a bookcase he had bought out to his car. He didn't ask me to help him--he expected me to help him. I hate that kind of "You're my servant" attitude, and I told him that carrying stuff out to cars wasn't my job. Ordinarily I go out of my way to give people a hand, but not guys like him. . . .

Here are two general ideas stemming from the journal entry that the writer might develop into paragraphs:

> Working at a department store means that you have to deal with some irritating customers.
>
> Certain preparations are advisable before you quit a job.

See if you can construct another general point from the journal entry that might be the basis for a detailed and interesting paragraph; write the point in the space below.

____

■ 4 Writing a Dialog

Make up and write a *realistic* dialog between two or more people. Don't have your characters talk like cardboard figures; have them talk the way people would in real life. Also, make sure their voices are consistent. (Do not have them suddenly talk out of character.)

The dialog should deal with a lifelike situation. It may, for example, be a discussion or argument of some kind between two friends or acquaintances, or a husband and wife, or a parent and child, or a brother and sister, or a boyfriend and girlfriend, or a clerk and customer, or other persons. The conversation may or may not lead to a decision or action of some kind.

When writing dialog, enclose characters' exact words within quotation marks. (You should first review the material on quotation marks on pages 432–439.) Also, include brief descriptions of whether your characters smile, sit down or stand up, or make other facial gestures or movements during the conversation. And be sure to include a title for your dialog. The example that follows can serve as a guide.

A Supermarket Conversation

The supermarket checker rang up the total and said to the young woman in line, "That'll be $43.61."

The young woman fumbled with her pocketbook and then said in an embarrassed voice, "I don't think I have more than $40. How much did you say it was again?"

"It's $43.61," the checker said in a sharp, impatient tone.

As the young woman searched her pocketbook for the dollars she needed, the checker said loudly, "If you don't have enough money, you'll have to put something back."

A middle-aged man behind the young woman spoke up. "Look, Ma'am, I'll lend you a couple of dollars."

"No, I couldn't do that," said the young woman. "If . . . I don't think I need those sodas," she said hesitantly.

"Look, lady, make up your mind. You're holding up the line," the checker snapped.

The man turned to the checker and said coldly, "Why don't you try being a little more courteous to people? If we weren't here buying things, you'd be out of a job."

■ 5 Annoyances in Everyday Life

Make up a list of things that bother you in everyday life. One student's list of "pet peeves" included the following items:

Drivers that suddenly slow down to turn without having signaled

The cold floor in my bathroom on a winter morning

Not having cable television to watch football and basketball games

The small napkin holder in my parents' home that is always running out of napkins

Not being able to fall asleep at night when I know I have to get up at 6:30 the next morning

Suggestions on How to Proceed

a Brainstorm a list of everyday annoyances by asking yourself questions: "What annoys me at home (or about my kitchen, bathroom, closets, and so on)?" "What annoys me about getting to school?" "What annoys me at school or work?" "What annoys me while I am driving or shopping?" You will probably be able to think of other questions.

b Decide on the annoyances that seem most promising to develop. Which are the most interesting or important? Which ones can be developed with specific, vivid details? Cross out the items you will not use. Next, number the annoyances you have listed in the order in which you will present them. You may want to group related items together (all the ones that are connected with shopping, for instance). Be sure to end with the item that annoys you the most.

c Now write a rough draft of the paragraph. Begin with a topic sentence that makes clear what your paragraph is about. Concentrate on providing plenty of details about each of the annoyances you are describing.

d In a second or third draft, add word signals (such as *one, also, another,* and *last*) to set off each annoyance.

e Use the checklist on the inside back cover to edit your paper for sentence-skills mistakes, including spelling.

■ 6 Getting Comfortable

Getting comfortable is a quiet pleasure in life that we all share. Write a paper about the special way you make yourself comfortable, providing plenty of specific details so that the reader can really see and understand your particular method. Use transition words such as *first, next, then, in addition, also, finally,* and so on to guide readers through your paper. Transitions act like signposts on an unfamiliar route—they prevent your readers from getting lost.

A student paragraph on getting comfortable is on page 41.

■ 7 A Special Person

Write in detail about a person who provided help at an important moment in your life. State in the first sentence who the person is and the person's relationship to you (friend, father, cousin, etc.). For example, "My grandmother gave me a lot of direction in the difficult time when my parents were getting divorced." Then show through specific examples (the person's words and actions) why he or she was so special for you.

■ 8 A Favorite Childhood Place

Describe a favorite childhood place that made you feel secure, safe, private, or in a world of your own. Here are some possibilities:

A closet
Under a piece of furniture
A grandparent's room
A basement or attic
The woods
A shed or barn
A tree
A bunk bed

Begin with a topic sentence something like this: "____________ was a place that made me feel ____________ when I was a child." Keep the point of your topic sentence in mind as you describe this place. Include only details that will support the idea that your place was one of *security, safety, privacy,* or the like.

■ 9 Expressing Uniqueness

Write a paragraph providing examples of one quality or habit that helps make you unique. One student's response to this assignment appears below.

Floor-Cleaning Freak

The one habit that makes me unique is that I am a floor-cleaning freak. I use my Dustbuster to snap up crumbs seconds after they fall. When a rubber heel mark appears on my vinyl floor, I run for the steel wool. As I work in my kitchen preparing meals, I constantly scan the tiles, looking for spots where some liquid has been spilled or for a crumb that has somehow miraculously escaped my vision. After I scrub and wax my floors, I stand to one side of the room and try to catch the light in such a way as to reveal spots that have gone unwaxed. As I travel from one room to the other, my experienced eye is faithfully searching for lint that may have invaded my domain since my last passing. If I discover an offender, I discreetly tuck it into my pocket. The amount of lint I have gathered in the course of the day is the ultimate test of how diligently I am performing my task. I give my vacuum cleaner quite a workout, and I spend an excessive amount on replacement bags. My floor-cleaner and wax expenses are alarmingly high, but somehow this does not stop me. Where my floors are concerned, money is not a consideration!

■ 10 Making It through the Day

Write about techniques you use to make it through a day of school or work. These may include:

Caffeine
A system of rewards
Humor
Food
Fantasizing

You might organize the paragraph by using time order. Show how you turn to your supports at various times during the day in order to cope with fatigue or boredom. For example, in the morning you might use coffee (with its dose of caffeine) to get started. In later parts of the day, you would go on to use other supports.

■ 11 Life without TV

Imagine that all the televisions of America go blank, starting tonight. What would you and your family do on a typical night without television? You may want to write about

What each individual would be doing
What the family could do together
Problems the lack of TV would cause
Benefits of a TV-less family life

Choose any of the above approaches, or some other single approach, in writing about your family life without TV.

■ 12 Ten Topics

Write a paper on one of the following topics. Begin with a clear, direct sentence that states exactly what your paper will be about. For example, if you choose the first topic, your opening sentence might be, "There were several delightful childhood games I played that occupied many of my summer days." An opening sentence for the second topic might be, "The work I had to do to secure my high school diploma is one of the special accomplishments of my life." Be sure to follow your opening sentence with plenty of specific supporting details that develop your topic.

A way you had fun as a child
A special accomplishment
A favorite holiday and why
Some problems a family member or friend is having
A superstition or fear
A disagreement you have had with someone
A debt you have repaid or have yet to repay
The sickest you've ever been
How your parents (or you and a special person in your life) met
Your father's or mother's attitude toward you

■ 13 Ten More Topics

Write a paper on one of the topics below. Follow the instructions given for the preceding assignment.

A wish or dream you have or have had
Everyday pleasures
Ways you were punished by your parents as a child
Ways you were rewarded by your parents as a child
A difficult moment in your life
An experience you or someone you know has had with drugs
Your weaknesses as a student
Your strengths as a student
A time a prayer was answered
Something you would like to change

■ 14 Fifteen Topics

Write a paper on one of the following topics:

Crime	Music	Books
Lies	Exercise	Transportation
Television	Debt	Exhaustion
Plants	Parking meters	Telephone
Comic books	Hunger	Drugs

Suggestions on How to Proceed

a You might begin by writing several statements about your general topic. For example, suppose that you choose to do a paper on the subject of *neighborhood*. Here are some statements you might write:

My neighborhood is fairly rural.

The neighborhood where I grew up was unique.

Many city neighborhoods have problems with crime.

My new neighborhood has no playgrounds for the children.

A neighborhood's appearance reflects the people who live in it.

Everyone in my neighborhood seems to cut the grass almost daily.

My neighborhood became a community when it was faced with a hurricane last summer.

My neighborhood is a noisy place.

b Choose (or revise) one of the statements that you could go on to develop in a paragraph. You should not select a narrow statement like "My new neighborhood has no playgrounds for the children," for it is a simple factual sentence that needs no support. Nor should you begin with a point such as "Many city neighborhoods have problems with crime," which is too broad for you to develop adequately in a single paragraph. (See also the information on topic sentences on pages 22–29.)

c After you have chosen a promising sentence, make a scratch outline of supporting details that will develop the point of that sentence. For example, one student provided the following outline:

My neighborhood is a noisy place.

1. Businesses
    a. Tavern with loud music
    b. Twenty-four-hour drive-in burger restaurant
2. Children
    a. Skating and biking while carrying loud radios
    b. Street games
3. Traffic
    a. Truck route nearby
    b. Horn-blowing during frequent delays at intersection

d While writing your paper, use the checklist on the inside front cover to make sure you can answer *Yes* to the questions about unity, support, and coherence. Also, refer to the checklist when you edit the next-to-final draft of your paper for sentence-skills mistakes, including spelling.

■ 15 Fifteen More Topics

Write a paper on one of the topics below. Follow the instructions given for the preceding assignment.

Comics	Tryouts
Babies	Pens
Vacation	Hospital
Red tape	Parties
Dependability	Criticism
Illness	Success
Failure	Wisdom teeth
Home	

PART FOUR

ESSAY DEVELOPMENT

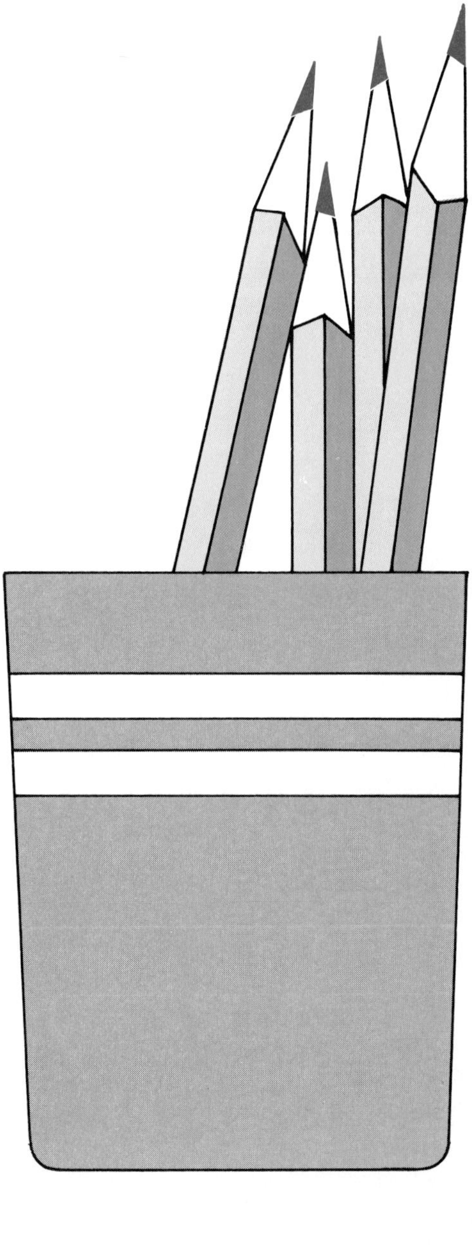

PREVIEW

Part Four moves from the single-paragraph paper to the several-paragraph essay. The differences between a paragraph and an essay are explained and then illustrated with a paragraph that has been expanded into an essay. You are shown how to begin an essay, how to tie together its supporting paragraphs, and how to conclude it. Three student essays are presented, along with questions to increase your understanding of the essay form. Finally, directions on how to plan an essay are followed by a series of essay writing assignments.

WRITING THE ESSAY

The Difference between a Paragraph and an Essay

An essay is simply a paper of several paragraphs, rather than one paragraph, that supports a single point. Subjects can and should be treated more fully in an essay than they would be in a single-paragraph paper.

The main idea or point developed in an essay is called the *thesis statement* rather than, as in a paragraph, the *topic sentence*. The thesis statement appears in the introductory paragraph, and it is then developed in the supporting paragraphs that follow. A short concluding paragraph closes the essay.

The diagram on the next page shows the form of an essay.

Introductory Paragraph

Introduction
Thesis sentence
Plan of development:
Points 1, 2, 3

The *introduction* attracts the reader's interest.

The *thesis sentence* states the main idea advanced in the paper.

The *plan of development* is a list of the points that support the thesis. The points are presented in the order in which they will be developed in the paper.

First Supporting Paragraph

Topic sentence (point 1)
Specific evidence

The *topic sentence* advances the first supporting point for the thesis, and the *specific evidence* in the rest of the paragraph develops that first point.

Second Supporting Paragraph

Topic sentence (point 2)
Specific evidence

The *topic sentence* advances the second supporting point for the thesis, and the *specific evidence* in the rest of the paragraph develops that second point.

Third Supporting Paragraph

Topic sentence (point 3)
Specific evidence

The *topic sentence* advances the third supporting point for the thesis, and the *specific evidence* in the rest of the paragraph develops that third point.

Concluding Paragraph

Summary, conclusion, or both

A *summary* is a brief restatement of the thesis and its main points. A *conclusion* is a final thought or two stemming from the subject of the paper.

A MODEL ESSAY

Gene, the writer of the paragraph on working in an apple plant (page 104), later decided to develop his subject more fully. Here is the essay that resulted.

My Job in an Apple Plant

Introductory paragraph

In the course of working my way through school, I have taken many jobs I would rather forget. I have spent nine hours a day lifting heavy automobile and truck batteries off the end of an assembly belt. I have risked the loss of eyes and fingers working a punch press in a textile factory. I have served as a ward aide in a mental hospital, helping care for brain-damaged men who would break into violent fits at unexpected moments. But none of these jobs was as dreadful as my job in an apple plant. The work was physically hard; the pay was poor; and, most of all, the working conditions were dismal.

First supporting paragraph

First of all, the job made enormous demands on my strength and energy. For ten hours a night, I took cartons that rolled down a metal track and stacked them onto wooden skids in a tractor-trailer. Each carton contained twelve heavy cans or bottles of apple juice. A carton shot down the track about every fifteen seconds. I once figured out that I was lifting an average of twelve tons of apple juice every night. When a truck was almost filled, I or my partner had to drag fourteen bulky wooden skids into the empty trailer nearby and then set up added sections of the heavy metal track so that we could start routing cartons to the back of the empty van. While one of us did that, the other performed the stacking work of two men.

Second supporting paragraph

I would not have minded the difficulty of the work so much if the pay had not been so poor. I was paid the minimum wage of that time, two dollars an hour, plus the minimum of a nickel extra for working the night shift. Because of the low salary, I felt compelled to get as much overtime pay as possible. Everything over eight hours a night was time-and-a-half, so I typically worked twelve hours a night. On Friday I would sometimes work straight through until Saturday at noon--eighteen hours. I averaged over sixty hours a week but did not take home much more than one hundred dollars.

Third supporting paragraph

But even more than the low pay, what upset me about my apple plant job was the working conditions. Our humorless supervisor cared only about his production record for each night and tried to keep the assembly line moving at a breakneck pace. During work I was limited to two 10-minute breaks and an unpaid half hour for lunch. Most of my time was spent outside on the truck loading dock in near-zero-degree temperatures. The steel floors of the trucks were like ice; the quickly penetrating cold made my feet feel like stone. I had no shared interests with the man I loaded cartons with, and so I had to work without job companionship. And after the production line shut down and most people left, I had to spend two hours alone scrubbing clean the apple vats, which were coated with a sticky residue.

Concluding paragraph

I stayed on the job for five months, hating all the while the difficulty of the work, the poor money, and the conditions under which I worked. By the time I quit, I was determined never to do such degrading work again.

Important Points about the Essay

INTRODUCTORY PARAGRAPH

An introductory paragraph should do three things:

1 Attract the reader's interest. Using one of the suggested methods of introduction described ahead can help draw the reader into your paper.

2 Present a *thesis sentence*—a clear, direct statement of the central idea that you will develop in your paper. The thesis statement, like a topic sentence, should have a key word or words that reflect your attitude about the subject. For example, in the essay on the apple plant job, the key word is *dreadful.*

3 Indicate a *plan of development*—a preview of the major points that will support your thesis statement, listed in the order in which they will be presented. In some cases, the thesis statement and plan of development may appear in the same sentence. In some cases, also, the plan of development may be omitted.

Activity

1. In "My Job in an Apple Plant," which sentences are used to attract the reader's interest?

   ______ First three sentences

   ______ First four sentences

   ______ First five sentences

2. The thesis in "My Job in an Apple Plant" is presented in the

   ______ Fourth sentence

   ______ Fifth sentence

   ______ Sixth sentence

3. The thesis is followed by a plan of development.

   ______ Yes

   ______ No

4. Write down the words in the plan of development that announce the three major supporting points in the essay.

   a. ______________________________

   b. ______________________________

   c. ______________________________

Common Methods of Introduction

Here are some common methods of introduction. Use any one method, or a combination of methods, to introduce your subject in an interesting way to the reader.

1 Begin with a broad, general statement of your topic and narrow it down to your thesis statement. Broad, general statements ease the reader into your thesis statement by providing a background for it. In ''My Job in an Apple Plant,'' Gene writes generally on the topic of his worst jobs and then narrows down to a specific worst job.

2 Start with an idea or situation that is the opposite of the one you will develop. This approach works because your readers will be surprised, and then intrigued, by the contrast between the opening idea and the thesis that follows it. Here is an example of a ''contrast'' introduction:

> When I was a girl, I never argued with my parents about differences between their attitudes and mine. My father would deliver his judgment on an issue, and that was usually the end of the matter. Discussion seldom changed his mind, and disagreement was not tolerated. But the situation is different with today's parents and children. My husband and I have to contend with radical differences between what our children think about a given situation and what we think about it. We have had disagreements with all three of our daughters, Stephanie, Diana, and Gisel.

3 Explain the importance of your topic. If you can convince your readers that the subject in some way applies to them, or is something they should know more about, they will want to continue reading. The introductory paragraph of ''Sports-Crazy America'' (page 223) provides an example of a ''relevance'' introduction.

4 Use an incident or brief story. Stories are naturally interesting. They appeal to a reader's curiosity. In your introduction, an anecdote will grab the reader's attention right away. The story should be brief and should be related to your central idea. The incident in the story can be something that happened to you, something that you have heard about, or something that you have read about in a newspaper or magazine. Here is an example of a paragraph that begins with a story:

The husky man pushes open the door of the bedroom and grins as he pulls out a .38 revolver. An elderly man wearing thin pajamas looks at him and whimpers. In a feeble effort at escape, the old man slides out of his bed and moves to the door of the room. The husky man, still grinning, blocks his way. With the face of a small, frightened animal, the old man looks up and whispers, "Oh God, please don't hurt me." The grinning man then fires four times. The television movie cuts now to a soap commercial, but the little boy who has been watching the set has begun to cry. Such scenes of direct violence on television must surely be harmful to children for a number of psychological reasons.

5 Ask one or more questions of your readers. The questions catch the readers' interest and make them want to read on. Here is an example of a paragraph that begins with questions:

What would happen if we were totally honest with ourselves? Would we be able to stand the pain of our own self-deception? Would the complete truth be too much for us to bear? Such questions will probably never be answered, for in everyday life we protect ourselves from the onslaught of too much reality. All of us cultivate defense mechanisms that prevent us from seeing and hearing and feeling too much. Included among such defense mechanisms are rationalization, reaction formation, and substitution.

6 Use a quotation. A quotation can be something you have read in a book or an article. It can also be something that you have heard: a popular saying or proverb ("Never give advice to a friend"); a current or recent advertising slogan ("Reach out and touch someone"); a favorite expression used by friends or family ("My father always says . . ."). Using a quotation in your introductory paragraph lets you add someone else's voice to your own. Here is an example of a paragraph that begins with a quotation:

"Evil," wrote Martin Buber, "is lack of direction." In my school days as a fatherless boy, with a mother too confused by her own life to really care for me, I strayed down a number of dangerous paths. Before my eighteenth birthday, I had been a car thief, a burglar, and a drug seller.

SUPPORTING PARAGRAPHS

Most essays have three supporting points, developed in three separate paragraphs. (Some essays will have two supporting points; others, four or more.) Each of the supporting paragraphs should begin with a topic sentence that states the point to be detailed in that paragraph. Just as the thesis provides a focus for the entire essay, the topic sentence provides a focus for each supporting paragraph.

Activity

1. What is the topic sentence for the first supporting paragraph of "My Job in an Apple Plant"?

   ____

   ____

2. What is the topic sentence for the second supporting paragraph?

   ____

   ____

3. What is the topic sentence for the third supporting paragraph?

   ____

TRANSITIONAL SENTENCES

Transitions and other connective devices (pages 43–47) are used to help link sentences in paragraphs. Similarly, *transitional sentences* are used to help tie together the supporting paragraphs in an essay. Such transitional sentences usually occur near the end of one paragraph or the beginning of the next. In the essay on the apple plant job, the first transitional sentence is:

> I would not have minded the difficulty of the work so much if the pay had not been so poor.

In the above sentence, the key word *difficulty* reminds us of the point of the first supporting paragraph, while *pay* tells us the point to be developed in the second supporting paragraph.

Activity

Here is the other transitional sentence in the essay:

> But even more than the low pay, what upset me about my apple plant job were the working conditions.

Complete the following statement: In the above sentence, the key words ____________________ echo the point of the second supporting paragraph, and the key words ____________________ announce the topic of the third supporting paragraph.

CONCLUDING PARAGRAPH

The concluding paragraph often summarizes the essay by briefly restating the thesis and, at times, the main supporting points of the essay. In addition, the writer often presents a concluding thought or two about the subject of the paper.

Activity

1. Which sentence in the concluding paragraph of "My Job in an Apple Plant" restates the thesis and supporting points of the essay?

   ______ First   ______ Second

2. Which sentence contains the concluding thought of the essay?

   ______ First   ______ Second

Essays to Consider

Read the three student essays below and then answer the questions that follow.

Giving Up a Baby

As I awoke, I overheard a nurse say, "It's a lovely baby boy. How could a mother give him up?" "Be quiet," another voice said. "She's going to wake up soon." Then I heard the baby cry, but I never heard him again. Three years ago, I gave up my child to two strangers, people who wanted a baby but could not have one. I was in pain over my decision, and I can still hear the voices of people who said I was selfish or crazy. But the reasons I gave up my child were important ones, at least to me.

I gave up my baby, first of all, because I was very young. I was only seventeen, and I was unmarried. Because I was so young, I did not yet feel the desire to have and raise a baby. I knew that I would be a child raising a child and that, when I had to stay home to care for the baby, I would resent the loss of my freedom. I might also blame the baby for that loss. In addition, I had not had the experiences in life that would make me a responsible, giving parent. What could I teach my child, when I barely knew what life was all about myself?

Besides my age, another factor in my decision was the problems my parents would have. I had dropped out of high school before graduation, and I did not have a job or a chance of one, at least for a while. My parents would have to support my child and me, possibly for years. My mom and dad had already struggled to raise their family and were not well off financially. I knew I could not burden them with an unemployed teenager and her baby. Even if I eventually got a job, my parents would have to help raise my child. They would have to be full-time baby-sitters while I tried to make a life of my own. Because my parents are good people, they would have done all this for me. But I felt I could not ask for such a big sacrifice from them.

The most important factor in my decision was, I suppose, a selfish one. I was worried about my own future. I didn't want to marry the baby's father. I realized during the time I was pregnant that we didn't love each other. My future as an unmarried mother with no education or skills would certainly have been limited. I would be struggling to survive, and I would have to give up for years my dreams of getting a job and my own car and apartment. It is hard to admit, but I also considered the fact that, with a baby, I would not have the social life most young people have. I would not be able to stay out late, go to parties, or feel carefree and irresponsible, for I would always have an enormous responsibility waiting for me at home. With a baby, the future looked limited and insecure.

In summary, thinking about my age, my responsibility to my parents, and my own future made me decide to give up my baby. As I look back today at my decision, I know that it was the right one for me at the time.

Sports-Crazy America

Almost all Americans are involved with sports in some way. They may play basketball or volleyball or go swimming or skiing. They may watch football or basketball games on the high school, college, or professional level. Sports may seem like an innocent pleasure, but it is important to look under the surface. In reality, sports have reached a point where they play too large a part in daily life. They take up too much media time, play too large a role in the raising of children, and give too much power and prestige to athletes.

The overemphasis on sports can be seen most obviously in the vast media coverage of athletic events. It seems as if every bowl game play-off, tournament, trial, bout, race, meet, and match is shown on one television channel or another. On Saturday and Sunday, a check of TV Guide will show almost forty sports programs on UHF and VHF alone, and many more on cable stations. In addition, sports makes up about 30 percent of local news at six and eleven, and network news shows often devote several minutes of world news to major American sports events. Radio offers a full roster of games and a wide assortment of sports talk shows. Furthermore, many daily papers such as USA Today are devoting more and more space to sports coverage, often in an attempt to improve circulation. The paper with the biggest sports section is the one people will buy.

The way we raise and educate our children also illustrates our sports mania. As early as six or seven, kids are placed into little leagues, often to play under screaming coaches and pressuring parents. Later, in high school, students who are singled out by the school and by the community are not those who are best academically but those who are best athletically. And college sometimes seems to be more about sports than about learning. America may be the only country in the world where people often think of their colleges as teams first and schools second. The names Penn State, Notre Dame, and Southern Cal mean "sports" to the public.

Our sports craziness is especially evident in the prestige given to athletes in America. For one thing, we reward them with enormous salaries. In 1980, for example, baseball players averaged $150,000 a year; the average annual salary in America is $15,000. Besides their huge salaries, athletes receive the awe, admiration, and sometimes the votes of the public. Kids look up to a Magic Johnson or a Roger Clemons as a true hero, while adults wear the jerseys and jackets of their favorite teams. Ex-players become senators and congressmen. And an athlete like Chris Evert or John Elway needs to make only one commercial for advertisers to see the sales of a product boom.

Americans are truly mad about sports. Perhaps we like to see the competitiveness we experience in our daily lives acted out on playing fields. Perhaps we need heroes who can achieve clear-cut victories in the space of only an hour or two. Whatever the reason, the sports scene in this country is more popular than ever.

An Interpretation of Lord of the Flies

Modern history has shown us the evil that exists in human beings. Assassinations are common, governments use torture to discourage dissent, and six million Jews were exterminated during World War II. In Lord of the Flies, William Golding describes a group of schoolboys shipwrecked on an island with no authority figures to control their behavior. One of the boys soon yields to dark forces within himself, and his corruption symbolizes the evil in all of us. First, Jack Merridew kills a living creature; then, he rebels against the group leader; and finally, he seizes power and sets up his own murderous society.

The first stage in Jack's downfall is his killing of a living creature. In Chapter 1, Jack aims at a pig but is unable to kill. His upraised arm pauses "because of the enormity of the knife descending and cutting into living flesh, because of the unbearable blood," and the pig escapes. Three chapters later, however, Jack leads some boys on a successful hunt. He returns triumphantly with a freshly killed pig and reports excitedly to the others, "I cut the pig's throat." Yet Jack twitches as he says this, and he wipes his bloody hands on his shorts as if eager to remove the stains. There is still some civilization left in him.

After the initial act of killing the pig, Jack's refusal to cooperate with Ralph shows us that this civilized part is rapidly disappearing. With no adults around, Ralph has made some rules. One is that a signal fire must be kept burning. But Jack tempts the boys watching the fire to go hunting, and the fire goes out. Another rule is that at a meeting, only the person holding a special seashell has the right to speak. In Chapter 5, another boy is speaking when Jack rudely tells him to shut up. Ralph accuses Jack of breaking the rules. Jack shouts: "Bollocks to the rules! We're strong--we hunt! If there's a beast, we'll hunt it down! We'll close in and beat and beat and beat--!" He gives a "wild whoop" and leaps off the platform, throwing the meeting into chaos. Jack is now much more savage than civilized.

The most obvious proof of Jack's corruption comes in Chapter 8, when he establishes his own murderous society. Insisting that Ralph is not a "proper chief" because he does not hunt, Jack asks for a new election. After he again loses, Jack announces, "I'm going off by myself. . . . Anyone who wants to hunt when I do can come too." Eventually, nearly all the boys join Jack's "tribe." Following his example, they paint their faces like savages, sacrifice to "the beast," brutally murder two of their schoolmates, and nearly succeed in killing Ralph as well. Jack has now become completely savage--and so have the others.

Through Jack Merridew, then, Golding shows how easily moral laws can be forgotten. Freed from grown-ups and their rules, Jack learns to kill living things, defy authority, and lead a tribe of murdering savages. Jack's example is a frightening reminder of humanity's potential for evil. The "beast" the boys try to hunt and kill is actually within every human being.

■ Questions

1. Circle the letter of the essay in which the thesis statement appears in the last sentence of the introductory paragraph.
   a. "Baby"
   b. "Sports"
   c. *"Flies"*
2. In *"Flies,"* which sentence of the introductory paragraph contains the plan of development?
   a. Third
   b. Fourth
   c. Fifth
3. Which method of introduction is used for "Baby"?
   a. General to narrow
   b. Stating importance of topic
   c. Incident or story
   d. Questions

4. Complete the following brief outline of "Baby":

   I gave up my baby for three reasons:

   a. ______________________________

   b. ______________________________

   c. ______________________________

5. Which two essays use a transitional sentence between the first and second supporting paragraphs?
   a. "Baby"
   b. "Sports"
   c. *"Flies"*

6. *Complete the following statement:* Emphatic order is shown in the last supporting paragraph of "Baby" with the words *most important factor;* in the last supporting paragraph of "Sports" with the words ____________; in the last supporting paragraph of *"Flies"* with the words ____________.

7. Which essay uses time order as well as emphatic order to organize its three supporting paragraphs?
   a. "Baby"
   b. "Sports"
   c. *"Flies"*

8. List four major transitions used in the supporting paragraphs of *"Flies."*

   a. ______________

   b. ______________

   c. ______________

   d. ______________

9. Which two essays include a sentence in the concluding paragraph that summarizes the three supporting points?
   a. "Baby"
   b. "Sports"
   c. *"Flies"*

10. Which essay includes two final thoughts in its concluding paragraph?
    a. "Baby"
    b. "Sports"
    c. *"Flies"*

Planning the Essay

When you write an essay, advance planning is crucial for success. You should plan your essay in two ways:

1 Prepare a scratch outline. This should consist of a short statement of the thesis followed by the main supporting points for the thesis. Here is Gene's scratch outline for his essay on the apple plant:

Working at an apple plant was my worst job.
1. Hard work
2. Poor pay
3. Bad working conditions

Do not underestimate the value of this initial outline—or the work involved in achieving it. Be prepared to do a good deal of plain hard thinking at this first and most important stage of your paper.

2 Prepare a more detailed outline. The outline form that follows will serve as a guide. Your instructor may ask you to submit a copy of this form either before you actually write an essay or along with your finished essay.

FORM FOR PLANNING AN ESSAY

To write an effective essay, first prepare an outline, using a form like the one that follows.

	Opening remarks
Introduction	***Thesis statement*** ______________________________
	______________________________
	Plan of development

Body	***Topic sentence 1*** ______________________________ ______________________________ Specific supporting evidence
	Topic sentence 2 ______________________________ ______________________________ Specific supporting evidence
	Topic sentence 3 ______________________________ ______________________________ Specific supporting evidence
Conclusion	Summary, closing remarks, or both

Essay Writing Assignments

Hints: Keep the following points in mind when writing an essay on any of the topics below.

1 Your first step must be to plan your essay. Prepare both a scratch outline and a more detailed outline, as explained on the preceding pages.

2 While writing your essay, use the checklist below to make sure your essay touches all four bases of effective writing.

Base 1: Unity

______ Clearly stated thesis in the introductory paragraph of your paper

______ All the supporting paragraphs on target in backing up your thesis

Base 2: Support

______ Three separate supporting points for your thesis

______ *Specific* evidence for each of the three supporting points

______ *Plenty* of specific evidence for each supporting point

Base 3: Coherence

______ Clear method of organization

______ Transitions and other connecting words

______ Effective introduction and conclusion

Base 4: Sentence Skills

______ Clear, error-free sentences (as listed on the inside front cover of this book)

1 Your House or Apartment

Write an essay on the advantages or disadvantages (not both) of the house or apartment where you live. In your introductory paragraph, describe briefly the place you plan to write about. End the paragraph with your thesis statement and a plan of development. Here are some suggestions for thesis statements:

> The best features of my apartment are its large windows, roomy closets, and great location.

The drawbacks of my house are its unreliable oil burner, tiny kitchen, and old-fashioned bathroom.

An inquisitive landlord, sloppy neighbors, and platoons of cockroaches came along with our rented house.

My apartment has several advantages, including friendly neighbors, lots of storage space, and a good security system.

■ 2 A Big Mistake

Write an essay about the biggest mistake you made within the past year. Describe the mistake and show how the effects of that action have convinced you it was the wrong thing to do. For instance, if you write about ''taking on a full-time job while going to school'' as your biggest mistake, show the problems that action caused. (You might discuss such matters as low grades, constant exhaustion, and poor performance at work, for example.)

To get started, make a list of all the things you did last year that, with hindsight, now seem to be mistakes. Then pick out the action that has had the most serious consequences for you. Make a brief outline to guide you as you write, as in the examples below.

Thesis: Separating from my husband was the worst mistake I made last year.
1. Children have suffered
2. Financial troubles
3. Loneliness

Thesis: Buying a used car to commute to school was the worst mistake of last year.
1. Unreliable--late for class or missed class
2. Expenses for insurance, repairs
3. Led to an accident

■ 3 A Valued Possession

Write an essay about a valued material possession you own. Here are some suggestions:

Car	Appliance
Portable radio	Cassette deck
TV set	Photograph album
Piece of furniture	Piece of clothing
Piece of jewelry	Stereo system (car or home)
Camera	Piece of hobby equipment

In your introductory paragraph, describe the possession: tell what it is, when and where you got it, and how long you have owned it. Your thesis statement should center on the idea that there are several reasons this possession is so important to you. In each of your supporting paragraphs, provide details to back up one of the reasons.

For example, here is a brief outline of an essay written about a leather jacket:

1. It is comfortable.
2. It wears well.
3. It makes me look and feel good.

4 Summarizing a Selection

Write an essay in which you summarize three of the study skills described on pages 247–259. Summarizing involves condensing material by highlighting main points and key supporting details. You can eliminate minor details and most examples given in the original material. You should avoid using the exact language in the original material; put the ideas into your own words.

The introductory paragraph of the essay and suggested topic sentences for the supporting paragraphs are provided below. In addition to developing the supporting paragraphs, you should write a brief conclusion for the essay.

Introductory Paragraph

Using Study Skills

Why do some students in a college class receive A grades, while others get D's and F's? Are some people just naturally smarter? Are other students doomed to failure? Motivation--willingness to do the work--is a factor in good grades. But the main difference between successful and unsuccessful students is that the ones who do well have mastered the specific skills needed to handle college work. Fortunately, these skills can be learned by anyone. Doing well in college depends on knowing how to . . . [*Complete this sentence with the three study skills you decide to write about.*]

Suggested Topic Sentences for the Supporting Paragraphs (Choose Any Three)

Time control is one aid to success as a student. . . .

Another aid is the use of memory techniques. . . .

Knowing how to concentrate is another essential skill. . . .

Studying a textbook effectively is another key to success. . . .

Perhaps the most crucial step of all is effective classroom note-taking. . . .

■ 5 How Study Skills Help

You may already be practicing some of the study skills described on pages 247–259. If so, write an essay on how study skills are helping you to succeed in school. Your thesis might be, "Study skills are helping me to succeed in college." You could organize the essay by describing, in separate paragraphs, how three different study skills have improved your work. Your topic sentences might be similar to these:

First of all, time control has helped me to make the best use of my time.

In addition, taking good notes in class has enabled me to do well in discussions and on tests.

Finally, I can study a textbook effectively now.

Alternatively, begin applying some of the techniques and be prepared to write an essay at a later time on how the study skills helped you become a better student. Or you might want to write about three study techniques of your own that have helped you succeed in your studies.

■ 6 Single Life

Write an essay on the advantages or drawbacks of single life. To get started, make a list of all the advantages and drawbacks you can think of for single life. Advantages might include:

Fewer expenses
Fewer responsibilities
More personal freedom
More opportunities to move or travel

Drawbacks might include:

Parental disapproval
Being alone at social events
No companion for shopping, movies, and so on
Sadness at holiday time

After you make up two lists, select the thesis for which you feel you have more supporting material. Then organize your material into a scratch outline. Be sure to include an introduction, a clear topic sentence for each supporting paragraph, and a conclusion.

Alternatively, write an essay on the advantages or drawbacks of married life. Follow the directions given above.

■ 7 Influences on Your Writing

Are you as good a writer as you want to be? Write an essay analyzing the reasons you have become a good writer or explaining why you are not as good as you'd like to be. Begin by considering some factors that may have influenced your level of writing ability.

Your family background: Did you see people writing at home? Did your parents respect and value the ability to write?

Your school experience: Did you have good writing teachers? Did you have a history of failure or success with writing? Was writing fun, or was it a chore? Did your school emphasize writing?

Social influences: How did your school friends do at writing? What were your friends' attitudes toward writing? What feelings about writing did you pick up from TV or the movies?

You might want to organize your essay by describing the three greatest influences on your writing skill (or lack of writing skill). Show how each of these has contributed to the present state of your writing.

■ 8 A Major Decision

All of us come to various crossroads in our lives—times when we must make an important decision about which course of action to follow. Think about a major decision you had to make (or one you are planning to make). Then write an essay on the reasons for your decision. In your introduction, describe the decision you have reached. Each of the body paragraphs that follow should fully explain one of the reasons for your decision. Here are some examples of major decisions that often confront people:

Enrolling in or dropping out of college
Accepting or quitting a job
Getting married or divorced
Breaking up with a boyfriend or girlfriend
Having a baby
Moving away from home

Student papers on this topic include the essay on page 222 and the paragraphs on page 16.

■ 9 Reviewing a TV Show or Movie

Write an essay about a television show or movie you have seen very recently. The thesis of your essay will be that the show (or movie) has both good and bad features. (Be sure that you evaluate only one episode if you are writing about a TV series.)

In your first supporting paragraph, briefly summarize the show or movie. Don't get bogged down in small details here; just describe briefly the major characters and give the highlights of the action.

In your second supporting paragraph, explain what you feel are the best features of the show or movie. Listed below are some examples of good features you might write about:

A suspenseful, ingenious, or realistic plot
Good acting
Good scenery or special effects
A surprise ending
Good music
Believable characters

In your third supporting paragraph, explain what you feel are the worst features of the show or movie. Here are some possibilities:

Farfetched, confusing, or dull plot
Poor special effects
Bad acting
Cardboard characters
Unrealistic dialog

Remember to cover only a few features in each paragraph; do not try to include everything.

■ 10 Good Qualities

We are often quick to point out a person's flaws, saying, for example, "That teacher is conceited," "My boss has no patience," or "My sister is lazy." We are usually equally hard on ourselves; we constantly analyze our own faults. We rarely, though, spend as much time thinking about another person's, or our own, good qualities. Write an essay on the good qualities of a particular person. The person might be a teacher, job supervisor, friend, relative, some other person you know well, or even yourself.

In your introductory paragraph, give some brief background information about the person you are describing. And include in your thesis statement a plan of development that names the three qualities you will write about. Here are several suggestions:

Patience, fairness, and kindness are my boss's best qualities.

My boyfriend is hardworking, ambitious, and determined.

Our psychology instructor has a good sense of humor, a strong sense of justice, and a genuine interest in his students.

When planning your paper, you may find it helpful to look at the positive qualities included in the list on page 122.

■ 11 Your High School

Imagine that you are an outside consultant called in as a neutral observer to examine the high school you attended. After your visit, you must send the school board a five-paragraph letter in which you describe the most striking features (good, bad, or a combination of both) of the school and the evidence for each of these features.

In order to write the letter, you may want to think about the following features of your high school:

The attitude of the teachers, student body, or administration

The condition of the buildings, classrooms, recreational areas, and so on

The curriculum

How classes are conducted

Extracurricular activities

Crowded or uncrowded conditions

Be sure to include an introduction, a clear topic sentence for each supporting paragraph, and a conclusion.

■ 12 Reacting to a Reading Selection

Read the following article about a boy who committed suicide. (The story is true, but the names of the persons involved have been changed for the sake of privacy.) Then do the activities that follow the article.

A Suicide at Twelve--"Why, Steve?"*
By Richard E. Meyer

He lived to be almost thirteen. Walnut eyes. Brown thatch. Boy Scout. Altar boy. He grew up in white, middle-class America. He played football, and he played baseball. His mother, father, two brothers, and sister loved him. On the fourth day of the eleventh month of his twelfth year, a sunny afternoon in suburban Cincinnati, he walked down his favorite trail in the woods behind his house, climbed a tree, knotted a rope, and hanged himself.

Why, Steve?

In the past year, at least 210 others as young as Steve Dailey killed themselves in the United States. Reported suicides among the very young have more than doubled in twenty years. Even adjusted for population growth, the rate has climbed. The story of Steve Dailey, all-American boy, is an American tragedy: a story about the good life and the possibilities it offers for hidden pressure, subtle loneliness, quiet frustration--and unanswered questions.

Why, Steve?

Steven Dailey was born July 30, 1961, in the Cincinnati suburb of Clifton. One month after his first birthday, his parents, Sue and Charles Dailey, presented him with a brother, Mike. The two boys would become good friends. When Steve was two or a little older, Grandpa Rafton, in charge of the tailors at MacGregor, the sporting goods company which made uniforms for the Cincinnati Reds, presented Steve and Mike with baseball uniforms of their own, cut in the Reds' own patterns from the Reds' own cloth. Steve's had pitcher Jimmy O'Toole's old number, 31, sewn on the back.

Almost from the day he was married, Charles Dailey worked with Boy Scouts, first as an assistant scoutmaster for a year, then as a scoutmaster for five. When Steve and Mike were still toddlers, he took them along to Scout meetings. One night, he told a meeting of Scout parents: "You know, these boys are growing up awfully fast. If you're ever going to get to know your sons, you better get to know them now--because soon they're going to be at an age when you can't really get to know them."

In the second grade, Steve entered St. Catherine's School, in the parish where the Daileys had moved in the suburb of Westwood. His father became a volunteer football coach in St. Catherine's growing athletic program. Steve Dailey was big enough to play second level, or "pony," football. But he got paired in practice against a youngster everybody called Mugsy. "After Mugsy kind of tore him up a few times, he decided that maybe he ought to play 'bandits' a year and kind of find out what it's all about first," his father remembers. "Bandits" are the beginners. "That kinda bugged the devil out of me," Steve's father says. Charles Dailey thinks he probably told his son he

* Richard E. Meyer, "A Suicide at Twelve: 'Why, Steve?' " Reprinted by permission of Associated Press.

was disappointed. "But Steve says, 'Well, I just don't want to play "pony" ball. I'm just not good enough.' And it was probably a good choice on his part. But that was at the stage when I really wanted him to be the best football player in the world, you know. And I wanted him to be better."

Steve preferred quieter pursuits. He started a stamp collection. At seven, he caught his first fish--a little bluegill he tugged from the lake at Houston Woods State Park on a camping trip with his family. In 1969, when he was eight years old, Steve joined the Cub Scouts. He advanced to Webelos, where he met Dan Carella, who would become his assistant scoutmaster. Just before becoming a full-fledged Boy Scout, Steve was given Cub Scouting's highest award, the Arrow of Light.

Steve was graduated from the "bandits" after a year of learning the fundamentals of football. He played "pony" football for two years. But he was a large boy, and he found himself paired off against Mugsy again. Charles Dailey resigned himself: "Steve didn't mind getting knocked down, getting blocked out and all that kind of stuff; but he just did not have the--what?--the killer instinct."

In school, Steve got B's and C's. He received his First Communion, was confirmed, and learned how to serve Mass. He was a faithful altar boy who kept his serving appointments on holidays and vacations. But he wasn't above draining the last few drops of altar wine--or clowning with the incense in the vestry. By 1972, when he was eleven, Steve was well on his way toward his most important goal: to become an Eagle Scout. He worked at it steadily. By now his father was a Scout commissioner. He went along with Steve and his troop on most of their hikes and campouts. And he counseled Steve on five of the dozen merit badges he earned.

"Steve went after the merit badges that took a little more brains and thought," says Dan Carella. "He was sensitive--not a rough kid. He wasn't a real loner, but he wasn't outgoing as much as some of the other kids. He liked to be with the older boys and the grown-ups. But there were a lot of older boys and younger ones, and he was in between. That's one of the reasons he had no real close buddies. I can't really remember ever seeing him with any close buddy."

At home, Steve and Mike started a beer-can collection. Steve learned to play chess. He read Hardy Boy mysteries. He got a new ten-speed bicycle for Christmas. And he went on a month-long camping trip to California with the whole family: Mike, sister Kay, and a new Dailey, his smallest brother, Jamie. Everybody visited Disneyland.

Back home, Sue and Charles Dailey noticed something--Mike was always outside playing baseball with the kids in the neighborhood. Steve preferred being alone. He worked on Scout projects or watched color television. His father thought it was because the other kids made up street rules for their game--and Steve insisted on playing by the correct rules.

By now Steve's father was athletic director at St. Catherine's. Steve worked long hours at fund-raising for the Dads' Club, which sponsored the parish teams. He took over the popcorn concession at basketball tournaments. "He'd get upset when I'd suggest he take a break and try to get some other kid to replace him so he could go watch the games," says Jay Deakin, past president of the Dads' Club.

During the 1972–1973 school year, Steve played "pee-wee" football, one level above "pony." So did Mugsy. "Steve always fought him off, but he'd get beat all the time," his father says. "There'd be nights when Steve'd say, 'Oh, he really wiped me out!' "

"It didn't frighten Steve to get hit," says coach Ray Bertran. "However, some boys, they go out and they look to hit the other kid. He wasn't that way. In 'pee-wee' I guess he was the biggest kid, but he just wasn't that aggressive."

Steve wasn't on the starting team. But one October evening, he came home from practice smiling.

"What happened?" asked his father.

"Boy, I really wiped him out tonight. I really got him."

Steve meant Mugsy. It was probably the only time that ever happened, Charles Dailey says.

"Steve never missed a Scout meeting. He added up the requirements to become an Eagle, allotted himself so much time to accomplish each, and put himself on a rigid schedule.

"Steve was really good at Scouting," says Charles Dailey, "and I really had a lot of pride in that."

Steve set his heart on a trip to the Philmont Scout Ranch in New Mexico, and started working at Scout projects to earn his way. He planned to work at a Scout car wash. And he never missed a Scout paper drive.

But he didn't go in for Scout roughhousing or free-for-alls. "Steve had sort of soft feelings," remembers Carella. "He was a very personal boy. He stuck up for the guys who were being picked on. During the district camporee in Mt. Airy Forest, there were a couple of kids who--well, they weren't mamma's boys, but they just didn't know how to handle themselves. A lot of the boys preferred to tent with other kids. But Steve said, 'Well, I'll go with them.' "

Last fall, Steve's father told him he had to play a fall sport. "I was thinking in terms of football," says Charles Dailey. But St. Catherine's had started soccer. Steve said he'd rather play that.

"He was aggressive on the soccer team," says football coach George Kugler. Dan Carella describes him as "a good soccer player." But soccer was not the prestige sport at St. Catherine's.

"Football at St. Catherine's is king," says Bill Coffey, a history teacher.

Carella discounts any attempt by Charles Dailey to pressure his son to play football. But he adds: "There probably was some pressure in the situation. His father is athletic director. The situation says, 'Hey, how come you're not playing, Steve?' "

To make enough money to go to the Philmont Scout Ranch, Steve wanted a summer job. His father arranged for the job with a company that shares space in the Cardinal Engineering Building, where he works as a civil engineer. But he didn't tell Steve about the arrangement. Better, he thought, to have Steve ask--and think he got the job himself. Lump in his throat, Steve accompanied his father to the Cardinal Building one morning in April. Fortified by a cup of chocolate milk and a donut from a bakery along the way, Steve marched in--and came out with a job making catalogs and cleaning up for 75 cents an hour starting when school let out this summer.

"Boy, he was a king then," Charles Dailey remembers.

Steve also got a newspaper route, with the weekly Press, which circulates in Westwood. That money would go toward Philmont. And he made arrangements with Aunt Beth McGinnis to mow her lawn for two dollars whenever it needed it. That would go toward Philmont, too.

In his own way, Steve Dailey was shy. When his mother went from room to room at night to check on her brood, she always got a kiss from Mike, a kiss from Kay, and a kiss from Jamie. But never from Steve. Kissing embarrassed him. His mother always thought: "Well, he'll come to me when he's ready."

On Mother's Day, Sunday, May 12, her children brought Sue Dailey breakfast in bed. Steve presented her with a terrarium he'd made in Scouts. And he put his arms around her and kissed her. By now, though, school wasn't going entirely well. Steve wasn't doing his homework for language arts. That was Margaret Linahan's class. And Steve was getting a D.

"In content subjects, like science and social studies, I suppose he could take his own path. But in English grammar there is only one way to go," Mrs. Linahan smiles. "As long as I'm your teacher." She told Sue and Charles Dailey their son's grades were falling.

"Hey, is something bothering you?" Steve's father asked him.

"No," Steve said.

"Hey, you know, if you fail anything you're going to be grounded in the yard the whole summer."

In Bill Coffey's history class, Steve slipped from an A to a B or B-plus. Coffey was one of his favorites. He, in turn, appreciated Steve's sense of humor. "In the last few weeks, he didn't talk as much," Coffey remembers. "He didn't participate. And his dry wit was no longer as present."

Steve paid a sentimental visit to Sister Marie Russell's fourth-grade classroom. "I wondered why he was not with his class," she recalls, eyes puzzled behind her glasses. "Why was he wandering in the hall? And why was he by himself? You'd think a twelve-year-old would be with the boys."

Though Steve was never what Bill Coffey calls "Joe Popularity," he was well-liked--and he was good friends with Ted Hutchinson, for instance, and Rick Flannery. But Charles Dailey was unaware that Steve had any close friends. He never went to any of his friends' houses to play--and never invited any of them to his house to play.

With spring came baseball, and a peak of activity in the Dailey household. "We would have to fix a pot of stew, where you could keep heating it up when people would come in and out, or chili, or something like that," Sue remembers. Her husband says: "Sometimes we'd just eat, and then the person that wasn't here, he'd have to warm up the stuff that was left."

Steve played on an intermediate-ability team. He was a starter. But manager Ray Kendrick says, "I'm not sure he really liked sports, at least not baseball. He wasn't that enthusiastic about it. . . ."

But now Charles Dailey headed in his spare time an athletic organization at St. Catherine's that totaled 110 coaches, almost all of them fathers who had volunteered. Four football teams . . . fourteen baseball teams . . . ten basketball teams . . . track . . . soccer . . . softball . . . volleyball . . . kickball. The parish sports budget totaled $11,491.

Steve's father says, "This year I think he wanted to play soccer again. But I told him that there wasn't any way, because in high school, well, he's just not going to be a soccer man . . . because he's plain too big, and never was real fast. I still had the hopes that this year he would finally find out, with the size and all on his side, that he would become more aggressive."

Steve Dailey, twelve years old, stood 5 feet, 5 inches, and weighed 140 pounds.

"Steve, you ready for football?" coach George Kugler asked him. "You ought to play. Get some fundamentals. You're gonna be a big kid. You can make tackle."

Ted Hutchinson remembers Steve Dailey saying: "My dad wants me to play football, but I'd rather play soccer."

Two weeks before the end of school, Bill Coffey asked him: "Steve, you gonna play football?"

"Yeah, I guess I have to," he shrugged. "My Dad wants me to lose 10 pounds because of the weight limit."

Steve put himself on another schedule, this time with weights. Across the top of a piece of notebook paper he marked places for the dates of each day until fall. Beneath that, he charted sit-ups, bench presses, snatches, lifts, push-ups, windmills, jumping jacks; he measured an oval in his backyard with a tape and started running laps.

Affectionately, Charles Dailey teased him about being a "big lop"--the nickname he'd been given when he'd grown to be 6 feet 2 inches, as a young man. But Mike told him Steve didn't like it. And he stopped.

On Sunday, May 26, Steve helped haul stones and build a form for the concrete foundation to a utility shed-workshop his father was putting up behind the house. He hurt his back and missed school on Monday. He missed baseball practice, too. And that was the second time--the first had been a short while before when he'd had to stay at home with Kay and Jamie while his mother took Mike to the doctor.

"Then he didn't show up for one of our games," says Ray Kendrick, the baseball manager. Charles Dailey thinks it was a make-up game. "I started someone else in his place," Kendrick says.

That week, smiling, Steve told Sister Marie Russell about his summer job. But he didn't dress up for Roaring Twenties Day in Bill Coffey's history class. Ted Hutchinson remembers: "He just sat there." And that week, Coffey remembers, he discussed Japanese hara-kiri in class. He recalls no reaction from Steve.

On Saturday, June 1, Steve's father took him to a Scout show. He bought Steve a souvenir patch. That evening Steve worked on his personal management merit badge, for which he drew up a budget. It set a fixed amount aside each month for the trip to Philmont. After dinner, he tried to show his family photo slides of Philmont, but the projector bulb blew out.

On Sunday, June 2, Steve helped clean the family camper for a Scout canoe trip the coming weekend. He wire-brushed the rust from its wheels and painted them white.

On Monday, June 3, he rode his bicycle in front of his house and hit a hole in the pavement. It pitched him over the handlebars. A neighbor was sure he'd been hurt, but he got up, looked around to be certain nobody had seen him and got back on his bike. One of its pedals was bent.

On Tuesday, June 4, two days before the end of school, Sue Dailey volunteered to staple the PTA bulletin together at St. Catherine's. She met Steve in the hall on his way to history. He called out, "Hi, Mom."

Margaret Linahan kept him after school to finish an assignment. When he got done, he found that Aunt Beth had already left. She was to have picked him up and taken him to her house so he could earn more Philmont money mowing the lawn. But she had biscuits in the oven and couldn't wait.

Steve walked home. He called his father at work: "I just want to tell you that Monday I wrecked my bike."

"Oh? Did you get hurt?"

"Yeah, I hurt my hand, and you know, it's pretty sore. I think I might have broken it."

Charles Dailey didn't think it was all that bad, or his son would have mentioned it before. He and Steve talked about the bicycle. Steve's father remembers saying, without raising his voice: "We'll take a look at it, and if you broke it that means you're going to have to pay for it."

"You know, I can't play ball, so I don't want to go to practice," Steve said.

"Well, you know, I think you ought to go, because you've missed here a few times, and if you're going to be part of the team you've got to go to practices, too."

"Well, I'm not gonna take my glove."

"I think that you ought to take the glove and all and just go on up."

Steve handed the telephone receiver to his mother, and she hung it up.

Steve walked out the back door. He had tears in his eyes. He went to the garage, found the rope, carried it down the trail to a dead tree in the woods. His father found his body the next morning. The baseball glove was nearby.

The terrible ifs accumulated:

Dan Carella: "If he'd come to me. . . ."

Sister Marie Russell: "Oh, if only I would have known, I would have gone out of my way to get him and really talk to him. . . ."

Margaret Linahan: "If I wouldn't have kept him after school. . . ."

Beth McGinnis: "If I would have just waited for him. . . ."

Sue Dailey: "If I'd have only said he didn't have to go to baseball practice. . . ."

Charles Dailey: "If I had gone back there [to the woods that night], he might have been able to keep his weight off the rope for a period of time, or something like that, and, you know, you could have helped him. . . ."

Steve's father says a police officer friend told him the rope wasn't tied, but only looped, around the tree limb. He believes his son didn't intend to die--but that the rope had held accidentally.

"Yet I don't question the fact that he got the rope and he went back there and he had tied the rope around his neck. You know, I just can't believe that Steve would really do that. Except that he had to have done it, I guess."

Other police officers and county coroner Philip Holman determined that the fastening around the tree limb was secure enough to rule out an accident. They declared Steve a suicide.

"Not infrequently, suicides are caused by intense anger or frustration," says Dr. Fedor Hagenauer, a pediatric psychiatrist at the University of Cincinnati. "Because this anger or frustration is addressed at people who are very important, children have a lot of guilty feelings about them. And then, because of the guilty feelings, and because the anger or frustration has to come out in some way, they might try to take it out on themselves . . . even with a token gesture, or going through the motions . . . maybe with a fantasy that they'll be rescued at the last minute . . . and they'll do it thinking, 'Everybody will see how unhappy I am and they'll learn and give in to what I'm unhappy about.' " It would have been impossible, he said, to predict Steve's fate.

The Rev. James Conway, who celebrated Requiem Mass at St. Catherine's, doesn't think Steve was morally responsible for his death.

During the Mass, Boy Scouts presented gifts to God symbolizing Steve's life. At Mike's suggestion, one was a soccer ball.

Your instructor may have you discuss the following questions with a small group of your classmates. If so, appoint one member to keep brief notes on how the group responds to each question, for a general class discussion may follow. Whether you work in a small group or answer the questions individually, be sure to provide *specific evidence from the text* to back up all your points and ideas.

Questions to Consider

1. What kind of boy was Steve? What words (for example, *quiet, active, bright, lazy, shy*) would you use to describe his personality? Be sure to provide details from the text to support the qualities that you name.
2. a. In what ways was Steve a highly organized person?
   b. Why was he so organized, do you think?
3. Why did Steve feel pressured to play football rather than soccer (which he preferred)?
4. a. What kind of person does Margaret Linahan, Steve's English teacher, seem to be?
   b. Do you think that she was a good teacher for Steve?
5. a. What kind of person does Steve's mother, Sue Dailey, seem to be?
   b. Do you think that she was a good mother for Steve?
6. a. What are some examples of how Charles Dailey was sensitive to his son?
   b. What are some examples of how Charles Dailey was insensitive to his son?
7. Why do you think Steve's father believes his death was accidental?
8. Do you think that Charles Dailey's love for his son was destructive?
9. Why do you think Steve killed himself at the point when he did?
10. Why does the writer end his piece with the detail of the soccer ball?

Writing Activity

Option 1: Imagine that you work for an adoption agency, and that Steve's father and mother have come to the agency to adopt a boy. After an investigation in which you learn all the details described in the article, would you deny or grant Steve's parents the right to adopt a boy? To make your decision, you will have to think carefully about and interpret the information about Steve's parents that is presented in the article.

Write a several-paragraph letter to your superior in which you recommend or do not recommend that they be granted the right of adoption. Include a brief introductory paragraph stating your recommendation (*thesis*) and summarizing briefly your reasons for the recommendation (*plan of development*). Then write a supporting paragraph for each of your reasons. Refer to specific words and actions of Steve's parents in developing the reasons for your recommendation.

Option 2: Write a several-paragraph essay in which you provide evidence from the text to support either one of the following points:

Steve's father and other adults in his life were insensitive to him and his needs.

Steve's father and other adults in his life should not be blamed for his suicide.

PART FIVE

SPECIAL SKILLS

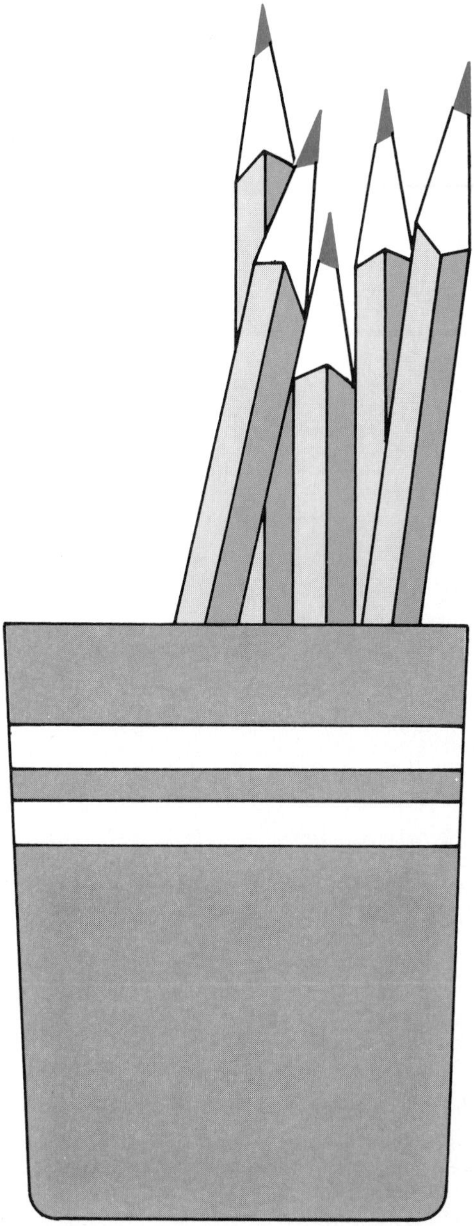

PREVIEW

Part Five presents skills that will help you in a variety of study or writing situations. "Key Study Skills" explains five skills that will make you a better student in all your courses. In "Writing an Exam Essay," you will learn how to prepare for and take the essay exams that are among the most common types of writing students do in college. Similarly, "Preparing a Summary," "Doing a Report," and "Writing a Résumé and Job Application Letter" provide explanations and models for three practical kinds of writing that you may need to know. Finally, "Using the Library" and "Writing a Research Paper" will prepare you for writing projects that require library research.

KEY STUDY SKILLS

Following are brief guides to several important reading and study skills needed for success in school. A short comprehension test follows each guide. The skills include class note-taking, time control, concentrating, studying a textbook, and memory training.

TAKING EFFECTIVE CLASSROOM NOTES

One of the most important single things you can do to perform well in a college course is to take effective class notes. The following hints should help you become a better note-taker.

First, attend class faithfully. Your alternatives—reading the text or someone else's notes, or both—cannot substitute for the experience of hearing ideas in person as someone presents them to you. Also, in class lectures and discussions, your instructor typically presents and develops the main ideas and facts of the course—the ones you will be expected to know on exams.

Another valuable hint is to make use of abbreviations while taking notes. Using abbreviations saves time when you are trying to get down a great deal of information. Abbreviate terms that recur frequently in a lecture and put a key to your abbreviations at the top of your notes. For example, in a sociology class, *eth* could stand for *ethnocentrism;* in a psychology class, *s-t mem* could stand for *short-term memory*. (When a lecture is over, you may want to go back and write out the terms you have abbreviated.) In addition, abbreviate words that often recur in any lecture. For instance, use *e* for *example; def* for *definition; info* for *information,* + for *and*), and so on. If you use the same abbreviations all the time, you will soon develop a kind of personal shorthand that makes taking notes much easier.

A third hint when taking notes is to be on the lookout for signals of importance. Write down whatever your teacher puts on the board. If he or she takes the time to put material on the board, it is probably important, and the chances are good that it will come up later on exams. Always write down definitions and enumerations. Enumerations are lists of items. They are signaled in such ways as: "The four steps in the process are . . ."; "There were three reasons for . . ."; "The two effects were . . ."; "Five characteristics of . . ."; and so on. Always number (1, 2, 3, etc.) such enumerations in your notes. They will help you understand relationships among ideas and organize the material of the lecture. Watch for emphasis words—words your instructor may use to indicate that something is important. Examples of such words are "This is an important reason . . ."; "A point that will keep coming up later . . ."; "The chief cause was . . ."; "The basic idea here is . . ."; and so on. Always write down the important statements announced by these and other emphasis words. Finally, if your instructor repeats a point, you can assume it is important. You might put an R for *repeated* in the margin, so that later you will know that your teacher has stressed it.

Next, be sure to write down the teacher's examples and mark them with an X. The examples help you understand abstract points. If you do not write them down, you are likely to forget them later when they are needed to help make sense of an idea.

Also, be sure to write down the connections between ideas. Too many students merely copy the terms the teacher puts on the board. They forget that, as time passes, the details that serve as connecting bridges between ideas quickly fade. You should, then, write down the relationships and connections in class. That way you'll have them to help tie together your notes later on.

Review your notes as soon as possible after class. You must make them as clear as possible while they are fresh in your mind. A day later may be too late, because forgetting sets in very quickly. Make sure that punctuation is clear, that all words are readable and correctly spelled, and that unfinished sentences are completed (or at least marked off so that you can check your notes with another student's). Add clarifying or connecting comments wherever necessary. Make sure important ideas are clearly marked. Improve the organization if necessary, so that you can see at a glance main points and relationships among them.

Finally, try in general to get down a written record of each class. You must do this because forgetting begins almost immediately. Studies have shown that within two weeks you are likely to have forgotten 80 percent or more of what you have heard. And in four weeks you are lucky if 5 percent remains! The significance of this is so crucial that it bears repeating: to guard against the relentlessness of forgetting, it is absolutely essential that you write down what you hear in class. Later on you can concentrate on working to understand fully and to remember the ideas that have been presented in class. And the more complete your notes are at this time of study, the more you are likely to learn.

Activity

Check your understanding by answering the following questions.

1. *True or false?* ______ Forgetting will begin several days after you have attended a class.
2. How would you abbreviate the term *traditional authority* during a fast-moving sociology lecture?

   ____

3. Often the most important single step you can take to perform well in a course is to
   a. sit where the instructor can see you and listen carefully.
   b. write down definitions and examples.
   c. be there and take effective notes.
   d. continue taking notes during discussion periods or at the end of a class.
4. Which of the following should be taken down in your notes?
   a. Enumerations
   b. Definitions
   c. Material written on the board
   d. All of the above
5. When you review your notes after a class, you should
   a. memorize them.
   b. clarify them.
   c. type them.
   d. reduce them.

ACHIEVING TIME CONTROL

Success in college depends on time control. Time control means that you deliberately organize and plan your time, instead of letting it drift by. Planning means that you should never be faced with a night-before-the-test "cram" session or an overdue term paper.

There are three steps involved in time control. *First,* you should prepare a large monthly calendar. Buy a calendar with a large white block around each date, or make one yourself. At the beginning of the college semester, circle important dates on this calendar. Circle the days on which tests are scheduled; circle the days papers are due. This calendar can also be used to schedule study plans. You can jot down your plans for each day at the beginning of the week. An alternative method would be to make plans for each day the night before. On Tuesday night, for example, you might write down "Read Chapter 5 in psychology" in the Wednesday block. Be sure to hang this calendar in a place where you will see it every day—your kitchen, your bedroom, even your bathroom!

The *second step* in time control is to have a weekly study schedule for the semester. To prepare this schedule, make up a chart that covers all the days of the week and all the waking hours in each day. Here is part of one student's schedule:

	Mon.	Tues.	Wed.	Thurs.	Fri.	Sat.	Sun.
6:00 A.M.							
7:00	B	B	B	B	B		
8:00	Math	STUDY	Math	STUDY	Math		
9:00	STUDY	Biology	STUDY	Biology	STUDY	Job	
10:00	Psychology	↓	Psychology	↓	Psychology	↓	
11:00	STUDY	English	English	English		↓	
12:00	L		L		L	↓	

On your schedule, mark in all the fixed hours in each day—hours for meals, classes, job (if any), and travel time. Next, mark in time blocks that you can *realistically* use for study each day. Depending on the number of courses you are taking and the demands of the courses, you may want to block off five, ten, or even twenty or more hours of study time a week. Keep in mind that you should not block off time for study that you do not truly intend to use for study. Otherwise, your schedule will be a meaningless gimmick. Also, remember that you should allow time for "rest and relaxation" in your schedule. You will be happiest, and able to accomplish the most, when you have time for both work and play.

The *third step* in time control is to make a daily or weekly "to do" list. This may be the most valuable time control method you ever use. On this list, you write down the things you need to do for the following day or the following week. If you choose to write a weekly list, do it on Sunday night. If you choose to write a daily list, do it the night before.

Here is part of one student's daily list:

To Do *Tuesday*

*1. *Review biology notes before class*
*2. *Proofread English paper due today*
3. *See Dick about game on Friday*
*4. *Gas for car*
5. *Read next chapter of psychology text*

You may use a three- by five-inch notepad or a small spiral-bound notebook for this list. Carry the list around with you during the day. Always concentrate on doing first the most important items on your list. Mark high-priority items with an asterisk and give them precedence over low-priority items in order to make the best use of your time. For instance, you may find yourself wondering what to do after dinner on Thursday evening. Among the items on your list are "Clean inside of car" and "Review chapter for math quiz." It is obviously more important for you to review your notes at this point; you can clean the car some other time. As you complete items on your "to do" list, cross them out. Do not worry about unfinished items. They can be rescheduled. You will still be accomplishing a great deal and making more effective use of your time.

Activity

Check your understanding by answering the following questions.

1. *True or false?* ______ Do not list personal chores on your "to do" list.
2. *True or false?* ______ On a large monthly calendar, you should circle the days that tests are scheduled and papers are due.
3. When you make up a "to do" list, you should
   a. schedule one-hour blocks of study time.
   b. mark down deadlines.
   c. decide on priorities.
   d. hang it on the wall.
4. On your weekly schedule, you should block out time periods for
   a. commuting time.
   b. study time.
   c. rest and relaxation.
   d. all of the above.

5. Circle the highest-priority item on the following ‘‘to do’’ list:
   a. Buy new shirt
   b. Study notes for tomorrow’s lab quiz
   c. Wax car
   d. Preview next chapter for Friday’s sociology class

SECRETS OF CONCENTRATION

Lack of concentration happens to everyone. But if you are a student, you cannot afford to let it happen too often. Nor can you merely say, ‘‘This time, I’m going to keep my mind on my work,’’ and have it magically happen. A much better method is to figure out what in particular is interfering with your concentration—and then to do something about it.

Causes of Lack of Concentration

What causes lack of concentration? It can happen, first of all, because of physical factors. If you are sick, hungry, thirsty, or sleepy, you will not be able to concentrate. Or the factors could be mental, not physical. You could be suffering from indecision: other things keep popping into your head, and you do not know what to do first. You could be distracted by daydreaming or worrying about a personal problem. Finally, the cause of your failure to concentrate could be external. Your study environment could be the problem if it is too warm or too cold, too noisy, or not properly lighted. If your study spot lacks the right equipment—yellow pads, pens and pencils, or a dictionary, for instance—distraction may result. Any of these factors can take your mind off the assignment.

How to Concentrate

Concentration allows you to focus on just one thought or bit of information at a time, eliminating the others. The first step in achieving a high level of concentration is having the right attitude. If you want to absorb something, you’ll do so, no matter what else is going on—as anyone glued to a television set in the middle of a family argument proves. Take a positive attitude—here’s a chance to learn something new. Or take a realistic attitude—the job simply has to be done today. And forget about how you felt or performed in the past. You are making a fresh start.

Next, create a good atmosphere if you want to concentrate. Choose a room or area where you can work without being disturbed. Find a desk or table and clear it off. Sit in a straight chair. On your desk or table, place a good light source, such as a gooseneck fluorescent lamp. Then, add the study equipment you'll need: textbooks and notebooks, dictionary, pens, pencils, paper, a clock, calendar, calculator, and so on. Keep this special area only for studying; when you sit down there, the atmosphere will say "Work!"

The third step toward concentration is planning study time. Make up a weekly schedule and block out regular study periods that you plan to stick to. Schedule at least one hour of study time for each hour of class time. Organized, preplanned study time can aid concentration—you know exactly when you will study, and you're sure that there won't be any conflicts then with other activities.

Finally, study with a goal in mind. Do not just read the history chapter; read it to discover the specific causes of World War II. Work quickly. Have a clock in sight or put your watch next to your book, and try to cover each page in a designated period of time. Plan to take a break after a certain number of pages; keep the break brief, however. Remember, you want to get the job done so you can go on to the next item on your schedule. If you do feel your concentration slipping as you study, put a pencil mark in the margin each time you get distracted. The mark will remind you to concentrate.

What Not to Do: A Few Warnings

When you are trying to concentrate, watch out for several pitfalls. For one thing, do not try to study when you are physically uncomfortable. If you are too warm, open a window. If you are hungry, eat. Make sure you get enough sleep. And make a real effort to exercise regularly. Your mind will concentrate better when your body is in shape.

In addition, do not allow distractions to disturb you. Some people claim that noise does not bother them when they are trying to study. In general, though, it helps to avoid noisy places such as a college cafeteria or a lounge, and to keep the radio and television turned off. Do not waste brain power blocking out sounds that intrude on your concentration. Should a distracting thought get in your way, write it down and go back to your studying. You can always deal with the idea later, and once it's written down, it can't be lost.

Last of all, don't be a passive learner. When you read, do not just sit quietly and let your eyes roam across the page. Get involved with the assignment. Have a pen or pencil in hand and use it to underline, check, and star material. Write key words and questions in the margins. Turn the chapter headings and subheadings into questions and look for the answers as you read. You might want to close your eyes after you have read several paragraphs and see if you can restate what you have learned. If you cannot, go back, re-read, and try again. If nothing else works, read aloud. You'll hear the words as well as see them—and the more senses you involve in studying, the easier the process will be.

Activity

Check your understanding by answering the following questions.

1. *True or false?* ______ Lack of concentration could be caused by hunger.
2. The first step in achieving a high level of concentration is
   a. buying a fluorescent light.
   b. solving a personal problem.
   c. studying with a goal in mind.
   d. having the right attitude.
3. *True or false?* ______ Concentrating means reading a textbook selection as slowly as you can.
4. Being an active learner means
   a. underlining material.
   b. turning headings into questions.
   c. trying to recall what you read.
   d. all of the above.
5. A good study area should have
   a. soothing music.
   b. a straight chair.
   c. a telephone.
   d. exercise equipment.

TEXTBOOK STUDY SYSTEM

In many college courses, success means being able to read and study a textbook skillfully. For many students, unfortunately, textbooks are heavy going. After an hour or two of study, the textbook material is as formless and as hard to understand as ever. But there is a way to attack even the most difficult textbook and make sense of it. Use a sequence in which you preview a chapter, mark it, take notes on it, and then study the notes.

Previewing

Previewing a selection is an important first step to understanding. Taking the time to preview a section or chapter can give you a bird's-eye view of the way the material is organized. You will have a sense of where you are beginning, what you will cover, and where you will end.

There are several steps in previewing a selection. First, study the title. The title is the shortest possible summary of a selection and will often tell you the limits of the material you will cover. For example, the title ''FDR and the

Supreme Court'' tells you to expect a discussion of President Roosevelt's dealing with the Court. You know that you will probably not encounter any material dealing with FDR's foreign policies or personal life. Next, read over quickly the first and last paragraphs of the selection; these may contain important introductions to, and summaries of, the main ideas. Then examine briefly the headings and subheadings in the selection. Together, the headings and subheadings are a mini-outline of what you are reading. Headings are often main ideas or important concepts in capsule form; subheadings are breakdowns of ideas within main areas. Finally, read the first sentence of some paragraphs, look for words set off in **boldface** or *italics,* and look at pictures or diagrams. After you have previewed a selection in this way, you should have a good general sense of the material to be read.

Marking

You should mark a textbook selection at the same time that you read it through carefully. Use a felt-tip highlighter to shade material that seems important, or use a regular ballpoint pen and put a symbol in the margin next to the material: a star, a check, or NB (for *nota bene,* a Latin phrase meaning ''note well''). What to mark is not as mysterious as some students believe. You should try to find main ideas by looking for the following clues: definitions and examples, enumerations, and emphasis words.

1 ***Definitions and examples:*** Definitions are often among the most important ideas in a selection. They are particularly significant in introductory courses in almost any subject area, where much of your learning involves mastering the specialized vocabulary of that subject. In a sense, you are learning the ''language'' of psychology or business or whatever the subject might be.

   Most definitions are abstract, and so they usually are followed by one or more examples to help clarify their meaning. Always mark off definitions and at least one example that makes a definition clear to you. In a psychology text, for example, we are told that ''rationalization is an attempt to reduce anxiety by deciding that you have not really been frustrated.'' Several examples follow, among them: ''A young man, frustrated because he was rejected when he asked for a date, convinces himself that the girl is not very attractive and is much less interesting than he had mistakenly supposed.''

2 ***Enumerations:*** Enumerations are lists of items (causes, reasons, types, and so on) that are numbered 1, 2, 3, . . . or that could easily be numbered in an outline. They are often signaled by addition words. Many of the paragraphs in this book use words like *First of all, Another, In addition,* and *Finally* to signal items in a series. Textbooks use this very common and effective organizational method as well.

3 ***Emphasis words:*** Emphasis words tell you that an idea is important. Common emphasis words include phrases such as *a major event, a key feature, the chief factor, important to note, above all,* and *most of all.* Here is an example: "The most significant contemporary use of marketing is its application to nonbusiness areas, such as political parties."

Note-Taking

Next, you should take notes. Go through the chapter a second time, re-reading the most important parts. Try to write down the main ideas in a simple outline form. For example, in taking notes on a psychology selection, you might write down the heading "Kinds of Defense Mechanisms." Below the heading you would number and describe each kind and give an example of each.

Defense Mechanisms

a. Definition: unconscious attempts to reduce anxiety

b. Kinds:

(1) Rationalization: An attempt to reduce anxiety by deciding that you have not really been frustrated
Example: A man turned down for a date decides that the woman was not worth going out with anyway

(2) Projection: Projecting onto other people motives or thoughts of one's own
Example: A wife who wants to have an affair accuses her husband of having one

Studying Notes

To study your notes, use the method of repeated self-testing. For example, look at the heading "Kinds of Defense Mechanisms" and say to yourself, "What are the kinds of defense mechanisms?" When you can recite them, then say to yourself, "What is rationalization?" "What is an example of rationalization?" Then ask yourself, "What is projection?" "What is an example of projection?" After you learn each section, review it, and then go on to the next section.

Do not simply read your notes; keep looking away and seeing if you can recite them to yourself. This self-testing is the key to effective learning.

In conclusion, remember this sequence in order to deal with a textbook: previewing, marking, taking notes, studying the notes. Approaching a textbook in this methodical way will give you very positive results. You will no longer feel bogged down in a swamp of words, unable to figure out what you are supposed to know. Instead, you will understand exactly what you have to do, and how to go about doing it.

Activity

Check your understanding by answering the following questions.

1. *True or false?* ______ Previewing a textbook means marking off definitions and examples.
2. A textbook writer might let you know an idea is important by using
   a. stars.
   b. emphasis signals.
   c. illustrations.
   d. addition signals.
3. Previewing a textbook selection includes
   a. reading the title.
   b. looking at diagrams.
   c. examining subheadings.
   d. all of the above.
4. *True or false?* ______ Headings are usually set off in larger type or different-colored ink.
5. Enumerations are
   a. definitions.
   b. outlines.
   c. lists of items.
   d. examples.

BUILDING A MORE POWERFUL MEMORY

The Two Basic Steps in Remembering

Effective studying and remembering require, first, that you organize the material to be learned. Organization means preparing study notes made up of headings and subheadings, definitions and examples, enumerations, and other important points. The very process of organizing material and condensing it to the main points will help you understand and remember it.

After you have organized your subject material, memorize it through repeated self-testing. Look at the first item in your notes; then look away and try to repeat it to yourself. When you can, look at the next item; then look away and try to repeat it. When you can repeat the second item, go back without looking at your notes and try to repeat both the first and second items. This constant review is at the heart of self-testing. After you can repeat the first two items without looking at your notes, go on to the third item. When you learn it, try to repeat all three items without looking at your paper. After you learn each new item, go back and test yourself on all the previous items you have studied.

Six Aids to Memorization

1 ***Intend to remember:*** The first aid to memory is intending to remember. This bit of advice appears to be so obvious that many people overlook its value. But if you have made the decision to remember something, and you then work at mastering it, you will remember. Anyone can have a bear-trap memory by working at it; no one is born with a naturally poor memory.

2 ***Overlearn:*** Overlearning is a second memory aid. If you study a subject beyond the time needed for perfect recall, you will increase the length of time that you will remember it. The method of repeated self-testing uses the principle of overlearning; you can also apply the principle by going over several times a lesson you have already learned perfectly.

3 ***Space memory work:*** Spacing memory work over several sessions, rather than a single long one, is the third aid. Just as with physical exercise, five two-hour sessions spaced over several days are more helpful than ten hours all at once. The spaced sessions allow material time to "sink in" (psychologists would say, "transfer from the short-term to the long-term memory"). Spacing the sessions also helps you "lock in" material you have studied in the first session but have begun to forget. Studies show that forgetting occurs most rapidly soon after learning ends—but that review within a day or two afterward counters much memory loss.

4 ***Study before bedtime:*** A fourth aid in memorizing material is studying just before going to bed. Do not watch the *Late Show* or allow any other interference between studying and sleep. Then be sure to review the material immediately upon arising in the morning. Set your clock a half hour earlier than usual so that you will have time to do this. The review in the morning will help "lock in" the material that you have studied the night before and that your mind has worked over during the night.

5 ***Use key words as "hooks":*** A fifth helpful tool is using key words in an outline as "hooks." Reduce your outline of a passage to a few key words and memorize those words. The key words you master will then serve as "hooks" that will help you pull back entire ideas into your memory.

6 ***Use memory formulas:*** Sixth and finally, another tool is using memory formulas to help you recall points under a main idea, items in a list, steps in a procedure, or other things arranged in a series. For example, you might remember the four methods used in behavior therapy (extinction, reinforcement, desensitization, and imitation) by writing down the first letter in each word (*e r d i*) and remembering the letters by forming an easily recalled catchphrase ("Ellen's rolling dice inside") or rearranging them to form an easily recalled word (*r i d e*). The letters serve as hooks that help you pull in words that are often themselves hooks for entire ideas.

Activity

Check your understanding by answering the following questions.

1. The two basic steps to remembering are organizing the material to be learned and
   a. studying before bedtime.
   b. testing yourself repeatedly.
   c. preparing study notes.
   d. memorizing definitions.
2. *True or false?* ______ Material is best studied in a single long session rather than spaced out over several sessions.
3. *True or false?* ______ Some people are born with naturally poor memories.
4. Overlearning means
   a. studying beyond the time needed for perfect recall.
   b. transferring facts to the short-term memory.
   c. using memory formulas.
   d. studying to the point of diminishing returns.
5. The first aid to memory is
   a. creating "hooks."
   b. self-testing.
   c. intending to remember.
   d. using study notes.

WRITING AN EXAM ESSAY

Examination essays are among the most common types of writing that you will do in college. They include one or more questions to which you must respond in detail, writing your answers in a clear, well-organized manner. This section describes five basic steps needed to prepare adequately for an essay test and to take the test. It is assumed, however, that you are already doing two essential things: first, attending class regularly and taking notes on what happens in class; second, reading your textbook and other assignments and taking notes on them. If you are not consistently going to class, reading your text, and taking notes in both cases, perhaps you should be asking yourself and talking with others (counselors, teachers, friends) about your feelings on being in school.

To write an effective exam essay, follow these five steps:

Step 1: Try to anticipate the probable questions on the exam.

Step 2: Prepare and memorize an informal outline answer for each question.

Step 3: Read exam directions and questions carefully, and budget your time.

Step 4: Prepare a brief outline before answering an essay question.

Step 5: Write a clear, well-organized essay.

Each step will be explained and illustrated on the pages that follow.

STEP 1: ANTICIPATE PROBABLE QUESTIONS

Anticipating probable questions is not as hard to do as you might think. Because exam time is limited, the instructor can give you only several questions to answer. He or she will reasonably focus on questions dealing with the most important parts of the subject. You probably can guess most of them as you make up a list of ten or more likely questions.

Your class notes are one key. What topics and ideas did your instructor spend a good deal of time on? Similarly, in your textbook, what ideas are emphasized? Usually the keys to the most important ideas are headings and subheadings, definitions and examples, enumerations, and ideas marked by emphasis signals. Also take advantage of any study guides that may have been given you, any questions you may have gotten on quizzes, and any review that your instructor may have provided in class. You should, then, be able to determine the most important areas of the subject and make up questions that cover them.

STEP 2: PREPARE AND MEMORIZE AN INFORMAL OUTLINE ANSWER FOR EACH QUESTION

Write out each question you have made up and, under it, list the main points that need to be discussed. Put important supporting information in parentheses after each main point. You now have an informal outline that you can memorize.

An Illustration of Step 2

One class was given a day to prepare for an essay exam. The students were told that the essay item would be "Describe six aids to memory." One student, Teri, made up the following outline answer.

Six Memory Aids

1. *Intend to remember (personal decision is crucial)*
2. *Overlearn (helps you remember longer)*
3. *Space memory work (several sessions rather than one long session)*
4. *Time before bed as a study period (no interference; review the next morning)*
5. *Use key words as "hooks" (help pull into memory whole ideas)*
6. *Memory formulas (letters serve as hooks to help you remember items in a series)*

IOSBKF (I often see Bill kicking footballs.)

Activity

See whether you can complete the following explanation of what Teri has done in preparing for the essay item.

> First, Teri wrote down the heading and numbered the different items under it. Also, in parentheses beside each point she added ________________. Next, she circled the key word for each hint and wrote down the first ________________ of each key word below her outline. She then used the first letter in each key word to make up a catchphrase she could remember easily. Finally, she ________________ herself repeatedly until she could recall the key words the letters stood for and the main points the key words represented.

STEP 3: LOOK AT THE EXAM CAREFULLY AND DO SEVERAL THINGS

First, read all test directions carefully. This seems like an obvious point, but people are often so anxious at the start of a test that they fail to read the instructions, and so they never understand clearly and completely just what they must do.

Second, read all the essay questions carefully, first noting the *direction word* or *words* in each question that tell you just what to do. For example, *enumerate,* or *list,* means "to number 1, 2, 3, and so on"; *illustrate* means "to explain by giving examples"; *compare* means "to give similarities"; *contrast* means "to give differences"; *summarize* means "to offer a condensed account of the main ideas."

Finally, roughly budget your time, depending on the point value of each question and its difficulty for you. Write in the test margin the time you give yourself to answer each question. This way you will not end the exam with too little time to respond to a question that you know you can answer.

An Illustration of Step 3

When Teri received the exam, she circled the direction word *Describe,* which she knew meant "Explain in detail." She also jotted a "30" in the margin when the teacher said that students would have a half hour to write their answers.

STEP 4: PREPARE A BRIEF OUTLINE BEFORE ANSWERING AN ESSAY QUESTION

Too many students make the mistake of anxiously and blindly starting to write. Instead, you should first jot down the main points you want to discuss in an answer. (Use the margin of the exam or a separate piece of scratch paper.) Then decide how you will order the points in your essay. Put 1 in front of the first point, 2 beside the second, and so on. You now have an informal outline to guide you as you write your essay answer.

If there is a question on an exam which is similar to the questions you anticipated and outlined at home, quickly write down the catchphrase that calls back the content of the outline. Below the catchphrase, write the key words represented by each letter in the catchphrase. The key words, in turn, will remind you of the ideas they represent. If you have prepared properly, this step will take only a minute or so, and you will have before you the guide you need to write a focused, supported, organized answer.

An Illustration of Step 4

Teri first recited her catchphrase to herself, using it as a guide to write down her memory formula (IOSBKF) at the bottom of the test sheet. The letters in the formula helped her call into memory the key words in her study outline, and she wrote down the words. Then in parentheses beside each word she added the supporting points she remembered.

By investing only a couple of minutes, Teri was able to reconstruct her study outline and give herself a clear and solid guide to use in writing her answer.

STEP 5: WRITE A CLEAR, WELL-ORGANIZED ESSAY

If you have followed the suggestions to this point, you have done all the preliminary work needed to write an effective essay. Be sure not to wreck your chances of getting a good grade by writing carelessly. Instead, as you prepare your response, keep in mind the principles of good writing: unity, support, coherence, and clear, error-free sentences.

First, start your essay with a sentence that clearly states what your paper will be about. Then make sure that everything in your paper relates to your opening statement.

Second, though you must obviously take time limitations into account, provide as much support as possible for each of your main points.

Third, use transitions to guide your reader through your answer. Words such as *first, next, then, however,* and *finally* make it easy for the reader to follow your train of thought.

Last, leave time to edit your essay for sentence-skills mistakes you may have made while you concentrated on writing your answer. Look for words omitted, miswritten, or misspelled (if it is possible, bring a dictionary with you); for awkward phrasings or misplaced punctuation marks; for whatever else may prevent the reader from understanding your thought. Cross out any mistakes and make your corrections neatly above the errors. If you want to change or add to some point, insert an asterisk at the appropriate spot, put another asterisk at the bottom of the page, and add the corrected or additional material there.

An Illustration of Step 5

Read through Teri's answer, reproduced here, and then do the activity that follows.

There are six aids to memory. One aid is to intend to remember. Making the ~~decison~~ decision that you are truly going to remember something is an important part of success. A second aid is overlearning. ~~Studing~~ Studying a lesson several more times after you know it will help you remember it longer. Also, space study over several sessions rather than ^just one long one. Another aid is to study just before bedtime and not watch TV or do anything else after study. The mind ~~ad~~ absorbs the material during the night. ~~The most~~ You should then review the material the next morning. A fifth memory aid is ^to use key words as hooks. For example, the key word "bed" helped me remember the entire idea about the value of studying right before sleep. A final aid to memory is memory formulas. I used the catchphrase "I often see Bill kicking footballs" and IOSBKF to recall the first letters of the six memory aids.*

** You need time in between for material to "sink in."*

Activity

The following sentences comment on Teri's essay. Fill in the missing word or words in each case.

1. Teri begins with a sentence that clearly states what her paper ________________. Always begin with such a clear signal!
2. The six transitions that Teri used to guide her reader, and herself, through the six points of her answer are:

   ________________, ________________, ________________,

   ________________, ________________, ________________.
3. Notice the various ________________ that Teri made when writing and proofreading her paper. She neatly crossed out miswritten or unwanted words; she used her ________________ after she had finished her essay to correct a misspelled word; she used insertion signs (∧) to add omitted words; and she used an asterisk (*) to add an omitted detail.

PRACTICE IN WRITING AN ESSAY EXAM

Activity 1

Check your understanding of the chapter by answering the following questions.

1. When you receive an essay exam in class, you should first
   a. Tackle the easiest question.
   b. Write a brief outline of each question.
   c. Read all test directions carefully.
   d. Memorize a catchphrase.
2. *True or false?* ______ Because of time limits, you do not have to worry about the four bases of good writing on an essay exam.
3. *True or false?* ______ It is possible to anticipate essay exam questions.
4. Clues to possible essay exam questions are
   a. enumerations.
   b. ideas marked by emphasis signals.
   c. reviews in class.
   d. all of the above.
5. A catchphrase can help you
   a. recall an informal outline prepared for a test question.
   b. proofread your essay for sentence-skills mistakes.
   c. budget your time on an essay.
   d. use transitions to guide the reader through your answer.

Activity 2

As the assignment for your next class, your instructor may ask you to study pages 247–248 so that you will be ready to write an in-class paper in response to the statement, "Describe seven hints that will make you a better note-taker."

You should do well on this paper if you follow the five basic steps to writing an effective essay exam that have been presented in this chapter.

Activity 3

1. Make up five questions you might be expected to answer on an essay exam in a social or physical science course (sociology, psychology, biology, or other).
2. Then make up for each of the five questions an outline answer comparable to the one on memory training.
3. Finally, write a full essay answer, in complete sentences, to one of the questions. Your outline will serve as your guide.

Be sure to begin your essay with a statement that makes the direction of your answer clear. For example, "The six different kinds of defense mechanisms are defined and illustrated below." If you are explaining in detail the different causes of, reasons for, or characteristics of something, you may want to develop each point in a separate paragraph. For instance, if you were answering a question in sociology about the primary functions of the family unit, you could, after starting with a statement that "There are three primary functions of the family unit," go on to develop and describe each function in a separate paragraph.

You will turn in the essay answer to your English instructor, who will evaluate it using the standards for effective writing applied to your other written assignments.

PREPARING A SUMMARY

At some point in a course, your instructor may ask you to write a summary of a book, article, TV show, or the like. In a *summary* (also referred to as a *précis* or an *abstract*), you reduce material in an original work to its main ideas and key supporting points. Unlike an outline, however, a summary does not use symbols such as I, A, 1, 2, and so on to indicate the relationships among parts of the original material.

A summary may be a word, a phrase, several sentences, or one or more paragraphs in length. The length of the summary you prepare will depend on your instructor's expectations and the length of the original work. Most often, you will be asked to write a summary of one or more paragraphs.

Writing a summary brings together a number of important reading, study, and writing skills. To condense the original matter, you must preview, read, evaluate, organize, and perhaps outline the material. Summarizing, then, can be a real aid to understanding; you must "get inside" the material and realize fully what is being said before you can reduce its meaning to a few words.

HOW TO SUMMARIZE AN ARTICLE

To write a summary of an article, follow the steps described below. If the assigned material is a TV show or film, adapt the suggestions accordingly.

1 Take a few minutes to preview the work. You can preview an article in a magazine by taking a quick look at the following.

   a ***Title:*** The title often summarizes what the article is about. Think about the title for a minute and how it may condense the meaning of an article.

   b ***Subtitle:*** A subtitle, if given, is a short summary appearing under or next to the title. For example, in a *Newsweek* article titled "Splitting Up the Family," the following caption appeared: "The courts are changing rules of divorce and child custody—and often making things worse." The subtitle, the caption, or any other words in large print under or next to the title often provide a quick insight into the meaning of an article.

   c ***First and last several paragraphs:*** In the opening paragraphs, the author may introduce the subject and state the purpose of the article. In the closing paragraphs, the writer may present conclusions or a summary. In either case, you get a quick overview of what the entire article is about.

   d ***Other items:*** Note any headings or subheadings that appear in the article. They often provide clues to the article's main points and give an immediate sense of the content of each section. Look carefully at any pictures, charts, or diagrams that accompany the article. Page space in a magazine or journal is limited, and such visual aids are generally used only when they help illustrate important points in the article. Note any words or phrases set off in *italic type* or **boldface type;** such words have probably been emphasized because they deal with important points.

2 Quickly read the article for a general understanding the first time through. Do not slow down or turn back. Mark off what seem to be main ideas and key supporting points. Pay special attention to all the items noted in the preview. Look for major enumerations (lists of items), since these often indicate key ideas. Also, try to identify important information by turning headings and subheadings into questions and by reading to find the answers to the questions.

3 Go back and re-read more carefully the areas you have identified as most important. Also, focus on other key points you may have missed in your first reading.

4 Keep the following items in mind when working on the rough drafts of your summary.
   a Express the author's ideas in your own words. Do not imitate or stay too close to the style of the original work.
   b Do not write an overly detailed summary. Remember that the purpose of a summary is to reduce the original material to its main ideas and essential supporting points. A paragraph summary should be between 150 and 200 words in length.
   c Do not begin your sentences with expressions like "the author says"; equally important, do not introduce your own opinions into the summary with comments like "another good point made by the author." Instead, concentrate on presenting directly and briefly the author's main ideas.
   d Preserve the balance and proportion of the original work. If the original devoted 70 percent of its space to one idea and only 30 percent to another, your summary should reflect that emphasis.
   e As you work on the summary, pay attention to the principles of effective writing (unity, support, coherence, and clear, error-free sentences) explained in Part One.
   f Write the final draft of the summary.

A MODEL SUMMARY

Here is a model summary of a magazine article.

> In "Grays on the Go" (Time, February 22, 1988), Nancy R. Gibbs discusses benefits and problems of the growing percentage of the elderly in the United States. Americans sixty-five and over now make up 12 percent of the population. For many, retirement is a time of active enjoyment of friends, hobbies, sports, volunteer work, and part-time work. Old age, however, is a time of illness and poverty for many others, especially those over seventy-five and those in some ethnic groups. For the government, the growing numbers of the elderly mean more and more money going for Social Security and health care. While a fourth of all government spending goes to the elderly, aid to families with dependent children and to school-lunch programs has been cut dramatically. Some experts now fear "age wars" in which the young and old fight over government resources. There is also concern that unless Social Security and Medicare are reformed, they will run out of money. It is hoped that cooperation between families, government, business, and community groups will help the United States grow old gracefully, avoiding competition between the generations.

HOW TO SUMMARIZE A BOOK

To write a summary of a book, first preview the book by taking a quick look at the following:

1 ***Title:*** The title is often the shortest possible summary of what a book is about. Think about the title for a minute and how it may summarize the whole meaning of the work.

2 ***Table of contents:*** The contents will tell you the number of chapters in the book and the subject of each chapter. Use the contents to get a general sense of how the book is organized. You should also note the number of pages in each chapter. If thirty pages are devoted to one episode or idea and an average of fifteen pages to other episodes or ideas in the book, you should probably give more space to the contents of the longer chapter in your summary.

3 ***Preface:*** Here you will probably find the author's reasons for writing the book. Also, the preface may summarize the main ideas developed in the book and may describe briefly how the book is organized.

4 ***First and last chapters:*** In these chapters, the author may preview and review important ideas and themes developed in the book.

5 ***Other items:*** Note the way the author has used headings and subheadings to organize the information in the book. Check the opening and closing paragraphs of each chapter to see if they contain introductions or summaries. Look quickly at charts, diagrams, and pictures in the book, since they are probably there to illustrate key points. Note any special features (index, glossary, appendices) that may appear at the end of the book.

After previewing the book, use steps 2 through 4 on pages 268–269 as a guide in preparing a summary.

PRACTICE IN PREPARING A SUMMARY

Activity 1

Check your understanding of the chapter by answering the following questions.

1. Key ideas in an article may be signaled by
   a. the table of contents.
   b. the title and subtitle.
   c. the preface.
   d. the index.

2. After previewing an article, you should
   a. read the article.
   b. take notes on the material.
   c. write a first draft of your summary.
   d. quote from the material.
3. *True or false?* ______ Use expressions such as "the author says" when writing your summary.
4. The table of contents in a book will give you an idea of
   a. how much space in the book is devoted to a particular idea.
   b. why the author wrote the book.
   c. the conclusions the author has reached.
   d. all of the above.
5. *True or false?* ______ A summary should include the key supporting points of a selection.

Activity 2

Use the guidelines in this chapter to write a one-paragraph summary of one of the following study-skill selections:

Achieving Time Control

Secrets of Concentration

A Textbook Study System

Building a More Powerful Memory

Your summary should be no fewer than 100 words and no more than 125 words. A summary of one study-skill selection is given below as a model.

A Summary of "Taking Effective Classroom Notes"

The following hints can help you take better notes in your classes. First, attend class faithfully. Copying another student's notes cannot substitute for hearing the ideas in person. Another important hint is to develop a system of abbreviations. Using abbreviations for often-used words and special terms will speed note-taking. Putting a key to abbreviations at the top of the page will prevent confusion. In addition, be alert for signals of importance: anything written on the board, definitions, enumerations, emphasis words, and repeated ideas. Writing down examples and connections between ideas is also essential. Next, review your notes after class to clarify and expand them. Finally, take notes in every class you attend. Otherwise, you are sure to forget most of what you hear.

Activity 3

Write a one-paragraph summary of an article of interest to you in a weekly or monthly magazine. Be sure to use the guidelines in this chapter when reading the article and preparing the summary. Hand in a copy of the article along with your summary.

Activity 4

Watch a television show. Then prepare a summary of the show. In your first sentence, give basic information about the show by using a format such as the following: "The January 6, 1985, broadcast of CBS's *60 Minutes* examined . . ."

DOING A REPORT

Each semester, you will probably be asked by at least one instructor to read a book or an article (or watch a TV show or a film) and to write a paper recording your response to the material. In these reports, or reaction papers, your instructor will most likely expect you to do two things: summarize the material and detail your reaction to it. The following pages explain both parts of a report.

PART 1 OF A REPORT: A SUMMARY OF THE WORK

To develop the first part of a report, do the following:

1 Identify the author and title of the work and include in parentheses the publisher and publication date. An example follows on page 275. For magazines, give the date of publication.

2 Write an informative summary of the material. Condense the content of the work by highlighting its main points and key supporting points. (See pages 267–272 for a complete discussion of summarizing techniques.) Use direct quotations from the work to illustrate important ideas.

Do not discuss in great detail any single aspect of the work and neglect to mention other equally important points. Summarize the material so that the reader gets a general sense of *all* key aspects of the original work. Also, keep the summary objective and factual. Do not include in the first part of the paper your personal reaction to the work; your subjective impression will form the basis of the second part of the paper.

PART 2 OF A REPORT: YOUR REACTION TO THE WORK

To develop the second part of a report, do the following:

1 Focus on any or all of the following questions. (Check with your instructor to see if he or she wants you to emphasize specific points.)
   a How is the assigned work related to ideas and concerns discussed in the course for which you are preparing the paper? For example, what points made in the course textbook, class discussions, or lectures are treated more fully in the work?
   b How is the work related to problems in our present-day world?
   c How is the material related to your life, experiences, feelings, and ideas? For instance, what emotions did the work arouse in you? Did the work increase your understanding of a particular issue? Did it change your perspective in any way?

2 Evaluate the merit of the work: the importance of its points, its accuracy, completeness, organization, and so on. You should also indicate here whether or not you would recommend the work to others, and why.

POINTS TO KEEP IN MIND WHEN WRITING THE REPORT

Here are some important matters to consider as you prepare the report.

1 Apply the four basic standards of effective writing (unity, support, coherence, and clear, error-free sentences) when writing the report.
   a Make sure each major paragraph presents and then develops a single main point. For example, in the model report in the next section, the first paragraph summarizes the book, and the three paragraphs that follow detail three separate reactions of the student writer to the book. The student then closes the report with a short concluding paragraph.
   b Support any general points or attitudes you express with specific reasons and details. Statements such as "I agreed with many ideas in this article" or "I found the book very interesting" are meaningless without specific evidence that shows why you feel as you do. Look at the model report closely to see the way the main point or topic sentence of each paragraph is developed by specific supporting evidence.
   c Organize the material in the paper. Follow the basic *plan of organization:* a summary of one or more paragraphs, a reaction of two or more paragraphs, and a conclusion. Also, use *transitions* to make the relationships among ideas in the paper clear.
   d Edit the paper carefully for errors in grammar, mechanics, punctuation, word use, and spelling.

2 Document quotations from all works by placing the page number in parentheses after the quoted material. Look at the example in the first paragraph of the model report. You may use quotations in the summary and reaction parts of the paper, but do not rely on them too much. Use them only to emphasize key ideas.

A MODEL REPORT

Here is a report written by a student in an introductory psychology course. Look at the paper closely to see how it follows the guidelines for report writing described in this chapter.

A Report on Man's Search for Meaning

PART 1: SUMMARY Topic sentence for summary paragraph

Dr. Viktor Frankl's book Man's Search for Meaning (New York: Washington Square Press, 1966) is both an autobiographical account of his years as a prisoner in Nazi concentration camps and a presentation of his ideas about the meaning of life. The three years of deprivation and suffering he spent at Auschwitz and other Nazi camps led to the development of his theory of Logotherapy, which, very briefly, states that the primary force in human beings is "a striving to find a meaning in one's life" (154). Without a meaning in life, Frankl feels, we experience emptiness and loneliness that lead to apathy and despair. This need for meaning was demonstrated to Frankl time and again with both himself and other prisoners who were faced with the horrors of camp existence. Frankl was able to sustain himself partly through the love he felt for his wife. In a moment of spiritual insight, he realized that this love was stronger and more meaningful than death, and would be a real and sustaining force within him even if he knew his wife was dead. Frankl's comrades also had reasons to live that gave them strength. One had a child waiting for him; another was a scientist who was working on a series of books that needed to be finished. Finally, both Frankl and his friends found meaning through their decision to accept and bear their fate with courage. He says that the words of Dostoevski came frequently to mind: "There is one thing that I dread: not to be worthy of my suffering." When Frankl's prison experience was over and he returned to his profession of psychiatry, he found that his theory of meaning held true not only for the prisoners but with all people. He has since had great success in working with patients by helping them locate in their own lives meanings of love, work, and suffering.

PART 2: REACTION Topic sentence for first reaction paragraph

One of my reactions to the book was the relationship I saw between the "Capos" and ideas about anxiety, standards, and aggression discussed in our psychology class. The Capos were prisoners who acted as trustees, and Frankl says they acted more cruelly toward the prisoners than the guards or the SS men. Several psychological factors help explain this cruelty. The Capos must have been suppressing intense anxiety about "selling themselves out" to the Nazis in return for small favors. Frankl and other prisoners must have been a constant reminder to the Capos of the courage and integrity they themselves lacked. When our behavior and values are threatened by someone else acting in a different way, one way we may react is with anger and aggression. The Capos are an extreme example of how, if the situation is right and we will not risk our "civilized image," we may be capable of great cruelty to those whose actions threaten our standards.

Topic sentence for second reaction paragraph

I think that Frankl's idea that meaning is the most important force in human beings helps explain some of the disorder and discontent in the world today. Many people are unhappy because they are caught in jobs where they have no responsibility and creativity; their work lacks meaning. Many are also unhappy because our culture seems to stress sexual technique in social relationships rather than human caring. People buy popular books that may help them become better partners in bed, but that may not make them more sensitive to each other's human needs. Where there is no real care, there is no meaning. To hide the inner emptiness that results from impersonal work and sex, people busy themselves with the accumulation of material things. With television sets, stereos, cars, expensive clothes, and the like, they try to forget that their lives lack true meaning. Instead of working or going to school to get a meaningful job, or trying to be decent human beings and friends with the people around them, or accepting their troubles with quiet determination and dignity, they frantically buy, buy, buy to distract themselves from the lack of real meaning within.

Topic sentence for third reaction paragraph

I have also found that Frankl's idea that suffering can have meaning helps me understand the behavior of people I know. I have a friend named Jim who was always poor and did not have much of a family--only a stepmother who never cared for him as much as for her own children. What Jim did have, though, was determination. He worked two jobs to save money to go to school, and then he worked and went to school at the same time. The fact that his life was hard seemed to make him bear down all the more. On the other hand, I can think of a man in my neighborhood who for all the years I've known him has done nothing with his life. He spends whole days standing on his front porch, or on the sidewalk, or on the street corner, smoking and looking at cars go by. He is a burned-out case. Somewhere in the past his problems must have become too much for him, and he gave up. He could have found meaning in his life by deciding to fight his troubles like Jim, but he didn't, and now he is a sad shadow of a man. Without determination and the desire to face his hardships, he lost his chance to make his life meaningful.

Concluding paragraph

In conclusion, I would strongly recommend Frankl's book to persons who care about why they are alive, and who want to truly think about the purpose and meaning of their lives.

PRACTICE IN DOING A REPORT

Activity 1

Check your understanding of the chapter by answering the following questions.

1. *True or false?* ______ Each major paragraph in a report should develop a single main point.
2. A summary of a work should
   a. be opinionated.
   b. focus on one key idea.
   c. be objective and factual.
   d. show how the work relates to your life.
3. *True or false?* ______ Quotations should be documented by placing the page number in parentheses after the quoted material.
4. The two basic parts of a report are
   a. a summary and supporting details.
   b. a summary and a reaction.
   c. a plan of organization and quotations.
   d. a reaction and a final draft.
5. A reaction to a work could include
   a. how the work relates to a certain course.
   b. how the work relates to current problems.
   c. how the work relates to your own life.
   d. all of the above.

Activity 2

Read a magazine article that interests you. Then write a report on the article. Include a one-paragraph summary, a reaction of one or more paragraphs, and a brief concluding paragraph. You may, if you like, quote briefly from the article. Be sure to enclose in quotation marks the words that you take from the article and put the page number in parentheses at the end of the quoted material.

Activity 3

Read a book suggested by your instructor. Then write a report on the book. Include a summary of at least one paragraph, a reaction of two or more paragraphs, and a brief concluding paragraph. Also, make sure that each major paragraph in your report develops a single main point. You may quote some sentences from the book, but they should be only a small part of your report. Follow the directions in Activity 2 above when you quote material.

WRITING A RÉSUMÉ AND JOB APPLICATION LETTER

When applying for a job through the mail, you should ordinarily send (1) a résumé and (2) a job application letter.

RÉSUMÉ

A résumé is a summary of your personal background and your qualifications for a job. It helps your potential employer see at a glance whether you are suited for a job opening. A sample job résumé is shown on the following page.

Points to Note about the Résumé

1 Your résumé, along with your letter of application, is your introduction to a potential employer. First impressions count, so it is extremely important that you make the résumé neat!

- a If possible, type the résumé on good-quality letter (8½- by 11-inch) paper. Keep at least a 1-inch margin on all sides.
- b Edit and proofread very carefully for sentence-skills and spelling mistakes. A potential employer may regard such mistakes as signs of carelessness in your character. You might even want to get someone else to proofread the résumé for you.
- c If possible, be brief and to the point: use only one page.
- d Use a format like that of the model résumé. (See also the variations described ahead.) Balance your résumé on the page so that you have at least a 1-inch margin on all sides.
- e Note that you should start with your most recent education or job experience and work backward in time.

ROBERTA LYONS
715 Baltic Avenue
Atlantic City, New Jersey 08401
609-821-8715

Education

1987–Present	Atlantic Community College Mays Landing, New Jersey 08330 By June I will have completed my Associate of Science degree, including twenty-four hours of courses in my major, Hotel-Motel Management. In addition, I will have taken twelve hours of courses in accounting. Presently I have a B+ average in my major and a B in my other courses.
1983–1987	Pleasantville High School Pleasantville, New Jersey 08310

Job Experience

1987–Present	Checker and Assistant to the Manager, A & P Supermarket, Atlantic City, New Jersey 08401 During holiday periods in the two years I have worked at the A & P, I have served as an assistant to the manager by supervising the preparation of party trays.
1986–1987	Clerk, Seven-Eleven Food Store, Absecon, New Jersey 08300 My job also included some bookkeeping and stock inventory.

Special Training

As part of one of my courses, Seminar in Hospitality Management, I have helped plan and supervise the preparation of luncheons for several college affairs. I have also privately catered several baptisms and weddings for relatives and friends.

References

My references are available upon request from the Placement Office at Atlantic Community College, Mays Landing, New Jersey 08330.

2 Your résumé should point up strengths, not weaknesses.
   a Do not include "Special Training" if you have had none. Do not refer to your grade-point average if it is a low C.
   b On the other hand, include a main heading like "Extracurricular Activities" if the activities or awards seem relevant. For example, if Roberta Lyons had been a member of the Management Club or vice president of the Hospitality Committee in high school or college, she should have mentioned these facts.
   c If you have no work experience related to the job for which you are applying, then list the jobs you have had. Any job that shows a period of responsible employment may favorably impress a potential employer.

3 You can list the names of your references directly on the résumé. Be sure to get the permission of people you cite before listing their names. You can also give the address of a placement office file that holds references, as shown on the model report. Or you can simply say that you will provide references on request.

JOB APPLICATION LETTER

The purpose of the letter of application that goes with your résumé is to introduce yourself briefly and to try to make an employer interested in you. You should include only the high points of the information about yourself in the résumé.

Shown on the next page is the letter of application that Roberta Lyons sent with her résumé.

Points to Note about the Job Application Letter

1 Your letter should do the following:
   a In the first paragraph, state that you are an applicant for the job and tell the source through which you learned about the job.

   Here is how Roberta's letter might have opened if her source had been a newspaper: "I would like to apply for the position of Assistant Banquet Manager which was advertised in yesterday's *Philadelphia Inquirer*."

   Sometimes an ad will list only a box number (such as Y-140) to reply to. Your inside address should then be:

   Y-140
   Philadelphia Inquirer
   Philadelphia, Pennsylvania 19101

   Dear Sir or Madam:

715 Baltic Avenue
Atlantic City, New Jersey 08401
March 3, 1989

Mr. Philip McGuire
Banquet Manager
Sheraton Hotel
1725 John F. Kennedy Boulevard
Philadelphia, Pennsylvania 19103

Dear Mr. McGuire:

I learned through the Placement Office at Atlantic Community College of the Assistant Banquet Manager position at the Sheraton Hotel. I would like to be considered as a candidate for the job.

I will graduate from Atlantic Community College in June with an Associate of Science degree in Hotel-Motel Management. The degree will include twenty-four hours of courses related to the hospitality industry and twelve hours of accounting. Also, you will see from my résumé that I have work-related experience as well, including two years as an assistant to the manager at an A & P Supermarket.

If my qualifications and experience are of interest to you, I will be happy to come for an interview at your convenience. I think you will find me an eager, motivated, and able person, truly interested in working in the hospitality field.

Sincerely yours,

Roberta Lyons

Roberta Lyons

b In the second paragraph, state briefly your qualifications for the job and refer the reader to your résumé.

c In the last paragraph, state your willingness to come for an interview. If you can be available for an interview at only certain times, indicate this.

2 As with the résumé, neatness is crucial. Follow the same hints for the letter that you did for the résumé:

a Type the letter on good-quality letter (8½- by 11-inch) paper.

b Proofread very carefully for sentence-skills and spelling mistakes. Use the checklist of sentence skills on the inside front cover.

c Be brief and to the point: use no more than one page.

d Use a format like the model letter. Keep at least a 1-inch margin on all sides.

e Use punctuation and spelling in the model letter as a guide. For example:

Skip two spaces between the inside address and the salutation ("Dear Mr. McGuire:").

Use a colon after the salutation.

Sign your name at the bottom, in addition to typing it.

PRACTICE IN WRITING A RÉSUMÉ AND JOB APPLICATION LETTER

Activity 1

Check your understanding of the chapter by answering the following questions.

1. *True or false?* ______ A job application letter should tell an employer about your family and hobbies.
2. A résumé should always list
   a. names of references.
   b. previous jobs.
   c. height and weight.
   d. your grades.
3. *True or false?* ______ A résumé should be brief—one page if possible.
4. On a résumé, you should
   a. admit your weak areas.
   b. list your most recent job last.
   c. highlight your strengths.
   d. do all of the above.

5. The purpose of a job application letter is to
   a. try to make an employer interested in you.
   b. repeat all the information in your résumé.
   c. take the place of an interview.
   d. do all of the above.

Activity 2

Clip a job listing from a newspaper or copy a job description posted in your school placement office. The job should be one you feel you are presently qualified for or that you would be qualified for in the future.

Write a résumé and a letter of application for the job. Use the models already considered as guides. Your instructor may let you invent some of the specific supporting material needed to make you appear a strong candidate for the job.

Use the checklist of the four bases on the inside front cover as a guide in your writing. Be sure to edit and proofread both the résumé and the application letter carefully, and give them to someone else to check as well. Each should be nothing less than perfect, because a prospective employer will use them as a first indication of whether you are a good candidate for a job.

USING THE LIBRARY

A surprising number of students seem overwhelmed by their college library. They do not understand how the library is set up and so are not sure how to use its many services. If you share these students' confusion, this chapter will help you. It will provide the basic information you need to use your college library with confidence.

Libraries vary in size, layout, and the services they offer. Most libraries, however, have a main desk, a card catalog, stacks, a reference section, and a periodical area. Each of these will be discussed on the pages that follow.

THE MAIN DESK

The main desk, often located in a central spot, is usually staffed by at least one professional librarian and several assistants. Check with the staff to see if there are any brochures or pamphlets that describe the layout and services of the library. Many college libraries give tours of the facilities, particularly at the beginning of the school year. If descriptive pamphlets or tours are available, take advantage of them. The more familiar you are with the library, the more effectively you will be able to use it.

Many libraries provide the following services: interlibrary loan system; copying machines; typing facilities; study carrels; record and film collections; a vertical file containing pamphlets and clippings; a government document room; and microfilm and microfiche files for out-of-date newspapers, magazines, and the like. Check with the main desk to find out which of these services are available.

Instructors often put on reserve materials that many students will use. These materials must usually be kept in the library, although at times they may be taken out overnight. Books on reserve are often shelved behind the main desk.

Activity

Put a check beside each of the following services that is available at your library. Ask someone at the main desk if you are in doubt about whether the library offers a particular service.

_______ Descriptive pamphlet about library

_______ Typing facilities

_______ Vertical file of pamphlets and clippings

_______ Copying machines

_______ Study carrels

_______ Reserve book area

THE CARD CATALOG

Author, Title, and Subject Cards

The card catalog is a file of cards alphabetically arranged in drawers; it lists all the books in the library. You can find out whether the library has a certain book, and where it is located, by looking it up in the card catalog according to subject, author, or title.

For example, if you wanted to see if the library had *Megatrends* by John Naisbitt, you could look up the author's name under *N* (Naisbitt) in the *Authors* section of the card catalog. Or you could look up *Megatrends* under *M* in the *Titles* section of the catalog. Or you could look it up under the category *Social Prediction* in the *Subjects* section of the catalog.

Shown on the following page is the most important information on subject, author, and title cards for a single book. Note carefully the kinds of information provided on the author card and how the information is presented.

Hints about Using the Card Catalog

You may at times have trouble locating material in the card catalog because you are not familiar with some of the conventions most libraries use when filing cards. Keeping the following points in mind should make it easier for you to find the information you need.

1 A book is not alphabetized using *A, An, The* when one of these is the first word in its title. Instead, the book is catalogued according to the second word in the title. For example, the book *The Lives of a Cell* would be found under *Lives*.

Subject card

HF
5387 BUSINESS ETHICS
B56

Blanchard, Kenneth H., and Norman Vincent Peale.
The Power of Ethical Management / by Kenneth H.
Blanchard and Norman Vincent Peale. -- New York:
William Morrow and Company, 1988.

139 p.

Author card

HF
5387 Blanchard, Kenneth H., and Norman Vincent Peale.
B56 The Power of Ethical Management / by Kenneth H.
Blanchard and Norman Vincent Peale. -- New York:
William Morrow and Company, 1988.

139 p.

Title card

Power of Ethical Management, The.

HF Blanchard, Kenneth H., and Norman Vincent Peale.
5387 The Power of Ethical Management / by Kenneth H.
B56 Blanchard and Norman Vincent Peale. -- New York:
William Morrow and Company, 1988.

139 p.

ISBN 0-688-07062-0

1. Business ethics. 2. Conduct of life.

HF5387.B56 174′.4--dc19 87-24210

Title

Call number (how to find the book)

Author

Place of publication publisher, and year of publication

Subject headings (refer to these headings to find related books)

Dewey decimal number

Library of Congress number

2 Near the bottom of many cards in the catalog, you will find a number of headings. For instance, on the card shown on the previous page, there are three headings: "1. United States—Social conditions—1970– 2. Social indicators—United States. 3. Social prediction." These headings tell you the subject areas in the card catalog under which the book in question is filed. You can refer to these subject areas for related books on your topic.

Activity

Use the library card catalog to answer the following questions.

1. What is the title of one book by Mortimer Adler?

 ____

2. What is the title of a book by Alice Walker?

 ____

3. Who is the author of *The Making of the President?* (Remember to look up the title under *Making,* not *The.*)

 ____

4. Who is the author of *Passages?*

 ____

5. List two authors and titles of books dealing with the subject of divorce:

 a. ______________________________

 b. ______________________________

6. List two authors and titles of books dealing with the subject of Martin Luther King, Jr.:

 a. ______________________________

 b. ______________________________

7. Look up *Slouching toward Bethlehem* or *The Mature Mind* or *Escape from Freedom* and give the following information:

 a. Author ______________________________

 b. Place of publication ______________________________

 c. Publisher ______________________________

 d. Date of publication ______________________________

 e. Subject headings at the bottom of the card ______________________________

 ____

 ____

 f. Call number ______________________________

8. Look up a book written by Bruce Catton or Barbara Tuchman or Dee Brown and give the following information:
   a. Title ______________________________
   b. Place of publication ______________________________
   c. Publisher ______________________________
   d. Date of publication ______________________________
   e. Subject headings at the bottom of the card ______________________________
   ____
   ____
   f. Call number ______________________________

THE STACKS

The stacks are the library shelves where books are arranged according to their call numbers. The call number is printed in the upper left corner of each card in the catalog and is as distinctive as a social security number. It is also printed on the spine of every book in the library.

In a library having open stacks (ones that you are permitted to enter), follow these steps to find a book. If, for example, you are looking for Blanchard and Peale's book *The Power of Ethical Management,* you first use the card catalog to get the call number, which is HF/5387/B56 in the Library of Congress system. (Libraries that use the Dewey Decimal System provide call letters that are made up entirely of numbers, rather than letters and numbers. However, the same basic method of locating a book is involved.) Then you go to the section of the stacks that holds the H's. After you locate the H's, you look for the HF's. After that, you look for HF/5387. Finally, you look for HF/5387/B56.

If the library has closed stacks, you will have to make out a call slip, supplying the call number and other identifying information about the book. A staff person will then locate the book and bring it to you.

Activity

Use the library stacks to answer the questions on the following page. (Note that the questions assume that your library classifies books according to the Library of Congress System.)

1. What author is the subject of the books that fall between PS2380 and PS2388?

___

2. What author is the subject of the books that fall between PR2754 and PR3106? ___

3. What is the general subject of the books that fall between ND1 and ND1500?

___

4. What is the general subject of the books that fall between BL and BX?

___

5. What country is the subject of the books that fall between DA1 and DA690?

___

THE REFERENCE SECTION

The reference section stocks such general resource materials as indexes, encyclopedias, atlases, and yearbooks. People sometimes conduct their preliminary research here before going to the card catalog for more specific materials. Resources in the reference section are generally large, expensive volumes which cannot be taken out of the library. They usually must be used on the premises.

It would be impractical to give here all the reference materials carried by even a small library, and so only a brief list of such materials has been provided.

Atlases

Hammond Medallion World Atlas
National Atlas of the United States

Biographical References

Biography Index: A Cumulative Index to Biographical Material in Books and Magazines
Current Biography: Who's News and Why
Who's Who

Encyclopedias

Colliers Encyclopedia
Encyclopedia Americana
Encyclopaedia Britannica

Dictionaries of Quotations

Dictionary of Quotations
Familiar Quotations

Government Publications

Guide to U. S. Government Serials Periodicals
Monthly Catalog of U. S. Government Publications
Vertical File Index

References in Business

Business Periodicals Index
Encyclopedia of Banking and Finance
Sources of Business Information

References in Education

Current Index to Journals in Education
Education Index
ERIC Research in Education

References in Psychology

American Journal of Psychology
A Dictionary of Psychology
Psychology Abstracts

References in Sociology

American Journal of Sociology
American Sociological Review
Sociological Abstracts

Yearbooks

Guinness Book of World Records
Information Please Almanac
The World Almanac and Book of Facts

THE PERIODICAL AREA

Periodicals are magazines, journals, and newspapers that are printed at periodic (regular or intermittent) intervals during the year. Because these materials contain current information, they are often particularly valuable when doing research. Just as you can use the card catalog to locate a specific book, so you can use one of several periodical guides or indexes to locate a specific article in a magazine or other publication.

The *Readers' Guide*

The most common of these indexes is *Readers' Guide to Periodical Literature.* This guide lists articles in over one hundred general-interest magazines, such as *Newsweek, Time,* and *Reader's Digest,* as well as more specialized magazines, such as *Popular Electronics, Ebony,* and *National Review.* Articles are listed under both subject and author. If, for example, you wanted to learn the names of articles published on the subject of intelligence tests, you would look under the heading "Intelligence Tests." If you wanted to identify articles written by Ralph Nader, you would look under his last name.

Some students are confused by entries in the *Readers' Guide*. However, the sequence of information in each entry is always the same; also, any abbreviations used are explained at the front of each issue.

Here is a typical entry in the *Readers' Guide:*

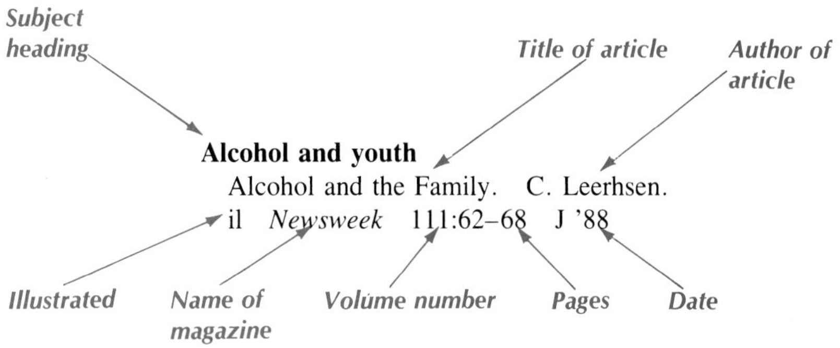

Note the sequence in which information about the article is given:

1. The subject heading (or author, last name first) in boldface type
2. The title of the article
3. The author—if it is a signed article
4. Whether or not the article has a bibliography (*bibl*). Look in the key in the front of an issue of *Readers' Guide* to find out what *il* and *por* mean and write their meanings here:

   il = ______________________ por = ______________________

5. The name of the magazine. The magazine abbreviated in the entry is *Newsweek*. Refer to the list of magazines in the front of the index to identify the following abbreviations:

   Bus W ______________________ Sat R ______________________

6. The volume number of the magazine (preceding the colon)
7. The numbers of the pages on which the article appears (after the colon)
8. The date of the issue of the magazine in which the article appears. Look in the front of the index to identify the following abbreviations for months of the year:

   J ________________ Je ________________ O ________________

Activity 1

Use the excerpt below from *Readers' Guide to Periodical Literature* to answer the questions that follow.

Alcohol
See also
Prohibition
Physiological effects
See also
Alcohol antagonists
Fetal alcohol syndrome
Drinking downs exercise gains. il *Prevention* 38:8 D '86
Eat, drink . . . and be wary. C. A. Pearce. il *Harpers Bazaar* 120:92+ D '86
Heavy drinking increases stroke risk. J. Silberner. *Sci News* 130:276 N 1 '86
Alcohol and air pilots
16,000 pilots with drunk driving history reported. *Jet* 71:33 N 24 '86
Airborne and hung over [research by Jerome A. Yesavage and Von Otto Leirer] *Sci News* 130:398 D 20-27 '86
Alcohol and automobile drivers
16,000 pilots with drunk driving history reported. *Jet* 71:33 N 24 '86
Death of a daughter [J. Clymer] A. Clymer, il *N Y Times Mag* p59-63 N 2 '86
Drunk driving: what not to do. H. L. Ross and G. Hughes. il *Nation* 243:663-4 D 13 '86
Stranger than true: why I defend guilty clients. B. Winston. *Harpers* 273:70-1 D '86
Alcohol and crime
A judge who lets them go [Chicago judge L. Passarella's leniency with drunken offenders] M. Royko. il *Read Dig* 129:29-32 O '86
Alcohol and sex
Sex under the influence: the hazards of drugs and alcohol. K. McCoy. *Seventeen* 45:50+ D '86
Alcohol and women
See also
Fetal alcohol syndrome
Alcohol and youth
Campus drinking blues [college students thwart drinking age laws] E. Salholz. il *Newsweek* 108:60+ N 3 '86
Detecting and preventing drug and alcohol abuse. J. P. Comer. il *Parents* 61:228 O '86
When your child drinks. S. L. Englebardt. il *Read Dig* 129:110-14 N '86
Alcohol antagonists
An alcohol antidote: in search of a better cup of coffee [S. M. Paul's research on a compound that erases the symptoms of alcohol intoxication] J. Hammer. il por *Esquire* 106:218-20 D '86
Coming: a drug to sober you up? [work of Peter D. Suzdak and others with Ro 15-4513] J. Raloff. *Sci News* 130:358 D 6 '86
New drug counters alcohol intoxication [Ro 15-4513] G. Kolata. il *Science* 234:1198-9 D 5 '86
A selective imidazobenzodiazepine antagonist of ethanol in the rat [Ro 15-4513] P. D. Suzdak and others. bibl f il *Science* 234:1243-7 D 5 '86

Alcoholic beverages

See also

Beer

Cocktails

Liqueurs

Wine

Great American Christmas treats. J. F. Mariani. il *Harpers Bazaar* 120:182-3+ D '86

Great drinks with red wine. M. B. Johnson. il *McCalls* 114:132 O '86

Spirits aflame: autumn chill-chasers. W. Cook. il *Harpers Bazaar* 120:106 N '86

Contamination

The dangers in your drink [urethane in alcoholic beverages may cause cancer] T. Monmaney. il *Newsweek* 108:60+ D 22 '86

Labeling

Congress considers warning labels on liquor. C. Holden. *Science* 233:517-18 Ag 1 '86

Alcoholics and alcoholism

See also

Alcohol—Physiological effects

Children of alcoholics

Therapy

See also

Alcohol antagonists

Alcoholics Anonymous

Alcoholics Anonymous

A drunkards progress: AA and the sobering strength of myth. Elpenor. il *Harpers* 273:42-8 O '86

1. How many articles are listed that deal with drunken driving?

____

2. What is the title of an article by B. Winston?

____

3. What is the date of the issue of *Reader's Digest* that includes an article about children who drink?

____

4. Who wrote the article titled "Congress Considers Warning Labels on Liquor"?

____

5. Under what four headings besides "Alcoholic beverages" would you find articles about alcoholic beverages?

____

Activity 2

1. Look up a recent article on exercise in *Readers' Guide to Periodical Literature* and fill in the information below:
   a. Article title ______________________________
   b. Author (if given) ______________________________
   c. Name of periodical ______________________________
   d. Volume ____________________ Page(s) ____________________
   e. Date ______________________________
2. Look up a recent article on occupations in *Readers' Guide* and fill in the information below:
   a. Article title ______________________________
   b. Author (if given) ______________________________
   c. Name of periodical ______________________________
   d. Volume ____________________ Page(s) ____________________
   e. Date ______________________________

If you are doing a research paper in a special subject area, your instructor or a librarian should be able to tell you whether one of the specialized indexes below, or some other index, will be a helpful source for articles.

Applied Science and Technology Index
Art Index
Book Review Digest
Business Periodicals Index
Education Index
Nursing Index
Social Sciences and Humanities Index
Essay and General Literature Index
New York Times Index
Public Affairs Information Service

Entries in the specialized indexes follow roughly the same format as that used in *Readers' Guide*. If you have trouble understanding an entry, refer to the front of the index for an explanation of the symbols used.

The File of Periodical Holdings

After using the appropriate index to identify articles you would like to read, you need to determine (1) if the library receives the periodicals you want and (2) whether it has the particular issues you want. For this information, check the file (sometimes a booklet) of periodical holdings; the file is located in the periodical area.

Most libraries provide an explanatory key so you can interpret the information entered in the periodical holding file. This key will tell you whether a particular magazine is on microfilm or microfiche or is available in loose or bound copies.

A Final Note about Periodicals

Current issues of magazines and journals remain unbound and are usually shelved on open stacks in the periodical area. Back issues, however, are bound in annual or semiannual volumes and may be in the periodical area or in some other spot in the library. Most libraries keep loose copies of selected recent newspapers on open stacks in the periodical area. Past issues of particularly important newspapers may be on microfilm. Check with the library staff for the locations of these materials.

PRACTICE IN USING THE LIBRARY

Activity 1

Check your understanding of the chapter by answering the following questions.

1. *True or false?* ______ In order to locate a book called *The Member of the Wedding,* you would look in the title section of the card catalog under *T*.
2. *True or false?* ______ The library stacks consist of books on reserve and books in special collections.
3. After locating the name of an article you would like to read, you need to find out
   a. if the library receives the periodical you want.
   b. whether or not the library has that particular issue.
   c. where in the library the article can be found.
   d. all of the above.
4. The bottom of a card in the card catalog lists
   a. subject areas under which the book is filed.
   b. the author's previous books.
   c. the titles of other books about the same subject.
   d. all of the above.

5. *Readers' Guide to Periodical Literature* lists articles under author and
   a. Library of Congress number.
   b. periodical title.
   c. subject.
   d. volume number.

Activity 2

Make up a floor plan of your college library. Label the main desk, card catalog, stacks, reference section, and periodical area.

Activity 3

Answer the following questions about your library.

1. What are the library's hours during the week and on the weekend?

   ____

2. For how long may books be taken out? ______________________________
3. What is the fine on overdue books? ______________________________
4. Which system, the Library of Congress System or the Dewey Decimal System, is used to catalog books? ______________________________
5. Are the stacks open or closed? ______________________________
6. Where are books located that teachers have placed on reserve?

   ____

7. Are there any typewriters? ____________ Study carrels? ____________

   Copying machines? ____________ Microfilm machines? ____________

Activity 4

Use the library to do some preliminary research on a subject that interests you. Choose one of the following areas.

Adoption	Weather control
Overpopulation	Violence on television
Handicapped children	Robert Kennedy
Jesse Jackson	UFOs
Heart disease	Leukemia
Sharks	Witchcraft

Organ transplants	Exercise
Fairy tales	AIDS
Fire prevention	Feminism—history
Terrorism	Mental retardation
Asthma	Stress

Research the topic first through the *Subjects* section of the card catalog and then in the periodical indexes indicated below. On a separate sheet of paper, provide the following information:

1. The topic
2. Five books on the topic. Include these items:

   Author
   Title
   Publisher
   Place of publication
   Date of publication

3. Three articles on the topic from *Readers' Guide to Periodical Literature*. Include these items:

   Title of article
   Author (if given)
   Title of periodical
   Volume (if given)
   Page(s)
   Date

4. Three articles on the topic from other indexes (*New York Times Index* or *Social Science and Humanities Index* or *Essay and General Literature Index* or others). Include these items:

   Title of article
   Author (if given)
   Title of periodical
   Volume (if given)
   Page(s)
   Date

WRITING A RESEARCH PAPER

The process of writing a research paper can be divided into seven steps:

1 Select a topic that interests you.
2 Limit your topic.
3 Prepare a list of sources of information on your topic.
4 Read about your topic and make the purpose of your paper clear.
5 Plan your paper and take notes that support your purpose.
6 Write the paper.
7 Use an acceptable format and method of documentation in the final version.

This chapter explains and illustrates each of the steps.

STEP 1: SELECT A TOPIC THAT INTERESTS YOU

At the same time, make sure that your library has sufficient information on your subject. To do this, go to the *Subjects* section of the library card catalog and see whether there are at least four books on your general topic. For example, if you initially choose the general topic of handicaps, you should find at least four books listed on handicaps. In addition, check the library stacks to make sure that the books are available on the shelves.

You should also go through a recent volume of *Readers' Guide to Periodical Literature* or the appropriate specialized periodical index to see whether articles on your subject are listed. Then check the file of periodical holdings (you may have to ask a library assistant to point out the file to you) to see if the library actually has the periodicals you may need.

If both books and articles are immediately at hand, then pursue your topic. Otherwise, you may have to choose another topic. You cannot write a paper on a topic for which research materials are not available.

STEP 2: LIMIT YOUR TOPIC

A research paper should develop a specific, limited topic. It should be narrow and deep rather than broad and shallow. Therefore, skim through several books or articles on the topic, looking for a way to limit it.

In reading through the available books on handicaps, for example, you may decide that you could limit your paper to the problems of sight-impaired students. The general topic of sports might be narrowed to drug use among Olympic athletes; the broad subject of death could be reduced to unfair pricing practices in funeral homes; education might be limited to sex education in primary schools; animals could be narrowed to endangered species in your state.

STEP 3: PREPARE A LIST OF SOURCES OF INFORMATION ON YOUR TOPIC

Your list of possible sources of information (also called a *working bibliography*) should consist of books, articles, pamphlets, and the like that seem relevant to your subject. Go to the following places in your library to prepare your list of sources:

1 The *Subjects* section of the card catalog.
2 The subject cards will tell you which books on your topic have bibliographies. Locate the books in the library stacks and consult their bibliographies for additional references on your topic.
3 *Readers' Guide to Periodical Literature.*
4 Appropriate specialized periodical indexes.
5 The pamphlet file (you may have to ask a library assistant to tell you where this file is located).

Keep a written record of all sources that you think will help you. On three- by five-inch cards, or on one side only of sheets of loose-leaf paper, record the information below about each source:

For Books

Author (last name first)
Title (underlined)
Place of publication
Publisher
Date of publication
Call number (upper right corner)

For Periodicals

Author (last name first)
Title of article (in quotation marks)
Title of periodical (underlined)
Volume (if available)
Pages
Date

Here is a copy of a bibliography card for a book:

SF411
5
F64

Fogel, Bruce

Pets and Their People
New York: The Viking Press, 1984

Fogel describes the use of pets in private and institutional therapy programs.

Note that at the bottom of the card, the writer has briefly described the relevance of the book to the paper.

STEP 4: READ ABOUT YOUR TOPIC AND MAKE THE PURPOSE OF YOUR PAPER CLEAR

Locate and read accounts of your subject in books, magazines, or other sources. As you develop knowledge about your subject, work at clearly defining and limiting your *purpose* in writing the paper. Your purpose might be to *make and defend a point of some kind*. For example, your concern in the paper might be to provide evidence for your belief that gambling should be legalized. On the other hand, depending on your course and instructor, your purpose might simply be to *present information about a particular subject*. For example, you might be asked to explain the theories of several psychologists on the stages of development in children.

STEP 5: PLAN YOUR PAPER AND TAKE NOTES THAT SUPPORT YOUR PURPOSE

When you have made your purpose clear, you can start to plan the specific content and organization of your paper. You can, in other words, begin making decisions about the exact information and ideas you will present, and the arrangement of the information and ideas.

At this point, you should begin taking notes on whatever seems relevant or significant. And as you continue to read and take notes, you should think constantly about how you will use the material gathered to support your purpose in the paper.

Write your notes on four- by six-inch or five- by eight-inch cards or on sheets of loose-leaf paper. Do not worry about taking too many notes. You can put aside what may turn out to be unnecessary notes more easily than you can make a second search of library sources. (If your library has a copying machine, you may want to copy important sections from magazine articles or books that are kept on reserve. Also, some libraries can copy for you any article that is on microfilm.)

The notes you take may be in the form of *direct quotation* or *summary in your own words* or *a combination of the two*. Put quotation marks around all material which you take word for word from any source. If you omit material from a quoted passage, show the omission by using three spaced periods (. . .) called *ellipses* or an *ellipsis*. When omission is from the end of a quoted sentence use four dots (. . . .), with the first dot indicating the period at the end of the sentence. In a summary, condense the original material by stating its main points briefly in your own words.

Here is a copy of a note card that combines both direct quotation and summary:

> *Pets and the handicapped*
>
> *Dogs have been trained to be listeners for the deaf in this country since the 1970s. One reason is that "a properly trained dog will act as ears for his or her owner." The other reason is that whether or not dogs understand their owners' moods, most people feel they do. Thus dogs can provide the deaf with a greater sense of communication. "There is understanding, and one little bit of the loneliness of deafness is lifted."*
>
> *Fogel, 208-209*

Keep in mind the following points about note cards:

1 Write on one side of the card only.

2 Put only one kind of information, from one source, on any one card. For example, the sample card above has information on only one idea (pets and the handicapped) from one source (Fogel).

3 Include at the top of each card a label, or heading, that summarizes the content of the card. This heading will help you organize the different kinds of information that you gather on your topic.

4 Identify the source and page number at the bottom of each card.

When you take notes, you should generally try to summarize in your own words rather than quote. With either method, however, be sure to record the exact source and page from which you take each piece of information. In your research paper, you must document through footnoting all information that is not "common knowledge." For example, the birth and death dates of John F. Kennedy, the site of the first atomic test, and the Academy Award winners for a given year are established facts and do not need documenting. On the other hand, the number of animals destroyed in experimental research every year, the percentage of high school students who use drugs regularly, and the total amount of oil imported by the United States last year are specialized facts that should be documented. As you read several sources on a subject, you will develop a sense of what authors regard as generally shared or common information about a subject and what is more specialized information that must be documented.

If you do not document specialized information or ideas that are not your own, you will be stealing. (The formal term is *plagiarizing*—using someone else's work as your own work.) A good deal of the material in research writing, it can usually be assumed, will need to be documented.

STEP 6: WRITE THE PAPER

After you have finished your reading and note-taking, you should have a fairly clear idea of the plan of your paper. Make a final outline and use it as a guide to write the first draft of your paper. In your introductory paragraph, include a thesis statement expressing the purpose of your paper and indicate the plan of development that you will follow. The section on writing an introductory paragraph for the essay on page 218 is appropriate for the introductory section of the research paper as well. Note also the opening paragraph in the model research paper on page 306.

As you move from introduction to main body to summary or conclusion, or both, strive for unity, support, and coherence in your writing so that your paper will be clear and effective. In particular, repeatedly ask yourself the question, "Does each of my supporting paragraphs develop the thesis of my paper?" Use the checklist on the inside front cover to make sure that your paper touches all four bases of effective writing.

STEP 7: USE AN ACCEPTABLE FORMAT AND METHOD OF DOCUMENTATION IN THE FINAL VERSION OF YOUR PAPER

Format is discussed below; documentation is discussed beginning on page 309.

FORMAT

The following sample pages from a student research paper illustrate an acceptable format for a research paper. Be sure to note the directions set in special color print next to each sample page.

This is the title page of a sample research paper.

The title should be centered and in capitals.

PETS AS THERAPISTS

by

Your name should be placed two spaces under by.

Carla Morrell

At the bottom put the course title and date; you may also include the course section number and the instructor's name.

English 102

January 8, 1989

Include an unnumbered outline page, similar in format to this one, if your instructor requests it.

OUTLINE

Thesis: Pets have been found to provide important therapeutic benefits to the mentally ill, the physically ill, and the handicapped.

I. Benefits to the mentally ill
   A. History of the use of animals for the mentally disturbed
   B. Recent use of animals to help mentally ill patients
   C. Use of pets to help the criminally insane

II. Benefits to the physically ill
   A. Higher survival rates for heart-disease patients who own pets
   B. Improved blood pressure in those patients with pets
   C. Improvements to hospital patients who are visited by pets

III. Benefits to the handicapped and disabled
   A. Physical assistance
      1. Seeing-eye dogs
      2. Hearing-ear dogs
      3. Animals that run errands
   B. Emotional support
      1. Emotional benefits of guide dogs
      2. Increased confidence to disabled from horseback riding
      3. Improvement of morale in nursing homes

Leave about 3 inches of blank space between the top of the first page and the title of the paper. The text of the pages that follow should begin about 1 inch from the top.

PETS AS THERAPISTS

(3 spaces)

Double-space between lines of the text.

1½-inch margin at left

Few would be surprised to hear that animals delight and entertain humans. After all, there are numerous pet owners throughout the country, and the pet industry is thriving. But how many would believe that pets can be good for our health? Yet a growing number of experiences and studies are showing that pets do provide therapeutic benefits to the mentally ill, the physically ill, and the handicapped.

About 1-inch margin at right

That animals can be useful in treating the mentally ill is not a new idea. In fact, the first known use of animals for that purpose began in 1792, when the Society of Friends established the York Retreat in England as a humane alternative to the brutal lunatic asylums of the time. With the hope that patients would learn self-control through caring for others, they were encouraged to care for rabbits, poultry, and other small animals (White, Pet-Love,

1

Page numbering starts with the first page of the text. Page 1 is numbered at the bottom. Leave about a 1-inch margin at the bottom of the page.

Page numbers after the first page are put in the upper right-hand corner.

2

94-95). The formal use of animals in therapy wasn't initiated in the United States until 1942, when the American Red Cross set up a program to help rehabilitate emotionally and physically disabled airmen at the American Air Force Convalescent Center in Pawling, New York (96).

The use of pets in psychological therapy for individuals was pioneered by child psychologist Dr. Boris Levinson, who first thought of that approach with his own dog, Jingles.

Direct quotes of four lines or more are single-spaced and indented five spaces. Quotation marks are not used. The spaced periods show that material is omitted from the quotation.

> He certainly did not set out with the idea of using Jingles as a co-therapist; it happened quite unintentionally when a woman and her very disturbed little boy arrived at his door one day, hours early for an appointment. As a rule, Jingles would be excluded from the office during consultations, but this was unexpected. The little boy immediately made contact with the dog, cuddling and petting him. . . . It was the beginning of successful therapy for the boy, and the start of a fourteen-year career as a co-therapist for Jingles (149).

In 1961, Dr. Levinson introduced his method of using pets in psychotherapy at an American Psychological Association convention.

The heading should be in capitals and centered.
Three spaces should follow before the first entry.

10

WORKS CITED

Beck, Alan, and Aaron Katcher. Between Pets and People: The Importance of Animal Companionship. New York: Putnam, 1983.

"Bedside Petting Perks Up Patients." Consumers Digest. May 1986: 10.

Cusack, Odean, and Elaine Smith, eds. Pets and the Elderly: The Therapeutic Bond. New York: Haworth Press, 1984.

Fogle, Bruce. Pets and Their People. New York: The Viking Press, 1984.

Levinson, Boris M. Pet-Oriented Child Psychotherapy. Springfield, Illinois: C. C. Thomas, 1969.

Sifford, Darrell, "Pets Can Play Therapeutic Roles." The Philadelphia Inquirer Oct. 12 1987: 2C.

Toufexis, Anastasia, "Furry and Feathery Therapists." Time 30 Mar. 1987: 74.

White, Betty. In Person. New York: Doubleday, 1987.

---------------------. Pet-Love. New York: William Morrow and Company, 1983.

DOCUMENTATION OF SOURCES

You must tell the reader the sources (books, articles, and so on) of the borrowed material in your paper. Whether you quote directly or summarize ideas in your own words, you must acknowledge your sources. In the past, you may have used footnotes and a bibliography to cite your sources. Now, you will learn to use the simplified documentation style recently provided by the Modern Language Association. The easy-to-learn style resembles the documentation used by the social sciences and natural sciences.

Citations within a Paper

Here are four guidelines for doing citations:

1 When citing a source for the first time, you must mention the author's name and the relevant page number. The author's name may be given either in the sentence you are writing or in parentheses following the sentence. Here are examples:

> Theodore Sizer explains, "The only way to learn to think well and usefully is by practice. The way a teacher assists this learning is by coaching" (216).
>
> One educator explains, "The only way to learn to think well and usefully is by practice. The way a teacher assists this learning is by coaching" (Sizer, 216).

2 The second reference to a source, if it comes immediately after the first reference, requires only the page number. You'll see on page 307, in the sample research paper, that the second reference to *Pet-Love* uses the page number alone (96).

3 If you are using more than one work by the same author or authors, include the title within the text. Notice how the title is used in the sample research paper on pages 306–307 (White, *Pet-Love*, 94–95). If there were only one book by White listed in the "Works Cited," then her name alone and the page number would suffice.

When you include a title within the text, shorten any long title. For example, if there were two books by Alan Beck and Aaron Katcher, and you were citing from their *Between Pets and People: The Importance of Animal Companionship*, you might shorten the title to simply *Pets and People*.

4 Finally, any notes in your paper should be informational—in other words, they should contain material of interest that is not essential to the discussion. These content notes (if any), titled "Notes," should be included before your list of "Works Cited."

Citations at the End of a Paper

Your paper should end with a list of "Works Cited" which includes all sources mentioned in the paper. Look at the "Works Cited" in the model research paper (page 308) and note the following points:

- The list is organized alphabetically according to the author's last name. Entries are not numbered.
- After the first line of each entry, there is an indentation of five spaces for each additional line in the entry.
- Entries are single-spaced, with a double space between entries.
- Entries without an author (such as "Bedside Petting Perks Up Patients") are listed alphabetically by the first word.
- When more than one work by the same author or authors is listed, a line followed by a period should be substituted for the author's or authors' names after the first entry. Thus a line is used with the second of two works by White.

Model entries for a list of "Works Cited" are given below. Use these entries as a guide when you prepare your own list.

Model Entries for a List of "Works Cited"

Book by One Author

Newman, Katherine. Falling From Grace. New York: The Free Press, 1988.

Book by Two Authors

Fisher, Roger, and Scott Brown. Getting Together. Boston: Houghton Mifflin, 1988.

Magazine Article

Clark, Matt, "What You Should Know about Heart Attacks." Newsweek 8 Feb. 1988: 50–54.

Write the date of the issue as follows: day, month (abbreviated in most cases to three letters), and year. The final numbers refer to pages 50–54 of the issue.

Newspaper Article

Spencer, Hal. "Miners Protect the Wild While Seeking Treasure." The New York Times 11 Feb. 1988: A.16.1–5.

The final numbers refer to section A, page 16, columns 1–5.

Signed Encyclopedia Article

H[utton], J[ohn] H[enry]. "Head-Hunting." Encyclopaedia Britannica. 1968 ed.

The brackets indicate that the article is signed with the author's *initials* only.

Selection in an Edited Collection

Fagin, Helene. "Creativity and Dreams." The Variety of Dream Experience. Ed. Montague Ullman and Claire Limmer. New York: Continuum, 1987. 59–81.

Revised or Later Edition

Verderber, Rudolph F. Communicate! 5th ed. Belmont, California: Wadsworth, 1987.

Pamphlet

Super Sitter, The. Washington: U.S. Consumer Product Safety Commission, Aug. 1986.

Film

School Daze. Directed by Spike Lee. Columbia Pictures, 1988.

Television Program

Reasoner, Harry. "Elizabeth of Toro." 60 Minutes. CBS-TV, 7 Feb. 1988.

Recording

Springsteen, Bruce, "Brilliant Disguise." Tunnel of Love. Columbia Records, CD-40999.

Personal or Telephone Interview

Heider, Dr. Janet. Personal interview. 735 North Front Street, Cleveland, Ohio 44102, 4 Jan. 1989.

Activity 1

Check your understanding of the chapter by answering the following questions.

1. *True or false?* ______ One purpose of a research paper might be to defend a point of some kind.
2. *True or false?* ______ Entries in a list of "Works Cited" are always numbered.
3. When you cite a source for the first time in your paper, you should
   a. use a footnote.
   b. use quotation marks.
   c. mention the author's name.
   d. mention the author's name and the page number.
4. A research paper topic should be
   a. general.
   b. unusual.
   c. plagiarized.
   d. narrow.
5. A list of possible sources of information for your paper is called
   a. a summary.
   b. a working bibliography.
   c. an outline.
   d. *Readers' Guide to Periodical Literature.*

Activity 2

On a separate sheet of paper, convert the information in each of the following references into the correct form for a list of "Works Cited." Use the appropriate model on pages 310–312 as a guide.

1. A book by Nancy Lieberman called Trained To Win and published in New York by Henry Holt and Company in 1988.
2. An article by Annetta Miller titled "The new Volunteerism" on pages 42–43 of the February 8, 1988 issue of Newsweek.
3. An article by Tom Goldstein titled "Women in the Law Aren't Yet Equal Partners" on page 7 of section B of the February 11, 1988 issue of The New York Times and occupying columns 3 to 6.
4. A book by Diana E. Papalia and Sally W. Olds titled Human Development and published in a fourth edition by McGraw-Hill Book Company in 1989.
5. An article by Ethel S. Person titled "Love Triangles" on pages 41–52 of the February issue of The Atlantic.

PART SIX

SENTENCE SKILLS

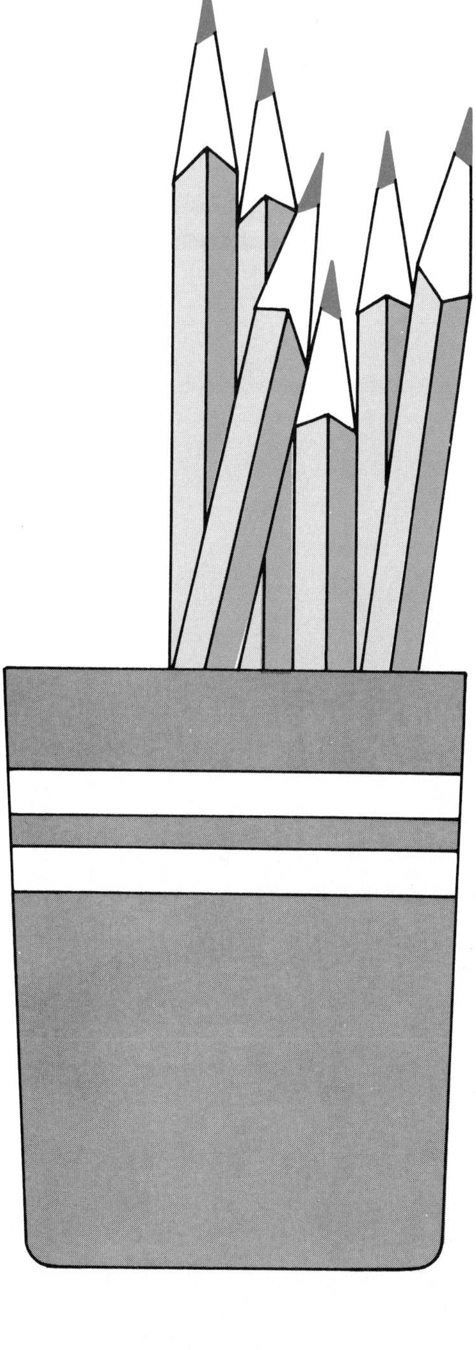

PREVIEW

As explained in Part One, there are four steps, or bases, in effective writing. Part Six is concerned with the *fourth step: the ability to write clear, error-free sentences*. First a diagnostic test is given so that you can check your present understanding of important sentence skills. Then the skills themselves appear under the general headings of ''Grammar,'' ''Mechanics,'' ''Punctuation,'' and ''Word Use.'' Following the skills is a chapter on sentence variety which helps develop your sense of the various options and methods available for composing sentences. Next come editing tests that reinforce many basic writing skills and give you work in editing and proofreading. Then an achievement test helps you measure your improvement in important sentence skills.

SENTENCE-SKILLS DIAGNOSTIC TEST

PART 1

This test will help you check your knowledge of important sentence skills. Certain parts of the following word groups are underlined. Place an X in the answer space if you think a mistake appears at the underlined part. Place a C in the answer space if you think the underlined part is correct.

A series of headings (''Sentence Fragments,'' ''Run-Ons,'' and so on) will give you clues to the mistakes to look for. However, you do not have to understand the label to find a mistake. What you are checking is your own sense of effective written English.

Sentence Fragments

X 1. Because Tom had eaten and drunk too much. He had to leave the party early. His stomach was like a volcano ready to erupt.

C 2. After I slid my aching bones into the hot water of the tub, I realized there was no soap. I didn't want to get out again.

X 3. I spent two hours on the phone yesterday. Trying to find a garage to repair my car. Eventually I had to have the car towed to a garage in another town.

X 4. Sweating under his heavy load. Brian staggered up the stairs to his apartment. He felt like his legs were crumbling beneath him.

C 5. I love to eat and cook Italian food, especially lasagna and ravioli. I make everything from scratch.

X 6. One of my greatest joys in life is eating desserts. Such as blueberry cheesecake or vanilla cream puffs. Almond fudge cake makes me want to dance.

Run-Ons

C ______ 7. He decided to stop smoking, for he didn't want to die of lung cancer.

X ______ 8. The window shade snapped up like a gunshot her cat leaped four feet off the floor.

X ______ 9. Billy is the meanest little kid on his block, he eats only the heads of animal crackers.

X ______ 10. He knew he had flunked the driver's exam, he ran over a stop sign.

C ______ 11. My first boyfriend was five years old. We met everyday in the playground sandbox.

X ______ 12. Lola wanted to go disco dancing, Tony preferred going to a movie.

Standard English Verbs

______ 13. Jed tows away cars for a living and is ashamed of his job.

______ 14. You snored like a chain saw last night.

______ 15. When I was about to finish work last night, a man walk into the restaurant and ordered two dozen hamburgers.

______ 16. Charlotte react badly whenever she gets caught in a traffic jam.

Irregular Verbs

______ 17. I knowed her from somewhere, but I couldn't remember just where.

______ 18. I had eaten so much food at the buffet dinner that I went into the bathroom just to loosen my belt.

______ 19. When the mud slide started, the whole neighborhood began going downhill.

______ 20. Juan has rode the bus to school for two years while saving for a car.

Subject-Verb Agreement

______ 21. There is long lines at the checkout counter.

______ 22. The camping blanket have to be washed.

______ 23. One of the crooked politicians was jailed for a month.

______ 24. The cockroaches behind my stove gets high on Raid.

Consistent Verb Tense

______ 25. I played my stereo and watched television before I decides to do some homework.

______ 26. The first thing Jerry does everyday is weigh himself. The scale informs him what kind of meals he can eat that day.

______ 27. Sandy eats a nutritional breakfast, skips lunch, and then enjoys a big dinner.

______ 28. His parents stayed together for his sake; only after he graduates from college were they divorced.

Misplaced Modifiers

______ 29. He swatted the wasp that stung him with a newspaper.

______ 30. Charlotte returned the hamburger that was spoiled to the supermarket.

______ 31. My aunt once met Jerry Lewis at a benefit, whom she found to be a very engaging person.

______ 32. I adopted a dog from a junkyard which is very close to my heart.

Dangling Modifiers

______ 33. Going to work, Clyde saw a three-car accident.

______ 34. Flunking out of school, my parents demanded that I get a job.

______ 35. While I was waiting for the bus, rain began to fall.

______ 36. Braking the car suddenly, the shopping bags tumbled onto the floor.

Faulty Parallelism

______ 37. Bill enjoys hunting for rabbits, socializing with friends, and to read the funnies.

______ 38. Lola likes to wear soft sweaters, to eat exotic foods, and to bathe in Calgon bath oil.

______ 39. When I saw my roommate with my girlfriend, I felt worried, angry, and embarrassment as well.

______ 40. Frances enjoys shopping for new clothes, trying different cosmetics, and reading beauty magazines.

Pronoun Agreement, Reference, and Point of View

_________ 41. I work at a clothes shop where you do not get paid for all the holidays I should.

_________ 42. I enjoy movies like *The Return of the Vampire* that frighten me.

_________ 43. A student should write their own papers.

_________ 44. Persons camping in those woods should watch their step because of wild dogs.

_________ 45. Angry at striking out, Tony hurled the baseball bat at the fence and broke it.

_________ 46. I love Parmesan cheese, but it does not always agree with me.

Capital Letters

_________ 47. Clyde uses certs mints after smoking his pipe or a cigar.

_________ 48. During july, Frank's company works a four-day week.

_________ 49. I asked my dad, "When's Uncle Bill getting his toupee?"

_________ 50. On Summer days I like to sit in the backyard and sunbathe.

Apostrophe

_________ 51. The Wolfman's bite is worse than his bark.

_________ 52. Clydes quick hands reached out to break his son's fall.

_________ 53. I'll be with you shortly if youll just wait a minute.

_________ 54. You shouldn't drink any more if you're hoping to get home safely.

Quotation Marks

_________ 55. Mark Twain once said, "The more I know about human beings, the more I like my dog."

_________ 56. Say something tender to me, "whispered Tony to Lola."

_________ 57. "I hate that commercial, he muttered."

_________ 58. "If you don't leave soon," he warned, "you'll be late for work."

Comma

________ 59. Bill relaxes by reading Donald Duck Archie and Bugs Bunny comic books.

________ 60. Although I have a black belt in karate I decided to go easy on the demented bully who had kicked sand in my face.

________ 61. Dracula, who had a way with women, is his favorite movie hero.

________ 62. We could always tell when our teacher felt disorganized for his shirt would not be tucked into his pants.

________ 63. You, my man, are going to get yours.

________ 64. His father shouted "Why don't you go out and get a job?"

Commonly Confused Words

________ 65. Some stores will accept your credit cards but not you're money.

________ 66. That issue is to hot for any politician to handle.

________ 67. They're planning to trade in their old car.

________ 68. Its important to get this job done properly.

________ 69. You should have the brakes on your car replaced write away.

________ 70. Who's the culprit who left the paint can on the table?

Effective Word Use

________ 71. I comprehended her statement.

________ 72. I understood what she said.

________ 73. The movie was a real bomb, so we left early.

________ 74. The victims of the car accident were shaken but none the worse for wear.

________ 75. Anne is of the opinion that the death penalty should be abolished.

Answers are on page 531.

PART 2 (OPTIONAL)

Do the following at your instructor's request. This second part of the test will provide more detailed information about skills you need to know. On separate paper, number and correct all the items you have marked with an X. For example, suppose you had marked the word groups below with an X. (Note that these examples are not taken from the test.)

4. If football games disappeared entirely from television. I would not even miss them. Other people in my family would perish.
7. The kitten suddenly saw her reflection in the mirror, she jumped back in surprise.
15. The tree in my cousins front yard always sheds its leaves two weeks before others on the street.
29. When we go out to a restaurant we always order something we would not cook for ourselves.

Here is how you should write your corrections on a separate sheet of paper.

4. television, I
7. mirror, and
15. cousin's
29. restaurant, we

There are over forty corrections to make in all.

SUBJECTS AND VERBS

The basic building blocks of English sentences are subjects and verbs. Understanding them is an important first step toward mastering a number of sentence skills.

Every sentence has a subject and a verb. Who or what the sentence speaks about is called the subject; what the sentence says about the subject is called the verb.

The children laughed.
Several branches fell.
Most students passed the test.
That man is a crook.

A SIMPLE WAY TO FIND A SUBJECT

To find a subject, ask *who* or *what* the sentence is about. As shown below, your answer is the subject.

Who is the first sentence about? Children
What is the second sentence about? Several branches
Who is the third sentence about? Most students
Who is the fourth sentence about? That man

A SIMPLE WAY TO FIND A VERB

To find a verb, ask what the sentence *says about* the subject. As shown below, your answer is the verb.

What does the first sentence *say about* the children? They laughed.

What does the second sentence *say about* the branches? They fell.

What does the third sentence *say about* the students? They passed.

What does the fourth sentence *say about* that man? He is (a crook).

A second way to find the verb is to put *I, you, he, she, it,* or *they* in front of the word you think is a verb. If the result makes sense, you have a verb. For example, you could put *they* in front of *laughed* in the first sentence above, with the result, *they laughed,* making sense. Therefore you know that *laughed* is a verb. You could use *they* or *he* to test the other verbs as well.

Finally, it helps to remember that most verbs show action. In the sentences already considered, the three action verbs are *laughed, fell,* and *passed.* Certain other verbs, known as *linking verbs,* do not show action. They do, however, give information about the subject. In ''That man is a crook,'' the linking verb *is* tells us that the man is a crook. Other common linking verbs include *am, are, was, were, feel, appear, look, become,* and *seem.*

Activity

In each of the following sentences, draw one line under the subject and two lines under the verb.

1. The heavy purse cut into my shoulder.
2. Small stones pinged onto the windshield.
3. The test directions confused the students.
4. Cotton shirts feel softer than polyester ones.
5. The fog rolled into the cemetery.
6. Sparrows live in the eaves of my porch.
7. A green bottle fly stung her on the ankle.
8. Every other night, garbage trucks rumble down my street on their way to the river.
9. The family played badminton and volleyball, in addition to a game of softball, at the picnic.
10. With their fingers, the children drew pictures on the steamed window.

MORE ABOUT SUBJECTS AND VERBS

1 A pronoun (a word like *he, she, it, we, you,* or *they* used in place of a noun) can serve as the subject of a sentence. For example:

He seems like a lonely person.

They both like to gamble.

Without a surrounding context (so that we know who *He* or *They* refers to), the sentences may not seem clear, but they *are* complete.

2 A sentence may have more than one verb, more than one subject, or several subjects and verbs:

My heart skipped and pounded.

The radio and tape player were stolen from the car.

Dave and Ellen prepared the report together and presented it to the class.

3 The subject of a sentence never appears within a prepositional phrase. A prepositional phrase is simply a group of words that begins with a preposition. Following is a list of common prepositions:

about	before	by	inside	over
above	behind	during	into	through
across	below	except	of	to
among	beneath	for	off	toward
around	beside	from	on	under
at	between	in	onto	with

Cross out prepositional phrases when looking for the subject of a sentence.

~~Under my pillow~~ I found a quarter left ~~by the Tooth Fairy.~~

One ~~of the yellow lights at the school crossing~~ began flashing.

The funny pages ~~of the newspaper~~ disappeared.

~~In spite of my efforts,~~ Bob dropped out of school.

~~During a rainstorm,~~ I sat ~~in my car~~ reading magazines.

4 Many verbs consist of more than one word. Here, for example, are some of the many forms of the verb *smile*.

smile	smiled	should smile
smiles	were smiling	will be smiling
does smile	have smiled	can smile
is smiling	had smiled	could be smiling
are smiling	had been smiling	must have smiled

Notes

a Words like *not, just, never, only,* and *always* are not part of the verb although they may appear within the verb.

Larry did not finish the paper before class.

The road was just completed only last week.

b No verb preceded by *to* is ever the verb of a sentence.

My car suddenly began to sputter on the freeway.

I swerved to avoid a squirrel on the road.

c No *-ing* word by itself is ever the verb of a sentence. (It may be part of the verb, but it must have a helping verb in front of it.)

They leaving early for the game. (not a sentence, because the verb is not complete)

They are leaving early for the game. (a sentence)

Activity

Draw a single line under the subjects and a double line under the verbs in the following sentences. Be sure to include all parts of the verb.

1. A burning odor from the wood saw filled the room.
2. At first, sticks of gum always feel powdery on your tongue.
3. Vampires and werewolves are repelled by garlic.
4. Three of my checks have bounced in the past week.
5. The driving rain had pasted wet leaves all over the car.
6. She has decided to buy a condominium.
7. The trees in the mall were glittering with tiny white lights.
8. The puppies slipped and tumbled on the vinyl kitchen floor.
9. Tony and Lola ate at Pizza Hut and then went to a movie.
10. We have not met our new neighbors in the apartment building.

■ Review Test

Draw a single line under subjects and a double line under verbs. Crossing out prepositional phrases may help to find the subjects.

1. A cloud of fruit flies hovered over the bananas.
2. Candle wax dripped onto the table and hardened into pools.
3. Nick and Fran are both excellent Frisbee players.
4. The leaves of my dying rubber plant resembled limp brown rags.
5. During the first week of vacation, Ken slept until noon every day.
6. They have just decided to go on a diet together.
7. Psychology and word processing are my favorite subjects.
8. The sofa in the living room has not been cleaned for over a year.
9. The water stains on her suede shoes did not disappear with brushing.
10. Fred stayed in bed too long and, as a result, arrived late for work.

SENTENCE SENSE

WHAT IS SENTENCE SENSE?

As a speaker of English, you already possess the most important of all sentence skills. You have *sentence sense*—an instinctive feel for where a sentence begins, where it ends, and the ways a sentence can be developed. You automatically and naturally learned sentence sense as part of learning the English language, and you have practiced it through all the years that you have been speaking English. It is as much a part of you as your ability to speak and understand English is a part of you.

The Value of Sentence Sense

Sentence sense can help you recognize and avoid fragments and run-ons, two of the most common and serious sentence-skills mistakes in written English. Sentence sense will also help you to place commas, to spot awkward and unclear phrasings, and to add variety to your sentences. You may ask, "If I already have this 'sentence sense,' why do I still make skills mistakes in punctuating sentences?" One answer could be that your past school experiences in writing were unrewarding or unpleasant. English may have been a series of dry writing topics, heavy doses of "correct" grammar and usage, or in some cases no attention to sentence skills at all. For any of these or other reasons, the instinctive sentence skills you practice while *speaking* may turn off when you start *writing*. The very act of picking up a pen may shut down your whole natural system of language abilities and skills.

How to Turn On the Sentence Sense within You

Chances are you don't *read a paper aloud* after you write it. Or you don't do the next best thing: read it aloud in your head. But it's essential to read aloud to turn on the natural language system within you. By reading aloud, you will be able to hear the points where your sentences begin and end. In addition, you will be able to pick up any trouble spots where your thoughts are not communicated clearly and well.

The practice activities that follow will help you turn on and rediscover the enormous language power within you. You will be able to see how your built-in sentence sense can guide your writing just as it does your speaking.

Activity

Each selection that follows lacks basic sentence punctuation. There is no period to mark the end of one sentence and no capital letter to mark the start of the next. Read each selection aloud (or in your head) so that you "hear" where each sentence begins and ends. Your voice will tend to drop and come to a pause at the point of each sentence break. Put a light slash mark (/) at every point where you hear a break. Then go back and read over the selection a second time. If you are now sure of each place where a split occurs, insert a period and change the first small letter after it to a capital. Minor pauses are often marked in English by commas; these are already inserted. Part of the first selection is done for you.

1. I take my dog for a walk on Saturdays in the big park by the lake/ I do this very early in the morning before children come to the park. That way I can let my dog run freely/ he jumps out the minute I open the car door and soon sees the first innocent squirrel/ then he is off like a shot and doesn't stop running for at least half an hour.

2. Lola hates huge tractor trailers that sometimes tailgate her Honda Civic/ the enormous smoke-belching machines seem ready to swallow her small car/ she shakes her fist at the drivers, and she rips out a lot of angry words/ recently she had a very satisfying dream/ she broke into an army supply depot and stole a bazooka/ she then became the first person in history to murder a truck

3. When I sit down to write, my mind is blank all I can think of is my name, which seems to me the most boring name in the world often I get sleepy and tell myself I should take a short nap other times I start daydreaming about things I want to buy sometimes I decide I should make a telephone call to someone I know the piece of paper in front of me is usually still blank when I leave to watch my favorite television show

4. One of the biggest regrets of my life is that I never told my father I loved him I resented the fact that he had never been able to say the words "I love you" to his children even during the long period of my father's illness, I remained silent and unforgiving then one morning he was dead, with my words left unspoken a guilt I shall never forget tore a hole in my heart I determined not to hold in my feelings with my daughters they know they are loved, because I both show and tell them this all people, no matter who they are, want to be told that they are loved

5. Two days ago, Greg killed several flying ants in his bedroom he also sprayed a column of ants that was forming a colony along the kitchen baseboard yesterday, he picked the evening newspaper off the porch and two black army ants scurried onto his hand this morning, he found an ant crawling on a lollipop he had left in his shirt pocket if any more insects appear, he is going to call Orkin Pest Control he feels like the victim in a Hitchcock movie called *The Ants* he is half afraid to sleep tonight he imagines the darkness will be full of tiny squirming things waiting to crawl all over him

SUMMARY

You probably did well in locating the end stops in the selections and helped prove to yourself that you *do* have sentence sense. This instinctive sense will help you deal with sentence fragments and run-ons, perhaps the two most common sentence-skills mistakes that people make.

Remember the importance of *reading your paper aloud*. By doing so, you turn on all the natural language skills that come from a lifetime of speaking English. The same sentence sense that helps you communicate effectively in speaking will help you communicate effectively in writing.

SENTENCE FRAGMENTS

Introductory Project

Every sentence must have a subject and a verb and must express a complete thought. A word group that lacks a subject or a verb and that does not express a complete thought is a fragment.

Listed below are a number of fragments and sentences. See if you can complete the statement that explains each fragment.

1. People. *Fragment*

   People gossip. *Sentence*

   "People" is a fragment because, while it has a subject (*People*), it lacks a verb (*gossip*) and so does not express a complete thought.

2. Wrestles. *Fragment*

   Tony wrestles. *Sentence*

   "Wrestles" is a fragment because, while it has a verb (*Wrestles*), it lacks a Subject (*Tony*) and so does not express a complete thought.

3. Drinking more than anyone else at the bar. *Fragment*

   Grandmother was drinking more than anyone else at the bar. *Sentence*

   "Drinking more than anyone else at the bar" is a fragment because it lacks a Subject (*Grandmother*) and also part of the verb (*was*) and so does not express a complete thought.

4. When Lola turned eighteen. *Fragment*

   When Lola turned eighteen, she began looking for pickups at dances. *Sentence*

   "When Lola turned eighteen" is a fragment because we want to know *what happened when* Lola turned eighteen. The word group does not follow through and Does not Express a Complete Thought

Answers are on page 532.

WHAT SENTENCE FRAGMENTS ARE

Every sentence must have a subject and a verb and must express a complete thought. A word group that lacks a subject or a verb and that does not express a complete thought is a *fragment*. Following are the most common types of fragments that people write:

1 Dependent-word fragments
2 *-ing* and *to* fragments
3 Added-detail fragments
4 Missing-subject fragments

Once you understand the specific kind or kinds of fragments that you may write, you should be able to eliminate them from your writing. The following pages explain all four fragment types.

DEPENDENT-WORD FRAGMENTS

Some word groups that begin with a dependent word are fragments. Here is a list of common dependent words:

after	if, even if	when, whenever
although, though	in order that	where, wherever
as	since	whether
because	that, so that	which, whichever
before	unless	while
even though	until	who, whoever
how	what, whatever	whose

Whenever you start a sentence with one of these words, you must be careful that a fragment does not result. The word group beginning with the dependent word *After* in the example below is a fragment.

After I learned the price of new cars. I decided to keep my old Buick.

A *dependent statement*—one starting with a dependent word like *After*—cannot stand alone. It depends on another statement to complete the thought. "After I learned the price of new cars" is a dependent statement. It leaves us hanging.

We expect in the same sentence to find out *what happened after* the writer learned the price of new cars. When a writer does not follow through and complete a thought, a fragment results.

To correct the fragment, simply follow through and complete the thought:

After I learned the price of new cars, I decided to keep my old Buick.

Remember, then, that *dependent statements by themselves are fragments.* They must be attached to a statement that makes sense standing alone.

Here are two other examples of dependent-word fragments:

My daughter refused to stop smoking. Unless I quit also.

Bill asked for a loan. Which he promised to pay back in two weeks.

"Unless I quit also" is a fragment; it does not make sense standing by itself. We want to know in the same statement *what would not happen unless* the writer quit also. The writer must complete the thought. Likewise, "Which he promised to pay back in two weeks" is not in itself a complete thought. We want to know in the same statement what *which* refers to.

How to Correct a Dependent-Word Fragment

In most cases you can correct a dependent-word fragment by attaching it to the sentence that comes after it or the sentence that comes before it:

After I learned the price of new cars, I decided to keep my old Buick.
(The fragment has been attached to the sentence that comes after it.)

My daughter refused to quit smoking unless I quit also.
(The fragment has been attached to the sentence that comes before it.)

Bill asked for a loan which he promised to pay back in two weeks.
(The fragment has been attached to the sentence that comes before it.)

Another way of correcting a dependent-word fragment is simply to eliminate the dependent word:

I learned the price of new cars and decided to keep my old Buick.

She wanted me to quit also.

He promised to pay it back in two weeks.

Do not use this method of correction too frequently, however, for it may cut down on interest and variety in your writing style.

Notes

1 Use a comma if a dependent-word group comes at the beginning of a sentence (see also page 442):

After I learned the price of new cars, I decided to keep my old Buick.

However, do not generally use a comma if the dependent-word group comes at the end of a sentence:

My daughter refused to stop smoking unless I quit also.
Bill asked for a loan which he promised to pay back in two weeks.

2 Sometimes the dependent words *who, that, which,* or *where* appear not at the very start, but near the start, of a word group. A fragment often results:

The town council decided to put more lights on South Street. A place where several people have been mugged.

"A place where several people have been mugged" is not in itself a complete thought. We want to know in the same statement *where was the place* that several people were mugged. The fragment can be corrected by attaching it to the sentence that comes before it:

The town council decided to put more lights on South Street, a place where several people have been mugged.

Activity 1

Turn each of the following dependent-word groups into a sentence by adding a complete thought. Put a comma after the dependent-word group if a dependent word starts the sentence.

Examples Although I arrived in class late

Although I arrived in class late, I still did well on the test.

The little boy who plays with our daughter

The little boy who plays with our daughter just came down with German measles.

1. Because the weather is bad

   Because The weater is bad, we will stay home.

2. If I lend you twenty dollars

   IF I lend You twenty dollars, will You Pay me back interest.

3. The car that we bought

   the Car that we bought needs unleaded Gas.

4. Since I was tired

   Since I was tired, I stayed Home.

5. Before the teacher entered the room

   Before the teacher entered the Room She looked through the Window.

Activity 2

Underline the dependent-word fragment or fragments in each selection. Then rewrite the selections, correcting the fragments by attaching them to the sentence that comes before or the sentence that comes after—whichever sounds more natural. Put a comma after the dependent-word group if it starts the sentence.

1. Whenever our front and back doors are open. The air current causes the back door to slam shut. The noise makes everyone in the house jump.

   Whenever our front and back doors are open, The air

2. Bill always turns on the radio in the morning to hear the news. He wants to be sure that World War III has not started. Before he gets on with his day.

   Started before he gets on whith his day

3. Since the line at the Motor Vehicle Bureau crawls at a snail's pace. Fred waited two hours there. When there was only one person left in front of him. The office closed for the day.

Since the line at the Motor Vehicle Bureau crawls at a snails pace, Fred waited two hours there, When there was only one person left in front of him, The. The office closed for the day.

4. My dog ran in joyous circles on the wide beach. Until she found a dead fish. Before I had a chance to drag her away. She began sniffing and nudging the smelly remains.

5. When the air conditioner broke down. The temperature was over ninety degrees. I then found an old fan. Which turned out to be broken also.

-ING AND *TO* FRAGMENTS

When an *-ing* word appears at or near the start of a word group, a fragment may result. Such fragments often lack a subject and part of the verb. Underline the word groups in the selections below that contain *-ing* words. Each is a fragment.

Selection 1

I spent almost two hours on the phone yesterday. Trying to find a garage to repair my car. Eventually I had to have it towed to a garage in another town.

Selection 2

Maggie was at first very happy with the blue sports car she had bought for only five hundred dollars. Not realizing until a week later that the car averaged seven miles per gallon of gas.

Selection 3

He looked forward to the study period at school. It being the only time he could sit unbothered and dream about his future. He imagined himself as a lawyer with lots of money and women to spend it on.

People sometimes write *-ing* fragments because they think the subject in one sentence will work for the next word group as well. Thus, in the first selection, the writer thinks that the subject *I* in the opening sentence will also serve as the subject for "Trying to find a garage to repair my car." But the subject must actually be *in* the sentence.

How to Correct *-ing* Fragments

1 Attach the fragment to the sentence that comes before it or the sentence that comes after it, whichever makes sense. Selection 1 could read: "I spent two hours on the phone yesterday, trying to find a garage to repair my car."

2 Add a subject and change the *-ing* verb part to the correct form of the verb. Selection 2 could read: "She realized only a week later that the car averaged seven miles per gallon of gas."

3 Change *being* to the correct form of the verb *be* (*am, are, is, was, were*). Selection 3 could read: "It was the only time he could sit unbothered and dream about his future."

How to Correct *to* Fragments

When *to* appears at or near the start of a word group, a fragment sometimes results:

> I plan on working overtime. To get this job finished. Otherwise, my boss may get angry at me.

The second word group is a fragment and can be corrected by adding it to the preceding sentence:

> I plan on working overtime to get this job finished.

Activity 1

Underline the *-ing* fragment in each of the selections that follow. Then make it a sentence by rewriting it, using the method described in parentheses.

Example A thunderstorm was brewing. A sudden breeze shot through the windows. Driving the stuffiness out of the room.
(Add the fragment to the preceding sentence.)

A sudden breeze shot through the windows, driving the stuffiness out of the room.

1. Sweating under his heavy load. Brian staggered up the stairs to his apartment. He felt like his legs were crumbling beneath him.
(Add the fragment to the sentence that comes after it.)
Sweating under his heavy load Brian staggered up the stairs to his Apartment.

2. He works 10 hours a day. Then going to class for 2½ hours. It is no wonder he writes sentence fragments.
(Correct the fragment by adding the subject *he* and changing *going* to the proper form of the verb, *goes*.)
Then He goes to Class For 2½ hours.

3. Charlotte loved the movie *Gone with the Wind,* but Clyde hated it. His chief objection being that it lasted four hours.
(Correct the fragment by changing *being* to the proper verb form, *was*.)
His chief objection was that it lasted Four hours.

Activity 2

Underline the *-ing* or *to* fragment or fragments in each selection. Then rewrite each selection, correcting the fragments by using one of the three methods of correction described on page 337.

1. A mysterious package arrived on my porch yesterday. Bearing no return address. I half expected to find a bomb inside.
Bearing no return address, I half expected to Find a Bomb inside

2. Jack bundled up and went outside on the bitterly cold day. To saw wood for his fireplace. He returned half frozen with only two logs.
Jack bundled up and went outside on the bitterly Cold day to saw Wood For his Fire Place.

3. Looking tired and drawn. The little girl's parents sat in the waiting room. The operation would be over in a few minutes.
Looking tired and drawn, the little Jirl's ...

4. Sighing with resignation. Jill switched on her television set. She knew that the picture would be snowy and crackling with static. Her house being in a weak reception area.

Sighing with resignation, Jill switched on her television set. . . .

Her house was in a weak reception area.

5. Jabbing the ice with a screwdriver. Bill attempted to speed up the defrosting process in his freezer. However, he used too much force. The result being a freezer compartment riddled with holes.

Jabbing the ice with a screwdriver, Bill attempted. . . .

his result was a freezer compartment. . . .

ADDED-DETAIL FRAGMENTS

Added-detail fragments lack a subject and a verb. They often begin with one of the following words:

also	except	including
especially	for example	such as

See if you can locate and underline the one added-detail fragment in each of the selections that follow:

Selection 1

I love to cook and eat Italian food. Especially spaghetti and lasagna. I make everything from scratch.

Selection 2

The class often starts late. For example, yesterday at quarter after nine instead of at nine sharp. Today the class started at five after nine.

Selection 3

He failed a number of courses before he earned his degree. Among them, English I, Economics, and General Biology.

People often write added-detail fragments for much the same reason they write *-ing* fragments. They think the subject and verb in one sentence will serve for the next word group as well. But the subject and verb must be in *each* word group.

How to Correct Added-Detail Fragments

1 Attach the fragment to the complete thought that precedes it. Selection 1 could read: "I love to cook and eat Italian food, especially spaghetti and lasagna."

2 Add a subject and a verb to the fragment to make it a complete sentence. Selection 2 could read: "The class often starts late. For example, yesterday it began at quarter after nine instead of at nine sharp."

3 Change words as necessary to make the fragment part of the preceding sentence. Selection 3 could read: "Among the courses he failed before he earned his degree were English I, Economics, and General Biology."

Activity 1

Underline the fragment in each of the selections below. Then make it a sentence by rewriting it, using the method described in parentheses.

Example I am always short of pocket money. Especially for everyday items like magazines and sodas. Luckily my friends often have change. (Add the fragment to the preceding sentence.)

I am always short of pocket money, especially for everyday items like magazines and sodas.

1. Nina is trying hard for a promotion. For example, through night classes and a Dale Carnegie course. She is also working overtime for no pay. (Correct the fragment by adding the subject and verbs *she is taking*.)

For example, she is taking night...

2. I could feel Bill's anger building. Like a land mine ready to explode. I was silent because I didn't want to be the one to set it off.
(Add the fragment to the preceding sentence.)

I could feel Bill's anger building like a mine...

3. We went on vacation without several essential items. Among other things, our sneakers and sweat jackets.
(Correct the fragment by adding the subject and verb *we forgot*.)

We forgot our sneakers...

Activity 2

Underline the added-detail fragment in each selection. Then rewrite that part of the selection needed to correct the fragment. Use one of the three methods of correction described on the preceding page.

1. It's always hard for me to get up for work. Especially on Mondays after a holiday weekend. However, I always wake up early on free days.

It's always hard for me to get up for work, especially on...

2. Tony has enormous endurance. For example, the ability to run five miles in the morning and then play basketball all afternoon.

For example, he can run five miles...

X 3. A counselor gives you a chance to talk about your problems. Whether with your family or the boss at work. You learn how to cope better with life.

, whether with your family or the boss. A counselor

4. Fred and Martha do most of their shopping through mail-order catalogs. Especially the Sears and J. C. Penney catalogs.

catalogs, especially the...

5. One of my greatest joys in life is eating desserts. Such as cherry cheesecake or vanilla cream puffs. Almond fudge cake makes me want to dance.

deserts, such as...

MISSING-SUBJECT FRAGMENTS

In each selection below, underline the word group in which the subject is missing.

Selection 1

The truck skidded on the rain-slick highway. But missed a telephone pole on the side of the road.

Selection 2

Michelle tried each of the appetizers on the table. And then found that, when the dinner arrived, her appetite had gone.

People write missing-subject fragments because they think the subject in one sentence will apply to the next word group as well. But the subject, as well as the verb, must be in each word group to make it a sentence.

How to Correct Missing-Subject Fragments

1 Attach the fragment to the preceding sentence. Selection 1 could read: "The truck skidded on the rain-slick highway but missed a telephone pole on the side of the road."

2 Add a subject (which can often be a pronoun standing for the subject in the preceding sentence). Selection 2 could read: "She then found that, when the dinner arrived, her appetite had gone."

Activity

Underline the missing-subject fragment in each selection. Then rewrite that part of the selection needed to correct the fragment. Use one of the two methods of correction described above.

1. I tried on an old suit hanging in our basement closet. And discovered, to my surprise, that it was too tight to button.

 I discovered, . . .

 ____

 ____

2. When Mary had a sore throat, friends told her to gargle with salt water. Or suck on an ice cube. The worst advice she got was to avoid swallowing.

water, or suck on an . . .

3. One of my grade-school teachers embarrassed us with her sarcasm. Also, seated us in rows from the brightest student to the dumbest. I can imagine the pain the student in the last seat must have felt.

She seated us . . .

A Review: How to Check for Sentence Fragments

1 Read your paper aloud from the *last* sentence to the *first.* You will be better able to see and hear whether each word group you read is a complete thought.

2 Ask yourself of any word group you think is a fragment: Does this contain a subject and a verb and express a complete thought?

3 More specifically, be on the lookout for the most common fragments:

- Dependent-word fragments (starting with words like *after, because, since, when,* and *before*)
- *-ing* and *to* fragments (*-ing* or *to* at or near the start of a word group)
- Added-detail fragments (starting with words like *for example, such as, also,* and *especially*)
- Missing-subject fragments (a verb is present but not the subject)

■ Review Test 1

Turn each of the following word groups into a complete sentence. Use the space provided.

Example With sweaty palms

With sweaty palms, I walked in for the job interview.

Even when it rains

The football teams practice even when it rains.

1. When the alarm sounded

____

2. In order to save some money

____

3. Was late for the game

____

4. To pass the course

____

5. Peter, who is very impatient

____

6. During the holiday season

____

7. The store where I worked

____

8. Before the movie started

____

9. Down in the basement

____

10. Feeling very confident

____

■ Review Test 2

Each word group in the student paragraph below is numbered. In the space provided, write C if a word group is a *complete sentence;* write F if it is a *fragment.* You will find seven fragments in the paragraph.

A Disastrous First Date

[1]My first date with Donna was a disaster. [2]I decided to take her to a small Italian restaurant. [3]That my friends told me had reasonable prices. [4]At the restaurant, things started to go wrong. [5]Looking over the large menu and realizing I couldn't pronounce the complete names of any of the dishes. [6]Such as "veal piccante," "spaghetti Bolognese," and "fettucini Alfredo." [7]Then, I noticed a burning smell. [8]The candle on the table was starting to blacken and scorch the back of my plastic menu. [9]Trying to be casual. [10]I quickly poured half my glass of water down the melting menu. [11]The waiter eventually returned to our table. [12]And asked me if I wanted to order some wine. [13]I hoped I sounded sophisticated as I ordered a bottle of Blue Nun. [14]The only wine that I had heard of and could pronounce. [15]When the waiter brought the wine, he poured a small amount into my glass, held the bottle, and waited. [16]Wondering what was going on, I said, "You don't have to stand there. We can pour the wine ourselves." [17]When he left, Donna told me I was supposed to taste the wine. [18]Feeling like a complete fool. [19]I managed to get through the dinner. [20]However, for weeks afterward, I felt like jumping out a tenth-story window.

1. C
2. C
3. F
4. C
5. F
6. F
7. C
8. C
9. F
10. C
11. C
12. F
13. C
14. F
15. C
16. C
17. C
18. F
19. C
20. C

■ Review Test 3

Underline the two fragments in each selection. Then make whatever changes are needed to turn the fragments into sentences.

Example The people at the diner save money~~.~~ ~~B~~*b*y watering down the coffee. Also, *they use* ~~using~~ the cheapest grade of hamburger. Few people go there anymore.

1. Gathering speed with enormous force. The plane was suddenly in the air. Then it began to climb sharply. And several minutes later leveled off.
2. Before my neighbors went on vacation. They asked me to watch their house. I agreed to check the premises once a day. Also, to take in their mail.
3. Running untouched into the end zone. The halfback raised his arms in triumph. Then he slammed the football to the ground. And did a little victory dance.
4. It's hard to keep up with monthly payments. Among others, telephone, electric, and gas bills. After you finally mail the checks. New ones seem to arrive a day or two later.
5. Customers at the counter waited impatiently. While a woman ordered ten pounds of cold cuts. And fifteen pounds of potato salad. She explained that she was in charge of a Cub Scout picnic.

■ Review Test 4

Write quickly for five minutes about what you like to do in your leisure time. Don't worry about spelling, punctuation, finding exact words, or organizing your thoughts. Just focus on writing as many words as you can without stopping.

After you have finished, go back and make whatever changes are needed to correct any sentence fragments in your writing.

RUN-ONS

Introductory Project

A run-on occurs when two sentences are run together with no adequate sign given to mark the break between them. Shown below are four run-on sentences and four correctly marked sentences. See if you can complete the statement that explains how each run-on is corrected.

1. He is the meanest little kid on his block he eats only the heads of animal crackers. *Run-on*

   He is the meanest little kid on his block. He eats only the heads of animal crackers. *Correct*

   The run-on has been corrected by using a __Period__ and a capital letter to separate the two complete thoughts.

2. Fred Grencher likes to gossip about other people, he doesn't like them to gossip about him. *Run-on*

   Fred Grencher likes to gossip about other people, but he doesn't like them to gossip about him. *Correct*

   The run-on has been corrected by using a joining word, __but__, to connect the two complete thoughts.

3. The chain on my bike likes to chew up my pants, it leaves grease marks on my ankle as well. *Run-on*

   The chain on my bike likes to chew up my pants; it leaves grease marks on my ankle as well. *Correct*

   The run-on has been corrected by using a __as well__ to connect the two closely related thoughts.

4. The window shade snapped up like a gunshot, her cat leaped four feet off the floor. *Run-on*

   When the window shade snapped up like a gunshot, her cat leaped four feet off the floor. *Correct*

   The run-on has been corrected by using the subordinating word __Then__ to connect the two closely related thoughts.

Answers are on page 532.

WHAT RUN-ONS ARE AND HOW TO CORRECT THEM

A *run-on* is two complete thoughts that are run together with no adequate sign given to mark the break between them.* Some run-ons have no punctuation at all to mark the break between the thoughts. Such run-ons are known as *fused sentences:* they are fused or joined together as if they are only one thought.

Fused Sentence

My grades are very good this semester my social life rates only a C.

Fused Sentence

Our father was a madman in his youth he would do anything on a dare.

In other run-ons, known as *comma splices,* a comma is used to connect or ''splice'' together the two complete thoughts. However, a comma alone is *not enough* to connect two complete thoughts. Some stronger connection than a comma alone is needed.

Comma Splice

My grades are very good this semester, my social life rates only a C.

Comma Splice

Our father was a madman in his youth, he would do anything on a dare.

Comma splices are the most common kind of run-on mistake. Students sense that some kind of connection is needed between two thoughts, and so put a comma at the dividing point. But the comma alone is not sufficient, and a stronger, clearer mark between the two thoughts is needed.

Here are three common methods of correcting a run-on:

1 Use a period and a capital letter to break the two complete thoughts into separate sentences:

My grades are very good this semester. My social life rates only a C.

Our father was a madman in his youth. He would do anything on a dare.

* *Note:* Some instructors refer to each complete thought in a run-on as an *independent clause.* A *clause* is simply a group of words having a subject and a verb. A clause may be *independent* (expressing a complete thought and able to stand alone) or *dependent* (not expressing a complete thought and not able to stand alone). A run-on is two independent clauses that are run together with no adequate sign given to mark the break between them.

2 Use a comma plus a joining word (*and, but, for, or, nor, so, yet*) to connect the two complete thoughts:

My grades are very good this semester, but my social life rates only a C.

Our father was a madman in his youth, for he would do anything on a dare.

3 Use a semicolon to connect the two complete thoughts:

My grades are very good this semester; my social life rates only a C.

Our father was a madman in his youth; he would do anything on a dare.

A fourth method of correcting a run-on is to use *subordination*. The following activities will give you practice in the first three methods. The use of subordination will be described fully on page 494, in a section of the book that deals with sentence variety.

METHOD 1: PERIOD AND A CAPITAL LETTER

One way of correcting a run-on is to use a period and a capital letter at the break between the two complete thoughts. Use this method especially if the thoughts are not closely related or if another method would make the sentence too long.

Activity

Locate the split in each of the following run-ons. Each is a *fused sentence*—that is, each consists of two sentences that are fused or joined together with no punctuation at all between them. Reading each sentence aloud will help you "hear" where a major break or split in the thought occurs. At such a point, your voice will probably drop and pause.

Correct the run-on sentence by putting a period at the end of the first thought and a capital letter at the start of the next thought.

Example Martha Grencher shuffled around the apartment in her slippers. Her husband couldn't stand their slapping sound on the floor.

1. The down jacket was not well-made little feathers leaked out of the seams.
2. Phil cringed at the sound of the dentist's drill it buzzed like a fifty-pound mosquito.
3. Last summer no one swam in the lake a little boy had dropped his pet piranhas into the water.

4. A horse's teeth never stop growing they will eventually grow outside the horse's mouth.
5. Sue's doctor told her he was an astrology nut she did not feel good about learning that.
6. Ice water is the best remedy for a burn, using butter is like adding fat to a flame.
7. In the apartment the air was so dry that her skin felt parched, the heat was up to eighty degrees.
8. My parents bought me an ant farm it's going to be hard to find tractors that small.
9. Lobsters are cannibalistic this is one reason they are hard to raise in captivity.
10. Julia placed an egg timer next to the phone, she did not want to talk more than three minutes on her long-distance calls.

Activity 2

Locate the split in each of the following run-ons. Some of the run-ons are fused sentences, and some of them are *comma splices*—run-ons spliced or joined together only with a comma. Correct each run-on by putting a period at the end of the first thought and a capital letter at the start of the next thought.

1. A bird got into the house through the chimney we had to catch it before our cat did.
2. Some so-called health foods are not so healthy, many are made with oils that raise cholesterol levels.
3. We sat only ten feet from the magician, we still couldn't see where all the birds came from.
4. Rich only needs five hours of sleep each night his wife needs at least seven.
5. Our image of dentistry will soon change, dentists will use lasers instead of drills.
6. Gale entered her apartment and jumped with fright someone was leaving through her bedroom window.

7. There were several unusual hair styles at the party, one woman had bright green braids.

8. Jon saves all of his magazines, once a month, he takes them to a nearby nursing home.

9. The doctor seemed to be in a rush, I still took time to ask all the questions that were on my mind.

10. When I was little, my brother tried to feed me flies, he told me they were raisins.

A Warning: Words That Can Lead to Run-Ons

People often write run-on sentences when the second complete thought begins with one of the following words:

I	we	there	now
you	they	this	then
he, she, it		that	next

Remember to be on the alert for run-on sentences whenever you use one of these words in writing a paper.

Activity

Write a second sentence to go with each of the sentences that follow. Start the second sentence with the word given in italics. Your sentences can be serious or playful.

Example *She* Jackie works for the phone company. *She climbs telephone poles in all kinds of weather.*

It 1. The alarm clock is unreliable. It rings every hour.

He 2. My uncle has a peculiar habit. He eats Raw Potatoes.

Then 3. Lola studied for the math test for two hours. Then She went out to a Party.

It 4. I could not understand why the car would not start. IT JUST Failed TO GO.

There 5. We saw all kinds of litter on the highway. There were Loads of Paper.

METHOD 2: COMMA AND A JOINING WORD

Another way of correcting a run-on sentence is to use a comma plus a joining word to connect the two complete thoughts. Joining words (also called *conjunctions*) include *and, but, for, or, nor, so,* and *yet.* Here is what the four most common joining words mean:

and in addition to, along with

His feet hurt from the long hike, and his stomach was growling.

(*And* means ''in addition'': His feet hurt from the long hike; *in addition,* his stomach was growling.)

but however, except, on the other hand, just the opposite

I remembered to get the cocoa, but I forgot the marshmallows.

(*But* means ''however'': I remembered to get the cocoa; *however,* I forgot the marshmallows.)

He Does not want us to use this

for because, the reason why, the cause for something

She was afraid of not doing well in the course, for she had always had bad luck with English before.

(*For* means ''because'' or ''the reason why'': She was afraid of not doing well in the course; *the reason why* was that she had always had bad luck with English before.)

If you are not comfortable using *for,* you may want to use *because* instead of *for* in the activities that follow. If you do use *because,* omit the comma before it.

so as a result, therefore

The windshield wiper was broken, so she was in trouble when the rain started.

(*So* means "as a result": The windshield wiper was broken; *as a result,* she was in trouble when the rain started.)

Activity 1

Insert the joining word (*and, but, for, so*) that logically connects the two thoughts in each sentence.

1. The couple wanted desperately to buy the house, but they did not qualify for a mortgage.
2. A lot of men today get their hair styled, and they use perfume and other cosmetics as well.
3. Clyde asked his wife if she had any bandages, but he was dressed so sharply he was liable to cut himself to death.
4. He failed the vision part of his driver's test, ________ he did not get his driver's license that day.
5. The restaurant was beautiful, ________ the food was overpriced.

Activity 2

Add a complete and closely related thought to go with each of the following statements. Use a comma plus the italicized joining word when you write the second thought.

Example *for* Lola spent the day walking barefoot, *for the heel of one of her shoes had come off.*

but 1. She wanted to go to the party, but she had no ride.

and 2. Tony washed his car in the morning, and it was dirty by night.

so 3. The day was dark and rainy, So we could not Play Catch.

for 4. I'm not going to eat in the school cafeteria anymore ________________________________

but 5. I asked my brother to get off the telephone ________________________________

Activity 3

Correct each run-on with either (1) a period and a capital letter or (2) a comma and a logical joining word. Do not use the same method of correction for each sentence. You will notice that some of the run-ons are fused sentences (there is no punctuation between the two complete thoughts) and some are comma splices (there is only a comma between the two complete thoughts).

Example I can't study for the test this weekend my boss wants me to work overtime.

1. Martha quickly looked around the supermarket then she left the box of cookies she didn't want on the soup shelf.
2. My brother's asthma was worsening, he quit the soccer team.
3. The children begged to stay up for the vampire movie fifteen minutes later they wanted to go to bed.
4. Bill ate an entire pizza for supper, he had a big hunk of pound cake for dessert.
5. ''All Natural'' was printed in large letters on the yogurt carton, the fine print of the ingredients told a different story.
6. It took several minutes for my eyes to adjust to the light I had just come out of the dark movie theater.
7. My uncle has an electric pacemaker, the garage door opens whenever he sneezes.
8. The Olympic games may soon include events for disabled people wheelchair athletes and amputee skiers, for example, will compete in special races.
9. Lola loves the velvety texture of cherry Jell-O she also loves to squish it between her teeth.
10. The man leaned against the building was in obvious pain soon a passerby stopped to help him.

METHOD 3: SEMICOLON

A third method of correcting a run-on sentence is to use a semicolon to mark the break between two thoughts. A *semicolon* (;) is made up of a period and a comma and is sometimes called a *strong comma*. The semicolon signals more of a pause than a comma alone but not quite the full pause of a period.

Semicolon Alone

Here are some earlier sentences that were connected with a comma plus a joining word. Notice that a semicolon, unlike the comma alone, can be used to connect the two complete thoughts in each sentence:

> A lot of men today get their hair styled; they use perfume and other cosmetics as well.
>
> She was afraid of not doing well in the course; she had always had bad luck with English before.
>
> I can't study for the test this weekend; my boss wants me to work overtime.

The use of the semicolon can add to sentence variety. For some people, however, the semicolon is a confusing mark of punctuation. Keep in mind that if you are not comfortable using it, you can and should use one of the first two methods of correcting a run-on sentence.

Activity

Insert a semicolon where the break occurs between the two complete thoughts in each of the following sentences.

Example I missed the bus by seconds;there would not be another for half an hour.

1. I spend eight hours a day in a windowless office it's a relief to get out in the open air after work.
2. The audience howled with laughter the comedian enjoyed a moment of triumph.
3. It rained all week parts of the highway were flooded.
4. Tony never goes to a certain gas station anymore he found out that the service manager overcharged him for a valve job.
5. The washer shook and banged with its unbalanced load then it began to walk across the floor.

Semicolon with a Transitional Word

A semicolon is sometimes used with a transitional word and a comma to join two complete thoughts:

> We were short of money; therefore, we decided not to eat out that weekend.
>
> The roots of a geranium have to be crowded into a small pot; otherwise, the plants may not flower.
>
> I had a paper to write; however, my brain had stopped working for the night.

Here is a list of common transitional words (also known as *adverbial conjunctions*). Brief meanings are given for most of the words.

Transitional Word	*Meaning*
however	but
nevertheless	however
on the other hand	however
instead	as a substitute
meanwhile	in the intervening time
otherwise	under other conditions
indeed	in fact
in addition	
also	in addition
moreover	in addition
furthermore	in addition
as a result	
thus	as a result
consequently	as a result
therefore	as a result

Activity

Choose a logical transitional word from the above group and write it in the space provided. Put a semicolon *before* the connector and a comma *after* it.

Example Exams are over ___*; however,*___ I still feel tense and nervous.

1. I did not understand her point ___; Therefore,___ I asked her to repeat it.

2. With his thumbnail, Tony tried to split open the cellophane covering on the new record album ; Nevertheless, the cellophane refused to tear.
3. Post offices are closed for today's holiday ; therefore, no mail will be delivered.
4. They decided not to go to the movie ; instead, they went to play miniature golf.
5. I had to skip lunch ; otherwise, I would be late for class.

A NOTE ON SUBORDINATION

A fourth method of joining together related thoughts is to use subordination. *Subordination* is a way of showing that one thought in a sentence is not as important as another thought. (Subordination is explained in full on page 496.) Here are three earlier sentences that have been recast so that one idea is subordinated to (made less important than) the other idea:

When the window shade snapped up like a gunshot, her cat leaped four feet off the floor.

Because it rained all week, parts of the highway were flooded.

Although my grades are very good this year, my social life rates only a C.

A Review: How to Check for Run-On Sentences

1 To see if a sentence is a run-on, read it aloud and listen for a break marking two complete thoughts. Your voice will probably drop and pause at the break.

2 To check an entire paper, read it aloud from the *last* sentence to the *first*. Doing so will help you hear and see each complete thought.

3 Be on the lookout for words that can lead to run-on sentences:

I	he, she, it	they	this	next
you	we	there	that	then

4 Correct run-on sentences by using one of the following methods:

- Period and capital letter
- Comma and joining word (*and, but, for, or, nor, so, yet*)
- Semicolon
- Subordination (as explained on page 496)

■ Review Test 1

Some of the run-ons that follow are fused sentences, having no punctuation between the two complete thoughts; others are comma splices, having only a comma between the two complete thoughts. Two sentences are correctly punctuated.

Write C beside the two sentences that are correctly punctuated. Correct each run-on by using either (1) a period and a capital letter, (2) a comma and a joining word, or (3) a semicolon. Do not use the same method of correction in each sentence.

Example Three people did the job, but I could have done it alone.

1. The impatient driver tried to get a jump on the green light he kept edging his car into the intersection.
2. The course on the history of UFOs sounded interesting, it turned out to be very dull.
3. That clothing store is a strange place to visit you keep walking up to dummies that look like real people.
4. Everything on the menu of the Pancake House sounded delicious they wanted to order the entire menu.
5. Bill pressed a cold washcloth against his eyes, it helped relieve his headache.
6. Craig used to be a fast-food junkie now all he eats are vegetables and sunflower seeds.
7. I knew my term paper was not very good, so I placed it in a shiny plastic cover to make it look better.
8. Lola enjoys watching a talk show, Tony prefers watching a late movie.
9. My boss does not know what he is doing half the time then he tries to tell me what to do.
10. In the next minute, 100 people will die, and over 240 babies will be born.

Review Test 2

Follow the directions given for Review Test 1.

1. My car sounds like a motorcycle, rust has eaten a hole in the muffler.
2. The lady beside me on the bus fell asleep she began leaning her head on my shoulder.
3. There were a number of shirts and jackets on sale, they all had very noticeable flaws.
4. I can tell the pollen count is high my eyes have been watering all day.
5. Sixty-five is no longer a compulsory retirement age; many people continue working beyond that point.
6. Hank Aaron holds the home-run hitting record he hit forty-one more homers than Babe Ruth.
7. Electric cars eliminate automobile pollution, the limited power of the car's battery is a serious problem.
8. All the clocks in the house must be fixed, for the power went off during the night for ten minutes.
9. The apartment is beautifully decorated it is very cozy and comfortable as well.
10. Offices of the future will need very little paper, all memos and files will be stored in computers.

Review Test 3

Write quickly for five minutes about what you did this past weekend. Don't worry about spelling, punctuation, finding exact words, or organizing your thoughts. Just focus on writing as many words as you can without stopping.

After you have finished, go back and make whatever changes are needed to correct any run-ons in your writing.

STANDARD ENGLISH VERBS

Introductory Project

Underline what you think is the correct form of the verb in each of the sentences below:

As a boy, he (enjoy, enjoyed) watching *Wild Kingdom* on television.
He still (enjoy, enjoys) watching the show today as an adult.

When my car was new, it always (start, started) in the morning.
Now it (start, starts) only sometimes.

A couple of years ago, when Alice (cook, cooked) dinner, you needed an antacid tablet.
Now, when she (cook, cooks), neighbors invite themselves over to eat with us.

On the basis of the above examples, see if you can complete the following statements:

1. The first example in each pair refers to a (past, present) action, and the regular verb has an ________________ ending.
2. The second example in each pair refers to a (past, present) action, and the regular verb has an ________________ ending.

Answers are on page 532.

Many people have grown up in communities where nonstandard verb forms are used in everyday life. Such forms include *I thinks, he talk, it done, we has, you was,* and *she don't.* Community dialects have richness and power but are a drawback in college and the world at large, where standard English verb forms must be used. Standard English helps ensure clear communication among English-speaking people everywhere, and it is especially important in the world of work.

This chapter compares the community dialect and the standard English forms of a regular verb and three common irregular verbs.

REGULAR VERBS: DIALECT AND STANDARD FORMS

The chart below compares the community dialect (nonstandard) and the standard English forms of the regular verb *smile.*

SMILE

Community Dialect (Do not use in your writing)		*Standard English* (Use for clear communication)	
	Present tense		
~~I smiles~~	~~we smiles~~	I smile	we smile
~~you smiles~~	~~you smiles~~	you smile	you smile
~~he, she, it smile~~	~~they smiles~~	he, she, it smiles	they smile
	Past tense		
~~I smile~~	~~we smile~~	I smiled	we smiled
~~you smile~~	~~you smile~~	you smiled	you smiled
~~he, she, it smile~~	~~they smile~~	he, she, it smiled	they smiled

One of the most common nonstandard forms results from dropping the endings of regular verbs. For example, people might say "David never *smile* anymore" instead of "David never *smiles* anymore." Or they will say "Before he lost his job, David *smile* a lot" instead of "Before he lost his job, David *smiled* a lot." To avoid such nonstandard usage, memorize the forms shown above for the regular verb *like.* Then use the activities that follow to help make the inclusion of verb endings a writing habit.

Present Tense Endings

The verb ending *-s* or *-es* is needed with a regular verb in the present tense when the subject is *he, she, it,* or any *one person* or *thing.*

He	He yell*s*.
She	She throw*s* things.
It	It really anger*s* me.
One person	Their son storm*s* out of the house.
One person	Their frightened daughter crouch*es* behind the bed.
One thing	At night the house shake*s*.

All but one of the ten sentences that follow need *-s* or *-es* endings. Cross out the nonstandard verb forms and write the standard forms in the spaces provided. Mark the one sentence that needs no change with a C for *correct.*

Example wants ________ Pat always ~~want~~ the teacher's attention.

________ 1. That newspaper print nothing but bad news.

________ 2. The gourmet ice cream bar sell for almost two dollars.

________ 3. Pat gossip about me all the time.

________ 4. Whole-wheat bread taste better to me than rye bread.

________ 5. Bob weaken his lungs by smoking so much.

________ 6. The sick baby scream whenever her mother puts her down.

___C___ 7. You make me angry sometimes.

________ 8. Clyde drive twenty-five miles to work each day.

________ 9. She live in a rough section of town.

________ 10. Martha relax by drinking a glass of wine every night.

Activity 2

Rewrite the short selection below, adding present *-s* or *-es* verb endings wherever needed.

The man lounge^s on his bed and watch a spider as it crawl^s across the ceiling. It come^s closer and closer to a point directly above his head. It reach^es the point and stop. If it drop^s now, it will fall right into his mouth. For a while he attempt^s to ignore the spider. Then he move^s nervously off the bed.

____

____

____

____

____

____

____

Past Tense Endings

The verb ending *-d* or *-ed* is needed with a regular verb in the past tense.

A midwife deliver*ed* my baby.

The visitor puzzle*d* over the campus map.

The children watch*ed* cartoons all morning.

Activity 1

All but one of the ten sentences that follow need *-d* or *-ed* endings. Cross out the nonstandard verb forms and write the standard forms in the spaces provided. Mark the one sentence that needs no change with a C.

Example *failed* ______ This morning I ~~fail~~ a chemistry quiz.

________ 1. The customer twist^ed his ankle on the diner's slippery steps.

________ 2. The Vietnamese student struggle with the new language.

________ 3. The sick little boy start to cry again.

C ________ 4. The tired mother turned on the TV for him.

______ 5. I miss quite a few days of class early in the semester.

______ 6. The weather person promise blue skies, but rain began early this morning.

______ 7. Sam attempt to put out the candle flame with his finger.

______ 8. However, he end up burning himself.

______ 9. Carlo thread the film through the reels of the projector.

______ 10. As Alice was about to finish work last night, a man came into the diner and order two dozen hamburgers.

Activity 2

Rewrite the short selection below, adding past tense *-d* or *-ed* verb endings wherever needed.

I smoke for two years and during that time suffer no real side effects. Then my body attack me. I start to have trouble falling asleep, and I awaken early every morning. My stomach digest food very slowly, so that at lunchtime I seem to be still full with breakfast. My lips and mouth turn dry and I swallow water constantly. Also, mucus fill my lungs and I cough a lot. I decide to stop smoking when my wife insist I take out more life insurance for our family.

____

____

____

____

____

____

____

____

____

____

____

____

THREE COMMON IRREGULAR VERBS: DIALECT AND STANDARD FORMS

The following charts compare the community dialect and the standard English forms of the common irregular verbs *be, have,* and *do.* (For more on irregular verbs, see pages 369–376.)

BE

Community Dialect (Do not use in your writing)		*Standard English* (Use for clear communication)	
	Present tense		
~~I be (*or* is)~~	~~we be~~	I am	we are
~~you be~~	~~you be~~	you are	you are
~~he, she, it be~~	~~they be~~	he, she, it is	they are
	Past tense		
~~I were~~	~~we was~~	I was	we were
~~you was~~	~~you was~~	you were	you were
~~he, she, it were~~	~~they was~~	he, she, it was	they were

HAVE

Community Dialect (Do not use in your writing)		*Standard English* (Use for clear communication)	
	Present tense		
~~I has~~	~~we has~~	I have	we have
~~you has~~	~~you has~~	you have	you have
~~he, she, it have~~	~~they has~~	he, she, it has	they have
	Past tense		
~~I has~~	~~we has~~	I had	we had
~~you has~~	~~you has~~	you had	you had
~~he, she, it have~~	~~they has~~	he, she, it had	they had

DO

Community Dialect (Do not use in your writing)		*Standard English* (Use for clear communication)	
	Present tense		
~~I does~~	~~we does~~	I do	we do
~~you does~~	~~you does~~	you do	you do
~~he, she, it do~~	~~they does~~	he, she, it does	they do
	Past tense		
~~I done~~	~~we done~~	I did	we did
~~you done~~	~~you done~~	you did	you did
~~he, she, it done~~	~~they done~~	he, she, it did	they did

Note: Many people have trouble with one negative form of *do*. They will say, for example, "He don't agree" instead of "He doesn't agree," or they will say "The door don't work" instead of "The door doesn't work." Be careful to avoid the common mistake of using *don't* instead of *doesn't*.

Activity 1

Underline the standard form of *be, have,* or *do*.

1. When Walt (have, has) his own house, he will install built-in stereo speakers in every room.
2. The children (is, are) ready to go home.
3. Whenever we (do, does) the laundry, our clothes are spotted with blobs of undissolved detergent.
4. Ed and Arlene (was, were) ready to leave for the movies when the baby began to wail.
5. Our art class (done, did) the mural on the wall of the cafeteria.
6. If Maryanne (have, has) the time, she will help us set up the projector and tape the wires to the floor.
7. Curtis (be, is) the best Ping-Pong player in the college.
8. That mechanic always (do, does) a good job when he fixes my car.
9. The mice in our attic (have, has) chewed several holes in our ceiling.
10. The science teacher said that the state of California (be, is) ready for a major earthquake any day.

Activity 2

Fill in each blank with the standard form of *be, have,* or *do.*

1. My car ________ a real personality.
2. It acts as if it ________ human.
3. On cold mornings, it ________ not want to start.
4. Like me, the car ________ a problem dealing with freezing weather.
5. I don't want to get out of bed, and my car ________ not like leaving the garage.
6. Also, we ________ the same feeling about rainstorms.
7. I hate driving to school in a downpour and so ________ the car.
8. When the car ________ stopped at a light, it stalls.
9. The habits my car ________ may be annoying.
10. But they ________ understandable.

■ Review Test 1

Underline the standard verb form.

1. Martha (argue, argues) just to hear herself talk.
2. Those shoppers (do, does) not seem to know their way around the market; they keep retracing their steps.
3. The cheap ballpoint pen (leak, leaked) all over the lining of my pocketbook.
4. Pat (bag, bagged) the dirty laundry and threw it into the car.
5. If you (has, have) any trouble with the assignment, give me a call.
6. Whenever the hairdresser (do, does) my hair, she cuts one side shorter than the other.
7. Lola often (watch, watches) TV after her parents have gone to bed.
8. Two of the players (was, were) suspended from the league for ten games for using drugs.
9. Jeannie (has, have) only one eye; she lost the other years ago after falling on some broken glass.
10. I remember how my wet mittens (use, used) to steam on the hot school radiator.

■ Review Test 2

Cross out the two nonstandard verb forms in each sentence below. Then write the standard English verbs in the spaces provided.

Example __*is*__ / __*begins*__ When our teacher ~~be~~ angry, his eyelid ~~begin~~ to twitch.

works / takes — 1. My mother work for the local newspaper; she take classified ads over the phone.

towed / Picked — 2. Last week the city tow away my car; this morning I paid sixty dollars and pick it up from the towing company.

is / rushes — 3. When my wife be late for work, she rush around the house like a speeded-up cartoon character.

loves / removed — 4. Henry love to go camping until two thieves in the campground remove his cooler, stove, and sleeping bag from his tent.

_____ / _____ 5. If the baby have a bad cold, I takes her into a steamy bathroom for a while to ease her breathing.

_____ / _____ 6. Although my little girls knows they shouldn't tease the cat, they often dresses up the animal in doll clothes.

_____ / _____ 7. When my brothers watches their favorite *Star Trek* reruns, they knows exactly what Captain Kirk is going to say next.

_____ / _____ 8. Last week my cousin attempt to sell some property in Florida to me, but I refuse to listen to him.

_____ / _____ 9. I show the receipt to the manager to prove that the clerk had accidentally overcharge me.

is / tastes — 10. As far as our son be concerned, oatmeal taste like soggy cardboard.

IRREGULAR VERBS

Introductory Project

You may already have a sense of which common English verbs are regular and which are not. To test yourself, fill in the past tense and past participle of the verbs below. Five are regular verbs and so take *-d* or *-ed* in the past tense and past participle. Five are irregular verbs and will probably not sound right when you try to add *-d* or *-ed*. Put *I* for irregular in front of these verbs. Also, see if you can write in their irregular verb forms.

Present	*Past*	*Past Participle*
shout	*shouted*	*shouted*
1. crawl	Crawled	Crawled
2. bring	brought	Braught
3. use	Used	used
4. do	did	done
5. give	Gave	given
6. laugh	laughed	laughed
7. go	Went	Gone
8. scare	Scared	Sared
9. dress	dressed	dressed
10. see	Saw	seen

Answers are on page 532.

A BRIEF REVIEW OF REGULAR VERBS

Every verb has four principal parts: the present, the past, the past participle, and the present participle. These parts can be used to build all the verb tenses (the times shown by a verb).

The past and past participle of a regular verb are formed by adding *-d* or *-ed* to the present. The *past participle* is the form of the verb used with the helping verbs *have, has,* or *had* (or some form of *be* with passive verbs). The *present participle* is formed by adding *-ing* to the present. Here are the principal forms of some regular verbs:

Present	*Past*	*Past Participle*	*Present Participle*
crash	crashed	crashed	crashing
shiver	shivered	shivered	shivering
kiss	kissed	kissed	kissing
apologize	apologized	apologized	apologizing
tease	teased	teased	teasing

Most verbs in English are regular.

LIST OF IRREGULAR VERBS

Irregular verbs have irregular forms in the past tense and past participle. For example, the past tense of the irregular verb *know* is *knew;* the past participle is *known.*

Almost everyone has some degree of trouble with irregular verbs. When you are unsure about the form of a verb, you can check the list of irregular verbs on the following pages. (The present participle is not shown on this list because it is formed simply by adding *-ing* to the base form of the verb.) Or you can check a dictionary, which gives the principal parts of irregular verbs.

Present	*Past*	*Past Participle*
arise	arose	arisen
awake	awoke *or* awaked	awoken *or* awaked
be (am, are, is)	was (were)	been
become	became	become
begin	began	begun
bend	bent	bent
bite	bit	bitten
blow	blew	blown
break	broke	broken
bring	brought	brought
build	built	built
burst	burst	burst
buy	bought	bought
catch	caught	caught
choose	chose	chosen
come	came	come
cost	cost	cost
cut	cut	cut
do (does)	did	done
draw	drew	drawn
drink	drank	drunk
drive	drove	driven
eat	ate	eaten
fall	fell	fallen
feed	fed	fed
feel	felt	felt
fight	fought	fought
find	found	found
fly	flew	flown
freeze	froze	frozen
get	got	got *or* gotten
give	gave	given
go (goes)	went	gone
grow	grew	grown

Present	*Past*	*Past Participle*
have (has)	had	had
hear	heard	heard
hide	hid	hidden
hold	held	held
hurt	hurt	hurt
keep	kept	kept
know	knew	known
lay	laid	laid
lead	led	led
leave	left	left
lend	lent	lent
let	let	let
lie	lay	lain
light	lit	lit
lose	lost	lost
make	made	made
meet	met	met
pay	paid	paid
ride	rode	ridden
ring	rang	rung
run	ran	run
say	said	said
see	saw	seen
sell	sold	sold
send	sent	sent
shake	shook	shaken
shrink	shrank	shrunk
shut	shut	shut
sing	sang	sung
sit	sat	sat
sleep	slept	slept
speak	spoke	spoken
spend	spent	spent
stand	stood	stood
steal	stole	stolen

Present	*Past*	*Past Participle*
stick	stuck	stuck
sting	stung	stung
swear	swore	sworn
swim	swam	swum
take	took	taken
teach	taught	taught
tear	tore	torn
tell	told	told
think	thought	thought
wake	woke *or* waked	woken *or* waked
wear	wore	worn
win	won	won
write	wrote	written

Activity 1

Cross out the incorrect verb form in each of the following sentences. Then write the correct form of the verb in the space provided.

Example drew ______ The little boy ~~drawed~~ on the marble table with permanent ink.

grown ______ 1. Tomatoes were once thought to be poisonous, and they were growed only as ornamental shrubs.

ridden ______ 2. Juan has rode the bus to school for two years while saving for a car.

torn ______ 3. My cats have tore little holes in all my good wool sweaters.

Froze ______ 4. The pipes in the bathroom freezed last winter, and they burst when they thawed.

rung ______ 5. Every time my telephone has rang today, there has been bad news on the line.

Known ______ 6. Only seven people have ever knowed the formula for Coca-Cola.

blew ______ 7. Amy blowed up animal-shaped balloons for her son's birthday party.

lit ______ 8. The woman lighted a cigarette and then decided to put it out.

sat ______ 9. While waiting for the doctor to arrive, I sitted in a plastic chair for over two hours.

eaten ______ 10. The pile of bones on the plate showed how much chicken the family had ate.

Activity 2

For each of the italicized verbs, fill in the three missing forms in the following order:

a Present tense, which takes an *-s* ending when the subject is *he, she, it,* or any *one person* or *thing* (see page 362)

b Past tense

c Past participle—the form that goes with the helping verb *have, has,* or *had*

Example My uncle likes to *give* away certain things. He (*a*) ___gives___ old, threadbare clothes to the Salvation Army. Last year he (*b*) ___gave___ me a worthless television set in which the picture tube was burned out. He (*c*) has ___given___ away stuff that a junk dealer would reject.

1. I like to *freeze* Hershey bars. A Hershey bar (*a*) ___Freezes___ in half an hour. Once I (*b*) ___~~ran~~ Froze___ a bottle of Yoo-Hoo. I put it in the freezer to chill and then forgot about it. Later I opened the freezer and discovered that it had (*c*) ___~~burst~~ Frozen___ and exploded.
2. I *know* the girl in the lavender bikini. She (*a*) ___Knows___ me, too. I (*b*) ___Knew___ her brother before I met her. I have (*c*) ___Known___ him since boyhood.
3. An acquaintance of mine is a shoplifter, although he knows it's wrong to *steal.* He (*a*) ___Steals___ candy bars from supermarkets. Last month he (*b*) ___Stole___ a Sony Walkman and was caught by a detective. He has (*c*) ___Stolen___ pants and shirts by wearing several layers of clothes out of a store.
4. I *go* to parties a lot. Often Camille (*a*) ___goes___ with me. She (*b*) ___~~she~~ went___ with me just last week. I have (*c*) ___gone___ to parties every Friday for the past month.
5. My brother likes to *throw* things. Sometimes he (*a*) ___throws___ socks in his bureau drawer. In high school he (*b*) ___threw___ footballs while quarterbacking the team. And he has (*c*) ___Thrown___ Frisbees in our backyard for as long as I can remember.

6. I *see* her every weekend. She (*a*) ______________ her other friends during the week. We first (*b*) ______________ each other on a cold Saturday night last winter, when we went for supper at an Indian restaurant. Since then we have (*c*) ______________ each other every weekend except when my car was broken down.
7. I often *lie* down for a few minutes after a hard day's work. Sometimes my cat (*a*) ______________ down near me. Yesterday was Saturday, so I (*b*) ______________ in bed all morning. I probably would have (*c*) ______________ in bed all afternoon, but I wanted to get some planting done in my vegetable garden.
8. I *do* not understand the assignment. It simply (*a*) ______________ not make sense to me. I was surprised to learn that Shirley (*b*) ______________ understand it. In fact, she had already (*c*) ______________ the assignment.
9. I often find it hard to *begin* writing a paper. The assignment that I must do (*a*) ______________ to worry me while I'm watching television, but I seldom turn off the set. Once I waited until the late movie had ended before I (*b*) ______________ to write. If I had (*c*) ______________ earlier, I would have gotten a decent night's sleep.
10. Martha likes to *eat*. She (*a*) ______________ as continuously as some people smoke. Once she (*b*) ______________ a large pack of cookies in half an hour. Even if she has (*c*) ______________ a heavy meal, she often starts munching snacks right afterward.

■ Review Test 1

Underline the correct verb in the parentheses.

1. I (shaked, shook) the bottle of medicine before I took a teaspoon of it.
2. Chico came into the gym and (began, begun) to practice on the parallel bars.
3. Over half the class has (taken, took) this course on a pass-fail basis.
4. Even though my father (teached, taught) me how to play baseball, I never enjoyed any part of the game.
5. Because I had (lended, lent) him the money, I had a natural concern about what he did with it.

6. The drugstore clerk (gave, gived) him the wrong change.
7. Lola (brang, brought) a sweatshirt with her, for she knew the mountains got cold at night.
8. My sister (was, be) at school when a stranger came asking for her at our home.
9. The mechanic (did, done) an expensive valve job on my engine without getting my permission.
10. The basketball team has (broke, broken) the school record for most losses in one year.
11. Someone (leaved, left) his books in the classroom.
12. That jacket was (tore, torn) during the football game.
13. If I hadn't (threw, thrown) away the receipt, I could have gotten my money back.
14. I would have (become, became) very angry if you had not intervened.
15. As the flowerpot (fell, falled) from the windowsill, the little boy yelled, "Geronimo!"

■ Review Test 2

Write short sentences that use the form requested for the following irregular verbs.

Example Past of *grow* I grew eight inches in one year.

1. Past of *know* I Knew
2. Past of *take* I Took
3. Past participle of *give* given
4. Past participle of *write* written
5. Past of *bring* brought
6. Past participle of *speak* Spoken
7. Present of *begin* begins
8. Past of *go* Went
9. Past participle of *see* Seen
10. Past of *drive* drove

SUBJECT-VERB AGREEMENT

Introductory Project

As you read each pair of sentences below, place a check mark beside the sentence that you think uses the underlined word correctly.

There was too many people talking at once. ______

There were too many people talking at once. __✓__

The onions in that spaghetti sauce gives me heartburn. ______

The onions in that spaghetti sauce give me heartburn. __✓__

The mayor and her husband attends our church. ______

The mayor and her husband attend our church. __✓__

Everything seem to slow me down when I'm in a hurry. ______

Everything seems to slow me down when I'm in a hurry. __✓__

Answers are on page 532.

A verb must agree with its subject in number. A *singular subject* (one person or thing) takes a singular verb. A *plural subject* (more than one person or thing) takes a plural verb. Mistakes in subject-verb agreement are sometimes made in the following situations:

1 When words come between the subject and the verb
2 When a verb comes before the subject
3 With compound subjects
4 With indefinite pronouns

Each of these situations is explained on the following pages.

WORDS BETWEEN THE SUBJECT AND THE VERB

Words that come between the subject and the verb do not change subject-verb agreement. In the sentence

The mean cockroaches behind my stove get high on Raid.

the subject (cockroaches) is plural and so the verb (get) is plural. The words *behind my stove* that come between the subject and verb do not affect subject-verb agreement.

To help find the subject of certain sentences, you should cross out prepositional phrases (see page 325):

Nell, ~~with her three dogs close behind,~~ runs around the park every day.

The seams ~~in my new coat~~ have split after only two wearings.

Activity

Underline the subject and lightly cross out any words that come between the subject and the verb. Then double-underline the verb choice in parentheses that you believe is correct.

1. The decisions of the judge (seems, seem) questionable.
2. A hamburger with a double order of french fries (is, are) my usual lunch.
3. One of my son's worst habits (is, are) leaving an assortment of dirty plates on the kitchen counter every morning.
4. The rust spots ~~on the back of Emily's car~~ (needs, need) to be cleaned with a special polish.

5. The collection of medicine bottles in my bathroom (overflows, overflow) the cabinet shelves.

VERB BEFORE THE SUBJECT

A verb agrees with its subject even when the verb comes *before* the subject. Words that may precede the subject include *there, here,* and, in questions, *who, which, what,* and *where.*

> On Bill's doorstep were two police officers.
>
> There are many pizza places in our town.
>
> Here is your receipt.
>
> Where are they going to sleep?

If you are unsure about the subject, ask *who* or *what* of the verb. With the first example above, you might ask, "*Who* were on the doorstep?" The answer, *police officers,* is the subject.

Activity

Write the correct form of the verb in the space provided.

was, were 1. There ______________ not enough glasses for all the guests at the party.

is, are 2. Here ______________ the tickets for tonight's ball game.

do, does 3. Where ______________ you go when you want to be alone?

is, are 4. There ______________ too many people in the room for me to feel comfortable.

was, were 5. Stuffed into the mailbox ______________ ten pieces of junk mail and three ripped magazines.

COMPOUND SUBJECTS

Subjects joined by *and* generally take a plural verb.

> Maple syrup and sweet butter taste delicious on pancakes.
>
> Fear and ignorance have a lot to do with hatred.

When subjects are joined by *either . . . or, neither . . . nor, not only . . . but also,* the verb agrees with the subject closer to the verb.

> Either the Rolling Stones or Stevie Wonder deserves the award for the best album of the year.

The nearest subject, *Stevie Wonder,* is singular, and so the verb is singular.

Activity

Write the correct form of the verb in the space provided.

is, are 1. An egg and a banana ______________ required for the recipe.

was, were 2. Owning a car and having money in my pocket ______________ the chief ambitions of my adolescence.

visits, visit 3. My aunt and uncle from Ireland ______________ us every other summer.

was, were 4. Before they saw a marriage therapist, Peter and Jenny ______________ planning to get divorced.

acts, act 5. Not only the landlady but also her children ______________ unfriendly to us.

INDEFINITE PRONOUNS

The following words, known as *indefinite pronouns,* always take singular verbs:

(*-one* words)	(*-body* words)	(*-thing* words)	
one	nobody	nothing	each
anyone	anybody	anything	either
everyone	everybody	everything	neither
someone	somebody	something	

Note: *Both* always takes a plural verb.

Activity

Write the correct form of the verb in the space provided.

pitches, pitch 1. If each of us ________________ in, we can finish this job in an hour.

was, were 2. Everybody in the theater ________________ getting up and leaving before the movie ended.

provides, provide 3. Neither of the restaurants ________________ facilities for the handicapped.

likes, like 4. No one in our family ________________ housecleaning, but we all take a turn at it.

steals, steal 5. Someone in our neighborhood ________________ vegetables from people's gardens.

■ Review Test

Underline the correct verb in parentheses.

1. The lettuce in most of the stores in our area now (costs, cost) almost one dollar a head.
2. Nobody in the class of fifty students (understands, understand) how to solve the equation on the blackboard.
3. The packages in the shopping bag (was, were) a wonderful mystery to the children.
4. My yoga class of five students (meets, meet) every Thursday afternoon.
5. Anyone who (steals, steal) my purse won't find much inside it.
6. Business contacts and financial backing (is, are) all that I need to establish my career as a dress designer.
7. Each of those breakfast cereals (contains, contain) a high proportion of sugar.
8. The serious look in that young girl's eyes (worries, worry) me.
9. All of the cars on my block (has, have) to be moved one day a month for street cleaning.
10. The job is not for people who (stumbles, stumble) over tough decisions.

CONSISTENT VERB TENSE

Introductory Project

See if you can find and underline the two mistakes in verb tense in the following selection.

> Tony's eyes burned and itched all day long. When he looked at them in a mirror, he also discovers there were red blotches on his neck. He spoke to his mother about the symptoms, and she said that maybe he was allergic to something. Then he remembers he had been cuddling the kitten that Lola had just bought the day before. ''Good grief. I must be allergic to cats,'' he said to himself.

Answers are on page 532.

KEEPING TENSES CONSISTENT

Do not shift verb tenses unnecessarily. If you begin writing a paper in the present tense, don't shift suddenly to the past. If you begin in the past, don't shift without reason to the present. Notice the inconsistent verb tenses in the following selection:

> The shoplifter *walked* quickly toward the front of the store. When a clerk *shouts* at him, he *started* to run.

The verbs must be consistently in the present tense:

> The shoplifter *walks* quickly toward the front of the store. When a clerk *shouts* at him, he *starts* to run.

Or the verbs must be consistently in the past tense:

> The shoplifter *walked* quickly toward the front of the store. When a clerk *shouted* at him, he *started* to run.

Activity 1

In each selection one verb must be changed so that it agrees in tense with the other verbs. Cross out the incorrect verb and write the correct form in the space provided.

Example *carried* Ted wanted to be someplace else when the dentist carries in a long needle.

decided 1. I played my stereo and watched television before I decide to do some homework.

says 2. The hitchhiker stopped me as I walks from the turnpike rest station and said, "Are you on your way to San Jose?"

_______ 3. Some students attend all their classes in school. They listen carefully during lectures but they don't take notes. As a result, they often failed tests.

graduated 4. His parents stayed together for his sake; only after he graduates from college were they divorced.

tossed 5. In the movie, artillery shells exploded on the hide of the reptile monster. It just grinned, tosses off the shells, and kept eating people.

______ 6. Several months a year, monarch butterflies come to live in a spot along the California coast. Thousands and thousands of them hang from trees and fluttered through the air in large groups.

______ 7. After waking up each morning, Harry stays in bed for a while. First he stretches and yawned loudly, and then he plans his day.

______ 8. The salespeople at Biggs' Department Store are very helpful. When people asked for a product the store doesn't carry or is out of, the salesperson recommends another store.

______ 9. Part-time workers at the company are the first to be laid off. They are also paid less, and they received no union representation.

______ 10. Smashed cars, ambulances and police cars blocked traffic on one side of the highway. On the other side, traffic slows down as drivers looked to see what happened.

Activity 2

Change verbs where needed in the following selection so that they are consistently in the past tense. Cross out each incorrect verb and write the correct form above it, as shown in the example. You will need to make nine corrections.

Late one rainy night, Sheila woke to the sound of steady dripping. When she got out of bed to investigate, a drop of cold water ~~splashes~~ *splashed* onto her arm. She looks up just in time to see another drop form on the ceiling, hang suspended for a moment, and fall to the carpet. Stumbling to the kitchen, Sheila reaches deep into one of the cabinets and lifts out a large roasting pan. As she did so, pot lids and baking tins clattered out and crash onto the counter. Sheila ignored them, stumbled back to the bedroom, and places the pan on the floor under the drip. But a minute after sliding her icy feet under the covers, Sheila realized she is in trouble. The sound of each drop hitting the metal pan echoed like a gunshot in the quiet room. Sheila feels like crying, but she finally thought of a solution. She got out of bed and returns a minute later with a thick bath towel. She lined the pan with the towel and crawls back into bed.

■ Review Test

Follow the directions given for Activity 2.

Balancing the green plastic bag full of trash, Craig yanked the front door open. As he stepped onto the front porch, he ~~notices~~ *noticed* that a light snow was already falling. He remembers that when he called to rent the cabin, he was told that it was not too early to expect snow in this mountain community. He glances up at the sky and then walks briskly to the end of the driveway. There he deposited the overflowing bag into one of the large trash cans. Shivering from the cold, he turned around and starts back toward the house, but then he pauses suddenly. At the southwest corner of the cabin, standing on its hind legs, was an enormous black bear. For a long terrible second, Craig was positive the bear was staring right at him. Looking for a promising direction to run, Craig turns around and saw a small bear cub scampering away from behind another garbage can. Before Craig had time to react, the large bear went down on all fours, sprints past the house, and started after the cub. Craig breathed a sigh of relief, races into the cabin, and locks the door behind him.

MISPLACED MODIFIERS

Introductory Project

Because of misplaced words, each of the sentences below has more than one possible meaning. In each case, see if you can explain the intended meaning and the unintended meaning. Also, circle the words that you think create the confusion because they are misplaced.

1. The sign in the restaurant window reads, "Wanted: Young Man—To Open Oysters with References."

   Intended meaning: ____________________

   Unintended meaning: ____________________

2. Clyde and Charlotte decided to have two children on their wedding day.

   Intended meaning: ____________________

   Unintended meaning: ____________________

3. The students no longer like the math teacher who failed the test.

   Intended meaning: ____________________

   Unintended meaning: ____________________

Answers are on page 532.

WHAT MISPLACED MODIFIERS ARE AND HOW TO CORRECT THEM

Misplaced modifiers are words that, because of awkward placement, do not describe the words the writer intended them to describe. Misplaced modifiers often confuse the meaning of a sentence. To avoid them, place words as close as possible to what they describe.

Misplaced Words	*Correctly Placed Words*
Tony bought an old car from a crooked dealer *with a faulty transmission.* (The dealer had a faulty transmission?)	Tony bought an old car with a faulty transmission from a crooked dealer. (The words describing the old car are now placed next to "car.")
I *nearly* earned a hundred dollars last week. (You just missed earning a hundred dollars, but in fact earned nothing?)	I earned nearly a hundred dollars last week. (The meaning—that you earned a little under a hundred dollars—is now clear.)
Bill yelled at the howling dog *in his underwear.* (The *dog* wore underwear?)	Bill, in his underwear, yelled at the howling dog. (The words describing Bill are placed next to him.)

Activity

Underline the misplaced word or words in each sentence. Then rewrite the sentence, placing related words together and thereby making the meaning clear.

Examples The suburbs nearly had five inches of rain.

The suburbs had nearly five inches of rain.

We could see the football stadium driving across the bridge.

Driving across the bridge, we could see the football stadium.

1. I saw mountains of uncollected trash walking along the city streets.

Walking along the city streets, I saw mountains

2. I almost had a dozen job interviews after I sent out my résumé.

I had almost a dozen job interviews

3. Bill swatted the wasp that stung him with a newspaper.

With a newspaper, Bill swatted the wasp

4. Joanne decided to live with her grandparents when she attended college to save money.

to save money, Joanne decided

5. Charlotte returned the hamburger to the supermarket that was spoiled.

Charlotte returned the hamburger that was spoiled to

6. Roger visited the old house still weak with the flu.

Still weak with the flu, Roger visited the

7. The phone almost rang fifteen times last night.

The phone rang almost fifteen times last

8. My uncle saw a kangaroo at the window under the influence of whiskey.

under the influence of whiskey, My uncle saw a

9. We decided to send our daughter to college on the day she was born.

On the day she was born, we decided to send

10. Fred always opens the bills that arrive in the mailbox with a sigh.

With a sigh, Fred always opens the bills that

■ Review Test

Place an M for *misplaced* or a C for *correct* in front of each sentence.

M 1. Rita found it difficult to mount the horse wearing tight jeans.

C 2. Rita, wearing tight jeans, found it difficult to mount the horse.

M 3. I noticed a crack in the window walking into the delicatessen.

C 4. Walking into the delicatessen, I noticed a crack in the window.

M 5. A well-worn track shoe was found on the locker bench with holes in it.

C 6. A well-worn track shoe with holes in it was found on the locker bench.

M 7. I almost caught a hundred lightning bugs.

C 8. I caught almost a hundred lightning bugs.

C 9. In a secondhand store, Willie found a television set that had been stolen from me last month.

M 10. Willie found a television set in a secondhand store that had been stolen from me last month.

C 11. Willie found, in a secondhand store, a television set that had been stolen from me last month.

M 12. There were four cars parked outside the café with Minnesota license plates.

C 13. There were four cars with Minnesota license plates parked outside the café.

C 14. The President was quoted on the *NBC Evening News* as saying that the Chinese might attack the Russians.

M 15. The President was quoted as saying that the Chinese might attack the Russians on the *NBC Evening News*.

DANGLING MODIFIERS

Introductory Project

Because of dangling words, each of the sentences below has more than one possible meaning. In each case, see if you can explain the intended meaning and the unintended meaning.

1. While smoking a pipe, my dog sat with me by the crackling fire.

   Intended meaning: ______________________________

   Unintended meaning: ______________________________

2. Looking at the leather-skirted woman, his sports car went through a red light.

   Intended meaning: ______________________________

   Unintended meaning: ______________________________

3. After baking for several hours, Grandmother removed the beef pie from the oven.

   Intended meaning: ______________________________

   Unintended meaning: ______________________________

Answers are on page 532.

WHAT DANGLING MODIFIERS ARE AND HOW TO CORRECT THEM

A modifier that opens a sentence must be followed immediately by the word it is meant to describe. Otherwise, the modifier is said to be dangling, and the sentence takes on an unintended meaning. For example, in the sentence

> While smoking a pipe, my dog sat with me by the crackling fire.

the unintended meaning is that the *dog* was smoking the pipe. What the writer meant, of course, was that *he,* the writer, was smoking the pipe. He should have said,

> While smoking a pipe, *I* sat with my dog by the crackling fire.

The dangling modifier could also be corrected by placing the subject within the opening word group:

> While *I* was smoking my pipe, my dog sat with me by the crackling fire.

Here are other sentences with dangling modifiers. Read the explanations of why they are dangling and look carefully at the ways they are corrected.

Dangling	*Correct*
Swimming at the lake, a rock cut Sue's foot. (*Who* was swimming at the lake? The answer is not *rock* but *Sue*. The subject *Sue* must be added.)	Swimming at the lake, Sue cut her foot on a rock. *Or:* When Sue was swimming at the lake, she cut her foot on a rock.
While eating my sandwich, five mosquitoes bit me. (*Who* is eating the sandwich? The answer is not *five mosquitoes,* as it unintentionally seems to be, but *I*. The subject *I* must be added.)	While *I* was eating my sandwich, five mosquitoes bit me. *Or:* While eating my sandwich, *I* was bitten by five mosquitoes.
Getting out of bed, the tile floor was so cold that Maria shivered all over. (*Who* got out of bed? The answer is not *tile floor* but *Maria*. The subject *Maria* must be added.)	Getting out of bed, *Maria* found the tile floor so cold that she shivered all over. *Or:* When *Maria* got out of bed, the tile floor was so cold that she shivered all over.

Dangling	*Correct*
To join the team, a C average or better is necessary. (*Who* is to join the team? The answer is not *C average* but *you*. The subject *you* must be added.)	To join the team, *you* must have a C average or better. *Or:* For *you* to join the team, a C average or better is necessary.

The preceding examples make clear the two ways of correcting a dangling modifier. Decide on a logical subject and do one of the following:

1 Place the subject *within* the opening word group:

When Sue was swimming at the lake, she cut her foot on a rock.

Note: In some cases an appropriate subordinating word such as *When* must be added, and the verb may have to be changed slightly as well.

2 Place the subject right *after* the opening word group:

Swimming at the lake, Sue cut her foot on a rock.

Ask *Who?* of the opening words in each sentence. The subject that answers the question should be nearby in the sentence. If it is not, provide the logical subject by using either method of correction described above.

Example While sleeping at the campsite, a Frisbee hit Bill on the head.

While Bill was sleeping at the campsite, a Frisbee hit him on the head.

or *While sleeping at the campsite, Bill was hit on the head by a Frisbee.*

1. Watching the horror movie, goose bumps covered my spine.

When watching the horror movie ...

____

2. After putting on a corduroy shirt, the room didn't seem as cold.

After She put on a corduroy shirt,

3. Flunking out of school, my parents demanded that I get a job.

When I Flunked out of school,

4. Covered with food stains, my mother decided to wash the tablecloth.

5. Joining the Glee Club, the social life of Mike became more active.

After he Joined the Gee Club,

6. While visiting the Jungle Park Safari, a baboon scrambled onto the hood of their car.

When they visited the Jungle Park Safari,

7. Under attack by beetles, Charlotte sprayed her roses with insecticide.

8. Standing at the ocean's edge, the wind coated my glasses with a salty film.

9. Braking the car suddenly, my shopping bags tumbled off the seat.

10. Sometimes covering thousands of miles, scientists are fascinated by the migration routes of birds.

■ Review Test

Place a D for *dangling* or a C for *correct* in front of each sentence. Remember that the opening words are a dangling modifier if they have no logical subject to modify.

______ 1. Advertising in the paper, Frank's car was quickly sold.

______ 2. By advertising in the paper, Frank quickly sold his car.

______ 3. After painting the downstairs, the house needed airing to clear out the fumes.

______ 4. After we painted the downstairs, the house needed airing to clear out the fumes.

______ 5. Frustrated by piles of homework, Wanda was tempted to watch television.

______ 6. Frustrated by piles of homework, Wanda's temptation was to watch television.

______ 7. After I waited patiently in the bank line, the teller told me I had filled out the wrong form.

______ 8. After waiting patiently in the bank line, the teller told me I had filled out the wrong form.

______ 9. When overweight, desserts are especially tempting.

______ 10. When overweight, I find desserts especially tempting.

______ 11. Looking through the telescope, I saw a brightly lit object come into view.

______ 12. As I was looking through the telescope, a brightly lit object came into view.

______ 13. Looking through the telescope, a brightly lit object came into my view.

______ 14. Weighing thousands of pounds, no one knows how the enormous stones were brought to Stonehenge.

______ 15. No one knows how the enormous stones, weighing thousands of pounds, were brought to Stonehenge.

FAULTY PARALLELISM

Introductory Project

Read aloud each pair of sentences below. Put a check mark beside the sentence that reads most smoothly and clearly and sounds most natural.

I made resolutions to study more, to lose weight, and watching less TV. _______

I made resolutions to study more, to lose weight, and to watch less TV. ___✓___

A consumer group rates my car as noisy, expensive, and not having much safety. _______

A consumer group rates my car as noisy, expensive, and unsafe. ___✓___

Lola likes wearing soft sweaters, eating exotic foods, and to bathe in Calgon bath oil. _______

Lola likes wearing soft sweaters, eating exotic foods, and bathing in Calgon bath oil. ___✓___

Single life offers more freedom of choice; more security is offered by marriage. _______

Single life offers more freedom of choice; marriage offers more security. ___✓___

Answers are on page 532.

PARALLELISM EXPLAINED

Words in a pair or a series should have a parallel structure. By balancing the items in a pair or a series so that they have the same kind of structure, you will make a sentence clearer and easier to read. Notice how the parallel sentences that follow read more smoothly than the nonparallel ones.

Nonparallel (Not Balanced)	*Parallel (Balanced)*
I made resolutions to lose weight, to study more, and *watching* less TV.	I made resolutions to lose weight, to study more, and to watch less TV. (A balanced series of *to* verbs: *to lose, to study, to watch*)
A consumer group rates my car as noisy, expensive, and *not having much safety*.	A consumer group rates my car as noisy, expensive, and unsafe. (A balanced series of descriptive words: *noisy, expensive, unsafe*)
Lola likes wearing soft sweaters, eating exotic foods, and *to bathe* in Calgon bath oil.	Lola likes wearing soft sweaters, eating exotic foods, and bathing in Calgon bath oil. (A balanced series of *-ing* words: *wearing, eating, bathing*)
The single life offers more freedom of choice; *more security is offered by marriage*.	The single life offers more freedom of choice; marriage offers more security. (Balanced verbs and word order: *single life offers . . . ; marriage offers . . .*)

Balanced sentences are not a skill you need worry about when writing first drafts. But when you rewrite, you should try to put matching words and ideas into matching structures. Such parallelism will improve your writing style.

Activity

The unbalanced part of each of the following sentences is *italicized.* Rewrite the unbalanced part so that it matches the rest of the sentence. The first one is done for you as an example.

1. Woody Allen's films are clever, well-acted, and *have a lot of humor.* humorous
2. Filling out an income tax form is worse than wrestling a bear or *to walk* on hot coals. walking
3. The study-skills course taught me how to take more effective notes, to read a textbook chapter, and *preparing* for exams. to prepare
4. Lola plans to become a model, lawyer, or *to go into nursing.* a nurse
5. Martha Grencher likes *to water* her garden, walking her fox terrier, and arguing with her husband. watering
6. Filled with talent and *ambitious,* Charlie plugged away at his sales job. ambition
7. When I saw my roommate with my girlfriend, I felt worried, angry, and *embarrassment* as well. embarrased
8. Cindy's cat likes sleeping in the dryer, lying in the bathtub, and *to chase* squirrels. Chaseing
9. The bacon was fatty, *grease was on the potatoes,* and the eggs were cold.
10. People in the lobby munched popcorn, sipped sodas, and *were shuffling* their feet impatiently. shuffled

■ Review Test 1

On separate paper, write five sentences of your own that use parallel structure.

■ Review Test 2

Draw a line under the unbalanced part of each sentence. Then rewrite the unbalanced part so that it matches the other item or items in the sentence. The first one is done for you as an example.

1. Our professor warned us that he would give surprise tests, the assignment of term papers, and allow no makeup exams.

   assign term papers

2. Pesky mosquitoes, humidity that is high, and sweltering heat make summer an unpleasant time for me.

   hish humid

3. I want a job that pays high wages, provides a complete benefits package, and offering opportunities for promotion.

   offers

4. My teenage daughter enjoys shopping for new clothes, to try different cosmetics, and reading beauty magazines.

   ____

5. My car needed the brakes replaced, the front wheels aligned, and the recharging of the battery.

   battery recharged

6. I had to correct my paper for fragments, misplaced modifiers, and there were apostrophe mistakes.

   ____

7. They did not want a black-and-white TV set, but a color set could not be afforded.

   but could not afford a color TV set

8. The neighborhood group asked the town council to repair the potholes and that a traffic light be installed.

   and install a traffic

9. Having a headache, my stomach being upset, and a bad case of sunburn did not put me in a good mood for the evening.

   an upset stomach

10. The Gray Panthers is an organization that not only aids older citizens but also providing information for their families.

    provides

PRONOUN AGREEMENT, REFERENCE, AND POINT OF VIEW

Introductory Project

Read each pair of sentences below. Then put a check mark beside the sentence that you think uses the underlined word or words correctly.

Someone in my neighborhood lets their dog run loose. ______

Someone in my neighborhood lets his or her dog run loose. ✓

After Tony reviewed his notes with Bob, he passed the exam with ease. ______

After reviewing his notes with Bob, Tony passed the exam with ease. ✓

I dislike waitressing, for you can never count on a fair tip. ______

I dislike waitressing, for I can never count on a fair tip. ✓

Answers are on page 533.

Pronouns are words that take the place of nouns (persons, places, or things). In fact, the word *pronoun* means "for a noun." Pronouns are shortcuts that keep you from unnecessarily repeating words in writing. Here are some examples of pronouns:

> Shirley had not finished *her* paper. (*Her* is a pronoun that takes the place of *Shirley's*.)
>
> Tony swung so heavily on the tree branch that *it* snapped. (*It* replaces *branch*.)
>
> When the three little pigs saw the wolf, *they* pulled out cans of Mace. (*They* is a pronoun that takes the place of *pigs*.)

This section presents rules that will help you avoid three common mistakes people make with pronouns. The rules are as follows:

1 A pronoun must agree in number with the word or words it replaces.
2 A pronoun must refer clearly to the word it replaces.
3 Pronouns should not shift unnecessarily in point of view.

PRONOUN AGREEMENT

A pronoun must agree in number with the word or words it replaces. If the word a pronoun refers to is singular, the pronoun must be singular; if that word is plural, the pronoun must be plural. (Note that the word a pronoun refers to is also known as the *antecedent*.)

> Barbara agreed to lend me her Willie Nelson albums.
>
> People walking the trail must watch their step because of snakes.

In the first example, the pronoun *her* refers to the singular word *Barbara;* in the second example, the pronoun *their* refers to the plural word *People*.

Activity

Write the appropriate pronoun (*their, they, them, it*) in the blank space in each of the following sentences.

Example I lifted the pot of hot potatoes carefully, but ___*it*___ slipped out of my hand.

1. The value that people receive for ____________ dollars these days is rapidly diminishing.
2. Fred never misses his daily workout; he believes ____________ keeps him healthy.
3. Sometimes, in marriage, partners expect too much from ____________ mates.
4. For some students, college is often their first experience with an undisciplined learning situation, and ____________ are not always ready to accept the responsibility.
5. Our new neighbors moved in three months ago, but I have yet to meet ____________.

Indefinite Pronouns

The following words, known as *indefinite pronouns,* are always singular.

(-*one* words)	(-*body* words)	
one	nobody	each
anyone	anybody	either
everyone	everybody	neither
someone	somebody	

If a pronoun in a sentence refers to one of the above singular words, the pronoun should be singular.

> Nobody feels worse than he does about the accident.
>
> One of the women could not find her purse.
>
> Everyone must be in his seat before the teacher takes the roll.

In each example, the circled pronoun is singular because it refers to one of the special singular words.

Note: The last example is correct if everyone in the class is a man. If everyone in the class was a woman, the pronoun would be *her*. If the class had both women and men, the pronoun form would be *his or her:*

> Everyone must be in his or her seat before the teacher takes the roll.

Some writers follow the traditional practice of using *his* to refer to both women and men. Many now use *his or her* to avoid an implied sexual bias. To avoid using *his* or the somewhat awkward *his or her,* a sentence can often be rewritten in the plural:

> Students must be in their seats before the teacher takes the roll.

Activity

Underline the correct pronoun.

1. Someone has blocked the parking-lot exit with (his, their) car.
2. Everyone in the women's group has volunteered some of (her, their) time for the voting drive.
3. Neither of the men arrested as terrorists would reveal information about (his, their) group.
4. Not one of the women coaches will be returning to (her, their) job next year.
5. Each of the President's advisers offered (his or her, their) opinion about the rail strike.

PRONOUN REFERENCE

A sentence may be confusing and unclear if a pronoun appears to refer to more than one word, or if the pronoun does not refer to any specific word. Look at this sentence:

> Joe almost dropped out of school, for he felt *they* emphasized discipline too much.

Who emphasized discipline too much? There is no specific word that *they* refers to. Be clear:

> Joe almost dropped out of school, for he felt *the teachers* emphasized discipline too much.

Here are sentences with other kinds of faulty pronoun references. Read the explanations of why they are faulty and look carefully at the ways they are corrected.

Faulty	***Clear***
June told Margie that *she* lacked self-confidence. (*Who* lacked self-confidence: June or Margie? Be clear.)	June told Margie, "You lack self-confidence." (Quotation marks, which can sometimes be used to correct an unclear reference, are explained on pages 433–434.)
Nancy's mother is a hairdresser, but Nancy is not interested in *it*. (There is no specific word that *it* refers to. It would not make sense to say, "Nancy is not interested in hairdresser.")	Nancy's mother is a hairdresser, but Nancy is not interested in becoming one.
Ron blamed the police officer for the ticket, *which* was foolish. (Does *which* mean that the officer's giving the ticket was foolish, or that Ron's blaming the officer was foolish? Be clear.)	Foolishly, Ron blamed the police officer for the ticket.

Activity

Rewrite each of the following sentences to make clear the vague pronoun reference. Add, change, or omit words as necessary.

Example Our cat was friends with our hamster until he bit him.

Until the cat bit the hamster, the two were friends.

1. Maria's mother let her wear her new earrings to school.

   maria's mother let maria wear her new

2. When I asked why I failed my driver's test, he said I drove too slowly.

   The instructor said, "You drove too slowly."

3. Dad ordered my brother to paint the garage because he didn't want to do it.

   Dad didn't want

4. Herb dropped his psychology courses because he thought they assigned too much reading.

   He thought the instructor assigned too much

5. I love Parmesan cheese on veal, but it does not always agree with me.

   but cheese does not always agree with

PRONOUN POINT OF VIEW

Pronouns should not shift their point of view unnecessarily. When writing a paper, be consistent in your use of first-, second-, or third-person pronouns.

Type of Pronoun	*Singular*	*Plural*
First-person pronouns	I (my, mine, me)	we (our, us)
Second-person pronouns	you (your)	you (your)
Third-person pronouns	he (his, him) she (her) it (its)	they (their, them)

Note: Any person, place, or thing, as well as any indefinite pronoun like *one, anyone, someone,* and so on (page 401), is a third-person word.

For instance, if you start writing in the third person *she,* don't jump suddenly to the second person *you.* Or if you are writing in the first person *I,* don't shift unexpectedly to *one.* Look at the examples.

Inconsistent	*Consistent*
I enjoy movies like *The Return of the Vampire* that frighten *you.* (The most common mistake people make is to let a *you* slip into their writing after they start with another pronoun.)	I enjoy movies like *The Return of the Vampire* that frighten me.
As soon as a person walks into Helen's apartment, *you* can tell that Helen owns a cat. (Again, the *you* is a shift in point of view.)	As soon as a person walks into Helen's apartment, *he or she* can tell that Helen owns a cat. (See also the note on *his or her* references on pages 401–402.)

Activity

Cross out inconsistent pronouns in the following sentences, and write the correct form of the pronoun above each crossed-out word.

Example My dreams are always the kind that haunt ~~you~~ *me* the next day.

1. Whenever we take our children on a trip, you have to remember to bring snacks, tissues, and toys.
2. In our society, we often need a diploma before you are hired for a job.
3. A worker can take a break only after a relief person comes to take your place.
4. If a student organizes his time carefully, you can accomplish a great deal of work.
5. Although I know you should watch your cholesterol intake, I can never resist an ear of corn dripping with melted butter.

■ Review Test

Underline the correct word in parentheses.

1. As we sat in class waiting for the test results, (you, we) could feel the tension.
2. Hoping to be first in line when (they, the ushers) opened the doors, we arrived two hours early for the concert.
3. If a person really wants to appreciate good coffee, (he or she, you, they) should drink it black.
4. I am hooked on science fiction stories because they allow (you, me) to escape to other worlds.
5. Lois often visits the reading center in school, for she finds that (they, the tutors) give her helpful instruction.
6. Nobody seems to know how to add or subtract without (his or her, their) pocket calculator anymore.
7. Cindy is the kind of woman who will always do (their, her) best.
8. Each of my brothers has had (his, their) apartment broken into.
9. If someone is going to write a composition, (he or she, you, they) should prepare at least one rough draft.
10. I've been taking cold medicine, and now (it, the cold) is better.

PAPER FORMAT

When you hand in a paper that is due for any one of your courses, probably the first thing you will be judged on is its format. It is important, then, that you do certain things to make your papers look attractive, neat, and easy to read. Here are guidelines to follow in preparing a paper for an instructor:

1 Use full-sized theme or typewriter paper, 8½ by 11 inches.

2 Keep wide margins (1 to 1½ inches) all around the paper. In particular, do not crowd the right-hand or bottom margins. The white space makes your paper more readable; also, the instructor has room for comments.

3 If you write by hand,
   - a Use a blue or black pen (*not* a pencil).
   - b Be careful not to overlap letters or to make decorative loops on letters. On narrow-ruled paper, write on every other line.
   - c Make all your letters distinct. Pay special attention to *a, e, i, o,* and *u*—five letters that people sometimes write illegibly.
   - d Keep your capital letters clearly distinct from small letters. You may even want to print all capital letters.

4 Center the title of your paper on the first line of page 1. Do not put quotation marks around the title or underline the title. Capitalize all the major words in a title, including the first word. Small connecting words within a title like *of, for, the, in,* and *to* are not capitalized.

5 Skip a line between the title and the first line of your text. Indent the first line of each paragraph about five spaces (half an inch) from the left-hand margin.

6 Make commas, periods, and other punctuation marks firm and clear. Leave a slight space after each period. When you type, leave a double space after a period.

7 If you break a word at the end of a line, break only between syllables (see page 456). Do not break words of one syllable.

8 Put your name, date, and course number where your instructor asks for them.

Also keep in mind these important points about the title and the first sentence of your paper:

9 The title should be several words that tell what the paper is about. The title should usually *not* be a complete sentence.

10 Do not rely on the title to help explain the first sentence of your paper. The first sentence must stand independent of the title.

Activity 1

Identify the mistakes in format in the following lines from a student theme. Explain the mistakes in the spaces provided. One mistake is described for you as an example.

"an unpleasant dining companion"

My little brother is often an unpleasant dining companion. Last
night was typical. For one thing, his appearance was disgusting
His shoes were not tied, and his shirt was unbuttoned and han-
ging out of his pants, which he had forgotten to zip up. Traces
of his afternoon snack of grape juice and chocolate cookies were

1. *Hyphenate only between syllables*
2. ______
3. ______
4. ______
5. ______
6. ______

Activity 2

As was already stated, a title should tell in several words (but *not* a complete sentence) what a paper is about. Often a title can be based on the topic sentence, the one that expresses the main idea of the paper. On the next page are five topic sentences taken from student papers. Write a suitable and specific title for each paper, basing the title on the topic sentence. (Note the example.)

Example *Compromise in a Relationship* ______________________

Learning how to compromise is essential to a good relationship.

1. Title: ______________________
   Some houseplants are dangerous to children and pets.
2. Title: ______________________
   A number of fears haunted me when I was a child.
3. Title: ______________________
   Several important steps should be taken to insulate a house properly.
4. Title: ______________________
   My husband is a compulsively neat person.
5. Title: ______________________
   There are a number of drawbacks to having a roommate.

Activity 3

In four of the five sentences that follow, the writer has mistakenly used the title to help explain the first sentence. But, as has already been stated, you must *not* rely on the title to help explain your first sentence.

Rewrite the sentences so that they stand independent of the title. Put *Correct* under the one sentence that is independent of the title.

Example Title: My Career Plans

First sentence: They have changed in the last six months.

Rewritten: *My career plans have changed in the last six months.*

1. Title: Contending with Dogs
   First sentence: This is the main problem in my work as a mail carrier.
   Rewritten: ______________________
   ____
2. Title: Study Skills
   First sentence: They are necessary if a person is to do well in college.
   Rewritten: ______________________
   ____
3. Title: Summer Vacation
   First sentence: Contrary to popular belief, a summer vacation can be the most miserable experience of the year.
   Rewritten: ______________________
   ____

4. Title: My Wife and the Sunday Newspaper
   First sentence: My wife has a peculiar way of reading it.

   Rewritten: ______________________________

5. Title: Traffic Circles
   First sentence: They are one of the chief hazards today's driver must confront.

   Rewritten: ______________________________

Review Test

In the space provided, rewrite the following sentences from a student paper. Correct the mistakes in format.

"disciplining our children"

My husband and I are becoming experts in disciplining our child-
ren. We have certain rules that we insist upon, and if there are
any violations, we are swift to act. When a child simply doesn't
do what he is told to do, he must write that particular action
twenty times. For example, if he doesn't brush his teeth, he
writes, "I must brush my teeth." If a child gets home after the

CAPITAL LETTERS

Introductory Project

You probably know a good deal about the uses of capital letters. Answering the questions below will help you check your knowledge.

1. Write the full name of a person you know: John E. Parker
2. In what city and state were you born? Danville Il
3. What is your present street address? ________
4. Name a country where you would like to travel: Africa
5. Name a school that you attended: Washington
6. Give the name of a store where you buy food: Jewel
7. Name a company where someone you know works: ________
8. What day of the week gives you the best chance to relax? ________
9. What holiday is your favorite? ________
10. What brand of toothpaste do you use? ________
11. Give the brand name of a candy or gum you like: ________
12. Name a song or a television show you enjoy: ________
13. Write the title of a magazine you read: ________

Items 14–16: Three capital letters are needed in the lines below. Underline the words that you think should be capitalized. Then write them, capitalized, in the spaces provided.

the masked man reared his silvery-white horse, waved good-bye, and rode out of town. My heart thrilled when i heard someone say, "that was the Lone Ranger. You don't see his kind much, anymore."

14. The 15. I 16. That

Answers are on page 533.

MAIN USES OF CAPITAL LETTERS

Capital letters are used with:

1. The first word in a sentence or direct quotation
2. Names of persons and the word *I*
3. Names of particular places
4. Names of days of the week, months, and holidays
5. Names of commercial products
6. Names of organizations such as religious and political groups, associations, companies, unions, and clubs
7. Titles of books, magazines, newspapers, articles, stories, poems, films, television shows, songs, papers that you write, and the like

Each use is illustrated on the pages that follow.

First Word in a Sentence or Direct Quotation

The panhandler touched me and asked, "Do you have any change?"

↑ (Capitalize the first word in the sentence.)

↑ (Capitalize the first word in the direct quotation.)

"If you want a ride," said Brenda, "get ready now. Otherwise, I'm going alone."

(*If* and *Otherwise* are capitalized because they are the first words of sentences within a direct quotation. But *get* is not capitalized because it is part of the first sentence within the quotation.)

Names of Persons and the Word *I*

Last night I ran into Tony Curry and Lola Morrison.

Names of Particular Places

Charlotte was graduated from Fargone High School in Orlando, Florida. She then moved with her parents to Bakersfield, California, and worked for a time there at Alexander's Gift House. Eventually she married and moved with her husband to the Naval Reserve Center in Atlantic County, New Jersey. She takes courses two nights a week at Stockton State College. On weekends she and her family often visit the nearby Wharton State Park and go canoeing on the Mullica River. She does volunteer work at Atlantic City Hospital in connection with the First Christian Church. In addition, she works during the summer as a hostess at Convention Hall and the Holiday Inn.

But: Use small letters if the specific name of a place is not given.

Charlotte sometimes remembers her unhappy days in high school and at the gift shop where she worked after graduation. She did not imagine then that she would one day be going to college and doing volunteer work for a church and a hospital in the community where she and her husband live.

Names of Days of the Week, Months, and Holidays

I was angry at myself for forgetting that Sunday was Mother's Day.

During July and August, Fred's company works a four-day week, and he has Mondays off.

Bill still has a scar on his ankle from a cherry bomb that exploded near him on a Fourth of July and a scar on his arm where he stabbed himself with a fishhook on a Labor Day weekend.

But: Use small letters for the seasons—summer, fall, winter, spring.

Names of Commercial Products

Clyde uses Scope mouthwash, Certs mints, and Dentyne gum to drive away the taste of the Marlboro cigarettes and White Owl cigars that he always smokes.

My sister likes to play Monopoly and Sorry; I like chess and poker; my brother likes Scrabble, baseball, and table tennis.

But: Use small letters for the *type* of product (mouthwash, mints, gum, cigarettes, and so on).

Names of Organizations such as Religious and Political Groups, Associations, Companies, Unions, and Clubs

Fred Grencher was a Lutheran for many years but converted to Catholicism when he married. Both he and his wife, Martha, are members of the Democratic Party. Both belong to the American Automobile Association. Martha works part time as a refrigerator salesperson at Sears. Fred is a mail carrier and belongs to the Postal Clerks' Union.

Tony met Lola when he was a Boy Scout and she was a Campfire Girl; she asked him to light her fire.

Titles of Books, Magazines, Newspapers, Articles, Stories, Poems, Films, Television Shows, Songs, Papers That You Write, and the Like

On Sunday Lola read the first chapter of *I Know Why the Caged Bird Sings,* a book required for her writing course. She looked through *The New York Times* that her parents had gotten. She then read an article titled "Thinking about a Change in Your Career" and a poem titled "Some Moments Alone" in *Cosmopolitan* magazine. At the same time she played an old Beatles album, *Abbey Road.* In the evening she watched *60 Minutes* on television and a movie, *Sudden Impact,* starring Clint Eastwood. Then from 11 P.M. to midnight she worked on a paper titled "Uses of Leisure Time in Today's Culture" for her sociology class.

Activity

Cross out the words that need capitals in the following sentences. Then write the capitalized forms of the words in the spaces provided. The number of spaces tells you how many corrections to make in each case.

Example I brush with ~~crest~~ toothpaste but get cavities all the time. Crest

1. A spokesperson for general motors announced that the prices of all chevrolets will rise next year.

   ______ ______ ______

2. Steve was graduated from Maplewood high school in june 1988.

   ______ ______ ______

3. The mild-mannered reporter named clark kent said to the Wolfman, "you'd better think twice before you mess with me, Buddy."

   ______ ______ ______

4. While watching television, Bill drank four pepsis, ate an entire package of ritz crackers, and finished up a bag of oreo cookies.

   ______ ______ ______

5. A greyhound bus almost ran over Tony as he was riding his yamaha to a friend's home in florida.

   ______ ______ ______

6. Before I lent my polaroid camera to Janet, I warned her, "be sure to return it by friday."

   ______ ______ ______

7. Last friday George took his entire paycheck, went to best, a discount store, and bought himself a nineteen-inch zenith color television.

   ______ ______ ______

8. On their first trip to New York city, Fred and Martha visited the empire State Building and Times square. They also saw the New York mets play at Shea Stadium.

   ______ ______ ______

9. Clyde was listening to Tina Turner's recording of "Proud mary," Charlotte was reading an article in the *Reader's digest* titled "let's Stop Peddling Sex," and their son was watching *sesame Street.*

   ______ ______ ______ ______

10. When a sign for a howard johnson's rest stop appeared on the turnpike, anita said, "let's stop here and stretch our legs for a bit."

    ______ ______ ______ ______

OTHER USES OF CAPITAL LETTERS

Capital letters are also used with:

1 Names that show family relationships
2 Titles of persons when used with their names
3 Specific school courses
4 Languages
5 Geographic locations
6 Historical periods and events
7 Races, nations, and nationalities
8 Opening and closing of a letter

Each use is illustrated on the pages that follow.

Names That Show Family Relationships

I got Mother to baby-sit for me.

I went with Grandfather to the church service.

Uncle Carl and Aunt Lucy always enclose five dollars with birthday cards.

But: Do not capitalize words like *mother, father, grandmother, aunt,* and so on when they are preceded by a possessive word (*my, your, his, her, our, their*).

I got my mother to baby-sit for me.

I went with my grandfather to the church service.

My uncle and aunt always enclose five dollars with birthday cards.

Titles of Persons When Used with Their Names

I wrote to Senator Grabbel and Congresswoman Punchie.

Professor Snorrel sent me to Chairperson Ruck, who sent me to Dean Rappers.

He drove to Dr. Helen Thompson's office after the cat bit him.

But: Use small letters when titles appear by themselves, without specific names.

I wrote to my senator and congresswoman.

The professor sent me to the chairperson, who sent me to the dean.

He drove to the doctor's office after the cat bit him.

Specific School Courses

I got an A in both Accounting I and Small Business Management, but I got a C in Human Behavior.

But: Use small letters for general subject areas.

I enjoyed my business courses but not my psychology or language courses.

Languages

She knows German and Spanish, but she speaks mostly American slang.

Geographic Locations

Johnny Carson grew up in the Midwest. He worked in the East for a number of years and then moved to the West Coast.

But: Use small letters in directions.

A new high school is being built at the south end of town.

Because I have a compass in my car, I know that I won't be going east or west when I want to go north.

Historical Periods and Events

Hector did well answering an essay question about the Second World War, but he lost points on a question about the Great Depression.

Races, Nations, Nationalities

The research study centered on low-income Caucasians and Hispanics.

They have German knives and Danish glassware in the kitchen, an Indian wood carving in the bedroom, African sculptures in the study, and an Oriental rug in the living room.

Opening and Closing of a Letter

Dear Sir:
Dear Madam:
Sincerely yours,
Truly yours,

Note: Capitalize only the first word in a closing.

Activity

Cross out the words that need capitals in the following sentences. Then write the capitalized forms of the words in the spaces provided. The number of spaces tells you how many corrections to make in each case.

1. Although my grandfather spoke german and polish, my mother never learned either language.

   ________ ________

2. The chain letter began, "dear friend—You must mail twenty copies of this letter if you want good luck."

   ________ ________

3. Tomorrow in our history class, dr. connalley will start lecturing on the civil war.

   ________ ________ ________ ________

4. aunt Sarah and uncle Hal, who are mormons, took us to their church services when we visited them in the midwest.

   ________ ________ ________ ________

5. My sister has signed up for a course titled eastern religions; she'll be studying buddhism and hinduism.

   ________ ________ ________ ________

UNNECESSARY USE OF CAPITALS

Many errors in capitalization are caused by adding capitals where they are not needed.

Activity

Cross out the incorrectly capitalized words in the following sentences. Then write the correct forms of the words in the spaces provided. The number of spaces tells you how many corrections to make in each sentence.

1. Although the Commercials say that Things go better with Coke, I prefer Root Beer.

   ________ ________ ________ ________

2. The old man told the Cabdriver, "I want to go out to the Airport and don't try to cheat me."

   ________ ________

3. A front-page Newspaper story about the crash of a commercial Jet has made me nervous about my Overseas trip.

   ________ ________ ________

4. During a Terrible Blizzard in 1888, People froze to Death on the streets of New York.

   ________ ________ ________ ________

5. I asked the Bank Officer at Citibank, "How do I get an identification Card to use the automatic teller machines?"

   ________ ________ ________

■ Review Test 1

Cross out the words that need capitals in the following sentences. Then write the capitalized forms of the words in the spaces provided. The number of spaces tells you how many corrections to make in each sentence.

1. wanda and i agreed to meet on saturday before the football game.

   ________ ________ ________

2. Between Long island and the atlantic Ocean lies a long, thin sandbar called fire island.

   ________ ________ ________ ________

3. When I'm in the supermarket check-out line, it seems as if every magazine on display has an article called "how You Can Lose Twenty pounds in two weeks."

_____ _____ _____ _____

4. At the bookstore, each student received a free sample pack of bayer aspirin, arrid deodorant, and prell shampoo.

_____ _____ _____

5. "can't you be quiet?" I pleaded. "do you always have to talk while I'm watching *general hospital* on television?"

_____ _____ _____ _____

6. On father's day, the children drove home and took their parents out to dinner at the ramada inn.

_____ _____ _____ _____

7. I will work at the holly Day School on mondays and fridays for the rest of september.

_____ _____ _____ _____

8. glendale bank, where my sister kathy works, is paying for her night course titled business accounting I.

_____ _____ _____ _____

9. I subscribe to one newspaper, the *daily planet,* and two magazines, *people* and *glamour.*

_____ _____ _____ _____

10. On thanksgiving my brother said, "let's hurry and eat so i can go watch the football game on our new sony TV."

_____ _____ _____ _____

■ Review Test 2

On separate paper,

1. Write seven sentences demonstrating the seven main uses of capital letters.
2. Write eight sentences demonstrating the eight other uses of capital letters.

NUMBERS AND ABBREVIATIONS

NUMBERS

1 Spell out numbers that take no more than two words. Otherwise, use numerals—the numbers themselves.

During the past five years, over twenty-five barracuda have been caught in the lake.

The parking fine was ten dollars.

In my grandmother's attic are eighty-four pairs of old shoes.

But

Each year about 250 baby trout are added to the lake.

My costs after contesting a parking fine in court were $135.

Grandmother has 382 back copies of *Reader's Digest* in her attic.

2 Be consistent when you use a series of numbers. If some numbers in a sentence or paragraph require more than two words, then use numerals throughout the selection:

During his election campaign, State Senator Mel Grabble went to 3 county fairs, 16 parades, 45 cookouts, and 112 club dinners, and delivered the same speech 176 times.

3 Use numerals to show dates, times, addresses, percentages, and parts of a book.

The letter was dated April 3, 1872.

My appointment was at 6:15. (*But:* Spell out numbers before *o'clock.* For example: The doctor didn't see me until seven o'clock.)

He lives at 212 West 19th Street.

About 20 percent of our class has dropped out of school.

Turn to page 179 in Chapter 8 and answer questions 1–10.

Activity

Cross out the mistakes in numbers and write the corrections in the spaces provided.

1. Rich was born on February fifteenth, nineteen seventy.

   15

   1970

2. When the 2 children failed to return from school, over 50 people volunteered to search for them.

   TWO

   FiFTY

3. At 1 o'clock in the afternoon last Thursday, an earthquake destroyed at least 20 buildings in the town.

   one o'clock

   twenty

ABBREVIATIONS

While abbreviations are a helpful time-saver in note-taking, you should avoid most abbreviations in formal writing. Listed below are some of the few abbreviations that can acceptably be used in compositions. Note that a period is used after most abbreviations.

1 Mr., Mrs., Ms., Jr., Sr., Dr. when used with proper names:

Mr. Tibble   Dr. Stein   Ms. O'Reilly

2 Time references:

A.M. or a.m.   P.M. or p.m.   B.C. or A.D.

3 First or middle name in a signature:

R. Anthony Curry   Otis T. Redding   J. Alfred Prufrock

4 Organizations, technical words, and trade names known primarily by their initials:

FBI   UN   CBS   FM   STP

Activity

Cross out the words that should not be abbreviated and correct them in the spaces provided.

1. On a Sat. morning I will never forget, Dec. 5, 1987, at ten min. after eight, I came downstairs and discovered that I had been robbed.

   ________ ________ ________

2. For six years I lived at First Ave. and Gordon St., right next to the Shore Memorial Hosp., in San Fran., Calif.

   ________ ________ ________ ________ ________

3. Before her biol. and Eng. exams, Linda was so nervous that her doc. gave her a tranq.

   ________ ________ ________ ________

Review Test

Cross out the mistakes in numbers and abbreviations and correct them in the spaces provided.

1. At three-fifteen p.m., an angry caller said a bomb was planted in a bus stat. locker.
   3:15 ______ station ______
2. Page eighty-two is missing from my chem. book.
   82 ______ Chemistry ______
3. Martha has over 200 copies of *People* mag.; she thinks they may be worth money someday.
   ______ Magazines ______
4. When I was eight yrs. old, I owned three cats, two dogs, and 4 rabbits.
   Years ______ Four ______
5. Approx. half the workers on strike returned to work on Jan. Third, nineteen eighty-five.
   Approximately ______ January ______ 3 ______ 1985 ______

APOSTROPHE

Introductory Project

1. Larry's motorcycle
   my sister's boyfriend
   Grandmother's shotgun
   the men's room
   Dionne Warwick's new album

   What is the purpose of the *'s* in all the examples above? ________

   ____

2. They didn't mind when their dog bit people, but now they're leashing him since he's eating all their garden vegetables.

   What is the purpose of the apostrophe in *didn't, they're,* and *he's?*

   ____

3. I used to believe that vampires lived in the old coal bin of my cellar.
   The vampire's whole body recoiled when he saw the crucifix.
   Fred ate two baked potatoes.
   One baked potato's center was still hard.

   In the sentence pairs above, why is the *'s* used in each second sentence but not in the first? ________________

   ____

Answers are on page 533.

The two main uses of the apostrophe are:

1 To show the omission of one or more letters in a contraction
2 To show ownership or possession

Each use is explained on the pages that follow.

APOSTROPHE IN CONTRACTIONS

A contraction is formed when two words are combined to make one word. An apostrophe is used to show where letters are omitted in forming the contraction. Here are two contractions:

have + not = haven't (the *o* in *not* has been omitted)
I + will = I'll (the *wi* in *will* has been omitted)

The following are some other common contractions:

I +	am =	I'm	it +	is =	it's
I +	have =	I've	it +	has =	it's
I +	had =	I'd	is +	not =	isn't
who +	is =	who's	could +	not =	couldn't
do +	not =	don't	I +	would =	I'd
did +	not =	didn't	they +	are =	they're

Note: Will + not has an unusual contraction: won't.

Activity 1

Combine the following words into contractions. One is done for you.

1.	we + are =	*we're*	6.	you + have =	You've
2.	are + not =	Aren't	7.	has + not =	hasn't
3.	you + are =	you're	8.	who + is =	Who's
4.	they + have =	they've	9.	does + not =	doesn't
5.	would + not =	wouldn't	10.	there + is =	there's

Activity 2

Write the contractions for the words in parentheses. One is done for you.

1. (Are not) ___Aren't___ you coming with us to the concert?
2. (I am) ___I'm___ going to take the car if (it is) ___it's___ all right with you.
3. (There is) ___there's___ an extra bed upstairs if (you would) ___You'd___ like to stay here for the night.
4. (I will) ___I'll___ give you the name of the personnel director, but there (is not) ___isn't___ much chance (he will) ___he'll___ speak to you.
5. Linda (should not) ___should'nt___ complain about the cost of food if (she is) ___she's___ not willing to grow her own by planting a backyard garden.

Note: Even though contractions are common in everyday speech and in written dialog, usually it is best to avoid them in formal writing.

APOSTROPHE TO SHOW OWNERSHIP OR POSSESSION

To show ownership or possession, we can use such words as *belongs to, possessed by, owned by,* or (most commonly) *of.*

the jacket that *belongs to* Tony
the gas station *owned by* our cousin
the footprints *of* the animal

But the apostrophe plus *s* (if the word does not end in *s*) is often the quickest and easiest way to show possession. Thus we can say:

Tony's jacket
our cousin's gas station
the animal's footprints

Points to Remember

1 The *'s* goes with the owner or possessor (in the examples given, *Tony, cousin, the animal*). What follows is the person or thing possessed (in the examples given, *the jacket, gas station, footprints*).

2 There should always be a break between the word and the *'s*.

Tony's not *Tony's*

Yes No

Activity 1

Rewrite the italicized part of each of the sentences below, using the *'s* to show possession. Remember that the *'s* goes with the owner or possessor.

Examples *The toys belonging to the children* filled an entire room.

The children's toys

1. *The roller skates owned by Pat* have been stolen.
   Pat's skates
2. *The visit of my cousin* lasted longer than I wanted it to.
   my Cousin's visit
3. *The fenders belonging to the car* are badly rusted.
   Car Fender's
4. *The prescription of a doctor* is needed for the pills.
   a doctor's Prescription
5. *The grade possessed by David* was the highest in our accounting class.
   David's grade
6. Is this *the hat of somebody*?
   somebody's hat
7. The broken saddle produced a sore on *the back of the horse*.
   horse's back
8. *The two dogs belonging to my neighbor* ripped open the trash bags.
   Neighbors dogs
9. *The energy level possessed by the little boy* is much higher than hers.
   Little boy's energy
10. *The foundation of the house* is crumbling.
    house's Foundation

Activity 2

Add *'s* to each of the following words to make them the possessors or owners of something. Then write sentences using the words. Your sentences can be serious or playful. One is done for you.

1. dog *dog's* *That dog's bite is worse than his bark.*
2. teacher teacher's ____________________
3. Lola Lola's ____________________
4. store Store's ____________________
5. mother Mother's ____________________

Apostrophe versus Possessive Pronouns

Do not use an apostrophe with possessive pronouns. They already show ownership. Possessive pronouns include *his, hers, its, yours, ours,* and *theirs.*

The bookstore lost its lease.	*not*	The bookstore lost its' lease.
The racing bikes were theirs.	*not*	The racing bikes were theirs'.
The change is yours.	*not*	The change is yours'.
His problems are ours, too.	*not*	His' problems are ours', too.
His skin is more sunburned than hers.	*not*	His' skin is more sunburned than hers.'

Apostrophe versus Simple Plurals

When you want to make a word plural, just add an *s* at the end of the word. Do *not* add an apostrophe. For example, the plural of the word *movie* is *movies,* not *movie's* or *movies'*. Look at this sentence:

Lola adores Tony's broad shoulders, rippling muscles, and warm eyes.

The words *shoulders, muscles,* and *eyes* are simple plurals, meaning more than one shoulder, more than one muscle, more than one eye. The plural is shown by adding *s* only. On the other hand, the *'s* after Tony shows possession—that Tony owns the shoulders, muscles, and eyes.

Activity

Insert an apostrophe where needed to show possession in the following sentences. Write *plural* above words where the *-s* ending simply means more than one thing.

Example Karen's tomato plants (*plural*) are taller than the six-foot stakes (*plural*) that support them.

1. Tonys favorite breakfast is five strips of bacon and fried potatoes.
2. My fathers influence on his brothers has been enormous.
3. When I walked into the doctors office, there were eight persons waiting who also had appointments.
4. Bills job of slaughtering pigs was enough to make him a vegetarian.
5. When the brakes failed on Phils jeep, he narrowly avoided hitting several parked cars and two trees.
6. As Ricks skill at guessing the essay questions on tests increased, his grades improved.
7. My friends cooking is not the greatest: she made spaghetti for us and the noodles were so tightly stuck together that I had to cut them with a knife.
8. His wifes habit of taking the hangers from his closet really bothers him.
9. I asked the record clerk for several blank cassette tapes and Carly Simons latest album.
10. After six weeks without rain, the nearby streams started drying up, and the lakes water level fell sharply.

Apostrophe with Words Ending in *-s*

If a word ends in *-s,* show possession by adding only an apostrophe. Most plurals end in *-s,* and so show possession simply by adding the apostrophe.

Charles' suede shirt
Doris' car
Ms. Rogers' briefcase
my parents' station wagon
the Beatles' last album
the students' class rings

Activity

Add an apostrophe where needed.

1. Phyllis grade was the best in the class.
2. The transit workers strike continued until a compromise was reached.
3. When the students gripes about the cafeteria were ignored, many of them started to bring their own lunches.
4. Lewis dog gets his exercise by biting people.
5. All the soldiers rifles were cleaned for inspection.

■ Review Test 1

In each sentence, cross out the two words that need apostrophes. Then write the words correctly in the spaces provided.

1. The contestants face fell when she learned she had won a years supply of Ajax cleanser.
2. Weve been trying for weeks to see that movie, but theres always a long line.
3. Freds car wouldnt start until the baby-faced mechanic replaced its spark plugs and points.
4. The citys budget director has trouble balancing his own familys books.
5. Taking Dianes elderly parents to church every week is one example of Toms generous behavior.

Here's / You're 6. Heres a checklist of points to follow when youre writing your class reports.

men's / Children's 7. Lola shops in the mens store for jeans and the childrens department for belts.

Cat's / Can't 8. The cats babies are under my chair again; I cant find a way to keep her from bringing them near me.

wasn't / Cousin's 9. Because of a family feud, Julie wasnt invited to a barbecue at her cousins house.

Show's / Ladies 10. During the shows intermission, a line formed quickly in front of the ladies room.

■ Review Test 2

Make the following words possessive and then use at least five of them in a not-so-serious paragraph that tells a story. In addition, use at least three contractions in the paragraph.

mugger	restaurant	Tony	student
New York	sister	children	vampire
duck	Miss Piggy	boss	Eddie Murphy
customer	bartender	police car	yesterday
professor	someone	mob	Chicago

QUOTATION MARKS

Introductory Project

Read the following scene and underline all the words enclosed within quotation marks. Your teacher may also have you dramatize the scene, with one person reading the narration and two persons acting the two speaking parts of the young man and the old woman. The two speakers should imagine the scene as part of a stage play and try to make their words seem as real and true-to-life as possible.

> An old woman in a Rolls-Royce was preparing to back into a parking space. Suddenly a small sports car appeared and pulled into the space. "That's what you can do when you're young and fast," the young man in the car yelled to the old woman. As he strolled away, laughing, he heard a terrible crunching sound. "What's that noise?" he said. Turning around, he saw the old woman backing repeatedly into and crushing his small car. "You can't do that, old lady!" he yelled.
>
> "What do you mean, I can't?" she chuckled, as metal grated against metal. "This is what you can do when you're old and rich."

1. On the basis of the above selection, what is the purpose of quotation marks?

   ____

2. Do commas and periods that come after a quotation go inside or outside quotation marks?

   ____

Answers are on page 533.

The two main uses of quotation marks are:

1 To set off the exact words of a speaker or a writer
2 To set off the titles of short works

Each use is explained on the pages that follow.

QUOTATION MARKS TO SET OFF THE EXACT WORDS OF A SPEAKER OR A WRITER

Use quotation marks when you want to show the exact words of a speaker or a writer.

''Say something tender to me,'' whispered Lola to Tony.
(Quotation marks set off the exact words that Lola spoke to Tony.)

Mark Twain once wrote, ''The more I know about human beings, the more I like my dog.''
(Quotation marks set off the exact words that Mark Twain wrote.)

''The only dumb question,'' the instructor said, ''is the one you don't ask.''
(Two pairs of quotation marks are used to enclose the instructor's exact words.)

Sharon complained, ''I worked so hard on this paper. I spent two days getting information in the library and two days writing it. Guess what grade I got on it.''
(Note that the end quotation marks do not come until the end of Sharon's speech. Place quotation marks before the first quoted word of a speech and after the last quoted word. As long as no interruption occurs in the speech, do not use quotation marks for each new sentence.)

Punctuation Hint: In the four examples above, notice that a comma sets off the quoted part from the rest of the sentence. Also observe that commas and periods at the end of a quotation always go *inside* quotation marks.

Complete the following statements that explain how capital letters, commas, and periods are used in quotations. Refer to the four examples as guides.

1. Every quotation begins with a Capital letter.
2. When a quotation is split (as in the sentence about dumb questions), the second part does not begin with a capital letter unless it is a new sentence.

3. _______________ are used to separate the quoted part of a sentence from the rest of the sentence.

4. Commas and periods that come at the end of a quotation go _______________ quotation marks.

The answers are *capital, new, Commas,* and *inside.*

Activity 1

Place quotation marks around the exact words of a speaker or writer in the sentences that follow.

1. Take some vitamin C for your cold, Lola told Tony.
2. How are you doing in school? my uncle always asks me.
3. An epitaph on a tombstone in Georgia reads, I told you I was sick!
4. Dave said, Let's walk faster. I think the game has already started.
5. Lincoln wrote, To sin by silence when they should protest makes cowards of men.
6. Thelma said, My brother is so lazy that, if opportunity knocked, he'd resent the noise.
7. It's extremely dangerous to mix alcohol and pills, Dr. Wilson reminded us. The combination could kill you.
8. Ice-cold drinks! shouted the vendor selling lukewarm drinks.
9. Be careful not to touch the fence, the guard warned. It's electrified.
10. Just because I'm deaf, Lynn said, many people treat me as if I were stupid.

Activity 2

1. Write a sentence in which you quote a favorite expression of someone you know. Identify the relationship of the person to you.

Example *One of my father's favorite expressions is, "Don't sweat the small stuff."*

____

____

____

2. Write a quotation that contains the words *Tony asked Lola.* Write a second quotation that includes the words *Lola replied.*

____

____

____

____

3. Copy a sentence or two that interests you from a book or magazine. Identify the title and author of the work.

Example *In Night Shift, Stephen King writes, "I don't like to sleep with one leg sticking out. Because if a cool hand ever reached out from under the bed and grasped my ankle, I might scream."*

____

____

____

____

Indirect Quotations

An indirect quotation is a rewording of someone else's comments, rather than a word-for-word direct quotation. The word *that* often signals an indirect quotation.

Direct Quotation	*Indirect Quotation*
Fred said, "The distributor cap on my car is cracked." (Fred's exact spoken words are given, so quotation marks are used.)	Fred said that the distributor cap on his car was cracked. (We learn Fred's words *in*directly, so no quotation marks are used.)
Sally's note to Jay read, "I'll be working late. Don't wait up for me." (The exact words that Sally wrote in the note are given, so quotation marks are used.)	Sally left a note for Jay that said she would be working late and that he should not wait up for her. (We learn Sally's words indirectly, so no quotation marks are used.)

Activity

Rewrite the following sentences, changing words as necessary to convert the sentences into direct quotations. The first one is done for you as an example.

1. Fred asked Martha if he could turn on the football game.
   Fred asked, "Martha, can I turn on the football game?"
2. Martha said that he could listen to the game on the radio.
   Martha said, "Fred Go ahead and listen"
3. Fred replied he was tired of being told what to do.
   Fred replied, "I am tired of . . . do"
4. Martha said that as long as she was bigger and stronger, she would make the rules.
   Martha said, " as long as
5. Fred said that the day would come when the tables would be turned.
   Fred Said, "The day will Come . . . Turned."

QUOTATION MARKS TO SET OFF THE TITLES OF SHORT WORKS

Short works are usually set off by quotation marks, while long works are underlined. Use quotation marks to set off the titles of such short works as articles in books, newspapers, or magazines; chapters in a book; short stories, poems, and songs.

On the other hand, you should underline the titles of books, newspapers, magazines, plays, movies, record albums, and television shows.

Quotation Marks	*Underlines*
the article "The Mystique of Lawyers"	in the book Verdicts on Lawyers
the article "Getting a Fix on Repairs"	in the newspaper The New York Times
the article "Animal Facts and Fallacies"	in the magazine Reader's Digest
the chapter "Why Do Men Marry?"	in the book Passages
the story "The Night the Bed Fell"	in the book A Thurber Carnival

Quotation Marks	*Underlines*
the poem "A Prayer for My Daughter"	in the book Poems of W. B. Yeats
the song "Beat It"	in the album Thriller
	the television show Hill Street Blues
	the movie Gone With the Wind

Note: In printed works titles of books, newspapers, etc. are set off by italics—slanted type that looks *like this*—instead of being underlined.

Activity

Use quotation marks or underlines as needed.

1. I Was a Playboy Bunny is the first chapter of Gloria Steinem's book Outrageous Acts and Everyday Rebellions.
2. No advertising is permitted in Consumer Reports, a nonprofit consumer magazine.
3. I cut out an article from Newsweek called The Bad News About Our High Schools to use in my sociology report.
4. Tony's favorite television show is Star Trek, and his favorite movie is The Night of the Living Dead.
5. Our instructor gave us a week to buy the textbook titled Personal Finance and to read the first chapter, Work and Income.
6. Every holiday season, our family watches the movie A Christmas Carol on television.
7. Fred bought the Ladies' Home Journal because he wanted to read the cover article titled Secrets Men Never Tell You.
8. Edgar Allan Poe's short story The Murders in the Rue Morgue and his poem The Raven are in a paperback titled Great Tales and Poems of Edgar Allan Poe.
9. When Elaine got her new TV Guide, she read an article titled The New Comedians and then thumbed through the listings to see who would be the guests that week on the Tonight Show.
10. The night before his exam, he discovered with horror that the chapter Becoming Mature was missing from Childhood and Adolescence, the psychology text that he had bought secondhand.

OTHER USES OF QUOTATION MARKS

1 To set off special words or phrases from the rest of a sentence:

> Many people spell the words ''a lot'' as *one* word, ''alot,'' instead of correctly spelling them as two words.
>
> I have trouble telling the difference between ''their'' and ''there.''

Note: In printed works, *italics* are often used to set off special words or phrases. That is usually done in this book, for example.

2 To mark off a quotation within a quotation:

> The instructor said, ''Know the chapter titled 'Status Symbols' in *Adolescent Development* if you expect to pass the test.''
>
> Lola said, ''One of my favorite Mae West lines is 'I used to be Snow White, but I drifted.' ''

Note: A quotation within a quotation is indicated by *single* quotation marks.

■ Review Test 1

Insert quotation marks where needed in the sentences that follow.

1. Don't you ever wash your car? Lola asked Tony.
2. When the washer tilted and began to buzz, Martha shouted, Let's get rid of that blasted machine!
3. Take all you want, read the sign above the cafeteria salad bar, but please eat all you take.
4. After scrawling formulas all over the board with lightning speed, my math instructor was fond of asking, Any questions now?
5. Move that heap! the truck driver yelled. I'm trying to make a living here.
6. I did a summary of an article titled Aspirin and Heart Attacks in the latest issue of Time.
7. Writer's block is something that happens to everyone at times, the teacher explained. You simply have to keep writing to break out of it.

8. A passenger in the car ahead of Clyde threw food wrappers and empty cups out the window. That man, said Clyde to his son, is a human pig.
9. If you are working during the day, said the counselor, the best way to start college is with a night course or two.
10. I told the dentist that I wanted Novocain. Don't be a sissy, he said. A little pain won't hurt you. I told him that a little pain wouldn't bother him, but it would bother me.

■ Review Test 2

Go through the comics section of a newspaper to find a comic strip that amuses you. Be sure to choose a strip where two or more characters are speaking to each other. Write a full description that will enable people who have not read the comic strip to visualize it clearly and appreciate its humor. Describe the setting and action in each panel, and enclose the words of the speakers in quotation marks.

COMMA

Introductory Project

Commas often (though not always) signal a minor break, or pause, in a sentence. Each of the six pairs of sentences below illustrates one of the six main uses of the comma. Read each pair of sentences aloud and place a comma wherever you feel a slight pause occurs.

1. a. Frank's interests are Maria television and sports.
   b. My mother put her feet up sipped some iced tea and opened the newspaper.
2. a. Although the Lone Ranger used lots of silver bullets he never ran out of ammunition.
   b. To open the cap of the aspirin bottle you must first press down on it.
3. a. Kitty Litter and Dredge Rivers Hollywood's leading romantic stars have made several movies together.
   b. Sarah who is my next-door neighbor just entered the hospital with an intestinal infection.
4. a. The wedding was scheduled for four o'clock but the bride changed her mind at two.
   b. The oranges in the refrigerator were covered with blue mold and the potatoes in the cupboard felt like sponges.
5. a. Lola's mother asked her "What time do you expect to get home?"
   b. "Don't bend over to pet the dog" I warned "or he'll bite you."
6. a. Roy ate seventeen hamburgers on July 29 1988 and lived to tell about it.
   b. Roy lives at 817 Cresson Street Detroit Michigan.

Answers are on page 533.

SIX MAIN USES OF THE COMMA

Commas are used mainly as follows:

1 To separate items in a series
2 To set off introductory material
3 On both sides of words that interrupt the flow of thought in a sentence
4 Between two complete thoughts connected by *and, but, for, or, nor, so, yet*
5 To set off a direct quotation from the rest of a sentence
6 For certain everyday material

You may find it helpful to remember that the comma often marks a slight pause, or break, in a sentence. Read aloud the sentence examples given for each rule, and listen for the minor pauses, or breaks, that are signaled by commas.

Comma between Items in a Series

Use commas to separate items in a series.

Do you drink tea with milk, lemon, or honey?

Today the dishwasher stopped working, the garbage bag split, and the refrigerator turned into an icebox.

The television game shows enraged him so much he did not know whether to laugh, cry, or throw up.

Jan awoke from a restless, nightmare-filled sleep.

Notes

a The final comma in a series is optional, but often it is used.

b A comma is used between two descriptive words in a series only if *and* inserted between the words sounds natural. You could say:

Jan awoke from a restless *and* nightmare-filled sleep.

But notice in the following sentence that the descriptive words do not sound natural when *and* is inserted between them. In such cases, no comma is used.

Wanda drove a bright blue Corvette. (A bright *and* blue Corvette doesn't sound right, so no comma is used.)

Activity

Place commas between items in a series.

1. Superman believes in truth justice and the American way.
2. My father taught me to swim by talking to me in a calm manner holding my hand firmly and throwing me into the pool.
3. Paul added white wine mushrooms salt pepper and oregano to his spaghetti sauce.
4. The baggy threadbare jeans feel more comfortable than pajamas to me.
5. Mark grabbed a tiny towel bolted out of the bathroom and ran toward the ringing phone.

Comma after Introductory Material

Use a comma to set off introductory material.

> After punching the alarm clock with his fist, Bill turned over and went back to sleep.
>
> Looking up in the sky, I saw a man who was flying faster than a speeding bullet.
>
> Holding a baited trap, Clyde cautiously approached the gigantic mousehole.
>
> In addition, he held a broom in his hand.
>
> Also, he wore a football helmet in case a creature should leap out at his head.

Note: If the introductory material is brief, the comma is sometimes omitted. In the activities here, you should include the comma.

Activity

Place commas after introductory material.

1. When the president entered the room became hushed.
2. Feeling brave and silly at the same time Tony volunteered to go on stage and help the magician.
3. While I was eating my tuna sandwich the cats circled my chair like hungry sharks.

4. Because my parents died when I was young I have learned to look after myself. Even though I am now independent I still carry a special loneliness within me.
5. At first putting extra hot pepper flakes on the pizza seemed like a good idea. However I felt otherwise when flames seemed about to shoot out of my mouth.

Comma around Words Interrupting the Flow of Thought

Use commas on both sides of words or phrases that interrupt the flow of thought in a sentence.

> My brother, a sports nut, owns over five thousand baseball cards.
>
> That game show, at long last, has been canceled.
>
> The children used the old Buick, rusted from disuse, as a backyard clubhouse.

Usually you can "hear" words that interrupt the flow of thought in a sentence. However, if you are not sure if certain words are interrupters, remove them from the sentence. If it still makes sense without the words, you know the words are interrupters and that the information they give is nonessential. Such nonessential information is set off with commas. In the following sentence

> Dody Thompson, who lives next door, won the javelin-throwing competition.

the words *who lives next door* are extra information, not needed to identify the subject of the sentence, Dody Thompson. Put commas around such nonessential information. On the other hand, in the sentence

> The woman who lives next door won the javelin-throwing competition.

the words *who lives next door* supply essential information—information needed for us to identify the woman being spoken of. If the words were removed from the sentence, we would no longer know who won the competition. Commas are not used around such essential information.

Here is another example:

> Wilson Hall, which the tornado destroyed, was ninety years old.

Here the words *which the tornado destroyed* are extra information, not needed to identify the subject of the sentence, *Wilson Hall.* Commas go around such nonessential information. On the other hand, in the sentence

The building which the tornado destroyed was ninety years old.

the words *which the tornado destroyed* are needed to identify the building. Commas are not used around such essential information.

Most of the time you will be able to ''hear'' words that interrupt the flow of thought in a sentence and will not have to think about whether the words are essential or nonessential.

Activity

Use commas to set off interrupting words.

1. On Friday my day off I went to get a haircut.
2. Dracula who had a way with women is Tony's favorite movie hero. He feels that the Wolfman on the other hand showed no class in handling women.
3. Many people forget that Franklin Roosevelt one of our most effective presidents was also handicapped.
4. Mowing the grass especially when it is six inches high is my least favorite job.
5. A jar of chicken noodle soup which was all there was in the refrigerator did not make for a very satisfying meal.

Comma between Complete Thoughts

Use a comma between two complete thoughts connected by *and, but, for, or, nor, so, yet.*

The wedding was scheduled for four o'clock, but the bride changed her mind at two.

We could always tell when our teacher felt disorganized, for his shirt would not be tucked in.

Rich has to work on Monday nights, so he tapes the TV football game on his video recorder.

Notes

a The comma is optional when the complete thoughts are short.

Grace's skin tans and Mark's skin freckles.

Her soda turned watery for the ice melted quickly.

The day was overcast so they didn't go swimming.

b Be careful not to use a comma in sentences having *one* subject and a *double* verb. The comma is used only in sentences made up of two complete thoughts (two subjects and two verbs). In this sentence

Bill will go partying tonight and forget all about tomorrow's exam.

there is only one subject (*Bill*) and a double verb (*will go* and *forget*). No comma is needed. Likewise, the following sentence

Rita was a waitress at the Holiday Inn last summer and probably will work there this summer.

has only one subject (*Rita*) and a double verb (*was* and *will work*); therefore, no comma is needed.

Activity

Place a comma before a joining word that connects two complete thoughts (two subjects and two verbs). Remember, do *not* place a comma within sentences that have only one subject and a double verb.

1. The oranges in the refrigerator were covered with blue mold and the potatoes in the cupboard felt like sponges.
2. All the slacks in the shop were on sale but not a single pair of them was in my size.
3. Martha often window-shops in the malls for hours and comes home without buying anything.
4. Tony left the dentist's office with his mouth still numb from Novocain and he talked with a lisp for two hours.
5. I covered the walls with three coats of white paint but the purple color still showed through underneath.
6. The car squealed down the entrance ramp and sped recklessly out onto the freeway.

7. The dancers in the go-go bar moved like wound-up Barbie dolls and the men in the audience sat as motionless as stones.
8. The aliens in the science fiction film visited our planet in peace but we greeted them with violence.
9. I felt like shouting at the gang of boys but didn't dare open my mouth.
10. Lenny claims he wants to succeed in college but he has missed classes all semester.

Comma with Direct Quotations

Use a comma to set off a direct quotation from the rest of a sentence.

> His father shouted, “Why don't you go out and get a job?”
>
> “Our modern world has lost a sense of the sacredness of life,” the speaker said.
>
> “No,” said Celia to Jerry. “I won't go to the roller derby with you.”
>
> “Can anyone remember,” wrote Emerson, “when the times were not hard and money not scarce?”

Note: Commas and periods at the end of a quotation go inside quotation marks. See also pages 433–434.

Activity

Use commas to set off quotations from the rest of the sentence.

1. The man yelled “Call an ambulance, somebody!”
2. My partner on the dance floor said “Don't be so stiff. You look as if you'd swallowed an umbrella.”
3. The question on the anatomy test read “What human organ grows faster than any other, never stops growing, and always remains the same size?”
4. The student behind me whispered “The human skin.”
5. “My stomach hurts” Bruce said “and I don't know whether it was the hamburger or the math test.”

Comma with Everyday Material

Use a comma with certain everyday material.

Persons Spoken To

Go to bed, Tina, if you're not feeling well.

Cindy, where did you put my shoes?

Are you coming with us, Bob?

Dates

March 4, 1978, is when Martha buried her third husband.

Addresses

Tony's grandparents live at 183 Roxborough Avenue, Cleveland, Ohio 44112.

Note: No comma is used to mark off the zip code.

Openings and Closings of Letters

Dear Santa,
Dear Larry,
Sincerely yours,
Truly yours,

Note: In formal letters, a colon is used after the opening: Dear Sir: *or* Dear Madam:

Numbers

The dishonest dealer turned the used car's odometer from 98,170 miles to 39,170 miles.

Activity

Place commas where needed.

1. I expected you to set a better example for the others Mike.
2. With your help Janet I passed the test.
3. The movie stars Kitty Litter and Dredge Rivers were married on September 12 1988 and lived at 3865 Sunset Boulevard Los Angeles California for one month.
4. They received 75000 congratulatory fan letters and were given picture contracts worth $3000000 in the first week of their marriage.
5. Kitty left Dredge on October 12 1988 and ran off with their marriage counselor.

■ Review Test 1

Insert commas where needed. In the space provided below each sentence, summarize briefly the rule that explains the use of the comma or commas.

1. The best features of my new apartment are its large kitchen its bay windows and its low rent.

2. Because we got in line at dawn we were among the first to get tickets for the concert.

3. ''When will someone invent a telephone'' Lola asked ''that will let you know who's calling before you answer it?''

4. Without opening his eyes Simon stumbled out of bed and opened the door for the whining dog.

5. I think David that you had better ask someone else for your $2500 loan.

6. Hot dogs are the most common cause of choking deaths in children for a bite-size piece can easily plug up a toddler's throat.

7. Tax forms though shortened and revised every year never seem to get any simpler.

8. Sandra may decide to go to college full-time or she may enroll in a couple of evening courses.

____

9. I remember how with the terrible cruelty of children we used to make fun of the retarded girl who lived on our street.

____

10. Although that old man on the corner looks like a Skid Row bum he is said to have a Swiss bank account.

____

■ Review Test 2

Insert commas where needed.

1. My dog who is afraid of the dark sleeps with a night-light.
2. "I wish there were some pill" said Chuck "that would give you the equivalent of eight hours' sleep in four hours."
3. The hot dogs at the ball park tasted delicious but they reacted later like delayed time bombs.
4. Janice attended class for four hours worked at the hospital for three hours and studied at home for two hours.
5. The loan shark may send a message to you a message you won't like unless you pay your money soon.
6. George and Ida sat down to watch the football game with crackers sharp cheese salty beer pretzels and two frosty bottles of beer.
7. Even though I knew exactly what was happening the solar eclipse gave me a strong feeling of anxiety.
8. The company agreed to raise a senior bus driver's salary to $28000 by January 1 1991.
9. Even though King Kong was holding her at the very top of the Empire State Building Fay Wray kept yelling at him "Let me go!"
10. Navel oranges which Margery as a little girl called belly-button oranges are her favorite fruit.

■ Review Test 3

On separate paper, write six sentences, with each sentence demonstrating one of the six main comma rules.

OTHER PUNCTUATION MARKS

No Dash
NO Parenteses on test

Introductory Project

Each of the sentences below needs one of the following punctuation marks:

; — - ( ) :

See if you can insert the correct mark in each sentence. Each mark is used once.

1. The following holiday plants are poisonous and should be kept away from children and pets holly, mistletoe, and poinsettias.
2. The freeze dried remains of Annie's canary were in a clear bottle on her bookcase.
3. William Shakespeare 1564–1616 married a woman eight years his senior when he was eighteen.
4. Grooming in space is more difficult than on Earth no matter how much astronauts comb their hair, for instance, it still tends to float loosely around their heads.
5. I opened the front door, and our cat walked proudly in with a live bunny hanging from his mouth.

Answers are on page 534.

COLON (:)

Use the colon at the end of a complete statement to introduce a list, a long quotation, or an explanation.

List

The following were my worst jobs: truck loader in an apple plant, assembler in a battery factory, and attendant in a state mental hospital.

Long Quotation

Thoreau explains in *Walden:* ‘‘I went to the woods because I wished to live deliberately, to front only the essential facts of life, and see if I could not learn what it had to teach, and not, when I came to die, discover that I had not lived.’’

Explanation

There are two softball leagues in our town: the fast-pitch league and the lob-pitch league.

Activity

Place colons where needed.

1. Foods that are high in cholesterol include the following: eggs, butter, milk, cheese, shrimp, and well-marbled meats.
2. All the signs of the flu were present: hot and cold spells, heavy drainage from the sinuses, a bad cough, and an ache through the entire body.
3. Carl Sagan has stated: ‘‘This nuclear madness is incredible. It’s like having the Soviet leaders and the American leaders standing in a room with gasoline up to their knees. The Soviets are holding a hundred matches and the Americans are holding ninety-eight matches. And they are arguing over how many more matches each should have.’’

SEMICOLON (;)

The main use of the semicolon is to mark the break between two complete thoughts, as explained on page 355. Another use of the semicolon is to mark off items in a series when the items themselves contain commas. Here are some examples:

> Winning prizes at the national flower show were Roberta Collins, Alabama, azaleas; Sally Hunt, Kentucky, roses; and James Weber, California, Shasta daisies.
>
> The following books must be read for the course: *The Color Purple,* by Alice Walker; *In Our Time,* by Ernest Hemingway; and *Man's Search for Meaning,* by Viktor Frankl.

Activity

Place semicolons where needed.

1. The specials at the restaurant today are eggplant Parmesan, for $3.95 black beans and rice, for $2.95 and chicken potpie, for $4.95.
2. The top of the hill offered an awesome view of the military cemetery thousands of headstones crisscrossed in perfect rows.
3. Lola's favorite old movies are *To Catch a Thief,* starring Cary Grant and Grace Kelly *Animal Crackers,* a Marx Brothers comedy and *The Wizard of Oz,* with Judy Garland.

DASH (—)

A dash signals a degree of pause longer than a comma but not as complete as a period. Use a dash to set off words for dramatic effect:

> I didn't go out with him a second time—once was more than enough.
>
> Some of you—I won't mention you by name—cheated on the test.
>
> It was so windy that the VW passed him on the highway—overhead.

Notes

a The dash is formed on the typewriter by striking the hyphen twice (--). In handwriting, the dash is as long as two letters would be.

b Be careful not to overuse dashes.

Activity

Place dashes where needed.

1. Riding my bike, I get plenty of exercise especially when dogs chase me.
2. I'm advising you in fact, I'm telling you not to bother me again.
3. The package finally arrived badly damaged.

HYPHEN (-)

1 Use a hyphen with two or more words that act as a single unit describing a noun.

The fast-talking salesman was so good that he went into politics. (*Fast* and *talking* combine to describe the salesman.)

I both admire and envy her well-rounded personality.

When the dude removed his blue-tinted shades, Lonnell saw the spaced-out look in his eyes.

2 Use a hyphen to divide a word at the end of a line of writing or typing. When you need to divide a word at the end of a line, divide it between syllables. Use your dictionary to be sure of correct syllable divisions (see also page 456).

When Tom lifted up the hood of his Toyota, he realized that one of the radi-ator hoses had broken.

Notes

a Do not divide words of one syllable.

b Do not divide a word if you can avoid doing so.

Activity

Place hyphens where needed.

1. High flying jets and gear grinding trucks are constant sources of noise pollution in our neighborhood, and consequently we are going to move.
2. When Linda turned on the porch light, ten legged creatures scurried every where over the crumb filled floor.
3. Fred had ninety two dollars in his pocket when he left for the supermarket, and he had twenty two dollars when he got back.

PARENTHESES ( )

Parentheses are used to set off extra or incidental information from the rest of a sentence:

> The section of that book on the medical dangers of abortion (pages 35 to 72) is outdated.
>
> Yesterday at Hamburger House (my favorite place to eat), the guy who makes french fries asked me to go out with him.

Note: Do not use parentheses too often in your writing.

Activity

Add parentheses where needed.

1. Certain sections of the novel especially Chapter Five made my heart race with suspense.
2. Did you hear that George Linda's first husband just got remarried?
3. Sigmund Freud 1856–1939 was the founder of psychoanalysis.

■ Review Test

At the appropriate spot, place the punctuation mark shown in the margin.

; 1. Mary's savings have dwindled to nothing she's been borrowing from me to pay her rent.

— 2. There's the idiot I'd know him anywhere who dumped trash on our front lawn.

\- 3. Today's two-career couples spend more money on eating out than their parents did.

: 4. Ben Franklin said ''If a man empties his purse into his head, no man can take it away from him. An investment in knowledge always pays the best interest.''

( ) 5. One-fifth of our textbook pages 401–598 consists of footnotes and a bibliography.

USING THE DICTIONARY

The dictionary is a valuable tool. To take advantage of it, you need to understand the main kinds of information that a dictionary gives about a word. Look at the information provided for the word *murder* in the following entry from *The American Heritage Dictionary of the English Language:**

Spelling and syllabication — *Pronunciation* — *Part of speech*

mur•der (mûr′dər) *n.* The unlawful killing of one human being by another, esp. with malice aforethought. —*v.* **1.** To kill (a human being) unlawfully. **2.** To mar or spoil by ineptness: *murder the English language.* [< OE *morthor.*] — **mur′der•er** *n.* —**mur′der•ess** *fem.n.*

← *Meanings*

← *Other forms of the word*

* © 1969, 1970, 1976, 1980, Houghton Mifflin Company. Reprinted by permission from *The American Heritage Dictionary of the English Language,* paperback edition.

SPELLING

The first bit of information, in the boldface (heavy type) entry itself, is the spelling of *murder*. You probably already know the spelling of *murder*, but if you didn't, you could find it by pronouncing the syllables in the word carefully and then looking it up in the dictionary.

Use your dictionary to correct the spelling of the following words:

compatable ____________	insite ____________
althogh ____________	troble ____________
aksident ____________	untill ____________
embelish ____________	easyer ____________
systimatise ____________	prepostrous ____________
shedule ____________	comotion ____________
attenshun ____________	Vasaline ____________
wierd ____________	fatel ____________
hurryed ____________	busines ____________
alright ____________	jenocide ____________
fony ____________	poluted ____________
kriterion ____________	perpose ____________
hetirosexual ____________	chalange ____________

SYLLABICATION

The second bit of information that the dictionary gives, also in the boldface entry, is the syllabication of *murder*. Note that a dot separates the syllables.

Use your dictionary to mark the syllable divisions in the following words. Also indicate how many syllables are in each word.

j i t t e r	(______ syllables)
m o t i v a t e	(______ syllables)
o r a n g u t a n	(______ syllables)
i n c o n t r o v e r t i b l e	(______ syllables)

Noting syllable divisions will enable you to *hyphenate* a word: divide it at the end of one line of writing and complete it at the beginning of the next line. You can correctly hyphenate a word only at a syllable division, and you may have to check your dictionary to make sure of a word's syllable divisions.

PRONUNCIATION

The third bit of information in the dictionary entry is the pronunciation of *murder:* (*mûr'dər*). You already know how to pronounce *murder,* but if you didn't, the information within the parentheses would serve as your guide. Use your dictionary to complete the following exercises that relate to pronunciation.

Vowel Sounds

You will probably use the pronunciation key in your dictionary mainly as a guide to pronouncing different vowel sounds. (Vowels are the letters *a, e, i, o,* and *u.*) Here is part of the pronunciation key in the *American Heritage Dictionary:*

ă bat / ā way / ĕ ebb / ē equal / ĭ if

The key tells you, for example, that the sound of the short *a* is pronounced like the *a* in *bat,* the sound of the long *a* is like the *a* in *way,* and the sound of the short *e* is like the *e* in *ebb.*

Now look at the pronunciation key in your dictionary. The key is probably located in the front of the dictionary or at the bottom of every page. What common word in the key tells you how to pronounce each of the following sounds?

ī ____________________ ŭ ____________________

ŏ ____________________ o͝o ____________________

ō ____________________ o͞o ____________________

(Note that the long vowel always has the sound of its own name.)

The Schwa (ə)

The symbol ə looks like an upside-down *e.* It is called a *schwa,* and it stands for the unaccented sound in such words as *ago, item, easily, gallop,* and *circus.* More approximately, it stands for the sound *uh*—like the *uh* that speakers sometimes make when they hesitate in their speech. Perhaps it would help to remember that *uh,* as well as ə, could be used to represent the schwa sound.

Here are some of the many words in which the sound appears: *imitation* (*im-uh-tā'shuhn* or *im*-ə-tā'shən); *elevate* (*el'uh-vāt* or *el'*ə-vāt); *horizon* (*huh-ri'zuhn* or *h*ə-rī'zən). Open your dictionary to any page and you will almost surely be able to find words that make use of the schwa in the pronunciation in parentheses after the main entry.

In the spaces below, write three words that make use of the schwa, and their pronunciations.

1. ____________________ (____________________)
2. ____________________ (____________________)
3. ____________________ (____________________)

Accent Marks

Some words contain both a primary accent, shown by a heavy stroke (ʹ), and a secondary accent, shown by a lighter stroke (′). For example, in the word *controversy* (*kon′trə vûr′se*), the stress, or accent, goes chiefly on the first syllable (*kon′*), and to a lesser extent, on the third syllable (*vûr′*).

Use your dictionary to add accent marks to the following words:

preclude (pri kloo̅d)
atrophy (at rə fē)
inveigle (in vā gəl)
ubiquitous (yoo̅ bik wi təs)
prognosticate (prog nos ti kāt)

Full Pronunciation

Now use your dictionary to write the full pronunciation (the information given in parentheses) for each of the following words.

1. inveigh ____________________
2. diatribe ____________________
3. raconteur ____________________
4. panacea ____________________
5. esophagus ____________________
6. Caesarean ____________________
7. clandestine ____________________
8. vicarious ____________________
9. quiescent ____________________
10. parsimony ____________________
11. penchant ____________________
12. antipathy ____________________

13. capricious ______________________________

14. schizophrenia ______________________________

15. euphemism ______________________________

16. internecine ______________________________

17. amalgamate ______________________________

18. quixotic ______________________________

19. laissez-faire ______________________________

20. antidisestablishmentarianism (This word is probably not in a paperback dictionary, but if you can say *establish* and if you break the rest of the word into individual syllables, you should be able to pronounce it.)

    ____

Now practice pronouncing each word. Use the pronunciation key in your dictionary as an aid to sounding out each syllable. Do *not* try to pronounce a word all at once; instead, work on mastering *one syllable at a time*. When you can pronounce each of the syllables in a word successfully, then say them in sequence, add the accent, and pronounce the entire word.

PARTS OF SPEECH

The next bit of information that the dictionary gives about *murder* is *n*. This abbreviation means that the meanings of *murder* as a noun will follow.

Use your dictionary if necessary to fill in the meanings of the following abbreviations:

v. = ______________	sing. = ______________
adj. = ______________	pl. = ______________

PRINCIPAL PARTS OF IRREGULAR VERBS

Murder is a regular verb and forms its principal parts by adding *-ed, -ed,* and *-ing* to the stem of the verb. When a verb is irregular, the dictionary lists its principal parts. For example, with *give* the present tense comes first (the entry itself, *give*). Next comes the past tense (*gave*), and then the past participle (*given*)—the form of the verb used with such helping words as *have, had,* and *was*. Then comes the present participle (*giving*)—the *-ing* form of the verb.

Look up the parts of the following irregular verbs and write them in the spaces provided. The first one is done for you.

Present	*Past*	*Past Participle*	*Present Participle*
tear	*tore*	*torn*	*tearing*
go			
know			
steal			

PLURAL FORMS OF IRREGULAR NOUNS

The dictionary supplies the plural forms of all irregular nouns. (Regular nouns like *murder* form the plural by adding *-s* or *-es*.) Give the plurals of the following nouns. If two forms are shown, write down both.

analysis ______

dictionary ______

criterion ______

activity ______

thesis ______

MEANINGS

When there is more than one meaning to a word, the meanings are numbered in the dictionary, as with the verb *murder*. In many dictionaries, the most common meanings of a word are presented first. The introductory pages of your dictionary will explain the order in which meanings are presented.

Use the sentence context to try to explain the meaning of the underlined word in each of the following sentences. Write your definition in the space provided. Then look up and record the dictionary meaning of the word. Be sure you pick out the meaning that fits the word as it is used in the sentence.

1. I spend an inordinate amount of time watching television.

   Your definition: ______

   Dictionary definition: ______

2. I appreciated her candid remark that my pants were so baggy they made me look like a clown.

   Your definition: ______________________________

   Dictionary definition: ______________________________

3. The FBI squelched the terrorists' plan to plant a bomb in the White House.

   Your definition: ______________________________

   Dictionary definition: ______________________________

4. One of the cardinal rules in our house was, "Respect other people's privacy."

   Your definition: ______________________________

   Dictionary definition: ______________________________

5. A special governor prevents the school bus from traveling more than fifty-five miles an hour.

   Your definition: ______________________________

   Dictionary definition: ______________________________

ETYMOLOGY

Etymology refers to the origin and historical development of a word. Such information is usually enclosed in brackets and is more likely to be present in a hardbound desk dictionary than in a paperback one. Good desk dictionaries include the following:

The American Heritage Dictionary of the English Language

The Random House College Dictionary

Webster's New Collegiate Dictionary

Webster's New World Dictionary

A good desk dictionary will tell you, for example, that the word *berserk* derives from the name of a tribe of Scandinavian warriors who would work themselves into a frenzy during battle. The word is now a general term to describe someone whose actions are frenzied or crazed.

See if your dictionary says anything about the origins of the following words:

bikini ______________________________

sandwich ______________________________

tantalize ______________________________

breakfast ______________________________

USAGE LABELS

As a general rule, use only standard English words in your writing. If a word is not standard English, your dictionary will probably give it a usage label like one of the following: *informal, nonstandard, slang, vulgar, obsolete, archaic, rare.*

Look up the following words and record how your dictionary labels them. Remember that a recent hardbound desk dictionary will always be the best source of information about usage.

flunk ______________________________

tough (meaning ''unfortunate, too bad'') ______________________________

creep (meaning ''an annoying person'') ______________________________

ain't ______________________________

scam ______________________________

SYNONYMS

A *synonym* is a word that is close in meaning to another word. Using synonyms helps you avoid unnecessary repetition of the same word in a paper. A paperback dictionary is not likely to give you synonyms for words, but a good desk dictionary will. (You might also want to own a *thesaurus,* a book that lists synonyms and antonyms. An *antonym* is a word approximately opposite in meaning to another word.)

Consult a desk dictionary that gives synonyms for the following words, and write the synonyms in the spaces provided.

heavy ______________________________

escape ______________________________

necessary ______________________________

IMPROVING SPELLING

Poor spelling often results from bad habits developed in early school years. With work, such habits can be corrected. If you can write your name without misspelling it, there is no reason why you can't do the same with almost any word in the English language. Following are six steps you can take to improve your spelling.

STEP 1: USE THE DICTIONARY

Get into the habit of using the dictionary. When you write a paper, allow yourself time to look up the spelling of all those words you are unsure about. Do not overlook the value of this step just because it is such a simple one. By using the dictionary, you can probably make yourself a 95 percent better speller.

STEP 2: KEEP A PERSONAL SPELLING LIST

Keep a list of words you misspell and study the words regularly. Use the space on page 537 as a starter. When you accumulate additional words, put them on the back page of a frequently used notebook or on a separate sheet of paper titled "Personal Spelling List."

To master the words on your list, do the following:

1 Write down any hint that will help you remember the spelling of a word. For example, you might want to note that *occasion* is spelled with two *c*'s, or that *all right* is two words, not one word.

2 Study a word by looking at it, saying it, and spelling it. You may also want to write out the word one or more times, or "air-write" it with your finger in large, exaggerated motions.

3 When you have trouble spelling long words, try to break the word down into syllables and see whether you can spell the syllables. For example, *inadvertent* can be spelled easily if you can hear and spell in turn its four syllables: *in ad ver tent*. Or the word *consternation* can be spelled easily if you hear and spell in turn its four syllables: *con ster na tion*. Remember, then: Try to see, hear, and spell long words in terms of their syllable parts.

4 Keep in mind that review and repeated self-testing are the keys to effective learning. When you are learning a series of words, go back after studying each new word and review all the preceding ones.

STEP 3: MASTER COMMONLY CONFUSED WORDS

Master the meanings and spellings of the commonly confused words on pages 474–484. Your instructor may assign twenty words for you to study at a time and give you a series of quizzes until you have mastered the words.

STEP 4: UNDERSTAND BASIC SPELLING RULES

Explained briefly here are three rules that may improve your spelling. While exceptions sometimes occur, the rules hold true most of the time.

1 Change *y* to *i*. When a word ends in a consonant plus *y*, change *y* to *i* when you add an ending.

try	+	ed	=	tried	easy	+	er	=	easier
defy	+	es	=	defies	carry	+	ed	=	carried
ready	+	ness	=	readiness	penny	+	less	=	penniless

2 Final silent *e*. Drop a final *e* before an ending that starts with a vowel (the vowels are *a, e, i, o,* and *u*).

create	+	ive	=	creative	believe	+	able	=	believable
nerve	+	ous	=	nervous	share	+	ing	=	sharing

Keep the final *e* before an ending that starts with a consonant.

extreme	+ ly	=	extremely		life	+ less	=	lifeless
hope	+ ful	=	hopeful		excite	+ ment	=	excitement

3 Doubling a final consonant. Double the final consonant of a word when all three of the following are true:

a The word is one syllable or is accented on the last syllable.
b The word ends in a single consonant preceded by a single vowel.
c The ending you are adding starts with a vowel.

shop	+ er	=	shopper		thin	+ est	=	thinnest
equip	+ ed	=	equipped		submit	+ ed	=	submitted
swim	+ ing	=	swimming		drag	+ ed	=	dragged

Activity

Combine the following words and endings by applying the three rules above.

1. worry + ed = ________________
2. write + ing = ________________
3. marry + es = ________________
4. run + ing = ________________
5. terrify + ed = ________________
6. dry + es = ________________
7. forget + ing = ________________
8. care + ful = ________________
9. control + ed = ________________
10. debate + able = ________________

STEP 5: STUDY A BASIC WORD LIST

Study the spellings of the words in the following list. They are five hundred of the most often used words in English. Your instructor may assign twenty-five or fifty words for you to study at a time and give you a series of quizzes until you have mastered the list.

Five Hundred Basic Words

ability
absent
accept
accident
ache
across
address
advertise
advice
after
again
against
agree
all right
almost
a lot
already
also
although
always
amateur
American
among
amount
angry 25
animal
another
answer
anxious
appetite
apply
approach
approve
argue
around
arrange
attempt
attention
August
automobile
autumn
avenue
awful
awkward
back
balance
bargain
beautiful
because
become 50
been
before
begin
being
believe
between
bicycle
black
blue
board
borrow
bottle
bottom
brake
breast
breathe
brilliant
brother
building
bulletin
bureau
business
came
can't
careful 75
careless
cereal
certain
chair
change
charity
cheap
cheat
cheek
chicken
chief
children
choose
church
cigarette
citizen
city
close
clothing
coffee
collect
college
color
come
comfortable 100
company
condition
conversation
copy
daily
danger
daughter
daybreak
dear
death
December
decide
deed
dentist
deposit
describe
did
died
different
dinner
direction
discover
disease
distance
doctor 125
does
dollar
don't
doubt
down
dozen
during
each
early
earth
easy
education
eight
either
empty

English
enough
entrance
evening
everything
examine
except
exercise
exit
expect 150
fact
factory
family
far
February
few
fifteen
fight
flower
forehead
foreign
forty
forward
found
fourteen
Friday
friend
from
gallon
garden
general
get
good
grammar
great 175
grocery
grow
guess
half
hammer
hand
handkerchief
happy
having
head
heard
heavy
high
himself
hoarse
holiday
home
hospital
house
however
hundred
hungry
husband
instead
intelligence 200
interest
interfere
interrupt
into
iron
itself
January
July
June
just
kindergarten
kitchen
knock
knowledge
labor
laid
language
last
laugh
learn
led
left
leisure
length
lesson 225
letter
life
light
listen
little
loaf
loneliness
long
lose
made
making
many
March
marry
match
matter
may
measure
medicine
men
middle
might
million
minute
mistake 250
Monday
money
month
more
morning
mother
mountain
mouth
much
must
nail
near
needle
neither
never
newspaper
nickel
niece
night
ninety
noise
none
not
nothing
November 275
now
number
ocean
o'clock
October
offer
often
old
omit

once
one
only
operate
opinion
opportunity
optimist
original
ought
ounce
overcoat
pain
paper
part
peace
pear 300
pencil
penny
people
perfect
period
person
picture
piece
pillow
place
plain
please
pocket
policeman
possible
post office
potato
power
prescription
president
pretty
probably
promise
psychology
public 325
pursue
put
quart
quarter
quick
quiet
quit
quite
quiz
raise
read
ready
really
reason
receive
recognize
refer
religion
remember
repeat
resource
restaurant
ribbon
ridiculous
right 350
said
same
sandwich
Saturday
say
school
scissors
season
see
sentence
September
service
seventeen
several
shoes
should
sight
since
sister
sixteenth
sleep
smoke
soap
soldier
something 375
sometimes
soul
soup
south
stamp
state
still
stockings
straight
street
strong
student
studying
such
suffer
sugar
suit
summer
Sunday
supper
sure
sweet
take
teach
tear 400
telegram
telephone
tenant
tenth
than
Thanksgiving
that
theater
them
there
they
thing
thirteen
this
though
thousand
thread
three
through
Thursday
ticket
time
tired
today
together 425
tomorrow
tongue
tonight

touch	vegetable	wear	winter
toward	very	weather	without
travel	view	Wednesday	woman
trouble	villain 450	week	wonder
trousers	visitor	weigh	won't
truly	voice	welcome	work
twelve	vote	well	world
uncle	wage	went	worth
under	wagon	were	would
understand	waist	what	writing
United States	wait	whether 475	written
until	wake	which	wrong
upon	walk	while	year
used	warm	white	yesterday
usual	warning	whole	yet
valley	Washington	whose	young
value	watch	wife	your
variety	water	window	you're 500

Note: Two spelling mistakes that students often make are to write *a lot* as one word (*alot*) and to write *all right* as one word (*alright*). Do not write either *a lot* or *all right* as one word.

STEP 6: BUY A TYPEWRITER WITH AN AUTOMATIC SPELLER

Some of the electronic typewriters on the market today will automatically find and correct your spelling errors. They include a built-in dictionary that beeps when you misspell or mistype a word. They can then erase your error and show you the correct spelling of a word.

These typewriters, like the pocket calculators of years ago, are the latest example of how technology can help the learning process. If you are a poor speller and want a helpful way to remove spelling and typing errors from your papers, seriously consider investing in such a machine. Smith-Corona, for example, has a series of portable typewriters with an "AutoSpell" feature in a two-hundred-dollar price range at discount stores.

VOCABULARY DEVELOPMENT

A good vocabulary is a vital part of effective communication. A command of many words will make you a better writer, speaker, listener, and reader. Studies have shown that students with strong vocabularies, and students who work to improve a limited vocabulary, are more successful in school. And one research study found that *a good vocabulary, more than any other factor, was common to people enjoying successful careers in life.* This section will describe three ways of developing your word power: (1) regular reading, (2) vocabulary wordsheets, and (3) vocabulary study books. You should keep in mind from the start, however, that none of the approaches will help unless you truly decide in your mind that vocabulary development is an important goal. Only when you have this attitude can you begin doing the sustained work needed to improve your word power.

REGULAR READING

Through reading a good deal, you will learn words by experiencing them a number of times in a variety of sentences. Repeated exposures to a word in context will eventually make it a part of your working language.

You should develop the habit of reading a daily newspaper and one or more weekly magazines like *Time, Newsweek,* or even *People,* as well as monthly magazines suited to your interests. In addition, you should try to do some book reading for pleasure. This may be especially difficult at times when you also have textbook reading to do. Try, however, to redirect a regular one-half to one hour of your recreational time to reading books, rather than watching television, listening to music, or the like. Doing so, you may eventually reap the rewards of an improved vocabulary *and* the discovery that reading can be truly enjoyable. If you would like some book recommendations, ask your instructor for a copy of the "List of Interesting Books" in the Instructor's Manual of *English Skills.*

VOCABULARY WORDSHEETS

Another means of vocabulary development is to use vocabulary wordsheets. You should first mark off words in your reading that you want to learn. After you have accumulated a number of words, sit down with a dictionary and look up basic information about each of them. Put this information on a wordsheet like the one shown below. Be sure also to write down a sentence in which each word appears. A word is always best learned not in a vacuum but in the context of surrounding words.

Study each word as follows. First, make sure you can correctly pronounce the word and its derivations. (Page 457 explains the dictionary pronunciation key that will help you properly pronounce each word.) Second, study the main meanings of the word until you can say them without looking at them. Finally, spend a moment looking at the example of the word in context. You should then go on to follow the same process with the second word. Then, after testing yourself on the first and the second words, go on to the third word. Remember to continue to test yourself on all the words you have studied after you learn each new word. Such repeated self-testing is the key to effective learning.

Activity

Locate four words in your reading that you would like to master. Enter them into the spaces on the vocabulary wordsheet below and fill in all the needed information. Your instructor may then check your wordsheet and perhaps give you a quick oral quiz on selected words.

You may receive a standing assignment to add five words a week to a wordsheet and to study the words. Note that you can create your own wordsheets using loose-leaf paper, or your instructor may give you copies of the wordsheet that appears below.

Vocabulary Wordsheet

1. Word: *formidable* Pronunciation: *(fôr′ mi də bəl)*

   Meanings: *1. feared or dreaded*

   2. extremely difficult

   Other forms of the word: *formidably formidability*

   Use of the word in context: *Several formidable obstacles stand between Matt and his goal.*

2. Word: ______________ Pronunciation: ______________

   Meanings: ______________

   ____

   ____

   Other forms of the word: ______________

   Use of the word in context: ______________

   ____

3. Word: ______________ Pronunciation: ______________

   Meanings: ______________

   ____

   ____

   Other forms of the word: ______________

   Use of the word in context: ______________

   ____

4. Word: ______________ Pronunciation: ______________

   Meanings: ______________

   ____

   ____

   Other forms of the word: ______________

   Use of the word in context: ______________

   ____

5. Word: ______________ Pronunciation: ______________

   Meanings: ______________

   ____

   ____

   Other forms of the word: ______________

   Use of the word in context: ______________

   ____

VOCABULARY STUDY BOOKS

A third means of increasing your word power is the use of vocabulary study books. One well-known series of books that may be available in the learning-skills center at your school is the EDL *Word Clues*. These books help you learn a word by asking you to look at the context, or the words around the unfamiliar word, to unlock its meaning. This method is called *using context clues,* or *word clues*.

Here are some individual vocabulary study books you can find at most bookstores:

1100 Words You Need to Know (Barron's)—Bromberg and Gordon

30 Days to a More Powerful Vocabulary (Pocket Books)—Funk and Lewis

Instant Word Power (Signet Books)—Lewis

Vocabulary through Pleasurable Reading (Amsco School Publications)

Many other vocabulary books and programs are available. The best are those that present words in one or more contexts and then provide several reinforcement activities for each word. The books will help you increase your vocabulary if you have the determination required to work with them on a regular basis.

COMMONLY CONFUSED WORDS

Introductory Project

Circle the five words that are misspelled in the following passage. Then see if you can write their correct spellings in the space provided.

You're mind and body are not as separate as you might think. Their is a lot of evidence, for instance, that says if you believe that a placebo (a substance with no medicine) will help you, then it will. One man is said to have rapidly recovered from an advanced case of cancer after only one dose of a drug that he believed was highly effective. Its not clear just how placebos work, but they do show how closely the mind and body are related.

1. Your ____________
2. there ____________
3. ____________
4. ____________
5. ____________

Answers are on page 534.

HOMONYMS

The commonly confused words (also known as *homonyms*) on the following pages have the same sounds but different meanings and spellings. Complete the activity for each set of words, and check off and study the words that give you trouble.

all ready completely prepared
already previously; before

We were *all ready* to start the play, but the audience was still being seated.

I have *already* called the police.

Fill in the blanks: I am __all Ready__ for the economics examination because I have __already__ studied the chapter three times.

brake stop; the stopping device in a vehicle
break come apart

His car bumper has a sticker reading, "I *brake* for animals."

"I am going to *break* up with Bill if he keeps seeing other women," said Rita.

Fill in the blanks: When my car's emergency __brake__ slipped, the car rolled back and demolished my neighbor's rose garden, causing a __break__ in our good relations with each other.

coarse rough
course part of a meal; a school subject; direction; certainly (as in *of course*)

By the time the waitress served the customers the second *course* of the meal, she was aware of their *coarse* eating habits.

Fill in the blanks: Ted felt the health teacher's humor was too __Coarse__ for his taste and was glad when he finished the __Course__.

hear perceive with the ear
here in this place

"The salespeople act as though they don't see or *hear* me, even though I've been standing *here* for fifteen minutes," the woman complained.

Fill in the blanks: "Did you Hear about the distinguished visitor who just came into town and is staying Here at this very hotel?"

hole an empty spot
whole entire

"I can't believe I ate the *whole* pizza," moaned Ralph. "I think it's going to make a *hole* in my stomach lining."

Fill in the blanks: The whole time I was at the party I tried to conceal the hole I had in my trousers.

its belonging to it
it's the shortened form for "it is" or "it has"

The car blew *its* transmission (the transmission belonging to it, the car).
It's (it has) been raining all week and *it's* (it is) raining now.

Fill in the blanks: it's hot and unsanitary in the restaurant kitchen I work in, and I don't think the restaurant deserves its good reputation.

knew past form of *know*
new not old

"I had *new* wallpaper put up," said Sarah.
"I *knew* there was some reason the place looked better," said Bill.

Fill in the blanks: Lola Knew that getting her hair cut would give her face a New look.

know to understand
no a negative

"I don't *know* why my dog Fang likes to attack certain people," said Martha. "There's *no* one thing the people have in common."

Fill in the blanks: I ____Know____ of ____no____ way of telling whether that politician is honest or not.

pair a set of two
pear a fruit

"What a great *pair* of legs Tony has," said Lola to Vonnie. Tony didn't hear her, for he was feeling very sick after munching on a green *pear*.

Fill in the blanks: In his lunch box were a ____Pair____ of ____Pears____s.

passed went by; succeeded in; handed to
past a time before the present; by, as in "I drove past the house"

Someone *passed* him a wine bottle; it was the way he chose to forget his unhappy *past*.

Fill in the blanks: I walked ____Past____ the teacher's office but was afraid to ask her whether or not I had ____Passed____ the test.

peace calm
piece a part

Nations often risk world *peace* by fighting over a *piece* of land.

Fill in the blanks: Martha did not have any ____Peace____ until she gave her pet dog a ____Piece____ of her meat loaf.

plain simple; a flat area
plane aircraft

> The *plain,* unassuming young man on the *plane* suddenly jumped up with a grenade in his hand and announced, "We're all going to Tibet."

Fill in the blanks: The game-show contestant opened the small box wrapped in __Plain__ brown paper and found inside the keys to his own jet __Plane__.

principal main; a person in charge of a school
principle a law, standard, or rule

Note: It might help to remember that the *e* in *principle* is also in *rule*—the meaning of *principle.*

> Pete's high school *principal* had one *principal* problem: Pete. This was because there were only two *principles* in Pete's life: rest and relaxation.

Fill in the blanks: The __Princital__ reason she dropped out of school was that she believed in the __Priciple__ of complete freedom of choice.

right correct; opposite of *left*
write what you do in English

> If you have the *right* course card, I'll *write* your name on the class roster.

Fill in the blanks: Eddie thinks I'm weird since I __write__ with both my __righT__ and left hands.

than (thăn) used in comparisons
then (thĕn) at that time

Note: It might help to remember that th*e*n is also a tim*e* signal.

When we were kids, my friend Elaine had prettier clothes *than* I did. I really envied her *then*.

Fill in the blanks: Marge thought she was better Than the rest of us, but Then she got the lowest grade on the history test.

their belonging to them
there at that place; a neutral word used with verbs like *is, are, was, were, have,* and *had*
they're the shortest form of "they are"

Two people own that van over *there* (at that place). *They're* (they are) going to move out of *their* apartment (the apartment belonging to them) and into the van, in order to save money.

Fill in the blanks: They're not going to invite us to their table because there is no room for us to sit down.

threw past form of *throw*
through from one side to the other; finished

The fans *threw* so much litter on the field that the teams could not go *through* with the game.

Fill in the blanks: When Mr. Jefferson was through screaming about the violence on television, he Threw the newspaper at his dog.

to a verb part, as in *to smile;* toward, as in "I'm going *to* heaven"
too overly, as in "The pizza was *too* hot"; also, as in "The coffee was hot, *too.*"
two the number 2

Tony drove *to* the park *to* be alone with Lola. (The first *to* means "toward"; the second *to* is a verb part that goes with *be.*)

Tony's shirt is *too* tight; his pants are tight, *too.* (The first *too* means "overly"; the second *too* means "also.")

You need *two* hands (2 hands) to handle a Whopper.

Fill in the blanks: ___Two___ times tonight, you have been ___Too___ ready ___To___ make assumptions without asking questions first.

wear to have on
where in what place

Fred wanted to *wear* his light pants on the hot day, but he didn't know *where* he had put them.

Fill in the blanks: ___Where___ exactly on my leg should I ___Wear___ this elastic bandage?

weather atmospheric conditions
whether if it happens that; in case; if

Some people go on vacations *whether* or not the *weather* is good.

Fill in the blanks: I always ask Bill ___Whether___ or not we're going to have a storm, for he can feel rainy ___Weather___ approaching in his bad knee.

whose belonging to whom
who's the shortened form for "who is" and "who has"

Who's the teacher *whose* students are complaining?

Fill in the blanks: __Who's__ the guy __whose__ car I saw you in?

your belonging to you
you're the shortened form of "you are"

You're (meaning "you are") not going to the fair unless *your* brother (the brother belonging to you) goes with you.

Fill in the blanks: __You're__ going to have to put aside individual differences and play together for the sake of __Your__ team.

OTHER WORDS FREQUENTLY CONFUSED

Following is a list of other words that people frequently confuse. Complete the activities for each set of words, and check off and study the words that give you trouble.

a, an Both *a* and *an* are used before other words to mean, approximately, "one."

Generally you should use *an* before words starting with a vowel (*a, e, i, o, u,*):

an ache an experiment an elephant an idiot an ox

Generally you should use *a* before words starting with a consonant (all other letters):

a Coke a brain a cheat a television a gambler

Fill in the blanks: The girls had __an__ argument over __a__ former boyfriend.

accept (ăk sĕpt′) receive; agree to
except (ĕk sĕpt′) exclude; but

> "I would *accept* your loan," said Bill to the bartender, "*except* that I'm not ready to pay 25 percent interest."

Fill in the blanks: EXcepT that she can't accepT any criticism, Lori is a good friend.

advice (ăd vīs′) a noun meaning "an opinion"
advise (ăd vīz′) a verb meaning "to counsel, to give advice"

> I *advise* you to take the *advice* of your friends and stop working so hard.

Fill in the blanks: I advise you to listen carefully to any advice you get from your boss.

affect (uh fĕkt′) a verb meaning "to influence"
effect (ĭ fĕkt′) a verb meaning "to bring about something"; a noun meaning "result"

> The full *effects* of marijuana and alcohol on the body are only partly known; however, both drugs clearly *affect* the brain in various ways.

Fill in the blanks: The new tax laws go into effecT next month, and they are going to affecT your income tax deductions.

among implies three or more
between implies only two

> We had to choose from *among* 125 shades of paint but *between* only two fabrics.

Fill in the blanks: The layoff notices distributed among the unhappy workers gave them a choice between working for another month at full pay or leaving immediately with two weeks pay.

beside along the side of
besides in addition to

I was lucky I wasn't standing *beside* the car when it was hit.

Besides being unattractive, these uniforms are impractical.

Fill in the blanks: besides the alarm system hooked up to the door, our neighbors keep a gun beside their beds.

desert (dĕz′ərt) a stretch of dry land; (di zûrt′) to abandon one's post or duty
dessert (dĭ zûrt′) last part of a meal

Camels are animals of the *desert;* they are also cigarettes people smoke after dinner with their coffee and *dessert.*

Fill in the blanks: After their meal, they carried their desserts into the living room so that they would not miss the start of the old desert movie about Lawrence of Arabia.

fewer used with things that can be counted
less refers to amount, value, or degree

There were *fewer* than seven people in all my classes today.

I seem to feel *less* tired when I exercise regularly.

Fill in the blanks: With Fewer people driving large cars, we are importing Less oil than we used to.

loose (loos) not fastened; not tight-fitting
lose (looz) misplaced; fail to win

Phil's belt is so *loose* that he always looks ready to *lose* his pants.

Fill in the blanks: At least once a week our neighbors Lose their dog; it's because they let him run Loose.

quiet (kwī′ĭt) peaceful
quite (kwīt) entirely; really; rather

After a busy day, the children were now *quiet,* and their parents were *quite* tired.

Fill in the blanks: The ___quiet___ halls of the church become ___quite___ lively during square-dance evenings.

though (thō) despite the fact that
thought (thôt) past form of *think*

Even *though* she worked, she *thought* she would have time to go to school.

Fill in the blanks: Susan ___thought___ she would like the job, but even ___though___ the pay was good, she hated the traveling involved.

■ Review Test 1

Underline the correct word in the parentheses. Rather than guessing, look back at the explanations of the words when necessary.

1. Please take my (advice, advise) and (where, wear) something warm and practical, rather (than, then) something fashionable and flimsy.
2. Glen felt that if he could (loose, lose) twenty pounds, the (affect, effect) on his social life might be dramatic.
3. (Their, There, They're) going to show seven horror films at (their, there, they're) Halloween night festival; I hope you'll be (their, there, they're).
4. (Your, You're) going to have to do (a, an) better job on (your, you're) final exam if you expect to pass the (coarse, course).
5. Those (to, too, two) issues are (to, too, two) hot for any politician (to, too, two) handle.
6. Even (though, thought) the (brakes, breaks) on my car were worn, I did not have (quiet, quite) enough money to get them replaced (right, write) away.

7. (Accept, Except) for the fact that my neighbor receives most of his mail in (plain, plane) brown wrappers, he is (know, no) stranger (than, then) anyone else in this rooming house.
8. Because the Randalls are so neat and fussy, (its, it's) hard (to, too, two) feel comfortable when (your, you're) in (their, there, they're) house.
9. (Whose, Who's) the culprit who left the paint can on the table? The paint has ruined a (knew, new) tablecloth, and (its, it's) soaked (threw, through) the linen and (affected, effected) the varnish stain on the table.
10. I would have been angry at the car that (passed, past) me at ninety miles an hour on the highway, (accept, except) that I (knew, new) it would not get (passed, past) the speed trap (to, too, two) miles down the road.

■ Review Test 2

On separate paper, write short sentences using the ten words shown below.

their	principal
its	except
you're	past
too	through
then	who's

EFFECTIVE WORD CHOICE

Introductory Project

Put a check beside the sentence in each pair that you feel makes more effective use of words.

1. I flipped out when Faye broke our date. ______

   I got very angry when Faye broke our date. ______
2. Doctors as dedicated as Dr. Curtin are few and far between. ______

   Doctors as dedicated as Dr. Curtin are rare. ______
3. Yesterday I ascertained that Elena and Judd broke up. ______

   Yesterday I found out that Elena and Judd broke up. ______
4. Judging by the looks of things, it seems to me that it will probably rain very soon. ______

   It looks as though it will rain soon. ______

Now see if you can circle the correct number in each case:

Pair (1, 2, 3, 4) contains a sentence with slang.
Pair (1, 2, 3, 4) contains a sentence with a cliché.
Pair (1, 2, 3, 4) contains a sentence with pretentious words.
Pair (1, 2, 3, 4) contains a word sentence.

Answers are on page 534.

Choose your words carefully when you write. Always take the time to think about your word choices rather than simply use the first word that comes to mind. You want to develop the habit of selecting words that are appropriate and exact for your purposes. One way you can show your sensitivity to language is by avoiding slang, clichés, pretentious words, and wordiness.

SLANG

We often use slang expressions when we talk because they are so vivid and colorful. However, slang is usually out of place in formal writing. Here are some examples of slang expressions:

I've *gotten into* science fiction lately.

Tom spent Saturday afternoon *messing around with* his car.

I don't *hang around* with Jerry anymore.

They enjoyed the party because it was a *real blast.*

The tires on my Camaro make the car look like *something else.*

Slang expressions have a number of drawbacks: they go out of date quickly, they become tiresome if used excessively in writing, and they may communicate clearly to some readers but not to others. Also, the use of slang can be an evasion of the specific details that are often needed to make one's meaning clear in writing. For example, in "The tires on my Camaro make the car look like something else," the writer has not provided the specific details about the tires necessary for us to understand the statement clearly. In general, then, you should avoid the use of slang in your writing. If you are in doubt about whether an expression is slang, it may help to check a recently published hardbound dictionary.

Activity

Rewrite the following sentences, replacing the italicized slang words with more formal ones.

Example The movie was a *real bomb,* so we *cut out* early.

The movie was terrible, so we left early.

1. My boss *came down on me* for *goofing off* on the job.

____

____

2. The car was a *steal* for the money until the owner *jacked up* the price.

____

____

3. If the teacher stops *hassling* me, I am going to *get my act together* in the course.

____

____

CLICHÉS

A cliché is an expression that has been worn out through constant use. Some typical clichés are:

pain in the neck	sad but true
know the ropes	taking a big chance
drop in the bucket	wear yourself out
sight for sore eyes	end of the affair
a spoiled brat	cold, cruel world
had a hard time of it	at a loss for words
work like a dog	it goes without saying
hour of need	break the ice

Clichés are common in speech but make your writing seem tired and stale. Also, they are often an evasion of the specific details that you must work to provide in your writing. You should, then, avoid clichés and try to express your meaning in fresh, original ways.

Activity

Underline the cliché in each of the following sentences. Then substitute specific, fresh words for the trite expression.

Example I passed the test by the skin of my teeth.
I barely passed the test.

1. Anyone turning in a paper late is throwing caution to the winds.
____

2. Judy doesn't make any bones about her ambition.
____

3. I met with my teacher to try to iron out the problems with my paper.
____

PRETENTIOUS WORDS

Some people feel they can improve their writing by using fancy and elevated words rather than simple and natural words. They use artificial and stilted language that more often obscures their meaning than communicates it clearly. Here are some unnatural-sounding sentences:

I comprehended her statement.

While partaking of our morning meal, we engaged in an animated conversation.

I am a stranger to excessive financial sums.

Law enforcement officers directed traffic when the lights malfunctioned.

The same thoughts can be expressed more clearly and effectively by using plain, natural language, as below:

I understood what she said.

While eating breakfast, we had a lively talk.

I have never had much money.

Police officers directed traffic when the lights stopped working.

Activity

Cross out the artificial words in each sentence. Then substitute clear, simple language for the artificial words.

Example The manager ~~reproached~~ me for my ~~tardiness~~.
The manager criticized me for being late.

1. One of Tina's objectives in life is to accomplish a large family.

____

____

2. Upon entering our residence, we detected smoke in the atmosphere.

____

____

3. I am not apprehensive about the test, which encompasses five chapters of the book.

____

____

WORDINESS

Wordiness—using more words than necessary to express a meaning—is often a sign of lazy or careless writing. Your readers may resent the extra time and energy they must spend when you have not done the work needed to make your writing direct and concise.

Here are examples of wordy sentences:

Anne is of the opinion that the death penalty should be allowed.

I would like to say that my subject in this paper will be the kind of generous person that my father was.

Omitting needless words improves the sentences:

Anne supports the death penalty.

My father was a generous person.

Activity

Rewrite the following sentences, omitting needless words.

1. After a lot of careful thinking, I have arrived at the conclusion that drunken drivers should receive jail terms.

____

____

2. The movie that I went to last night, which was fairly interesting, I must say, was enjoyed by me and my girlfriend.

____

____

3. Due to inclement weather conditions of wind and rain, we have decided not to proceed with the athletic competition about to take place on the baseball diamond.

____

____

4. Without any question, there should be a law making it a requirement for parents of young children to buckle the children into car seats for safety.

____

____

5. Beyond a doubt, the only two things you can rely, or depend, on would be the sure fact that death comes to everyone and that the government will tax your yearly income.

____

____

■ Review Test 1

Certain words are italicized in the following sentences. In the space provided, identify the words as *slang* (S), *clichés* (C), or *pretentious words* (PW). Then rewrite the sentences, replacing the words with more effective diction.

_______ 1. We're *psyched* for tonight's concert, which is going to be *totally awesome*.

____

____

_______ 2. Getting good grades in college courses is sometimes *easier said than done*.

____

____

_______ 3. I *availed myself* of the chance to *participate* in the computer course.

____

____

_______ 4. The victims of the car accident were shaken but *none the worse for wear*.

____

____

_______ 5. My roommate *pulled an all-nighter* and almost *conked out* during the exam.

____

____

■ Review Test 2

Rewrite the following sentences, omitting needless words.

1. Workers who are on a part-time basis are attractive to a business because they do not have to be paid as much as full-time workers for a business.

 ____

 ____

2. During the time that I was sick and out of school, I missed a total of three math tests.

 ____

 ____

3. The game, which was scheduled for later today, has been cancelled by the officials because of the rainy weather.

 ____

 ____

4. At this point in time, I am quite undecided and unsure about just which classes I will take during this coming semester.

 ____

 ____

5. A inconsiderate person located in the apartment next to mine keeps her radio on too loud a good deal of the time, with the result being that it is disturbing to everyone in the neighboring apartments.

 ____

 ____

SENTENCE VARIETY

One part of effective writing is to vary the kinds of sentences that you write. If every sentence follows the same pattern, writing may become monotonous to read. This section of the book explains four ways you can create variety and interest in your writing style. It will also describe coordination and subordination—two important techniques for achieving different kinds of emphasis in writing.

The following are four methods you can use to make simple sentences more complex and sophisticated:

1 Add a second complete thought (coordination)
2 Add a dependent thought (subordination)
3 Begin with a special opening word or phrase
4 Place adjectives or verbs in a series

Each method will be discussed in turn.

ADD A SECOND COMPLETE THOUGHT

When you add a second complete thought to a simple sentence, the result is a compound (or double) sentence. The two complete statements in a compound sentence are usually connected by a comma plus a joining, or coordinating, word (*and, but, for, or, nor, so, yet*).

A compound sentence is used when you want to give equal weight to two closely related ideas. The technique of showing that ideas have equal importance is called *coordination.*

Following are some compound sentences. Each contains two ideas that the writer regards as equal in importance.

> Bill has stopped smoking cigarettes, but he is now addicted to chewing tobacco.
>
> I repeatedly failed the math quizzes, so I decided to drop the course.
>
> Stan turned all the lights off, and then he locked the office door.

Activity

Combine the following pairs of simple sentences into compound sentences. Use a comma and a logical joining word (*and, but, for, so*) to connect each pair.

Note: If you are not sure what *and, but, for,* and *so* mean, review pages 352–353.

Example ■ The record kept skipping.
■ There was dust on the needle.
The record kept skipping, for there was dust on the needle.

1. ■ The line at the deli counter was long.
   ■ Jake took a numbered ticket anyway.
   ____

2. ■ Vandals smashed the car's headlights.
   ■ They slashed the tires as well.
   ____

3. ■ I married at age seventeen.
   ■ I never got a chance to live on my own.
   ____

4. ■ Mold grew on my leather boots.
   ■ The closet was warm and humid.
   ____
   ____

5. ■ My father has a high cholesterol count.
   ■ He continues to eat red meat almost every day.
   ____
   ____

ADD A DEPENDENT THOUGHT

When you add a dependent thought to a single sentence, the result is a complex sentence.* A dependent thought begins with one of the following subordinating words:

after	if, even if	when, whenever
although, though	in order that	where, wherever
as	since	whether
because	that, so that	which, whichever
before	unless	while
even though	until	who, whoever
how	what, whatever	whose

A complex sentence is used when you want to emphasize one idea over another in a sentence. Look at the following complex sentence:

Although I lowered the thermostat, my heating bill remained high.

The idea that the writer wishes to emphasize here—*my heating bill remained high*—is expressed as a complete thought. The less important idea—*Although I lowered my thermostat*—is subordinated to the complete thought. The technique of giving one idea less emphasis than another is called *subordination*.

Following are other examples of complex sentences. In each case, the part starting with the dependent word is the less emphasized part of the sentence.

Even though I was tired, I stayed up to watch the horror movie.

Before I take a bath, I check for spiders in the tub.

When Ivy feels nervous, she pulls on her earlobe.

* The two parts of a complex sentence are sometimes called an *independent clause* and a *dependent clause*. A *clause* is simply a word group that contains a subject and a verb. An independent clause expresses a complete thought and can stand alone. A dependent clause does not express a complete thought in itself and ''depends on'' the independent clause to complete its meaning. Dependent clauses always begin with a dependent, or subordinating, word.

Activity

Use logical subordinating words to combine the following pairs of simple sentences into sentences that contain a dependent thought. Place a comma after a dependent statement when it starts the sentence.

Example
- Our team lost.
- We were not invited to the tournament.

Because our team lost, we were not invited to the tournament.

1.
- I receive my degree in June.
- I will begin applying for jobs.

____

____

2.
- Lola doesn't enjoy cooking.
- She often eats at fast-food restaurants.

____

____

3.
- I sent several letters of complaint.
- The electric company never corrected my bill.

____

____

4.
- Neil's car went into a skid.
- He took his foot off the gas pedal.

____

____

5.
- The final exam covered sixteen chapters.
- The students complained.

____

____

BEGIN WITH A SPECIAL OPENING WORD OR PHRASE

Among the special openers that can be used to start sentences are *-ed* words, *-ing* words, *-ly* words, *to* words groups, and prepositional phrases. Here are examples of all five kinds of openers:

-ed *word*	Tired from a long day of work, Sharon fell asleep on the sofa.
-ing *word*	Using the hot comb, Mel dried his hair quickly.
-ly *word*	Reluctantly, I agreed to rewrite the paper.
to *word group*	To get to the church on time, you must leave now.
Prepositional phrase	With Fred's help, Martha planted the evergreen shrubs.

Activity

Combine the simple sentences into one sentence by using the opener shown in the margin and omitting repeated words. Use a comma to set off the opener from the rest of the sentence.

Example -ing *word:*
- The toaster refused to pop up.
- It buzzed like an angry hornet.

Buzzing like an angry hornet, the toaster refused to pop up.

-ed *word*

1. ■ Bill was annoyed by the poor TV reception.
   ■ He decided to get a new antenna.

____

____

-ing *word*

2. ■ The star player glided down the court.
   ■ He dribbled the basketball like a pro.

____

____

-ly *word*

3. ■ Food will run short on our crowded planet.
   ■ It is inevitable.

____

____

to word group

4. ■ Bill rented a limousine for the night.
   ■ He wanted to make a good impression.

____

____

prepositional phrase

5. ■ Lisa answered the telephone.
   ■ She did this at 4 A.M.

____

____

-ed word

6. ■ Nate dreaded the coming holidays.
   ■ He was depressed by his recent divorce.

____

____

-ing word

7. ■ The people pressed against the doors of the theater.
   ■ They pushed and shoved each other.

____

____

-ly word

8. ■ I waited in the packed emergency room.
   ■ I was impatient.

____

____

to word group

9. ■ The little boy likes to annoy his parents.
   ■ He pretends he can't hear them.

____

____

prepositional phrase

10. ■ People must wear white-soled shoes.
    ■ They must do this in the gym.

____

____

PLACE ADJECTIVES OR VERBS IN A SERIES

Various parts of a sentence may be placed in a series. Among these parts are adjectives (descriptive words) and verbs. Here are examples of both in a series.

Adjectives The *black, smeary* newsprint rubbed off on my *new butcher-block* table.

Verbs The quarterback *fumbled* the ball, *recovered* it, and *sighed* with relief.

Activity

Combine the simple sentences into one sentence by using adjectives or verbs in a series and by omitting repeated words. In most cases, use a comma between the adjectives or verbs in a series.

Example
- Before Christmas, I made fruitcakes.
- I decorated the house.
- I wrapped dozens of toys.

Before Christmas, I made fruitcakes, decorated the house, and wrapped dozens of toys.

1. ■ My lumpy mattress was giving me a cramp in my neck.
   ■ It was causing pains in my back.
   ■ It was making me lose sleep.

   ____

   ____

2. ■ Lights appeared in the fog.
   ■ The lights were flashing.
   ■ The lights were red.
   ■ The fog was gray.
   ■ The fog was soupy.

   ____

   ____

3. ■ Before going to bed, I locked all the doors.
   ■ I activated the burglar alarm.
   ■ I slipped a kitchen knife under my mattress.

   ____

   ____

4. ■ Lola picked sweater hairs off her coat.
   ■ The hairs were fuzzy.
   ■ The hairs were white.
   ■ The coat was brown.
   ■ The coat was suede.

   ____

   ____

5. ■ The contact lens fell onto the floor.
   ■ The contact lens was thin.
   ■ The contact lens was slippery.
   ■ The floor was dirty.
   ■ The floor was tiled.

   ____

   ____

■ Review Test 1

On separate paper, use coordination or subordination to combine the following groups of simple sentences into one or more longer sentences. Omit repeated words. Since a variety of combinations is possible, you might want to jot down several combinations in each case. Then read them aloud to find the combination that sounds best.

Keep in mind that, very often, the relationship among ideas in a sentence will be clearer when subordinating rather than coordinating words are used.

Example
■ I don't like to ask for favors.
■ I must borrow money from my brother-in-law.
■ I know he won't turn me down.
■ I still feel guilty about it.

I don't like to ask for favors, but I must borrow money from my brother-in-law. Although I know he won't turn me down, I still feel guilty about it.

Comma Hints

a Use a comma at the end of a word group that starts with a subordinating word (as in "Although I know he won't turn me down, . . .").

b Use a comma between independent word groups connected by *and, but, for, or, nor, so, yet* (as in "I don't like to ask for favors, but . . .").

1. ■ My grandmother is eighty-six.
   ■ She drives to Florida alone every year.
   ■ She believes in being independent.
2. ■ His name was called.
   ■ Luis walked into the examining room.
   ■ He was nervous.
   ■ He was determined to ask the doctor for a straight answer.
3. ■ They left twenty minutes early for class.
   ■ They were late anyway.
   ■ The car overheated.
4. ■ John failed the midterm exam.
   ■ He studied harder for the final.
   ■ He passed it.
5. ■ A volcano erupts.
   ■ It sends tons of ash into the air.
   ■ This creates flaming orange sunsets.
6. ■ Tony got home from the shopping mall.
   ■ He discovered his rented tuxedo did not fit.
   ■ The jacket sleeves covered his hands.
   ■ The pants cuffs hung over his shoes.
7. ■ The boys waited for the bus.
   ■ The wind shook the flimsy shelter.
   ■ They shivered with cold.
   ■ They were wearing thin jackets.
8. ■ The engine almost caught.
   ■ Then it died.
   ■ I realized no help would come.
   ■ I was on a lonely road.
   ■ It was very late.

9. ■ Miriam wanted white wall-to-wall carpeting.
   ■ She knew it was a bad buy.
   ■ It would look beautiful.
   ■ It would be very hard to clean.

10. ■ Gary was leaving the store.
    ■ The shoplifting alarm went off.
    ■ He had not stolen anything.
    ■ The clerk had forgotten to remove the magnetic tag.
    ■ The tag was on a shirt Gary had bought.

■ Review Test 2

On separate paper, write two sentences of your own that begin with (1) *-ed* words, (2) *-ing* words, (3) *-ly* words, (4) *to* word groups, and (5) prepositional phrases. Also write two sentences of your own that contain (1) a series of adjectives and (2) a series of verbs.

COMBINED MASTERY TESTS

SENTENCE FRAGMENTS AND RUN-ONS

■ Combined Mastery Test 1

The word groups below are numbered 1 through 20. In the space provided for each, write C if a word group is a complete sentence, write F if it is a sentence fragment, and write R-O if it is a run-on. Then correct the errors.

[1]I had a frightening dream last night, I dreamed that I was walking high up on an old railroad trestle. [2]It looked like the one I used to walk on recklessly. [3]When I was about ten years old. [4]At that height, my palms were sweating, just as they did when I was a boy. [5]I could see the ground out of the corners of my eyes, I felt a swooning, sickening sensation. [6]Suddenly, I realized there were rats below. [7]Thousands upon thousands of rats. [8]They knew I was up on the trestle, they were laughing. [9]Because they were sure they would get me. [10]Their teeth glinted in the moonlight, their red eyes were like thousands of small reflectors. [11]That almost blinded my sight. [13]Sensing there was something even more hideous behind me. [13]I kept moving forward. [14]Then I realized that I was coming to a gap in the trestle. [15]There was no way I could stop or go back I would have to cross over that empty gap. [16]I leaped out in despair. [17]Knowing I would never make it. [18]And felt myself falling helplessly down to the swarm of rejoicing rats. [19]I woke up bathed in sweat. [20]Half expecting to find a rat in my bed.

1. _____
2. _____
3. _____
4. _____
5. _____
6. _____
7. _____
8. _____
9. _____
10. _____
11. _____
12. _____
13. _____
14. _____
15. _____
16. _____
17. _____
18. _____
19. _____
20. _____

Score Number correct _____ × 5 = _____ percent

SENTENCE FRAGMENTS AND RUN-ONS

■ Combined Mastery Test 2

The word groups below are numbered 1 through 20. In the space provided for each, write C if a word group is a complete sentence, write F if it is a sentence fragment, and write R-O if it is a run-on. Then correct the errors.

1. _____
2. _____
3. _____
4. _____
5. _____
6. _____
7. _____
8. _____
9. _____
10. _____
11. _____
12. _____
13. _____
14. _____
15. _____
16. _____
17. _____
18. _____
19. _____
20. _____

[1]My sister asked my parents and me to give up television for two weeks. [2]As an experiment for her psychology class. [3]We were too embarrassed to refuse, we reluctantly agreed. [4]The project began on a Monday morning. [5]To help us resist temptation. [6]My sister unplugged the living room set. [7]That evening the four of us sat around the dinner table much longer than usual, we found new things to talk about. [8]Later we played board games for several hours, we all went to bed pleased with ourselves. [9]Everything went well until Thursday evening of that first week. [10]My sister went out after dinner. [11]Explaining that she would be back about ten o'clock. [12]The rest of us then decided to turn on the television. [13]Just to watch the network news. [14]We planned to unplug the set before my sister got home. [15]And pretend nothing had happened. [16]We were settled down comfortably in our respective chairs, unfortunately, my sister walked in at that point and burst out laughing. [17]"Ah ha! I caught you," she cried. [18]She explained that part of the experiment was to see if we would stick to the agreement. [19]Especially during her absence. [20]She had predicted we would weaken, it turned out she was right.

Score Number correct _____ × 5 = _____ percent

VERBS

■ Combined Mastery Test 1

Each sentence contains a mistake involving (1) standard English or irregular verb forms, (2) subject-verb agreement, or (3) consistent verb tense. Circle the letter that identifies the mistake. Then cross out the incorrect verb and write the correct form in the space provided.

________ 1. One of my apartment neighbors always keep the radio on loudly all night.
Mistake in: a. Subject-verb agreement b. Verb tense

________ 2. The more the teacher explained the material and the more he wroted on the board, the more confused I got.
Mistake in: a. Irregular verb form b. Verb tense

________ 3. I grabbed the last carton of skim milk on the supermarket shelf but when I checks the date on it, I realized it was not fresh.
Mistake in: a. Subject-verb agreement b. Verb tense

________ 4. This morning my parents argued loudly but later they apologized to each other and embrace.
Mistake in: a. Subject-verb agreement b. Verb tense

________ 5. When the bell rang, Mike takes another bite of his sandwich and then prepared for class.
Mistake in: a. Irregular verb form b. Verb tense

________ 6. Someone called Marion at the office to tell her that her son had been bit by a stray dog.
Mistake in: a. Irregular verb form b. Verb tense

________ 7. Because I had throwed away the sales slip, I couldn't return the microwave.
Mistake in: a. Irregular verb form b. Verb tense

________ 8. My dog and cat usually ignores each other, but once in a while they fight.
Mistake in: a. Subject-verb agreement b. Verb tense

________ 9. From the back of our neighborhood bakery comes some of the best smells in the world.
Mistake in: a. Subject-verb agreement b. Verb tense

________ 10. The cost of new soles and heels are more than those old shoes are worth.
Mistake in: a. Subject-verb agreement b. Verb tense

Score Number correct ______ × 5 = ______ percent

VERBS

■ Combined Mastery Test 2

Each sentence contains a mistake involving (1) standard English or irregular verb forms, (2) subject-verb agreement, or (3) consistent verb tense. Circle the letter that identifies the mistake. Then cross out the incorrect verb and write the correct form in the space provided.

_________ 1. My friend's bitter words had stinged me deeply.
Mistake in: a. Irregular verb form b. Verb tense

_________ 2. After she poured the ammonia in the bucket, Karen reels backward because the strong fumes made her eyes tear.
Mistake in: a. Subject-verb agreement b. Verb tense

_________ 3. Flying around in space is various pieces of debris from old space satellites.
Mistake in: a. Subject-verb agreement b. Verb tense

_________ 4. Eileen watched suspiciously as a strange car drived back and forth in front of her house.
Mistake in: a. Irregular verb form b. Verb tense

_________ 5. Both crying and laughing helps us get rid of tension.
Mistake in: a. Subject-verb agreement b. Verb tense

_________ 6. All my clothes were dirty, so I stayed up late and washes a load for tomorrow.
Mistake in: a. Subject-verb agreement b. Verb tense

_________ 7. McDonald's has selled enough hamburgers to reach to the moon.
Mistake in: a. Irregular verb form b. Verb tense

_________ 8. When Fred peeled back the bedroom wallpaper, he discovered another layer of wallpaper and uses a steamer to get that layer off.
Mistake in: a. Subject-verb agreement b. Verb tense

_________ 9. Rosie searched for the fifty-dollar bill she had hid somewhere in her dresser.
Mistake in: a. Irregular verb form b. Verb tense

_________ 10. The realistic yellow tulips on the gravestone is made of a weather-resistant fabric.
Mistake in: a. Subject-verb agreement b. Verb tense

Score Number correct _____ × 5 = _____ percent

CAPITAL LETTERS AND PUNCTUATION

■ Combined Mastery Test 1

Each of the following sentences contains an error in capitalization or punctuation. Refer to the box below to write, in the space provided, the letter identifying the error. Then correct the error.

a. missing capital	c. missing quotation marks
b. missing apostrophe	d. missing comma

_______ 1. Maggie's aerobics class has been canceled this week so she's decided to go running instead.

_______ 2. "One of the striking differences between a cat and a lie, wrote Mark Twain, "is that a cat has only nine lives."

_______ 3. My uncles checks are printed to look like Monopoly money.

_______ 4. Did you know someone is turning the old school on ninth Street into a restaurant named Home Economics?

_______ 5. My parents always ask me where Im going and when I'll be home.

_______ 6. She doesn't talk about it much, but my aunt has been a member of alcoholics Anonymous for ten years.

_______ 7. The sweating straining horses neared the finish line.

_______ 8. Whenever he gave us the keys to the car, my father would say, Watch out for the other guy."

_______ 9. If you're going to stay up late be sure to turn down the heat before going to bed.

_______ 10. I decided to have a glass of apple juice rather than order a pepsi.

Score Number correct _______ × 10 = _______ percent

CAPITAL LETTERS AND PUNCTUATION

■ Combined Mastery Test 2

Each of the following sentences contains an error in capitalization or punctuation. Refer to the box below to write, in the space provided, the letter identifying the error. Then correct the error.

a. missing capital	c. missing quotation marks
b. missing apostrophe	d. missing comma

_______ 1. Even though I hadn't saved the receipt I was able to return the blender to Sears.

_______ 2. "The diners food is always reliable," said Stan. "It's consistently bad."

_______ 3. Some people are surprised to hear that manhattan is an island.

_______ 4. "To love oneself, said Oscar Wilde, "is the beginning of a life-long romance."

_______ 5. The airplane was delayed for more than three hours and the passengers were getting impatient.

_______ 6. Leslie said to the woman behind her in the theatre, "will you stop talking, please?"

_______ 7. Charles corns are as good predictors of the weather as the TV weather report.

_______ 8. "Before you can reach your goals," says my grandfather, you have to believe you can reach them."

_______ 9. There is little evidence that king Arthur the legendary knight, really existed.

_______ 10. My cousin learned to cook when he was an Army cook during World war II.

Score Number correct _______ × 10 = _______ percent

WORD USE

■ Combined Mastery Test 1

Each of the following sentences contains a mistake identified in the left-hand margin. Underline the mistake and then correct it in the space provided.

Slang 1. Because Lisa had a lot of pull at work, she always has first choice of vacation time.

____

Wordiness 2. Truthfully, I've been wishing that the final could be postponed to a much later date sometime next week.

____

Cliché 3. Meg hoped her friends would be green with envy when they saw her new boyfriend.

____

Pretentious language 4. Harold utilizes old coffee cans to water his house plants.

____

Adverb error 5. The sled started slow and then picked up speed as the icy hill became steeper.

____

Error in comparison 6. When the weather is dry, my arthritis feels more better.

____

Confused word 7. If you neglect your friends, their likely to become former friends.

____

Confused word 8. She's the neighbor who's dog is courting my dog.

____

Confused word 9. If you don't put cans, jars, and newspapers on the curb for recycling, the township won't pick up you're garbage.

____

Confused word 10. "It's the most economical car you can buy," the announcer said.

____

Score Number correct ______ × 10 = ______ percent

WORD USE

■ Combined Mastery Test 2

Each of the following sentences contains a mistake identified in the left-hand margin. Underline the mistake and then correct it in the space provided.

Slang 1. After coming in to work late all last week, Sheila was canned.

____

Wordiness 2. At this point in time, I'm not really sure what my major will be.

____

Cliché 3. Jan and Stan knew they could depend on their son in their hour of need.

____

Pretentious language 4. I plan to do a lot of comparison shopping before procuring a new dryer.

____

Adverb error 5. The children sat very quiet as their mother read the next chapter of *Charlie and the Chocolate Factory*.

____

Error in comparison 6. The respectfuler you treat people, the more they are likely to deserve your respect.

____

Confused word 7. Insert the disk in the computer before you turn on its' power switch.

____

Confused word 8. "My advise to you," said my grandmother, "is to focus on your strengths, not your fears."

____

Confused word 9. The principle advantage to the school cafeteria is that its three blocks from a Wendy's.

____

Confused word 10. My parents mean well, but there goals for me aren't my goals.

____

Score Number correct _____ × 10 = _____ percent

EDITING TESTS

EDITING AND PROOFREADING FOR SENTENCE-SKILLS MISTAKES

The ten tests in this section will give you practice in editing and proofreading for sentence-skills mistakes. People often find it hard to edit and proofread a paper carefully. They have put so much work into their writing, or so little, that it's almost painful for them to look at the paper one more time. You may have to simply *force* yourself to edit and proofread. Remember that eliminating sentence-skills mistakes will improve an average paper and help ensure a strong grade on a good paper. Further, as you get into the habit of checking your papers, you will also get into the habit of using the sentence skills consistently. They are a basic part of clear and effective writing.

In the first five tests, the spots where errors occur have been underlined; your job is to identify each error. In the last five tests, you must locate as well as identify the errors.

Editing Test 1

Identify the sentence-skills mistakes at the underlined spots in the selection that follows. From the box below, choose the letter that describes each mistake and write it in the space provided. The same mistakes may appear more than once.

a. Sentence fragment	d. Apostrophe mistake
b. Run-on	e. Faulty parallelism
c. Nonstandard verb	

Looking Out for Yourself

It's sad but true that "If you don't look out for yourself, no one else will." For example, some people have a false idea about the power of a college <u>degree, they</u> (1) think that once they <u>possesses</u> (2) the degree, the world will be waiting on their doorstep. In fact, nobody is likely to be on their doorstep unless, through advance planning, they <u>has</u> (3) prepared themselves for a career. <u>The kind in which good job opportunities exist.</u> (4) Even after a person has landed a job, however, a healthy amount of self-interest is needed. People who hide in corners or <u>with hesitation</u> (5) to let others know about their skills <u>doesn't</u> (6) get promotions or raises. <u>Its</u> (7) important to take credit for a job well-done, whether it involves writing a report, <u>organized the office filing system,</u> (8) or calming down an angry customer. Also, people should feel free to ask the boss for a raise. <u>If they work hard and really deserve it.</u> (9) Those who look out for themselves get the <u>rewards, people</u> (10) who depend on others to help them along get left behind.

1. ______	3. ______	5. ______	7. ______	9. ______
2. ______	4. ______	6. ______	8. ______	10. ______

Editing Test 2

Identify the sentence-skills mistakes at the underlined spots in the selection that follows. From the box below, choose the letter that describes each mistake and write it in the space provided. The same mistake may appear more than once.

a. Sentence fragment	e. missing commas around an interrupter
b. Run-on	f. Mistake with quotation marks
c. Mistake in verb tense	g. Apostrophe mistake
d. Irregular verb mistake	

Deceptive Appearances

Appearances can be deceptive. While looking through a library window yesterday, I saw a neatly groomed woman walk by. Her clothes were skillfully tailored her (1) makeup was perfect. Then thinking no one was looking she (2) crumpled a piece of paper in her hand. And tossed it into a nearby hedge. (3) Suddenly she no longer looks (4) attractive to me. On another occasion, I started talking to a person in my psychology class named Eric. Eric seemed to be a great person. He always got the class laughing with his jokes, on (5) the days when Eric was absent, I think even the professor missed his lively personality. Eric asked me ''if I wanted to get a Coke in the cafeteria,'' (6) and I felt happy he had chose (7) me to be a friend. While we were sitting in the cafeteria. (8) Eric took out an envelope with several kinds of pills inside. ''Want one?'' he asked. ''They're uppers.'' I didn't want one, I (9) felt disappointed. Erics (10) terrific personality was the product of the pills he took.

1. ______ 3. ______ 5. ______ 7. ______ 9. ______

2. ______ 4. ______ 6. ______ 8. ______ 10. ______

■ Editing Test 3

Identify the sentence-skills mistakes at the underlined spots in the selection that follows. From the box below, choose the letter that describes each mistake and write it in the space provided. The same mistake may appear more than once.

a. Sentence fragment	e. Apostrophe mistake
b. Run-on	f. Dangling modifier
c. Irregular verb mistake	g. Missing quotation marks
d. Missing comma after introductory words	

A Horrifying Moment

The most horrifying moment in my life occurred in the dark hallway. Which led to my apartment house. (1) Though the hallway light was out I (2) managed to find my apartment door. However, I could not find the keyhole with my door key. I then pulled a book of matches from my pocket. Trying to strike a match (3), the entire book of matches bursted (4) into flames. I flicked the matches away but not before my coat sleeve catched (5) fire. Within seconds, my arm was like a torch. Struggling to unsnap the buttons of my coat, (6) flames began to sear my skin. I was quickly going into shock. And began screaming in pain. (7) A neighbors (8) door opened and a voice cried out, My God! (9) I was pulled through an apartment and put under a bathroom shower, which extinguished the flames. I suffered third degree burns on my arm, I (10) felt lucky to escape with my life.

1. ______ 3. ______ 5. ______ 7. ______ 9. ______

2. ______ 4. ______ 6. ______ 8. ______ 10. ______

Editing Test 4

Identify the sentence-skills mistakes at the underlined spots in the selection that follows. From the box below, choose the letter that describes each mistake and write it in the space provided. The same mistake may appear more than once.

a. Sentence fragment	e. Faulty parallelism
b. Run-on	f. Apostrophe mistake
c. Missing capital letter agreement	g. Missing quotation mark
d. Mistake in subject-verb	h. Missing comma after introductory words

Why I Didn't Go to Church

I almost never attended church in my boyhood years. There was an unwritten code that the guys on the corner was (1) not to be seen in churches' (2). Although there was (3) many days when I wanted to attend a church, I felt I had no choice but to stay away. If the guys had heard I had gone to church, they would have said things like, ''hey, (4) angel, when are you going to fly? (5) With my group of friends, its (6) amazing that I developed any religious feeling at all. Another reason for not going to church was my father. When he was around the house he (7) told my mother, ''Mike's not going to church. No boy of mine is a sissy.'' My mother and sister went to church, I (8) sat with my father and read the Sunday paper or watching television. (9) I did not start going to church until years later. When I no longer hung around with the guys on the corner or let my father have power over me. (10)

1. ______ 3. ______ 5. ______ 7. ______ 9. ______

2. ______ 4. ______ 6. ______ 8. ______ 10. ______

Editing Test 5

Identify the sentence-skills mistakes at the underlined spots in the selection that follows. From the box below, choose the letter that describes each mistake and write it in the space provided. The same mistake may appear more than once.

a. Sentence fragment	f. Missing comma between two complete thoughts
b. Run-on	g. Missing comma after introductory words
c. Nonparallel structure	h. Misspelled word
d. Missing apostrophe	
e. Missing quotation mark	

Anxiety and the Telephone

Not many of us would want to do without our telephones but [1] there are times when the phone is a source of anxiety. For example, you might be walking up to your front door. When you hear the phone ring. [2] You struggle to find your key, to unlock the door, and getting [3] to the phone quickly. You know the phone will stop ringing the instant you pick up the receiver, then [4] you wonder if you missed the call that would have made you a millionare [5] or introduced you to the love of your life. Another time, you may have called in sick to work with a phony excuse. All day long, youre [6] afraid to leave the house in case the boss calls back. And asks himself why you were feeling well enough to go out. [7] In addition, you worry that you might unthinkingly pick up the phone and say in a cheerful voice, "Hello, [8] completely forgeting [9] to use your fake cough. In cases like these having [10] a telephone is more of a curse than a blessing.

1. ______ 3. ______ 5. ______ 7. ______ 9. ______

2. ______ 4. ______ 6. ______ 8. ______ 10. ______

■ Editing Test 6

See if you can locate and correct the ten sentence-skills mistakes in the following passage. The mistakes are listed in the box below. As you locate mistakes, place checks in the spaces provided.

1 sentence fragment ______	2 missing commas between items in a series ______ ______
1 run-on ______	2 apostrophe mistakes ______ ______
1 nonstandard verb ______	1 capital letter mistake ______
1 missing comma around an interrupter ______	1 homonym mistake ______

Search for the Perfect Pajama Bottoms

I met a strange character in my job as an Orderly at a state mental hospital. Jacks illness was such that it led to a strange behavior. Jack, a middle-aged man spent most of the day obsessed with pajama bottoms. He seemed to think that someone might have a better pair of pajama bottoms than his. He would sneak into other patients rooms. And steal there pajama bottoms. Other times, he would undress a distracted patient to try on his pajamas. He would try them on find they were not perfect and discard them. Some days, I'd come upon three or four patients with no pajama bottoms on, I'd know Jack was on the prowl again. He were tireless in his search for the perfect pair of pajama bottoms. It was clearly a search that would never end in success.

■ Editing Test 7

See if you can locate and correct the ten sentence-skills mistakes in the following passages. The mistakes are listed in the box below. As you locate mistakes, place checks in the spaces provided.

2 sentence fragments ______ ______	1 missing comma after introductory words ______
1 run-on ______	2 apostrophe mistakes ______ ______
1 irregular verb mistake ______	1 nonparallel structure ______
1 missing comma between items in a series ______	1 missing quotation mark ______

Fred's Funeral

Sometimes when Fred feels undervalued and depression, he likes to imagine his own funeral. He pictures all the people who will be there. He hears their hushed words sees their tears, and feels their grief. He glows with a warm sadness as the minister begins a eulogy by saying, Fred Grencher was no ordinary man. . . .'' As the minister talks on Freds eyes grow moist. He laments his own passing and feels altogether appreciated and wonderful.

Feeding Time

Recently I was at the cathouse in the zoo. Right before feeding time. The tigers and lions were lying about on benches and little stands. Basking in the late-afternoon sun. They seemed tame and harmless. But when the meat was brung in, a remarkable change occurred. All the cats got up and moved toward the food. I was suddenly aware of the rippling muscles' of their bodies and their large claws and teeth. They seemed three times bigger, I could feel their power.

■ Editing Test 8

See if you can locate and correct the ten sentence-skills mistakes in the following passage. The mistakes are listed in the box below. As you locate mistakes, place checks in the spaces provided.

1 run-on ____	1 missing comma between items in a series ____
1 mistake in subject-verb agreement ____	2 apostrophe mistakes ____ ____
1 missing comma after introductory words ____	2 missing quotation marks ____ ____
2 missing commas around an interrupter ____ ____	

Walking Billboards

Many Americans have turned into driving, walking billboards. As much as we all claim to hate commercials on television we dont seem to have any qualms about turning ourselves into commercials. Our car bumpers for example advertise lake resorts underground caverns, and amusement parks. Also, we wear clothes marked with other peoples initials and slogans. Our fascination with the names of designers show up on the backs of our sneakers, the breast pocket of our shirts, and the right rear pocket of our blue jeans. And we wear T-shirts filled with all kinds of advertising messages. For instance, people are willing to wear shirts that read, "Dillon Construction," "Nike," or even I Got Crabs at Ed's Seafood Palace. In conclusion, we say we hate commercials, we actually pay people for the right to advertise their products.

■ Editing Test 9

See if you can locate and correct the ten sentence-skills mistakes in the following passage. The mistakes are listed in the box below. As you locate mistakes, place checks in the spaces provided.

3 sentence fragments ____ ____ ____	1 mistake in pronoun point of view ____
2 run-ons ____ ____	1 dangling modifier ____
1 irregular verb mistake ____	1 missing comma between two complete thoughts ____
1 nonparallel structure ____	

Too Many Cooks

The problem in my college dining hall was the succession of incompetent cooks who were put in charge. During the time I worked there, I watched several cooks come and go. The first of these was Irving. He was skinny and greasy like the undercooked bacon he served for breakfast. Irving drank, by late afternoon he begun to sway as he cooked. Once, he looked at the brightly colored photograph on the orange juice machine. And asked why the TV was on. Having fired Irving, Lonnie was hired. Lonnie had a soft, round face that resembled the Pillsbury Doughboy's but he had the size and temperament of a large bear. He'd wave one paw and growl if you entered the freezers without his permission. He also had poor eyesight. This problem caused him to substitute flour for sugar and using pork for beef on a regular basis. After Lonnie was fired, Enzo arrived. Because he had come from Italy only a year or two previously. He spoke little English. In addition, Enzo had trouble with seasoning and spices. His vegetables were too salty, giant bay leaves turned up in everything. Including the scrambled eggs. The cooks I worked for in the college dining hall would have made Julia Child go into shock.

■ Editing Test 10

See if you can locate and correct the ten sentence-skills mistakes in the following passage. The mistakes are listed in the box below. As you locate mistakes, place checks in the spaces provided.

2 sentence fragments ______ ______	1 missing comma between two complete thoughts ______
2 run-ons ______ ______	1 missing comma between items in a series ______
1 mistake in pronoun point of view ______	1 missing quotation mark ______
1 apostrophe mistake ______	1 misspelled word ______

My Ideal Date

Here are the ingredients for my ideal date, first of all, I would want to look as stunning as possible. I would be dressed in a black velvet jumpsuit. That would fit me like a layer of paint. My acessories would include a pair of red satin spike heels a diamond hair clip, and a full-length black mink coat. My boyfriend, Tony, would wear a sharply tailored black tuxedo, a white silk shirt, and a red bow tie. The tux would emphasize Tony's broad shoulders and narrow waist, and you would see his chest muscles under the smooth shirt fabric. Tony would pull up to my house in a long, shiny limousine, then the driver would take us to the most exclusive and glittery nightclub in Manhattan. All eyes would be on us as we entered and photographers would rush up to take our picture for *People* magazine. As we danced on the lighted floor of the club, everyone would step aside to watch us perform our moves. After several bottles of champagne, Tony and I would head for the top floor of the World Trade Center. As we gazed out over the lights' of the city, Tony would hand me a small velvet box containing a fifty-carat ruby engagement ring. And ask me to marry him. I would thank Tony for a lovely evening and tell him gently, "Tony, I don't plan to marry until I'm thirty.

SENTENCE-SKILLS ACHIEVEMENT TEST

PART 1

This test will help you measure your improvement in important sentence skills. Certain parts of the following word groups are underlined. Place an X in the answer space if you think a mistake appears at the underlined part. Place a C in the answer space if you think the underlined part is correct.

A series of headings (''Sentence Fragments,'' ''Run-Ons,'' and so on) will give you clues for the mistakes to look for. However, you do not have to understand the label to find a mistake. What you are checking for is your own sense of effective written English.

Sentence Fragments

_______ 1. After a careless driver hit my motorcycle, I decided to buy a car. At least I would have more protection against other careless drivers.

_______ 2. I was never a good student in high school. Because I spent all my time socializing with my group of friends. Good grades were not something that my group really valued.

_______ 3. The elderly couple in the supermarket were not a pleasant sight. Arguing with each other. People pretended not to notice them.

_______ 4. Using a magnifying glass, the little girls burned holes in the dry leaf. They then set some tissue paper on fire.

_______ 5. My brother and I seldom have fights about what to watch on television. Except with baseball games. I get bored watching this sport.

_______ 6. My roommate and I ate, talked, danced, and sang at a fish-fry party the other night. Also, we played cards until 3 A.M. As a result, we both slept until noon the next day.

Run-Ons

_______ 7. She decided to quit her high-pressured job, she didn't want to develop heart trouble.

_______ 8. His car's wheels were not balanced properly, for the car began to shake when he drove over forty miles an hour.

_______ 9. I got through the interview without breaking out in a sweat mustache, I also managed to keep my voice under control.

_______ 10. The craze for convenience in our country has gone too far. There are drive-in banks, restaurants, and even churches.

_______ 11. My most valued possession is my stoneware cooker, I can make entire meals in it at a low cost.

_______ 12. The shopping carts outside the supermarket seemed welded together, Rita could not separate one from another.

Standard English Verbs

_______ 13. I am going to borrow my father's car if he agree to it.

_______ 14. For recreation he sets up hundreds of dominoes, and then he knocks them over.

_______ 15. He stopped taking a nap after supper because he then had trouble sleeping at night.

_______ 16. There was no bread for sandwiches, so he decided to drive to the store.

Irregular Verbs

_______ 17. I learned that Dennis had began to see someone else while he was still going out with me.

_______ 18. That woman has never ran for political office before.

_______ 19. I knowed the answer to the question, but I was too nervous to think of it when the teacher called on me.

_______ 20. They had ate the gallon of natural vanilla ice cream in just one night.

Subject-Verb Agreement

_______ 21. Her watchband have to be fixed.

_______ 22. There is two minutes left in the football game.

_______ 23. He believes films that feature violence is a disgrace to our society.

_______ 24. The plastic slipcovers that she bought have begun to crack.

Consistent Verb Tense

________ 25. Myra wanted to watch the late movie, but she was so tired she falls asleep before it started.

________ 26. When the mailman arrived, I hoped the latest issue of *People* magazine would be in his bag.

________ 27. Juan ran down the hall without looking and trips over the toy truck sitting on the floor.

________ 28. Debbie enjoys riding her bike in the newly built park, which features a special path for bikers and runners.

Misplaced Modifiers

________ 29. I saw sharks scuba-diving.

________ 30. With a mile-wide grin, Betty turned in her winning raffle ticket.

________ 31. I bought a beautiful blouse in a local store with long sleeves and French cuffs.

________ 32. I first spotted the turtle playing tag on the back lawn.

Dangling Modifiers

________ 33. When seven years old, Jeff's father taught him to play ball.

________ 34. Running across the field, I caught the Frisbee.

________ 35. Turning on the ignition, the car backfired.

________ 36. Looking at my watch, a taxi nearly ran me over.

Faulty Parallelism

________ 37. Much of my boyhood was devoted to getting into rock fights, crossing railway trestles, and the hunt for rats in drainage tunnels.

________ 38. I put my books in my locker, changed into my gym clothes, and hurried to the playing field.

________ 39. Ruth begins every day with warm-up exercises, a half-hour run, and taking a hot shower.

________ 40. In the evening I plan to write a paper, to watch a movie, and to read two chapters in my biology text.

Pronoun Agreement, Reference, and Point of View

_______ 41. At the Saturday afternoon movie we went to, children were making so much noise that you could not relax.

_______ 42. We did not return to the amusement park, for we had to pay too much for the rides and meals.

_______ 43. Drivers should check the oil level in their cars every three months.

_______ 44. At the hospital, I saw mothers with tears in their eyes wandering down the hall, hoping that her child's operation was a success.

_______ 45. Sharon's mother was overjoyed when Sharon became pregnant.

_______ 46. You must observe all the rules of the game, even if you do not always agree with it.

Capital Letters

_______ 47. When the can of drano didn't unclog the sink, he called a plumber.

_______ 48. I asked Cindy, "what time will you be leaving?"

_______ 49. I have to get an allergy shot once a Week.

_______ 50. Mother ordered the raincoat at the catalog store on Monday, and it arrived four days later.

Apostrophe

_______ 51. I asked the record clerk if the store had Stevie Wonders latest album.

_______ 52. He's failing the course because he doesn't have any confidence in his ability to do the work.

_______ 53. Clyde was incensed at the dentist who charged him fifty dollars to fix his son's tooth.

_______ 54. I cant believe that she's not coming to the dance.

Quotation Marks

_______ 55. "Don't forget to water the grass, my sister said.

_______ 56. Martha said to Fred at bedtime, "Why is it that men's pajamas always have such baggy bottoms?" "You look like a circus clown in that flannel outfit."

_______ 57. The red sign on the door read, "Warning—open only in case of an emergency."

_______ 58. "I can't stand that commercial," said Sue. "Do you mind if I turn off the television?"

Comma

_______ 59. Hard-luck Sam needs a loan, a good-paying job, and someone to show an interest in him.

_______ 60. Even though I was tired I agreed to go shopping with my parents.

_______ 61. Power, not love or money, is what most politicians want.

_______ 62. The heel on one of Lola's shoes came off, so she spent the day walking barefoot.

_______ 63. "Thank goodness I'm almost done" I said aloud with every stroke of the broom.

_______ 64. I hated to ask Anita who is a very stingy person to lend me the money.

Commonly Confused Words

_______ 65. To succeed in the job, you must learn how to control your temper.

_______ 66. Fortunately, I was not driving very fast when my car lost its' brakes.

_______ 67. Put your packages on the table over their.

_______ 68. There are too many steps in the math formula for me to understand it.

_______ 69. The counseling center can advise you on how to prepare for an interview.

_______ 70. Who's white Eldorado is that in front of the house?

Effective Word Use

_______ 71. The teacher called to discuss Ron's social maladjustment difficulties.

_______ 72. The teacher called to discuss Ron's problems in getting along with others.

_______ 73. I thought the course would be a piece of cake, but a ten-page paper was required.

_______ 74. When my last class ended, I felt as free as a bird.

_______ 75. Spike gave away his television owing to the fact that it distracted him from studying.

PART 2 (OPTIONAL)

Do the following at your instructor's request. This second part of the test will provide more detailed information about skills you need to know. On separate paper, number and correct all the items you have marked with an X. For example, suppose you had marked the word groups below with an X. (Note that these examples are not taken from the test.)

4. If football games disappeared entirely from television. I would not even miss them. Other people in my family would perish.
7. The kitten suddenly saw her reflection in the mirror, she jumped back in surprise.
15. The tree in my cousins front yard always sheds its leaves two weeks before others on the street.
29. When we go out to a restaurant we always order something we would not cook for ourselves.

Here is how you should write your corrections on a separate sheet of paper.

4. television, I
7. mirror, and
15. cousin's
29. restaurant, we

There are over forty corrections to make in all.

APPENDIX

ANSWERS AND CHARTS

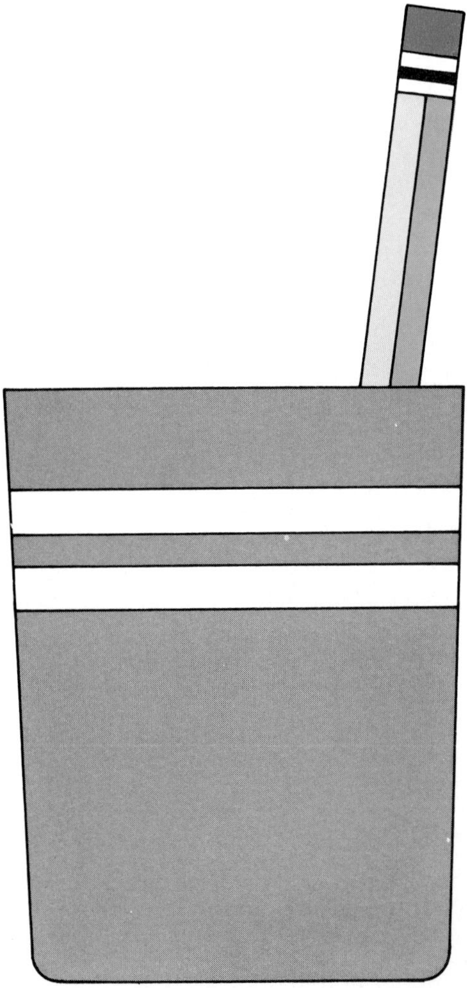

PREVIEW

This Appendix provides answers for the Sentence Skills Diagnostic Test on pages 317–322 and for the Introductory Projects in Part Six. It also gives three useful charts: an assignment chart and a spelling list to be filled in by the student, and a general form for planning a paragraph.

ANSWERS TO SENTENCE-SKILLS DIAGNOSTIC TEST AND INTRODUCTORY PROJECTS

SENTENCE-SKILLS DIAGNOSTIC TEST (pages 317–322)

Sentence Fragments

1. X
2. C
3. X
4. X
5. C
6. X

Run-Ons

7. C
8. X
9. X
10. X
11. C
12. X

Standard English Verbs

13. C
14. C
15. X
16. X

Irregular Verbs

17. X
18. C
19. C
20. X

Subject-Verb Agreement

21. X
22. X
23. C
24. X

Consistent Verb Tense

25. X
26. C
27. C
28. X

Misplaced Modifiers

29. X
30. C
31. X
32. X

Dangling Modifiers

33. C
34. X
35. C
36. X

Faulty Parallelism

37. X
38. C
39. X
40. C

Pronoun Agreement, Reference, and Point of View

41. X
42. C
43. X
44. C
45. X
46. C

Capital Letters

47. X
48. X
49. C
50. X

Apostrophe

51. C
52. X
53. X
54. C

Quotation Marks

55. C
56. X
57. X
58. C

Comma

59. X
60. X
61. C
62. X
63. C
64. X

Commonly Confused Words

65. X
66. X
67. C
68. X
69. X
70. C

Effective Word Use

71. X
72. C
73. X
74. X
75. C

INTRODUCTORY PROJECTS

Sentence Fragments (page 331)

1. verb
2. subject
3. subject . . . verb
4. express a complete thought

Run-Ons (page 347)

1. period
2. *but*
3. semicolon
4. *When*

Standard English Verbs (page 360)

enjoyed . . . enjoys; started . . . starts; cooked . . . cooks

1. past . . . *-ed*
2. present . . . *-s*

Irregular Verbs (page 369)

1. crawled, crawled (regular)
2. brought, brought (irregular)
3. used, used (regular)
4. did, done (irregular)
5. gave, given (irregular)
6. laughed, laughed (regular)
7. went, gone (irregular)
8. scared, scared (regular)
9. dressed, dressed (regular)
10. saw, seen (irregular)

Subject-Verb Agreement (page 377)

The second sentence in each pair is correct.

Consistent Verb Tense (page 382)

discovered . . . remembered

Misplaced Modifiers (page 386)

1. Intended: A young man with references is wanted to open oysters.
   Unintended: The oysters have references.
2. Intended: On their wedding day, Clyde and Charlotte decided they would have two childen.
   Unintended: Clyde and Charlotte decided to have two children who would magically appear on the day of their wedding.
3. Intended: The students who failed the test no longer like the math teacher.
   Unintended: The math teacher failed the test.

Dangling Modifiers (page 390)

1. Intended: My dog sat with me as I smoked a pipe.
   Unintended: My dog smoked a pipe.
2. Intended: He looked at a leather-skirted woman.
   Unintended: His sports car looked at a leather-skirted woman.
3. Intended: A beef pie baked for several hours.
   Unintended: Grandmother baked for several hours.

Faulty Parallelism (page 395)

The second sentence in each pair reads more smoothly and clearly.

Pronoun Agreement, Reference, and Point of View (page 399)

The second sentence in each pair is correct.

Capital Letters (page 410)

All the answers to the thirteen questions should be in capital letters.

11. The 15. I 16. ''That . . .''

Apostrophe (page 424)

1. The purpose of the *'s* is to show possession (that Larry owned the motorcycle, the boyfriend belonged to the sister, Grandmother owned the shotgun, and so on).
2. The purpose of the apostrophe is to show the omission of one or more letters in the contractions—two words shortened to form one word.
3. The *'s* shows possession in each of the second sentences: the body of the vampire; the center of the baked potato. In each first sentence, the *s* is used to form simple plurals: more than one vampire; more than one potato.

Quotation Marks (page 432)

1. The purpose of quotation marks is to set off the exact words of a speaker. (The words that the young man actually spoke aloud are set off with quotation marks, as are the words that the old woman spoke aloud.)
2. Commas and periods go inside quotation marks.

Comma (page 440)

1. a. Frank's interests are Maria, television, and sports.
   b. My mother put her feet up, sipped some iced tea, and opened the newspaper.
2. a. Although the Lone Ranger used lots of silver bullets, he never ran out of ammunition.
   b. To open the cap of the aspirin bottle, you must first press down on it.
3. a. Kitty Litter and Dredge Rivers, Hollywood's leading romantic stars, have made several movies together.
   b. Sarah, who is my next-door neighbor, just entered the hospital with an intestinal infection.
4. a. The wedding was scheduled for four o'clock, but the bride changed her mind at two.
   b. The oranges in the refrigerator were covered with blue mold, and the potatoes in the cupboard felt like sponges.
5. a. Lola's mother asked her, ''What time do you expect to get home?''
   b. ''Don't bend over to pet the dog,'' I warned, ''or he'll bite you.''
6. a. Roy ate seventeen hamburgers on July 29, 1984, and lived to tell about it.
   b. Roy lives at 817 Cresson Street, Detroit, Michigan.

Other Punctuation Marks (page 450)

1. pets; holly
2. freeze-dried
3. Shakespeare (1564–1616)
4. Earth; no
5. proudly—with

Commonly Confused Words (page 474)

Your mind and body . . . . *There* is a lot of evidence . . . .
then it will . . . . said *to* have . . . *It's* not clear

Effective Word Choice (page 486)

1. "Flipped out" is slang.
2. "Few and far between" is a cliché.
3. "Ascertained" is a pretentious word.
4. The first sentence here is wordy.

CHARTS

ASSIGNMENT CHART

Use this chart to record daily or weekly assignments in your composition class. You might want to print writing assignments and their due dates in capital letters so that they stand out clearly.

Date Given	*Assignment*	*Date Due*

Date Given	*Assignment*	*Date Due*

SPELLING LIST

Enter here the words that you misspelled in your papers. If you add to and study this list regularly, you will not repeat the same mistakes in your writing.

Incorrect Spelling	*Correct Spelling*	*Points to Remember*
alright	*all right*	*two words*
ocasion	*occasion*	*two "c"s*

FORM FOR PLANNING A PARAGRAPH

To write an effective paragraph, first prepare an outline. Often (though not always) you may be able to use a form like the one below.

Topic sentence: ____

____

____

Support (1): ____

____

Details:

Support (2): ____

____

Details:

Support (3): ____

____

Details:

INDEX